"[An] excellent new biography of the Boss . . . superb on the creation of the Tweed system and its expansion from acceptable petty skimming to the glittering fellowship of the ring . . . told in a crisp, clear way."

ok *Review*

"Based upon solid research . . tails and colorful anecdotes that bring o read."

Post Book World

"[An] absorbing account of Tweed's rise and fall . . Ackerman has fashioned a notable career chronicling with obvious relish the tarnished politics of the Gild

be

"Not only a compelling look at the colorful yet ruthless man who invented the big city political machine, it is also the gripping story of how dedicated newspapermen and zealous reformers brought down a notorious kingpin."

—*Publishers Weekly* (starred review)

Skillfully tells the story of the Tammany Hall chief . . . Ackerman makes it hard not to root for the old Boss in his final days when he faces his enemies."

—Jennifer Itzenson, *Denver Post*

A thoroughgoing, rayon-smooth biography of Boss Tweed . . . A fine piece of narrative historiography for a wide public, fron schiolars to the lay enthusiast of New York City's political past."

—*Kirkus Reviews*

"Kenneth D. Ackerman's superbly written biography of Boss Tweed is spellbinding . . . every bit as commanding as the man himself."

—Ed Koch, former mayor of New York City

"Engrossing and eye-opening . . ."

—*New York Post*

"A stark portrayal of the iconic Tammany Hall power wielder . . . Both an engrossing portrait of urban power and an in-depth reference source, this [is an] insightful and finely detailed work."

—*Library Journal*

"Ackerman shrewdly mixes together the reformist zeal and political opportunism that marked Tweed's career."

—*Booklist*

Also by Kenneth D. Ackerman

Young J. Edgar: Hoover and the Red Scare, 1919-1920

Dark Horse: The Surprise Election and Political Murder of President James A. Garfield

The Gold Ring: Jim Fisk, Jay Gould, and Black Friday, 1869.

www.ViralHistoryPress.com

Kenneth D. Ackerman

BOSS TWEED

The Corrupt Pol Who Conceived the Soul of Modern New York

VIRAL HISTORY PRESS, LLC
FALLS CHURCH, VIRGINIA

Boss Tweed
The Corrupt Pol Who Conceived the Soul of Modern New York

Viral History Press, LLC
Falls Church, VA 22044
www.viralhistorypress.com

First Carroll & Graf edition 2005
First Carroll & Graf trade paperback edition 2006

Library of Congress Cataloging-in-Publication Data is available.

ISBN-13: 978-1-61945-002-8

Designed by Zaccarine Design, Inc.
Printed in the United States of America

Dedicated to my mother, Ethel Ackerman,
And to my niece, Amanda Morrison,
Two beautiful women full of joy and life,
Both lost to a heartbroken family this year (2004),
And forever in our hearts and thoughts.

CONTENTS

• 1 • ALONE

April 12, 1878:

TWEED WAS DYING that morning, locked inside New York City's Ludlow Street Jail at Grand Street on the lower East Side. At about 11:40 am, he began to whisper; his lawyer William Edelstein had to lean close and place his ear by Tweed's lips to hear over the noise of horses and people on the street, women haggling at the nearby Essex Street Market. "Well, Tilden and Fairchild have killed me," he said.[1] Tweed had saved his last words for his tormentors: Charles Fairchild, the New York State Attorney General who had cheated him, broken his pledge to free him in exchange for a full confession, and Samuel Tilden, the New York Governor who'd built a national political career on Tweed's downfall and now demanded he die behind bars.

"I hope they are satisfied now."[2] He smiled faintly. A few minutes later, he lost consciousness.

For two weeks, Tweed had borne a cascade of ailments: fever, bronchitis, pneumonia. Months earlier, he'd suffered a heart attack, aggravated by kidney failure brought on by Bright's disease. His huge, 300-pound body, once known for its swagger, now sagged on the narrow bed, struggling to breathe; his sporadic coughs hung in the cool, dank air. Hollowed cheeks and a thin ghost-white beard dominated his long face. Blue eyes that once twinkled for friends and glared at enemies seemed vacant, haunted by depression.

At noon, just as mid-day bells sounded from the Essex Street Market tower, Tweed died, prematurely old at 55 years, surrounded by strangers.

It had been almost five years since Tweed had walked the streets of New York City, his life-long home, as a free man. A year before that, Tweed had stood at the height of power and could laugh at bureaucrats like Fairchild and Tilden who'd begged him for favors like everyone else. He, William M. Tweed, had been the single most influential man in New York City and a rising force on the national stage. Physically imposing and mentally sharp, Tweed reigned supreme. He was more than simply boss of Tammany Hall, commissioner of Public Works, and state senator. He controlled judges, mayors, governors, and newspapers. He flaunted his wealth, conspicuous and garish beyond anything supportable by his government salaries or even traditional "honest graft"*[3] as practiced by generations of politicians before and since. Tweed was the third-largest landowner in the city, director of the Erie Railroad, the Tenth National Bank, and the New-York Printing Company, proprietor of the Metropolitan Hotel, and president of the Americus Club. He owned two steam-powered yachts, a Fifth Avenue mansion, an estate in Greenwich, Connecticut, and a shirtfront diamond pin valued at over $15,000. Still, he gloried as friend to the poor, champion of immigrants, builder of a greater New York, and arbiter of influence and patronage. And he stole … on a massive scale.

Once the proof of Tweed's thefts from the city exploded in newspaper banner headlines, his house of cards collapsed. City investigators ultimately figured that Tweed and his city "ring," during a three-year period, had made off with a staggering $60 million from the local treasury—an amount larger than the entire annual U.S. federal budget up until the Civil War. Even then, political enemies and lawmen couldn't touch him; it would take a popular uprising to topple Tweed, led by a newspaper, the *New-York Times*, and a magazine, *Harpers Weekly*. Only after newspapers had produced the evidence did prosecutors like Tilden and Fairchild dare put Tweed behind bars.

In December 1873, a jury had convicted Tweed on 204 counts of criminal misdemeanor fraud growing from the famous "Tweed Ring" scandals and Judge Noah Davis had sentenced him to twelve years' imprisonment on Blackwell's Island.** Judge Davis had overstepped; the charges each actually carried a jail term of just a few months and an appeals court had freed Tweed a year later over the discrepancy, but Tilden had intervened again and or-

* "Honest graft" was defined by Tammany chief George Washington Plunkitt as "I seen my opportunities and I took 'em"—basically exploiting insider influence as opposed to direct stealing from the city treasury. In practice, it amounted to both, but with discretion and moderation.

** Located in the middle of the East River between Manhattan and Brooklyn, it is now called Roosevelt Island.

dered Tweed immediately rearrested and Judge Davis had set bail at an impossibly high $3 million.*

Now, six years later, Tweed alone remained in jail. All his friends and fellow thieves, the other Ring fugitives, had fled the country or settled their charges with the government. Tweed alone had become the scapegoat, the face of corruption. Increasingly, reformers criticized the prosecutors themselves for their clumsy handling of the case, running up huge legal costs while failing to recover more than a pittance of stolen city funds.

Tweed hated prison; it defied him—despite the fact that jailors gave him every comfort money could buy: a private room, hot meals, a bathtub, a window to the street, and friends to visit. He grew impatient at the lawyers' wrangling. In December 1875, he'd escaped and fled. One night that month, he snuck away from his jail guards and secretly crossed the Hudson River to New Jersey. He later admitted paying $60,000 in bribes to finance the dramatic breakout. Once loose, he traveled in disguise, wearing a wig, clean-shaven face, and workman's clothes, and using a false name. He reached Cuba and crossed the Atlantic Ocean to Spain, but only to face arrest. Spanish authorities had seized him on his arrival at Vigo and handed him back to a United States Navy frigate that returned him to New York City.

Then, back behind bars, exhausted, destitute, and sick, Tweed tried to surrender: "I am an old man, greatly broken in health, cast down in spirit, and can no longer bear my burden," he'd written from jail,[4] agreeing with Fairchild and Tilden to throw himself on their mercy. After years of denials, he now offered them a full confession of his crimes, including names of accomplices, surrender of all his property, and help in any legal steps to recover stolen city funds—all in exchange for his freedom. He wanted to be with his wife and children, he said, to live out his last years.

He delivered his confession both in writing and through eleven days of riveting public testimony before a committee of city aldermen investigating his crimes.[5] Newspapers carried full transcripts of the startling disclosures as Tweed appeared day after day in a packed City Hall chamber and unflinchingly poured out his secrets, explaining how he'd bribed the state legislature, fixed elections, skimmed money from city contractors, and systematically diverted public funds. Parts of his story had little or no corroboration, raising suspi-

* About $60 million in modern dollars. Generally, to compare modern dollars with dollars in the 1860s or 1870s, multiply by twenty.

cions he'd exaggerated his own guilt simply to flatter his jailers and help win his release.[6] He made no excuses, no alibis, and no complaints; sitting in the stuffy room he answered every question, rarely showing temper or impatience.

New Yorkers who earlier had despised Tweed for his arrogance and greed now grudgingly grew to respect "the old man"—for his terrible mistakes, his punishment, and his apparent atonement. The aldermen who took his testimony supported Tweed's plea for release from jail, as did old political rivals like "Honest John" Kelly, Tweed's replacement as leader of Tammany Hall.

But Tilden and Fairchild, sitting at the state capitol in Albany, were deaf to his pleas. Samuel Tilden had already run for president of the United States in 1876; he'd received more popular votes than Rutherford B. Hayes and lost the presidency by a single electoral vote in a contested outcome. He was considering a second try in 1880. Fairchild too saw higher political office in his future, including a possible run for the New York governor's mansion. Why should either risk his reputation now over Tweed?

His last appearance outside Ludlow Street Jail came on March 26, 1878, two weeks before his death. Sheriffs had taken Tweed to the state Supreme Court to testify in one of the many lawsuits resulting from his scandals. As guards led him through the marble courthouse corridors, he eagerly greeted the two or three old-timers who weren't ashamed to shake his hand, even though he was now the city's most notorious villain. Newsmen noticed how Tweed now walked with a limp and spoke in a rasping voice. When Tweed took the witness stand, he delivered a prepared statement: "Under promises made to me by the officials of the State and the city, I was induced to give evidence before the Common Council of this city… as to what are called 'Ring Frauds,'" he read. "I am advised by my counsel not to answer a single question put to me on this case… until the promises made to me… are fulfilled and I am liberated."[7]

The judge accepted Tweed's response at face value and allowed him to leave the court without being cross-examined by any of the lawyers.

Six days later, Tweed got his answer. Attorney General Fairchild issued a public letter denying he'd made any deals with Tweed—despite contrary statements he'd given earlier to Tweed's own lawyer and to John Kelly. Fairchild declared the whole incident a sham and a trick;[8] he never bothered even to send Tweed a copy of the letter. Tweed read it in the newspapers. When he saw Fairchild's denial, he knew his game was up. A few days later came the fever, then the cough, then pneumonia.

John Murray Carnochan, Tweed's physician at Ludlow Street Jail, didn't hesitate to pinpoint the cause of death. "Behind all these phases of disease," he told newspaper writers after the autopsy, "was [Tweed's] great nervous prostration, brought about by his prolonged confinement in an unhealthful locality"—the moldy jailhouse on Ludlow Street—"and by the unfavorable result of the efforts recently made to effect his release." [9]

Tweed's family had largely abandoned him by the time he died. Public shame had driven them away. Mary Jane, his wife of thirty-three years, had gone to Paris with their grown son William Jr.; she traveled under the false name "Weed" to avoid any connection with her disgraced husband. "My wife!... She is God's own workmanship," he confided to an interviewer. "The only thing against her is that she had such a worthless husband."[10] Tweed's two youngest sons, 10-year-old George and 14-year-old Charles, had been kept in a New England boarding school for the past five years and forbidden to see their father. Tweed's two oldest daughters, Mary Amelia and Lizzie, both lived with husbands in New Orleans, a thousand miles away, both taking the same married name, Maginnis.

Of all Tweed's children, only his daughter Josephine, 24 years old, still lived in New York City. She came frequently to the Ludlow Street Jail to visit her father and always tried to act cheerful around him. She'd come quickly this morning on hearing from the doctors, but had stepped away from her father's bedside to fetch him his favorite treat of tea and ice cream. She hadn't come back yet when he died at noon.

News of Tweed's death spread quickly through the busy metropolis of 900,000 souls. New Yorkers had known him for twenty-five years as hero, villain, and criminal. Tweed once had counted his friends and colleagues in the thousands. "Nine men out of ten either know me or I know them," he'd bragged back in the 1860s, when he still commanded the city's respect, "women and children you may include."[11] Now, crowds gathered at newspaper offices and government buildings with public bulletin boards—over a hundred people at City Hall alone. Boys selling extra editions of the *New York Sun*, the *World*, and the *Herald* made a fast business. The Boss dead? It couldn't be true! One rumor had it that Tweed had faked his own demise as just another gimmick to win release from jail.

Most New Yorkers sympathized at the news. "Poor old man, poor man, but perhaps it was best for him," Judge Van Vorst of the Court of Common Pleas told a reporter.[12] "Tweed had a great many friends among the poor and

Nast's final drawing of Tweed before the Boss's death.
Harper's Weekly, *January 26, 1878.*

friendless," added Bernard Reilly, sheriff of New York County. "Other people will regret his death because they think he has been rather harshly dealt with… he cannot be considered wholly as a bad man. He erred deplorably. And he has paid for his errors by dying in prison."[13]

But self-styled reformers rejected any pity for Tweed. They'd won a great victory by overthrowing Tweed's corrupt machine and refused to compromise now over misplaced sentiment for a sick old man. The *New-York Times* had dramatically unearthed and disclosed the Tweed Ring's secret accounts—the greatest journalistic scoop to that time, directly leading to Tweed's demise. Now it led the assault: "Such talents as [Tweed] had were devoted to cheating the people and robbing the public Treasury," insisted its lead editorial the next day, adding "his tastes were gross, his life impure, and his influence, both political and personal, more pernicious than that of any other public man of his generation."[14]

Thomas Nast, the brilliant young illustrator whose cartoons in *Harper's Weekly* had made Tweed a laughingstock to New York's illiterate masses, still featured the ex-Boss in his weekly drawings. These days he portrayed Tweed as a tiny parakeet—no longer the fierce Tammany Tiger but instead a pathetic "jailbird" with prison stripes on his feathers and a ball and chain locked to his ankle. Nast's final drawing of Tweed, published in January 1878, had mocked the appeals for Tweed's release by showing miniature jailbird Tweed gripped in a giant hand called "Prison," ready to crush him at a whim. "[I]f it be right that men should be punished for great offenses, there was nothing unkind, unjust, or unreasonable in the punishment of Tweed,"[15] echoed a *Harper's Weekly* editorial that week. It was right that Tweed should die in jail a broken man, others said. "Without his boldness and skill the gigantic Ring robberies would not have been committed," concluded James Gordon Bennett, Jr.'s *New York Herald*.[16] The "finger of scorn," as Tom Nast had drawn it, must follow him to the grave.

William Magear Tweed had left enormous footprints on his city; he had built as grandly as he'd stolen. His monuments dotted every corner of Manhattan—the new Brooklyn Bridge rising across the East River, the opulent new County Courthouse by City Hall, the widened, paved streets up Broadway and around Central Park. Just as striking were shadows of his crimes — the huge debt and ruined credit that would haunt city finances for a generation, the broken lives and shattered trust of former friends. Tweed had defined a grimy reality of American politics, perfecting forms of graft and voting-box abuse mimicked by political bosses for the next century, but never on so grand a scale. His fall had created a new role for a free press in the public arena, and his legal persecution had set a tone for political scandals lasting generations.

Fittingly, his most famous quotation is something he never said, at least publicly—"As long as I count the ballots, what are you going to do about it." Thomas Nast had put the words in his mouth in a *Harper's Weekly* cartoon in 1871.[17]

The morning after Tweed died in jail, newspapers crammed their front pages with stories of his life and times. Politicians rushed to claim credit for having a hand in his downfall; only a rare friend dared to wax nostalgic for old Tammany Hall. People bought extra copies of the newspapers to save for children and grandchildren; they sensed the passing of a monumental figure. Tweed's story would dominate church sermons and saloon arguments for weeks. "The career of Tweed was in many respects one of the most remarkable known to our peculiar land of peculiar institutions," the *Washington Post* noted.[18] How could one raised so high fall so low?

History would blacken Tweed's name, portraying him as the worst municipal thief, the most corrupt politician, the craftiest ballot-box fixer—a stereotype used to tarnish entire generations of American political professionals. Already, he'd become a caricature: More people knew Tweed as the comical thug in Nast's *Harper's Weekly* cartoons, the shameless villain in the *New-York Times* exposes, or the legendary wire-puller of Tammany Hall than as the vital flesh and blood person who'd walked the streets of Gotham for fifty-five years. He left a strange puzzle. Except for his stealing, Tweed would have been a great man; but had he been honest, he wouldn't have been Tweed and would not have left nearly so great a mark.

• PART I •

Rise

• 2 •
RIOTS

"As the representative of the Seventh Ward, I will not be bound by a paper from Judge Campbell or any other judge.... I will never permit [them] to direct me how to think or vote, and will continue to do my own thinking and voting despite injunctions or any other papers."

—TWEED, urging fellow aldermen to defy a judge's order forbidding their approval of a franchise to run streetcars on Broadway, December 28, 1852. The franchise motion carried; the judge, Campbell, cited Tweed and fourteen other aldermen for contempt.[1]

TWEED NEVER JOINED the Union army during the Civil War. He was 38 years old when fighting started in 1861, too old for the infantry though not for the officer corps. He stayed behind, but he didn't escape. Instead, the war with all its rage and violence came to Tweed where he lived in New York City.

New York Governor Horatio Seymour was spending a long summer weekend at the New Jersey seashore on Monday morning, July 13, 1863, traveling by carriage along the sand dunes near Long Branch, when two riders on horseback in military uniforms overtook him. One of the horsemen handed him a telegram which he immediately tore open and read: Violence had broken out in New York City. Seymour's presence was requested immediately. Sparking the outbreak—the military draft.[2]

The news didn't surprise Seymour. As governor, Seymour had warned President Abraham Lincoln for weeks against imposing the unpopular new draft law on New York City. People wouldn't stand for it, he'd argued. Seymour had seen New Yorkers' views turn ugly against Lincoln's war after two years of carnage and defeats. Whatever patriotic surge had followed the initial Confederate attack on Fort Sumter in 1861 had long since disappeared among poor families who saw husbands, fathers, and brothers butchered in

Virginia battlefields under Lincoln's incompetent generals. The draft—the first federal conscription in America, enacted only that March after Washington had grown alarmed over a sharp drop-off in volunteers—had become a special sore point. One enrolling officer in Indiana had already been shot dead by opponents that month trying to enforce it.

Seymour, a 53-year old Peace Democrat, had already made political hay by blasting Lincoln over the draft. He'd declared the law unconstitutional and demanded a court test before a single local conscript was called. He'd railed against the law's most hated feature, the "commutation" rule that allowed sons of wealthy families to buy their way out for $300—an impossible amount for most of New York's working poor. It only again proved that Lincoln's "rich man's war" against the South had become a "poor man's fight," the organized killing of northern Irishmen to save and coddle southern blacks.[3]

Enemies called Seymour a "copperhead"—like the poisonous snake, a favorite insult flung at anti-war Democrats—and New York had more than any other Northern city.

These passions had reached a breaking point in New York by mid-1863. The city's population had exploded in size since the 1830s, more than tripling to 800,000. Now, more than half its residents were foreign-born, mostly Irish and German immigrants crammed into teeming slums amid grinding poverty. Many immigrants had volunteered and fought bravely for the Union, but they saw no honor in a draft, only hardship for workingmen with families to feed. Irishmen particularly felt no quarrel with Southerners and no sympathy for blacks or slaves who, once freed, easily could come north to New York and steal their jobs.

Just weeks earlier, Irish workers had gone on strike at New York's riverside docks demanding better wages, only to see black strikebreakers brought in from Southern states and protected at bayonet-point by Union army soldiers. These tensions had caused even Horace Greeley, the Republican firebrand publisher of the *New York Tribune*, abolitionist and war hawk, to urge delay in starting the draft.

Speaking at Brooklyn's Academy of Music on July 4, Seymour had fanned the flames again by criticizing Lincoln's military failures and proclaimed "the bloody, treasonable, revolutionary doctrine of public necessity"—the basis for the draft law—"could be used by a mob as well as by a government."[4] Critics later would call Seymour's speech a call to arms, as if the riots a few days later were Seymour's own invention.

News the next week of a Union military victory at Gettysburg, Pennsylvania, brought little comfort; long lists of dead and crippled soldiers filled the newspapers, some 23,040 Union boys dead, wounded and missing—more seas of blood for Lincoln's war.

Army officials had ignored Seymour's warnings and decided to begin the draft on Saturday morning, July 11, at their office on Third Avenue and 46th street—an uptown neighborhood they considered safe and loyal. They spun a large wooden wheel to pick names of conscripts, which were then printed in the newspapers on Sunday. An unsettling quiet had hung over the city that Sabbath as troublemakers had a full day to sit around, stew at the news, and plan.

Now, on Monday morning, July 13, the street gave its answer.

Horatio Seymour, on receiving the news in his carriage by the New Jersey seashore, decided to leave at once for New York City. But he chose to travel alone and refused to let his nephew accompany him. Riots, after all, were nothing new to New York* and, as governor, he'd only be taking a back seat to police unless things got out of hand. Besides, the early reports Monday gave little warning of how ugly this latest outburst would turn.

Seymour took a wayward route. Instead of catching a direct steamboat from Long Branch to Manhattan or an immediate train and ferry through Jersey City—either of which would have gotten him to the city by mid-afternoon that day—he traveled inland, stopped and spent the night in New Jersey, and then waited until mid-morning the next day, Tuesday, July 14, before riding a steam-ferry from Jersey City across the Hudson to Manhattan, hoping perhaps the crisis would have blown over by then. Instead, things had deteriorated badly.

As Seymour reached the city and stepped onto the pier, he heard sounds of battle from all directions—gunshots, screams, breaking glass, angry voices. He saw smoke billowing from rows of burning buildings and smelled the acrid odor of gunpowder. Squads of police ran in all directions. Rioters had cut telegraph lines and crippled city communications—panic and rumor had replaced logic and sense. Seymour followed a small entourage to a line of carriages that snaked through narrow streets to Broadway and then north to the St. Nicholas Hotel near Spring Street where he kept a room. Here,

---

* Recent riots had included the 1857 melee between the rival Municipal and Metropolitan police forces as well as sporadic wars between gangs like the Dead Rabbits and Bowery Boys.

Seymour walked past rows of police guards; inside, he found New York Mayor George Opdyke, a 58-year old Republican millionaire dry-goods merchant, tall and gaunt, who'd been elected a year earlier with no political background beyond a single term in the state legislature. Opdyke had fled City Hall the prior morning fearing mob violence and moved his office to the Hotel.

Sitting with Opdyke behind closed doors, Seymour now heard the police, militia, and sheriff's office give their reports. They painted an awful picture: When army officials had resumed the draft Monday morning, July 13, bands of mostly Irish workmen had come prepared to stop them. They'd cut telegraph lines and congregated initially at the draft office on Third Avenue. There, led by a squad of volunteer firemen, they'd forced their way inside, smashed the selection wheel and set the building ablaze. Soon, the same firemen who'd led the initial charge—the so-called "Black Joke Company"—were fighting the mob to control flames spreading to surrounding buildings. Crowds then began murderous rampages through the city, burning shops, smashing windows, looting, and killing. They made blacks a special target, attacking and burning the Colored Orphan's Asylum on 43rd Street and lynching several black men from street-lamps. They'd threatened the Park Row buildings of the *New York Tribune* and *New-York Times*—both supporters of Lincoln and the war—and even mobbed Mayor Opdyke's house on Fifth Avenue. Early that morning, they'd recognized Police Superintendent John Kennedy walking on the street and beat him senseless.

Uptown, New York's wealthiest residents fled by the thousands, driven to panic as rioters targeted posh Republican homes for looting and window breaking. The rich packed rail cars, steamboats, stagecoaches, and any other conveyance headed across the Hudson or East Rivers for safety in Brooklyn, Westchester, or New Jersey. The timing couldn't have been worse. Only weeks earlier, Seymour had sent the bulk of New York's own state militia—over 16,000 armed men—marching into Pennsylvania to join in opposing Confederate General Robert E. Lee's invasion of the North, culminating in the Gettysburg bloodbath. As a result, the city stood unguarded.

Tuesday morning brought no let-up; the battle had resumed with even greater violence. Rioters fought police from behind street barricades they'd built; sounds of screams and gunfire filled the air along with the stench of burning wood and flesh. With no army to protect them and police badly outnumbered, citizens at the Stock Exchange, the Merchants Exchange, and the

New York Governor Horatio Seymour.

Union League had organized volunteers to take up rifles to defend their neighborhoods.

Horatio Seymour appeared shaken at the news. But after an hour or so, he seemed to find himself. As the highest-ranking government official present, he decided to act. He stood up from his seat, walked downstairs to the lobby of the hotel and stepped out into the street where people could see him; he heard a few cheers, then began to walk the dozen blocks down Broadway to City Hall as other officials straggled behind. Seymour recognized that many of these rioters were his own followers. Perhaps they'd listen to reason; perhaps they'd listen to him. He had decided to appeal directly, personally, to the mob and ask them to stop.

Since early that morning, crowds had gathered around City Hall and nearby Printing House Square where the newspaper offices stood; rioters had threatened again to burn down Greeley's *New York Tribune* and the *New-York Times*, while smashing windows and ransacking nearby shops. Worse violence was unfolding uptown on Ninth Avenue where rioters also had built barricades to fight police. Word of Governor Seymour's approach quickly rippled through the street and people began congregating at City Hall Park.

When Seymour reached City Hall itself, the building's marble, columned structure with its cupola and dome rising high above the neighborhood, he climbed up onto the front steps so the crowd could see him and recognize his familiar face: tufts of gray hair, slim build, high forehead, and quick glancing eyes. Seymour, an up-stater from Utica, normally felt more comfortable at a county fair than on teeming city streets, but now he appeared calm. He stood surrounded by police and a handful of officials; lines of armed militiamen—the few remaining in New York—ringed the square. A cheer rose from hoarse voices. Mayor Opdyke stood at Seymour's side visibly frightened—a newspaper writer described his face as "ghastly white" and his hands as visibly trembling. "In his person he symbolized the fear that possessed the town," he wrote.[5] Seymour glanced out at the crowd and saw mostly well-dressed, respectable-looking men and women. Whether these were rioters, shop owners, office clerks, curiosity seekers or some combination, he probably couldn't tell. But one thing was clear: they were anti-war, anti-Lincoln, and anti-draft.

Seymour began to speak. Shouting to be heard, he opened with the words "My friends,"[6] and announced that he'd just sent his state adjutant-general to Washington, D.C. to request that the government suspend the draft in New York City. Then he implored the crowd to disperse. "If the conscription law will not bear the test of the courts and the Constitution, it will not be enforced," he promised them,[7] and assured them he was their friend and the friend of their families. "[L]eave your interests in my hands and I will take care that justice is done you, and that your families shall be fully protected."[8]

At one point during the speech, he turned to a squad of soldiers and said, "Send away those bayonets."[9] After he'd finished, the crowd gave another cheer, loitered around the park some time, then slowly broke up.

Within hours, word of the governor's speech reverberated through the city. Telegraph wires flashed it across the country. Seymour had buckled; he'd groveled to law-breakers. Law-abiding New Yorkers, the majority of sensible people who feared for their lives and felt disgrace at the riots—whether they supported the draft or not—were appalled. Who would protect them? Certainly not the weak-kneed governor! Local merchant William Goodell took up his pen and scribbled a note to President Lincoln that afternoon saying: "Gov. Seymour has just made a speech to the rioters, the substance of which is—Desist from destroying private property, and I will help you break down the conscription—in other words, the Army of the National Government." He urged Lincoln immediately to declare martial law.[10]

If respectable New Yorkers cringed at the sight of Governor Seymour pandering to rioters and Mayor Opdyke trembling at his side, they still could find some confidence in two other men standing nearby that morning on the steps of City Hall as chaos unfolded around them. They had profiles long familiar to the crowd, no-nonsense, capable pillars of one institution in New York City that still seemed able to deal with the violent immigrant thugs. The two made an odd pair: skinny, wiry, energetic A. Oakey Hall, New York's long-time district attorney, and, at his side, a much larger, heavier man standing a full head taller than the others, looking strong enough to fight anyone he chose, with red hair, full red beard, and a broad face. Both were leaders at Tammany Hall, the "regular" voice of the Democratic Party in the city. The larger man, "Big Bill" Tweed, was a county supervisor and Tammany's general committee had recently voted him its new chairman.

Almost everyone around City Hall knew his name, but increasingly the Tammany men simply called him "the Boss."

⚙ ⚙ ⚙ ⚙ ⚙

Tweed kept his finger on the pulse of the city. Ever since violence had erupted Monday morning, he'd plunged head first into the maelstrom—mixing with rioters and shopkeepers on the street, huddling with political leaders, updating police with tips and rumors. At times, he and his Tammany men seemed all that stood between the city and chaos. When Mayor Opdyke had called New York's twenty-four aldermen for an emergency City Hall meeting Monday morning and only six came, it was Tweed who rounded up a quorum. Worried about Opdyke's safety, Tweed had joined those urging him to abandon City Hall for the St. Nicholas Hotel behind a strong police guard. When a vicious mob had surrounded Opdyke's own house on Fifth Avenue demanding "Bring out the Mayor" and threatening to burn the place down, it was George Barnard, one of Tweed's hand-picked judges on the state Supreme Court, who mounted a stoop and shouted: "We still have law" and that "the courts would protect us." Barnard had asked the crowd to disperse "for the honor of the City." They'd cheered him and went off to burn someplace else.[11]

Tweed had seen physical violence all his life on New York streets and didn't flinch from it now. He walked with the confidence of a man good with his fists. As a child in the 1820s, "Little Bill" Tweed, youngest of four siblings, had to fight for respect with older boys on Cherry Street near the East River where he grew up; eventually, he came to lead the gang of local toughs. Later, as a big strapping teenager, he'd joined the neighborhood volunteer fire squad—the Americus "Big-Six" company. Friends described Tweed as "a tall overgrown man, full of animal spirits [and] a swaggering gait, free and easy manner, the constant use of slang, and the display of a coarse humor greatly in vogue among his firemen associates."[12] The "Big Six" men prided themselves in wearing matching red shirts on their showy dashes to nearby rescues, pulling their shiny brass pump-wagon with ringing bells and a roaring tiger painted as an emblem on its side. Within a few years, they'd voted

Tweed their foreman. Their ranks, seventy-five strong, later gave Tweed a solid base for launching a political career, able to produce hundreds of votes on Election Day and provide a platoon of strong-arm bullies as tough as any other street gang.

Shrewd and outgoing, Tweed won friends. He attended the public school on Chrystie Street and showed a quick grasp of numbers. His father Richard, a chair-maker and third generation of Tweeds in America, traced his family's roots back to the Scottish town of Kelso on the river Tweed in the mid-1700s. Richard Tweed doted on his son and recognized talents in him. He stretched his money to send young Bill to a boarding school in New Jersey for a year of math and accounting. Tweed also taught his son business, making him an apprentice in his chair-making shop and then sending him to run errands and keep books for a nearby saddle-maker. When he bought into a brush-making business on Pearl Street—about two blocks from home—his son Bill became its bookkeeper and soon earned enough money to buy a stake in the business for himself. By the next spring, 1844, 21-year-old Bill Tweed had built a big enough nest-egg to marry 17-year-old Mary Jane Skaden, his sweetheart and neighbor since boyhood. He and his bride moved into a top-floor room in her father's house at 193 Madison Street to start their lives together.

Local Tammany politicos saw talent in the young Tweed whose sharp blue eyes, towering build, and friendly manner had already made him a popular figure. In 1843, they asked him to run for city alderman on their ticket, but he declined, still wanting to make money in brush-making. As a rising young businessman, though, Tweed saw politics all around him in New York City. He saw merchants prosper by playing ball with politicians and he enjoyed telling a story about the first time he came out to vote. It was on Election Day in 1844, a presidential year featuring a hard-fought contest between Democrat James K. Polk and Henry Clay, the Kentucky Whig. He watched outright vote-buying on the street and then pulled aside a local poll-watcher to ask how many votes he expected to be cast altogether in the city that day. The old-timer happily explained that of the 45,000 eligible voters, usually about 8 percent stayed home, even in a presidential year.

Tweed did the math for himself. That left about 41,000, which was the number actually cast four years earlier in 1840. The next morning, he laughed out loud at seeing the result printed in the newspapers: 55,086 ballots had been counted in New York for Polk and Clay, an abrupt jump of more than 14,000.[13]

Young Bill Tweed had marveled at the brazen theft, a product of ballot-box stuffing, bully-boy tactics, and pure lying, the stuff of New York "democracy" in the mid-1800s. Yet politicians got away with it, and they seemed like decent men in their own way. Many wouldn't steal a dime from a blind stranger and would move mountains to help friends, yet wouldn't sneeze at fixing a vote or skimming a city contract.

Now that he'd learned the game, Tweed jumped at the next chance. When Tammany made him another offer in 1851, he took it. Now 28 years old, Tweed lost a narrow contest for assistant alderman that year, but success came quickly. In 1852, voters in his Seventh Ward neighborhood* did make him an alderman—joining a group already famous as the "forty thieves"—and in 1853 they sent him to Washington, D.C. as United States congressman. Tweed hated the national legislature; he found it dull and spent most of his official time bickering over a postmastership for an obscure constituent and haggling over the Kansas-Nebraska Act, which he supported.[14] He lasted just one term. Asked years later about returning as a U.S. senator, he cringed: "what for? I can't talk, and I know it. And to spend my time in hearing a lot of snoozers discuss the tariff and the particulars of a contract to carry the mails from Paducah to Schoharie, I don't think I'm doing that just now."[15]

Back home in 1854, Tweed refused a nomination from the nativist "Know-Nothings,"** making him popular with Irish and German immigrants already swelling New York's poorer neighborhoods—despite his having been an officer in the Order of United Americans, a local anti-Catholic, anti-immigrant club, in the late 1840s.[16] He became a school commission member in 1856, a county supervisor in 1858, and deputy street commissioner in 1861, then bankrupted himself in a losing race for sheriff that year. By then, Tweed had given up brush-making to give politics his full attention and he'd figured out how to make money at it. He opened a private law office at 95 Duane Street where he used his city contacts to "fix" problems for paying customers.

Tammany's general committee had topped off Bill Tweed's rise by electing him its chairman in January of 1863—just six months before the draft

---

* Tweed's seventh ward stretched along the East River between Grand and Catherine Streets, east of East Broadway. Today, it is the area between the Manhattan and Williamsburg Bridges near the river.

** Formally called the Native American Party that peaked in the late 1850s, capturing many local offices and running former-president Millard Fillmore for the White House in 1856. After bloody anti-immigrant riots in the late 1840s, one branch, the "Order of the Star Spangled Banner," had answered police questions by saying "I know nothing," leading to the nickname.

riots. By now, Tweed and Mary Jane, his wife of 18 years, lived in their own home at 127 Henry Street. They'd moved out of Mary Jane's father's house in 1847 after the birth of their first child, William Jr., to avoid having him spoiled by doting grandparents: "If I don't [move] the folks will pet my boy to death," Tweed complained.[17] On July 10 that year, only three days before the riots, Mary Jane had made Tweed a father for the ninth time by giving birth to a new baby son, Charles. As two of their children had died in infancy, that left a total of seven, three sons and four daughters ranging in age from newborn to 18 years. Even with the maids Tweed hired as help, the load made Mary Jane a virtual household slave caring for their brood.

On Tuesday morning, July 14, 1863, as Governor Horatio Seymour arrived in New York by ferry from New Jersey to face the draft riots exploding through the city, it was Tammany chief Bill Tweed who met him at the Hudson River pier, shook his hand and escorted him to the St. Nicholas Hotel, then walked with him up Broadway to City Hall for his "My Friends" speech. Afterwards, it was Tweed who led Seymour through Manhattan for two more speeches in riot-torn neighborhoods. Tweed sat side-by-side with him that day in the governor's carriage as it threaded narrow streets behind police guards. Crowds recognized the two men instantly; as the carriage passed, rioters would stop for a moment as men raised hats, women waved handkerchiefs, and cheers rose.[18]

Tweed recognized the urgent need of being seen on the street that day. He had made Tammany his club, and Tammany over the years had linked its fate to these same immigrants who were now tearing up the city. Many were his constituents; no one knew them better than Tweed and company.

Tammany Hall—the "Tammany Society or Columbian Order"—had started in New York as a patriotic social club pre-dating the Revolutionary War. It had taken its name from the legendary Delaware Indian chief Tamanend, said to have welcomed William Penn to the New World in 1682 and to have defeated the Evil Spirit in a battle so fierce as to create the Niagara Falls, the Detroit Rapids, and the Ohio River in its wake. That's why it still called its members "warriors" or "braves," its leaders "Sachems," its buildings "Wigwams." But Tammany long ago had changed stripes and made itself an outright political organ. Its support had decided New York elections since the time of Aaron Burr and Martin Van Buren. Its current meeting hall, the Tammany Hotel at the corner of Nassau and Frankfort Streets near City Hall, had become a synonym for influence.[19]

Tammany had cast its lot with workingmen and immigrants as early as the 1840s. It campaigned to eliminate property requirements for voting, urged the repeal of New York's debtors' prison law, and opposed the Know Nothings in contests throughout the 1840s and 1850s. It had placed Irishmen in high, visible posts, such as Matthew Brennan as city comptroller, John Clancy as county clerk and editor of its newspaper, *The Leader*, and John Kelly as congressman and sheriff. These days, Tammany routinely arranged city jobs for poor men with families and supported Irish churches and charities; its clubs and committees reached deep into local neighborhoods. Any down-and-out New York greenhorn speaking a strange tongue and without a dime, could find a sympathetic Tammany man down at a corner saloon or walking nearby streets. These "ward heelers"—named for their worn-out shoes—became the immigrant's closest link to power in the strange new world of America.

Unlike rival Democratic clubs, Tammany also had taken a clear Union stand on the Civil War. It had organized its own regiment of soldiers for Lincoln's army* and required each of its candidates in the 1861 fall elections to sign a pledge supporting the war; once fighting began, it raised money for families of fallen soldiers. As a result, it remained one of the few New York political body credible to all sides: among loyalists for its patriotism, and immigrants for its friendship.

After Tweed had finished escorting Governor Seymour through the city on that second day of rioting, the governor returned to the St. Nicholas Hotel and Tweed returned to the streets. Seymour issued proclamations declaring the city in insurrection and urging crowds to disband, but with little impact. The carnage lasted four days; at its height, mobs captured the Second Avenue armory and looted its guns and rifles, burned several police stations, and pillaged the Brooks Brothers clothing store near Catherine Street. Throughout, Tweed and his allies patrolled the sidewalks, urging calm and keeping leaders abreast of developments. "Supervisor Tweed, Judge [John] McCunn, and Sheriff [Jimmy] Lynch were constantly around [the St. Nicholas Hotel] during the night and communicated to the Governor the news received from

---

* It was Fernando Wood, head of Mozart Hall, Tammany's chief rival among the Democratic clubs, who as mayor in 1861 had proposed that New York secede from the Union and become a "free city" doing business equally with both North and South. Tammany's army unit, the Tammany Jackson Guard, 42nd New York Infantry, was led by William Kennedy, Tammany's "Grand Sachem" at the time. Kennedy became an early war hero, dying shortly before the first battle of Bull Run on July 21, 1861. A monument to them, a statue of an Indian, stands today at Gettysburg.

up town," one newspaper noted at the height of battle, "which at one time was of a startling and serious character."[20]

By Thursday night, the fighting ended—crushed by force. Five regiments of regular Union army troops had rushed back from Gettysburg to join West Point cadets, police, and over 1,200 volunteers who had taken up arms to help restore order—including a corps of city street workers organized by Tweed as Deputy Street Commissioner. In its aftermath, Tweed saw a city shaken, feeling threatened on every side: by rebel armies, weak political leaders, and the seething mass of foreigners among them apparently ready to erupt as a violent mob. Worse still, crushing the riot had failed to settle the question: Would there be a military draft in New York? And if so, would it spark the city's poor to rise again in another violent spasm, perhaps more deadly than the first?

◎ ◎ ◎ ◎ ◎

The draft riots left blocks of New York buildings smoldering in ruin and hundreds of families homeless; the stench of death and burning, the sight of black smoke, the sound of marching soldiers, all would linger for days. Police piled dozens of dead near the waterfront—soldiers, bystanders, and rioters alike; newspapers trumpeted wild claims of over a thousand people killed in the melee, though more careful counts put the death toll at about 105. At least eleven black men were found murdered brutally, lynched or disfigured. Damage to property was measured in millions of dollars.

As the dust settled, anger erupted on all sides. Two opposing camps dominated a chorus of shrill voices: Loyal Republicans, nativists, and merchants all demanded a crackdown. Traitors must be crushed and the city surrendered to federal troops—martial law. Someone had to control the rowdy immigrants; why not the army? The draft must go forward, even at gunpoint, and Copperheads like their own Governor Seymour should be run out of town.[21] Just as defiantly, Peace Democrats demanded that Washington end the draft and threatened violence at any attempt to reinstate it. Many Irishmen felt shame for the July riots, but that didn't lessen their hatred of conscription. Governor Seymour, having returned to the state capitol in Albany, led the appeal. He barraged President Lincoln with letters and emissaries[22] pleading with him to abandon the draft, at least until the underlying statute, the Conscription Act, could be tested in the courts—a process promising to take months or years. New York already had furnished more than its fair share of soldiers through volunteer enlistments and state militia call-ups, he argued, and sent reams of statistics to prove his point.[23]

From the White House, the city heard only a hard line. Abraham Lincoln had a war to fight and his generals desperately needed soldiers. If he suspended the draft in New York, how could he continue it in Philadelphia, Chicago, or any other northern city? Lincoln had studied Seymour's appeals and rejected them all. "We are contending with an enemy who… drives every able bodied man he can reach into his ranks, very much as a butcher drives bullocks into a slaughter pen," he wrote to Seymour in early August.[24] When Seymour suggested waiting first to see the result of New York's volunteer recruitment drive before renewing the draft, Lincoln threw it back in his face: "Looking to *time*, as heretofore, I am unwilling to give up a drafted man now, even for the *certainty*, much less the mere *chance*, of getting a volunteer *hereafter*," he replied.[25]

Instead of delay, Lincoln demanded speed. He ordered that the draft resume immediately in New York, with new lotteries beginning in mid-August, and sent 10,000 federal troops marching to the city under command of Major General John A. Dix, a no-nonsense, 65-year-old officer with deep roots in New York politics. As a final step, Lincoln issued to Dix a blank-check authority to proclaim martial law at his discretion.[26] If military rule was the only way to force the draft on New York, then Lincoln was prepared to have Dix impose it.[27]

As this test of wills unfolded on the national stage, local officials fell into hopeless squabbling. In late July, New York's Copperhead-dominated aldermen met in City Hall and concocted a plan to sabotage any effort by Lincoln's War Department to reintroduce the draft. They proposed to make $3 million in City funds available to purchase a $300 exemption for any local man drafted into the army who refused to go—standing the Conscription Act's hated $300 commutation clause on its head. Mayor Opdyke had vetoed it promptly, arguing that the plan would yield no soldiers and was simply a slap at Lincoln. All July and August, Opdyke and the aldermen traded insults across City Hall.[28]

Bill Tweed, the new Boss of Tammany Hall, didn't involve himself directly in this haggling at first. He had other things in his life that summer: politics, money-making, and his new baby son, Charles, born just before the riots. But listening to the stream of visitors in his Duane Street office, hobnobbing around City Hall and Tammany, or visiting neighborhood clubs, he heard endless complaints: Was nobody capable of running the city? Anyone could see the danger: For Lincoln to force a federal draft on New York, someone had to convince the poor to accept it as fair. Otherwise, tempers would explode and violence would erupt again, just as in July.

This was no time for fancy speeches. It was a job for practical men: Politicians.

Among his official roles in New York in 1863, Tweed held a seat on the New York County Board of Supervisors, the local body that met in City Hall and held principal legislative power for the city and county—managing elections, approving treasury disbursements, hiring courtrooms and armories and issuing bonds.* State law required this twelve-member panel to be evenly balanced with six Democrats and six Republicans, but Tammany had dominated it for years. Tweed remembered first joining the board in 1858 when senior Democrats had paid $2,500 to one Republican simply for staying home when the board chose voting inspectors—allowing Tammany to place its own reliable men in charge on Election Day when it stuffed the ballot boxes.[29] Within a year, Tweed came to lead this hard-nosed group.

Usually, these supervisors busied themselves with one particular selfish matter: graft. Any contractor wanting to get paid by the county for work performed had to include in his bill an extra amount of padding—a "percentage," usually 15 percent—to pay the politicians. He'd pass the money directly to Tweed who'd split it with other supervisors who played the game. Tweed had an arrangement with two other Democratic supervisors; they'd meet privately before meetings in Tweed's office on Duane Street and decide which bills to approve and which to block. "[T]here was hardly a time when our three votes wouldn't carry most anything," he later boasted, and usually only the contractors who paid the tithe got their support.[30]

But now, in late July, things had changed. With the mayor, governor, and aldermen all locking horns and violence threatening the city, these county supervisors suddenly found themselves perhaps the only arm of local government able to function.

---

* New York City and County overlapped totally in the mid-1800s, and the line between city and county governments was often blurred. The city's mayor had county functions and the elected comptroller managed accounts for both entities. The state legislature had given the Supervisors added powers in 1857 due to concerns about corruption among the city's alderman. The overlap would continue until 1898 when the city expanded beyond Manhattan to include Brooklyn, Queens, and Staten Island.

Sometime in mid-August, Tweed pulled aside Orion Blunt, the senior Republican on the Board of Supervisors, for a private talk. The two men saw eye-to-eye; neither wanted to see their city plunged into another riot. Blunt was an industrialist, a gun-maker who'd seen his factories suffer in the July violence.*[31] Both recognized the problem: no new draft could go smoothly in New York unless it squarely addressed the basic unfairness of the federal law—its $300 commutation clause. The poor had to be treated equal to the rich; immigrants and workmen needed to know that the lottery was fair. At the same time, Lincoln needed troops for the army, and the only group able to fix things was the Board of Supervisors.

Tweed and Blunt decided to work together—and to avoid squabbling, they included Mayor Opdyke as well. On August 28, just as army offices around town were starting to select names in Lincoln's newest round of draft lotteries, Tweed and Blunt called together a special public meeting of the county supervisors at City Hall and quickly hammered out a plan.[32] The idea was simple: Certain categories of people—police, firemen, and state militiamen—had to be exempted from the draft to stay home and protect the city. Others, like poor workmen with families to feed—those who could never afford the $300 commutation fee—should be eligible for case-by-case relief. But instead of simply purchasing exemptions for these people—an approach that shortchanged the army—they'd find substitute recruits and use the city treasury to pay whatever bonus the market demanded, tapping a special $2 million fund financed by bonds to be sold on Wall Street. If a draftee chose to join the army, he could keep $300 as a reward. This way, Lincoln's army would get its soldiers and the people would get relief.

To make life and death rulings on individual cases, they'd create a special six-member County Substitute and Relief Committee with three Republicans and three Democrats, including the mayor, Orison Blunt, and Tweed.

So far, so good; city leaders all applauded the plan. But it lacked a crucial ingredient. Lincoln's government in Washington controlled the military draft and local county supervisors in New York City had no power to tamper with it. Unless Lincoln and his Secretary of War, Edwin Stanton, agreed to count the locally-bought New York substitutes toward their federal draft quotas, the

* Early in the war, Orison Blunt had invented an early machine gun called the "pepper-box gun" that could discharge seventy shots per minute operated by a crank handle. Lincoln himself tested it in Washington. Though never mass produced, one of them was sent to the front but captured by rebels before it could make an impact. Blunt discovered it years later in a junk shop.

plan could not take effect. To close this deal, someone had to go to Washington, D.C. and sell the plan to Lincoln's government, a tough job given Lincoln's hard line so far.

For this delicate diplomacy, the supervisors now voted to appoint a special committee of two: Orion Blunt and Big Bill Tweed.

Tweed and Blunt crossed the Hudson River one night in August and rode south by train, traveling in secret. On reaching the wartime Capital, they rode through mud streets cramped with army traffic and soon found themselves ushered into the War Department building on 17th Street—a beehive of activity with military officers dashing urgently with bulletins from the battlefront. At the personal office of the secretary, they found waiting to meet them Stanton himself and James Barnet Fry, the Army Provost Marshal-General responsible for administering the draft nationwide.

Stanton, a veteran Ohio lawyer with gray-streaked beard, spectacles, and prominent eyes, showed them in and gave them his full attention. Sitting face to face with Lincoln's war ministers, Orison Blunt probably spoke first. As a Republican whose factories sold rifles to the War Department, he spoke the same political dialect as Stanton and Fry. But apparently he turned to Tweed to make the case. "The committee [Blunt and Tweed] were received with great courtesy," they reported later, and the four men had a "full interchange of views."[33] Tweed probably addressed Stanton with the same frank directness he'd perfected through years of Tammany back-room huddles, looking him in the eye, patting his shoulder, sharing a confidence. Stanton listened with the weary patience borne after three years of bloodshed and frustration.

In fact, Lincoln and Stanton had been despairing for weeks at any chance of finding a reliable partner in New York City to help them implement the draft. Governor Seymour had resisted their every overture and Mayor Opdyke remained paralyzed in squabbles with city aldermen. Now this man Tweed had given them an answer. General John Dix, Lincoln's military overseer, who knew the political currents of Manhattan as well as anyone, had already put in a private good word on their behalf: "Tammany Hall, representing more than half the [Democratic Party], will stand by the government," he'd written to Stanton in late July, after the shock from the riots had begun to subside.[34]

Whether it was Dix's private advice, Lincoln's instructions, Blunt's political ties, or Tweed's own charm that won him over, Stanton bought the line. He agreed to the deal. Tammany Hall, through the county supervisors, would run Lincoln's August draft in New York City. Tweed's plan made practical sense and Tweed came across as someone he could trust. Stanton "highly commended [the plan] for its patriotism, and as evincing the determination of the citizens of the city and county of New York to aid and sustain the government in crushing this wicked rebellion, and in vindicating the majesty of the law," they could later report.[35] They'd become partners in a strange marriage.*[36]

With Stanton's blessing, Tweed and Blunt now hurried back to New York to put their plan in effect. The August draft came and went. Army offices around the city held lotteries, drawing large crowds to watch the spinning wooden wheels pick name after name. On its eve, Governor Seymour warned citizens against disorder and General Dix stationed army troops on the streets, but they weren't needed. Instead, Tammany vouched for the draft; at every office, its Sachems stood side by side with army officers in their crisp blue uniforms. The wooden wheels selected over a thousand names, and virtually every one of them appealed to the new County Substitute and Relief Committee—Tweed's committee. In the seventh ward by the East River, the army held its drawing at the old police station at 228 Broome Street and, after a few spins, the wheel actually selected the name of William M. Tweed, Boss of Tammany Hall. The announcement sparked a loud, good-natured cheer from the men in the room.[37] Tweed, if anyone, would have paid the $300 fee from his own pocket to avoid joining the infantry.

Then, all September, Tweed's committee met in the state Supreme Court chambers at 65 Duane Street, a few doors down from Tweed's private office. Tweed or Orison Blunt personally questioned almost every appellant under oath. "[I]f the duties of the Board are arduous they appear to be eminent and fair... invariably insisting that the would-be exempt shall first secure a substitute ere he is let off," a *New York Herald* reporter wrote after sitting through hours of sessions.[38] The *New-York Times* similarly complimented the committee members for "performing their duties with eminent satisfaction to all parties."[39] By September 29, out of 1,034 draftees appealing to them, Tweed's

* Tweed apparently did not meet with Lincoln personally on this trip. The War Department was just a few steps down Pennsylvania Avenue from the White House, though Lincoln may have been at the Soldier's Home, his summer residence outside Washington. It's tempting to savor what conversation might have occurred had Abraham Lincoln, America's most celebrated saint, had the chance to chat with Tweed, soon to become its most notorious sinner.

committee had found substitutes for 983, another 49 were excused, and only two chose to join the army and go to war.[40]

It was a remarkable accomplishment. Lincoln got his soldiers, the city had order, and the poor had relief from a law blatantly unfair to them. "No money, no trust was ever more honestly administered than the loan of the Board of Supervisors," crowed the journal destined soon to become Tweed's most bitter enemy—the *New-York Times*.[41]

At the same time, a few blocks away, two of Tweed's Tammany Hall proteges launched aggressive prosecutions against the July lawbreakers. District Attorney A. Oakey Hall and John Hoffman, the presiding judge of New York's Court of General Sessions—called the Recorder—won indictments against dozens of rioters and put them on immediate public trial. The daily spectacle of looters, arsonists, pickpockets, muggers, and killers from every ethnic background paraded in handcuffs through Hoffman's courtroom and sentenced to jail terms had a dramatic impact—a show of swift, tough law enforcement, even if juries had to release dozens of offenders because the cases against them were poorly prepared. Newspapers carried long transcripts of the daily court actions, soon making Hall and Hoffman two of the most popular political figures in New York.

Through the last two years of the Civil War, Tweed would position Tammany squarely with the Union. His county recruitment drive for the army would attract scandal: abusive bounty brokers, unqualified soldiers—either prisoners from local jails or immigrants literally straight from New York Harbor—and middlemen stealing fortunes in graft. But it hardly raised an eyebrow compared to the epidemic of war profiteering that had infected the country. Crooked contractors were charging Uncle Sam sky-high prices for everything from diseased horses to defective pistols, spoiled food, and frayed, tattered uniforms. In one case, bribed Brooklyn Navy Yard officers signed receipts for an estimated million dollars in non-existent hardware—nails, paint, and tools—paid for but never delivered.* By contrast, corruption aside, Tweed's committee in the last twenty months of the war could boast of paying 116,382 recruits for joining Lincoln's army.[43]

---

* Tweed, of course, was no innocent at war profiteering. By one story, when the city sold the old Harlem Hall in mid-1863, Tweed purchased 300 of its benches for $5 each, then used his influence as a member of the Supervisors' Committee on Armories to win approval for the county to buy all but 17 of the benches back to use as armory furniture for $600 each, costing taxpayers $169,800 in the turnaround.[42]

New Yorkers now trusted him, and inside the club his Tammany braves glorified him, electing him a Sachem in August 1863 on top of his chairmanship of the general committee. "He is a live man, in the most vigorous sense—energetic, industrious, courageous and indefatigable," John Clancy wrote of Tweed that summer in Tammany's newspaper, the *Leader*. "His vitality is felt in every movement with which he is connected, and he is withal a true man in the highest degree... He never turned his back on a friend or a foe."[44]

For now, the Boss of Tammany was a hero in New York City. Next to this, a few hearsay complaints about ballot box fraud, City Hall graft, and bribery at the Board of Supervisors seemed like very, very small things.

⊛ ⊛ ⊛ ⊛ ⊛

Thomas Nast, short and stocky with dark hair, small goatee beard, and boyish face with pointed nose and sharp eyes, stepped crisply along the sidewalk at Franklin Square near Pearl Street one morning in early November 1864—just sixteen months after the draft riots—carrying a large white folder under his arm, then entered the five-story stone edifice of Harper & Brothers, by far the largest building on the street.[45] He climbed the circular iron stairway to the editorial offices upstairs. All the while he noticed peoples' eyes following him.

Nast enjoyed his extraordinary fame: Harper and Brothers in 1864 was America's largest publishing house, its biggest book producer and home to its two most popular magazines, *Harper's Weekly* and *Harper's Magazine*. *Harper's Weekly* alone boasted a regular circulation of over 100,000 and a readership estimated at half a million; copies passed hand to hand, especially among soldiers at the front. The company employed over 500 machinists, editors, clerks, artists, writers, and arrangers, making it one of the largest businesses in New York City. And Thomas Nast was Harper's single most famous employee. Readers across the country, North and South, recognized the crisp "*Th. Nast*" scribbled in tiny neat letters at the bottom of his regular cartoons in *Harper's Weekly*. They might ignore the scholarly essays penned by editor George W. Curtis but they always jumped ahead to Nast's eye-catching pictures. What surprised people most on seeing Nast, though, was how young he looked. He was just 24 years old.

Nast's Civil War drawings had made him a sensation. Since joining the *Harpers Weekly* staff in August 1862, he'd produced a blizzard of work—over thirty featured illustrations in 1863 alone. His debut cover in September 1862, "A Gallant Color-Bearer"—showing a dying Union soldier passing his flag to comrades—had captured the country's wartime mood, its stark moral shades of right and wrong, courage and cowardice. Nast struck emotions in his work. He vilified Southerners so cuttingly, showing Confederate soldiers burning the land or harassing women and prisoners, that letters to *Harper's Weekly* from Dixie often contained death threats. His drawings of the home front—wives and children praying at windowsills for absent husbands alongside images of soldiers at the front dreaming of home—touched deep chords. His "Santa Claus in Camp" in late 1862 showed cheery old Saint Nick in stars and stripes handing out gifts to homesick troops.

Fame had come easily to young Tommy Nast, a favorite child of doting parents. Born in 1840 in a military barracks in Landau, Germany, a small town near Alsace, he was the younger of two children. Nast's father had played trombone in the ninth Bavarian Regiment Band. Settling the family in New York City when Tom was six years old, his father had joined the local Philharmonic Society and made a living playing at Burton's Theatre on Chambers Street. Young Tommy spoke no English at first—he had to learn it nearly from scratch—but he enjoyed carrying his father's trombone to the theatre for the chance to sit by Papa on a miniature seat in the orchestra pit.

Nast loved music, but he quickly showed another talent. He began picking up pencils and drawing pictures almost as soon as he could talk. As a child, he spent hours sketching anything that caught his eye: a favorite toy, Papa's musician friends, city streets and family members, even himself. His schoolteachers despaired: "Go finish your picture," one said. "You will never learn to read or figure."[46] Still, as a thirteen-year-old, Nast had drawn a portrait of Louis Kossuth, the Hungarian revolutionary who'd visited New York in 1851 to rousing cheers, so animated and lifelike that his school master put it on display. Nast saw the famed singer Jenny Lind perform for a huge crowd at New York's Castle Garden, at the tip of the Battery, and drew a portrait of her as well.

His talent won Nast admission to New York's respected Academy of Design on 13th Street near Broadway. Here he learned technique under teachers like German painter Theodore Kaufman and illustrator Alfred Fredericks, who jokingly called Nast the "little fat Dutch boy" but cultivated his interest in journalism. In 1856, just fifteen years old and fresh from school, Nast snagged an artist's job with *Frank Leslie's Illustrated Newspaper*. *Leslie's Illustrated* was a new journal launched by a *London Illustrated News* veteran who had brought to New York the latest technology sweeping Europe: commercial-scale wood engraving making possible a new generation of mass-circulation illustrated newspapers.* A revolution was changing the face of graphic arts in America in the 1850s and Tom Nast was arriving just on time to become its first major celebrity.

At the time, the change was dramatic. Up through the 1850s, very few Americans ever saw likenesses or photographs of popular leaders, places, or events. Most who voted for Jefferson or Jackson, for instance, had little idea what these people looked like. Rural farmers often had never seen cities like New York or Chicago, let alone ocean-going ships or European capitals. Most city dwellers could barely envision prairies, mountains, or small towns. Other than rare, expensive paintings, broadside posters during political campaigns, book illustrations, or engravings from printers like Currier and Ives, Americans had to rely on words to picture people and places beyond the immediate horizons of their lives.

By the late 1850s, New York alone had spawned almost a dozen new illustrated journals and readers began snapping them up; with the onset of Civil War, this demand exploded.

Leslie' Illustrated was a sixteen-page weekly costing ten cents when Nast started working there at a salary of $4 per week. Thrown into the fray, he quickly learned the symbolic language of image, caricature, and satire, using symbols like the British lion or Uncle Sam. By 1860, he'd moved his pen to another weekly, the *New York Illustrated News*, which gave him a chance to see the world. They sent Nast to England to cover the championship prizefight between American John Heenan and British champion Thomas Sayers—a great sporting event of its day.[47] Nast then traveled south to Italy to join patriot Giuseppi Garibaldi on his march of conquest from Genoa to Naples. For four months, Nast's drawings of the fighting in Italy appeared in New York weeklies; his exposure to the violence, courage, and devastation would later inspire his images on America's own Civil War. Returning home to New York City, he married his long-time friend Sarah Edwards, re-joined

* The process involved dividing a large single drawing into multiple pieces, having multiple engravers make separate wood engravings of each, and then reassembling the pieces for final printing—primitive and time-consuming by modern standards but a major breakthrough at the time. Sometimes, the artist would draw directly onto the wooden blocks in soft pencil.

"*Compromise with the South*,"
Harper's Weekly, *September 3, 1864*.

Leslie's Illustrated now at $50 per week, and followed newly-elected Abraham Lincoln to Washington, D.C. to draw pictures of Lincoln's inauguration. He became an unabashed admirer of the new president of the United States.

By then, his craft had matured. "It is full of life and character," one fellow artist said on seeing an early drawing, "as everything is which comes from Mr. Nast's pencil."[48]

Abraham Lincoln faced a difficult wartime reelection campaign in 1864 and Nast threw himself eagerly into the fray. Nast saw politics as a natural extension of the war. Democrats in 1864 had nominated former Union General George B. McClellan on a peace platform promising a negotiated end to fighting—what Nast, a Lincoln backer, saw as shameful surrender. New York Democrats had once again nominated for governor Horatio Seymour, the Copperhead who'd notoriously called draft rioters "My Friends."

Nast had seen the July 1863 riots firsthand; he'd just returned from the Virginia battlefront when they'd begun. At their height, an Irish mob had surrounded the Harper building on Franklin Square and forced it to close; employees—probably Nast among them—had barricaded the doors and taken up rifles against threatened attacks. Nast had ventured out onto the streets with pad and pencil at one point to sketch scenes of the mayhem, including one scene of children dancing around the body of a murdered soldier.

Nast saw the 1864 political campaign as a chance to get even with Copperhead politicians who'd allowed these outrages. Already, he'd produced one drawing that caused a national uproar. Titled "Compromise with the South," it showed an arrogant Confederate officer stepping with his boot on the grave of a dead Union soldier as a crippled Union veteran turns in shame and Columbia as a woman kneels in tears.[49] "Dedicated to the Chicago [Democratic] Convention," read the caption—directly fingering candidate McClellan. Lincoln's campaign printed an estimated million copies of Nast's cartoon and distributed them before Election Day.

Now, just days before the November voting, he'd produced another. A new scandal had erupted. The State of New York licensed agents to collect votes from tens of thousands of soldiers at the front line. These agents had been caught red-handed in a variety of frauds: tricking soldiers into signing blank ballots, forging signatures, filling in names of wounded, dead, or even non-existent men on Democratic papers—steps all designed to turn votes for Lincoln into votes for McClellan.* Nast pounced on this fraud for his new cartoon, barely a week before Election Day.

The charges had created a sensation. Many of the cheated soldiers were veterans of that summer's Wilderness campaign, a string of carnages across Virginia from Spotsylvania to Cold Harbor, whose units still faced Robert E. Lee's entrenched forces at Petersburg.[50] Hundreds lay crippled or dying in field hospitals. Thomas Nast's talent lay in his ability to translate such a complex scandal into a simple compelling image that even a child could understand.

Nast preferred to work from his home, a small house on West 44th Street, the city's upper fringe, on his drawings for *Harper's Weekly*.[51] His wife Sarah had recently given birth to their first child, a baby daughter. Sarah often read to him aloud from newspapers or books as he worked; novels by Thackeray became special favorites for them. Nast used Sarah as his model for Lady Columbia in several cartoons. "I think you are a lucky fellow to have so good a wife, and she's a lucky wife to have so good a husband," wrote

* The army had arrested five of these state agents; two had already been convicted by military commissions and given life sentences as three others awaited trial. The three were acquitted, but not until months after Election Day, prompting Democrats to complain the whole scandal had been overblown to intimidate Democratic voters.

Thomas Nast as a young prodigy.

his friend James Parton.[52] Nast sometimes drew so intensely that his hand would freeze in painful cramps.

Now he had produced an evocative new drawing based on the scandal. Reaching the top floor of the Franklin Square building, he quickly found the office of his publisher and stepped inside. Fletcher Harper liked what he saw. His broad face, deep eyes and wide whiskers, may have broken into a smirk at Nast's latest production; maybe he laughed out loud after laying it across his desk.

Harper, 57 years old, was the youngest of the four Harper brothers who'd started the publishing business decades earlier. A devout Methodist who wore black frock coats, he had an "earnest and definite way of expressing himself which was clear and impressive," his grandson John Harper wrote.[53] Within the company, he took responsibility for the two Harper journals, *Harper's New Monthly Magazine* launched in 1850 and now the political *Weekly* begun in 1857. He'd taken a quick liking to his magazine's young prodigy—he called him Tommy and used his work as an example for other staff artists. Beyond personal warmth, Harper appreciated that Nast made money for him and his brothers; a good Nast cartoon could boost wartime sales of *Harper's Weekly* by tens of thousands at ten cents apiece.

Harper studied Nast's newest drawing and saw it fitting nicely into his own political agenda: reelecting Abraham Lincoln. Its caption read simply: "How Copperheads Obtain their Votes." In it, Nast had focused on the scandal's most grisly detail—stealing the votes of dead soldiers. It showed two men dressed like grave robbers in a deserted cemetery at night, huddled in shadow around a fresh grave marked "Killed in the War of the Union." One man scribbles the name from the stone on a small paper as the other watches for intruders. But rising above them from the grave, visible only to the reader, is the ghost of the fallen soldier. He stands tall and glares down at his tormentors, his face torn by shock and anger. "Curse upon you," the ghost pronounces. "Curse upon you for making me appear disloyal to my country for which I have fought and died."[54]

In a few pencil strokes, Nast had created a deadly political weapon, evoking anger at the defilers, pride in the fallen soldier, and defiance at corruption! Harper approved it quickly and sent it to the engravers. *Harper's Weekly* would feature it in its November 12 edition hitting newsstands on the Saturday before Election Day, an edition devoted almost entirely to urging voters to cast the Lincoln ballot.

The strategy worked. Lincoln would carry New York State in 1864, but only by a whisker—50.5 percent for him versus 49.5 percent for McClellan. Separately, Horatio Seymour would be defeated as governor.[55] Afterward, Lincoln would praise the young artist who helped tilt the balance his way: "Thomas Nast has been our best recruiting sergeant," he'd write. "His emblematic cartoons have never failed to arouse enthusiasm and patriotism, and have always seemed to come just when these articles were getting scarce."[56] By the end of the Civil War, young Tommy Nast had emerged not just as a cartoonist and war illustrator but as a force in American politics. Through his pencil, he'd proven he could sway a national election and savage enemies from a national platform with a riveting new technology, the power of printed pictures.

In all his attacks against Democrats during the war, though, Nast in his cartoons never mentioned Tammany Hall itself, chronically the center of local corruption. Nast would have respected Tammany's pro-war stance and no evidence ever connected Tammany specifically with the 1864 soldier vote frauds. But perhaps there was something more: Tom Nast still held fondly to a memory from childhood. As a young boy in Manhattan in the late 1840s, he'd enjoyed running about in his knickers through city streets with friends and a favorite pastime had been to follow the showy firemen's companies and their loud, bell-ringing pump-engines racing to the scenes of giant fires, spectacles that terrified and fascinated him. Nast as a boy loved the excitement, the competition between rival fire teams, and clearly remembered his favorite, the "Big Six" volunteers. He'd particularly liked their emblem: the tiger painted in bright colors on the side of their shiny silver engine. He'd even made a point to study the original drawing of the tiger, a reproduction from a French lithograph hanging in a store on James and Madison Streets.

At the time, Nast didn't know the big strapping fellow in the red shirt, the chief of the fire company he so admired. But, years later, his drawings of corrupt politicians cheating voters like those frontline Civil War soldiers would lead to his downfall. By then, everyone would know the big man's name—Bill Tweed.

3
BALLOTS

"The fact is New York politics were always dishonest—long before my time. There never was a time you couldn't buy the Board of Aldermen.... A politician coming forward takes things as they are. The population is too hopelessly split up into races and factions to govern it under universal suffrage, except by the bribery of patronage or purchase."

—TWEED, in an interview from jail, October 25, 1877, about six months before his death.[1]

In the election of 1868, voting fraud reigned at the polls in New York City. Civil War hero General Ulysses Grant won the White House, defeating Democrat Horatio Seymour, the former New York governor, Civil War Copperhead and sympathizer with draft rioters. But Tammany Hall took all the important city and state prizes.

On Election Day, marshals arrested dozens of rabble-rousers after rival police forces threatened riots at the polls. Final vote counts clashed wildly with local registration lists and newspapers exploded with charges and countercharges. Republicans claimed at least ten thousand fake or illegal ballots had been cast; led by Tribune *editor Horace Greeley and the Union League Club, they demanded a thorough probe.*

The voting irregularities were so blatant that the United States Congress in Washington, D.C. assigned a special Select Committee to investigate.

SAMUEL JONES TILDEN KEPT HIS DISTANCE from Bill Tweed. They might be two top leaders in the New York Democratic Party, but they traveled in different circles. Tilden, nine years older, headed the state committee; he socialized with Swallowtails—wealthy Democrats named for the formal dinner jackets they wore at the posh Manhattan Club—and had amassed a fortune as a railroad lawyer. Tweed, by contrast, he considered merely a local chief and a post-war "shabby rich." Tilden's Manhattan Club would not offer Tweed a membership for years.[2]

Samuel J. Tilden.

Today, Tilden arrived at the snow-crusted sidewalk in front of the United States courthouse at 41 Chambers Street near City Hall just minutes before Tweed. He came in a separate horse-drawn carriage. The U.S. Congress' recently appointed Select Committee on Alleged Election Frauds had called him and Tweed both to testify on that same morning, December 30, 1868, one after the other.

The seven Committee members* had arrived from Washington, D.C. in mid-December and taken rooms at New York's Astor House on Broadway at Barclay Street, the elegant six-story hotel built by John Jacob Astor in the 1830s that featured central indoor heat and one of the city's best eateries. Some congressmen brought along their wives to enjoy the Christmas shopping on Broadway's "Ladies Mile" below Madison Square with its famous stores like A.T. Stewart's, Lord & Taylor, R.H. Macy's, and Tiffany's jewelry shop. City scions like William E. Dodge, founder of Phelps, Dodge & Company, feted the congressmen with private receptions.[3] America had prospered since the Civil War, and New York had gobbled up more than its share. Its population had surged past 900,000 and construction clogged streets as workmen erected a generation of elegant new buildings: the new Stock Exchange on Wall Street, A.T. Stewart's "Cast Iron Palace" on Union Square, spectacular mansions along Fifth Avenue, and the new County Courthouse aside City Hall. This wealth stood in stark contrast to the swarms of cold, crippled veterans begging for handouts and the squalor of slums like notorious Five Points, a stone's throw from City Hall.

Ships by the hundreds filled its harbor: steamers, schooners, sloops, brigs, and barks from around the world. Gray smoke rising from chimneys of thousands of small factories, breweries, tanneries, and steam-cars tinged the win-

* The committee consisted of congressmen William Lawrence as chairman (R-Ohio), Henry Dawes (R.-Ma.), Austin Blain (R.-Mi). Benjamin Hopkins (R.-Wis.), Oliver J. Dickey (R.-Pa) Michael Kerr (D.-In.), and Lewis Ross (D.-Ill.).

ter sky above rows of Manhattan rooftops, the steeple of Trinity Church towering higher than them all. On Wall Street, New York's financial markets gushed with wealth. Industries from railroads to telegraphs to textiles, each experiencing dramatic post-war booms, all brought their cash to New York's Stock Exchange that, in turn, became a battleground for elaborate power struggles among new corporate titans. The Erie Railway War, 1868's biggest, had pitted 74-year-old "Commodore" Cornelius Vanderbilt, Wall Street's richest operator, against two unscrupulous upstarts named Jay Gould and James Fisk, Jr. in a fierce battle of watered stock, dueling court orders, and legislative bribery, all for control of a company lamented as the "Scarlet Woman of Wall Street" after years of corrupt management. Stock traders—"a jolly, good-hearted, free-and-easy class of men" to one contemporary—made fortunes in a day and lost them just as quickly.[4]

The congressional investigators already had finished two weeks of testimony by the time Samuel Tilden arrived at the federal courthouse that late December morning; their witnesses so far had painted a damning picture. Robert Murray, the local United States marshal, a stern, clean-shaven man known for supplying Washington friends with the best cigars and brandy entering New York harbor,[5] had detailed the scandal's most eye-catching feature—an explosion of naturalizations, many fraudulent, turning thousands of greenhorn immigrants into instant certified voting citizens. "I take for granted that the stuffing of ballot-boxes is as great a crime against the law as the commission of burglary or highway robbery," Murray had told the committee on its opening day. The New York police, he said, obviously did not agree.[6]

Ballot box stuffing, gang intimidation, and repeat voting all had been long staples of New York "democracy," but the immigrant fraud was new. The city swarmed with foreign-born in 1868; long-term residents found the immigrant neighborhoods a confusion of strange languages and dialects. Tweed himself estimated that foreign-born constituted half to three-fifths of the vote that year in New York City.[7] Over five million immigrants had reached American shores in the 1850s and 1860s. Since the Civil War, record numbers of newcomers entered the city through Castle Garden each month*—English, French, Swiss, Swedes, and Danes, but by far the majority being Irish and Germans, crammed into the city's poorest wards.

* Castle Garden, at the lower tip of Manhattan, served as the principal immigration processing station for New York until Ellis Island opened in 1892. The site—Castle Clinton National Monument—is now the launch point for tourist ferries to Ellis Island and the Statue of Liberty.

Starting that October, Murray had begun tracing rumors of fake citizenship papers—obtained without the immigrant's actually appearing in court or swearing the required oath. The papers were being sold under-the-table by a man named Rosenberg, later identified in newspapers as a "Teutonic Israelite," operating from a lager-beer saloon at 6 Centre Street near the courthouse behind a sign reading "*Deutsche Amerikanische Demokratische Naturalizations Committee*."[8]

Murray had sent agents to Rosenberg's Centre Street saloon. They'd purchased dozens of the papers made out to fictitious names, each costing about $2 and carrying an official signature from the New York Supreme Court. Rosenberg himself had bragged to one agent of selling over 7,000 certificates but complained he'd kept only pennies of the fees, the rest going to bribe court officials and political higher-ups.

Murray had arrested Rosenberg on federal charges just two weeks before Election Day and locked him away in the Ludlow Street Jail.* When friendly newspapers began to dig deeper, they found local judges undeterred by the one arrest, stamping out new citizens at an alarming pace. One in particular, George Barnard of the State Supreme Court, had been running a virtual factory: "a system was established whereby four oaths could be administered at once.... Six or eight [immigrants] put their hands on the Bible—some put the right hand and some the left—and as many more place hands on another Bible." Many of the oath-takers lied, were underage, didn't meet the residency requirement, didn't understand the questions, or were imposters.[9]

The image of hordes of Irish Catholic vagabonds, fresh off the boat, cheating the system by the thousands and herded like cattle to vote the Tammany ticket, rankled old-time, affluent, taxpaying New Yorkers who saw their own votes being nullified by intruders. Beyond the usual anti-immigrant griping, they began voicing a new complaint: that universal suffrage itself, a reform of the 1840s, had failed in cities like New York, allowing mobs of ignorant sheep to prop up corrupt governments. Local New York judges stood for election and George Barnard specifically ran on Tweed's Tammany ticket. No wonder he'd been so helpful, critics charged. Ultimately, the congressional investigators would find that local judges like Barnard had processed 41,112 new citizenships in the weeks before that year's election—a startling

* Since selling fake naturalization papers violated *federal*, not *state* law, Murray as federal marshal had jurisdiction and could by-pass the Tammany-dominated local police and judges.

number comprising almost a third of all the votes cast in New York City that year. They'd claim that thousands of additional fake papers had been issued and used to doctor registration lists.

And that wasn't all: The prior afternoon, William Hendrick, an unemployed saloon gambler, had told the congressmen how he'd been part of a "gang of repeaters"—forty men who'd met in a liquor store on Bleecker Street just before Election Day, been lavished with whiskey, then went out and registered to vote up to twenty-five times each, using fake names and addresses provided by local party fixers.[10] During the hearings, the congressmen would hear dozens more such stories. Repeat voting might be an old game, but never before had they heard it done so brazenly and on such an organized large scale.

Samuel Tilden, of course, considered himself far above any such grimy street tricks. He was a nationally prominent figure. Ushered into the committee's private room that morning, he found himself facing four congressmen across a wooden table with a nearby clerk. The committee was meeting in a grand jury room designed for secrecy—they'd decided to take testimony behind closed doors. Witnesses had to appear alone without counsel. Michael Kerr, a red-bearded Indiana trial lawyer and senior Democrat on the panel, had been working for weeks with local Democrats to refute the fraud charges. He had arranged for Tilden and Tweed to come today and plead their innocence. But Tilden had a special problem—what we today would call a "smoking gun."

"State to the Committee what relations you bore during the last political campaign to the political parties in this State," Kerr asked Tilden once he'd taken his seat and sworn an oath.[11]

"I was chairman of the [D]emocratic State committee." Samuel Tilden had a round, clean-shaven face, short hair, blue eyes and high forehead; he spoke in a bland, colorless voice. Sickly since childhood, isolated and protected by his mother, treated with laudanum that would weaken his digestion for life, Tilden's skin had a sallow complexion—despite his daily regimen of walking or riding horseback. His mouth appeared uneven; Tilden had lost several teeth as a youngster and later had the rest removed and all replaced. A lifelong bachelor, he dressed formally: Prince Albert coats with stiff high collars and black ties though, according to one friend, "his clothes never seemed to fit him quite right."[12]

Kerr now reached across the table and handed Tilden a sheet of paper which showed signs of having been mass-printed. It bore the letterhead "Rooms of the Democratic State Committee"—Tilden's committee. It had the words "Privately and Strictly Confidential" written across the top and Tilden's own name signed at the bottom.

"Look at this circular... purporting to be issued by you," Kerr directed him, "and state to the committee whether you were the author of it or not."

"I was not," Tilden answered with a calm perfected in dozens of courtrooms over a long career.

"Do you know personally who was the author of it?"

"I do not."

The letter and Tilden's denial already had caused a public uproar. The letter had been telegraphed to hundreds of New York politicos just before Election Day. On its face, it looked like directions for a scam dictated by Tilden himself: "Please at once communicate with some reliable person in three or four principal towns and in each city of your county, and request him (expenses duly arranged for at this end) to telegraph to William M. Tweed, Tammany Hall, at the minute of closing the polls ... such person's estimate of the vote," it read. "*There is of course, an important object to be obtained.*" The letter then explained that by firing off preliminary vote counts instantly after the polls closed, they could exploit the usual half-hour delay before actual results normally began to flow over the wires. "Give orders to watch carefully the count," it went on. "Yours very truly, Samuel J. Tilden, chairman."[13]

Critics saw the implication clearly: that Tammany wire-pullers had wanted an early count of upstate votes—mostly Republican—so they could doctor the count downstate in New York City to produce a big enough Democratic majority to carry the state. In fact, that seemed to be exactly what had happened: Over 200 such telegrams, sent in reply to Tilden's letter, had reached Tammany Hall on election night, and Seymour had beaten Grant statewide by precisely 10,000 votes—a suspiciously neat margin.* Tilden had disowned the letter immediately when it first surfaced in newspapers in early November.[14] Now he repeated the same denials for the congressmen.

* Seymour had lost the national electoral count by 214 to 80, capturing only eight states for the Democrats: New York, Delaware, Georgia, Kentucky, Louisiana, Maryland, New Jersey, and Oregon. The popular vote margin was closer: 3,012,833 for Grant to 2,703,249 for Seymour.

Kerr continued: "State whether you, as chairman of the democratic State committee, distributed this circular by the mails, yourself, or procured it to be distributed."

"I did not," Tilden repeated. "I did not know of its being done, and I did not authorize it to be done"[15]

"Do you know whether Mr. Tweed did it or not?"

Tweed. Did he wince at the name? "I do not," Tilden said.

If any congressmen doubted Sam Tilden's word, they were gentlemen and didn't say so. But then Tilden went farther. "I will state what I do know of it," he said, apparently prompted by the mention of Tweed. But instead of taking the opportunity now to defend his honor by blasting the letter as a forgery and scam, he backtracked. He tried to brush it off as harmless—a well-intentioned safeguard against frauds by upstate Republicans.

"A day or two before the election, I was in the [Democratic State] committee room at the Metropolitan Hotel," Tilden explained, "and I then understood that a circular had been issued asking for early election returns.... Some gentleman, I think it was Mr. A. Oakey Hall"—Tilden was not likely to forget Oakey Hall, "Elegant Oakey," New York's district attorney and also secretary to Tilden's own committee—"spoke of it as having been intended to prevent the holding back of returns in the republican districts in the [upstate] country until our vote could be calculated, in order that the returns might then be manipulated." Hall was charging upstate Republicans with exactly the same scam they were alleging against Tammany.

Tilden then dismissed both charges as unrealistic: "I did not attach any importance to the statement, for the reason that I did not think it probable." Fixing the count, reporting fake returns simply could not be done, he argued, either by Democrats in New York City or by upstate Republicans.

In fact, later that day, Oakey Hall himself would appear as a witness and tell the congressmen that, yes, he did write the letter, he considered it proper, and he'd had Tilden's name signed to it "because it was the usage to sign the name of the chairman of the main committee."[16]

The congressmen must have scratched their heads. On its face, Tilden's story didn't add up. It was fog within fog. Listening to Tilden's monotone voice on that cold December morning with sunlight flooding in through wide windows from the street, they had to wonder: If the letter were harmless, then why had Tilden made such a fuss to deny his connection with it? Was he embarrassed at his own stupidity in being tricked? Or was it really a scam after all, with Tilden simply hiding behind a technicality? Was Tilden just as guilty as the others?

If his performance was vague, guarded, but purposeful, it was vintage Samuel Tilden. Tilden doubtless had spent hours planning it, shaping its nuances and calculating its impact. He was playing politics, something he'd done his entire life.

Born in New Lebanon, New York in 1814, Sam Tilden had grown up in a political household. His father, Elam Tilden, a well-connected farmer and grocery store owner, counted as personal friends old-style New York wire-pullers from future president Martin Van Buren to New York U.S. Senator Silas Wright and Governor William Marcy.* He invited them to plot strategy at the family dinner table for his son, young Sammy, to see. After studying at Yale and New York University, Tilden had settled in New York City in the 1840s to practice law and quickly joined the game. He became the city's Corporation Counsel in 1843, founded and edited a Democratic partisan newspaper, the *Morning News*, in 1844, and served a term in the state legislature in 1846. He joined Tammany Hall and became a Sachem in 1856. As a lawyer, he prospered—by one account, his clients included fully half the railroads in the northeast United States in the mid-1850s.[17] By the end of the Civil War he'd purchased a large townhouse at 15 Gramercy Park and counted himself financially independent, owning two iron mines, sheaves of railroad stocks, and an office at 43 Wall Street.

Along the way, Tilden also had shown an independent streak. Nominated for state Attorney General in 1856, he'd refused support both from the Know-Nothings and the anti-liquor Prohibitionists, denouncing each for its own intolerance. He lost the election and afterwards defeated the Know-Nothings in a high-profile courtroom drama when they'd challenged the election of a friendly city comptroller using doctored vote tallies.[18] He had campaigned against Lincoln in 1860 and, during the Civil War, co-founded New York's "Society for the Diffusion of Political Knowledge" which circulated anti-war, anti-Lincoln tracts.[19]

---

* All were members of the "Albany Regency" which ran the pre-Civil War party in New York. Martin Van Buren served as vice president under Andrew Jackson and then president from 1837 to 1841; Silas Wright represented New York in the U.S. Senate from 1833 to 1844 until resigning for a term as governor; William Marcy served as governor in the 1830s and later joined the cabinets of presidents James Polk and Franklin Pierce. It was Marcy who first pronounced what became the creed of the 19th century Democratic Party: "To the victor belongs the spoils."

Socially shy, frequently bedridden with colds and flues, Tilden distanced himself from casual human contact. He spent his free hours at the Manhattan Club at 96 Fifth Avenue where he'd paid $500 to become a charter member. "As a rule people did not like Tilden at a first meeting," a biographer explained. "He seemed cold, self-centered, vain, too cocksure, and too omniscient"; he had an irritating habit of telling people "I told you so" and hesitated about answering direct questions.[20] His bachelorhood raised eyebrows in New York, forcing even friendly biographers to explain how he "found a fairly satisfactory substitute for a sweetheart and children in his absorbing law work," as one wrote. "His deepest feelings were reserved for a great cause—a reform, a burning party issue or a sacred principle. To him love was merely sexual foolishness."[21]

Things had started well for Sam Tilden in 1868; friends had urged him to seek the New York governorship that year as a steppingstone for the future, perhaps even a run at the White House some day.[22] But then things had turned badly. Tilden found himself drawn into the woes of another person, one of his closest and oldest political friends, Horatio Seymour.

Lightning had struck in July 1868. A deadlocked Democratic convention in New York City had stampeded to Seymour on the 22nd ballot and made him its candidate for president. Seymour, who was chairing the convention at the time, had declined the honor at first; he enjoyed his life as retired elder statesman, practicing law in Utica and attending Democratic functions as a popular speaker.[23] In the excitement, he'd turned instantly to his long-time confidante Sam Tilden. By one account, Seymour ran out from the hall to a nearby lobby and found his friend: "My God Tilden, what shall I do?" he'd asked in a panic, to which Tilden had replied coolly: "Your party has called you, and you will accept."[24]

This reliance by Seymour on Tilden reflected a long bond. Both came from rural upstate towns and shared a background in pre-war New York politics. As wartime governor, Horatio Seymour had often turned to Tilden for advice: "Now that you and others have got me into [a] scrape, I wish you would tell me what to do," he'd written Tilden in 1862.[25] Tilden had been notably absent during the July 1863 draft riots. He later claimed to be sick in bed at the time, but afterwards he rose to face what he described as "many demands for attention and counsel amid ten days of excitement and bustle,"[26] including traveling to Washington, D.C., as Seymour's agent to try and convince President Lincoln to stop the draft.[27] Now in 1868, saddled with the nomination, Horatio Seymour turned again to his friend to manage the campaign, which became a disaster from the beginning.

Starting soon after the convention, enemies had dragged out Seymour's wartime Copperhead record and painted him as a weak-willed traitor and possibly insane. Then, after suffering weeks of attacks, Democrats lost contests in all four "October states"*—key indicators that the ticket was headed toward electoral doom. Party leaders who had forced the presidential nomination down Seymour's throat in July now panicked. Manton Marble, publisher of the *New York World* and one of Tilden's Manhattan Club cronies, led a chorus of demands: either drop Seymour's running mate, former Union General Frank Blair, from the ticket or drop Seymour himself. Telegrams flooded Tilden's New York office from across the country: "Call your committee together, withdraw Seymour & nominate [President Andrew] Johnson or [Supreme Court Justice Salmon P.] Chase. Act and win," wired one frustrated backer from Washington, D.C.; "Patriotism clearly commands withdrawal of Seymour and nomination of Chase," insisted another.**[8]

Facing collapse of the national campaign, Tilden had rushed to Utica and found Seymour himself willing to step aside. However, both agreed that such a last-minute shuffle would sink the party in local contests coast to coast. They decided to hold firm. "No authority or possibility to change front. All friends consider it totally impracticable, and equivalent to disbanding our forces," Tilden announced in a public letter cosigned with party leaders August Belmont and Augustus Schell. "We in New York are not panic-stricken."[29] Privately, Tilden knew the presidency was lost, and with it had gone his own chances for higher office for the foreseeable future.

After Election Day, he faced another indignity—bickering over money. Tilden had sunk $10,000 of his own cash into Seymour's 1868 defeat—an amount big enough to dent even his sizable bankroll—but the Democratic Party had spent thousands more based on Tilden's promises. In late October, Tweed—who'd given Tilden his own $5,000 check as an early campaign contribution—began pressing him to settle accounts. Tilden ignored repeated

* These states—Pennsylvania, Ohio, Indiana, and Nebraska—held elections for congressmen, governor, and local offices in October. Voters would have to return in November to cast ballots for president. In days before public opinion polls, the early voting was seen as a referendum on the national ticket.

** Such a change of presidential candidates by a party after its nominating convention and just weeks before Election Day would have been unprecedented either before then or since.

calls for a meeting to decide who should pay the mounting pile of bills. Tammany apparently got stuck with most of them.[30]

And now, sitting before a congressional committee, Tilden faced the final embarrassment of a voting scandal, complete with a forged letter dragging his name in the mud. He had a reputation to protect in 1868—a possible future in politics, his standing with the city's elite, his legal practice. This was no time to quarrel with Boss Tweed and his Tammany crowd. Tweed might be a rival but, so far, he wasn't an enemy. This day, December 30, 1868, testifying to the congressmen, Tilden would swallow his pride, make no damaging charges, and protect himself.

The more the congressmen pressed, the more Tilden back-pedaled. They asked him about the phony naturalizations and repeat voting and Tilden, the state party chairman, threw up his hands: "I did not know very much of the details of the minor committees," he claimed. "There was generally some officer about the City Hall who looked after all these matters; but I had nothing to do with naturalization at all."[31] The committee didn't keep him long in the grand jury room that morning—Tilden's testimony covers a scant three pages of the thousand-page transcript. On each point, the congressmen took Tilden's story at face value, even Tilden's explanation of the forged letter. In their final report, they'd describe it as "A. Oakey Hall's Secret Circular"—not Tilden's.

After he'd finished testifying, Tilden left the courthouse, stepped outside onto Chambers Street, and returned uptown to his busy legal practice. There was money to make in 1868 and plenty of time for politics later. But he couldn't shake the scandal that had tarred his name. Months later, long after the congressmen had issued their final report, Horace Greeley would publicly blast him in an open letter, published in the *New York Tribune*: "Mr. Tilden, you cannot escape responsibility," Greeley railed. "For you were at least a passive accomplice in the giant frauds of last November. Your name was used, without public protest … [a]nd you, not merely by silence but by positive assumption, have covered those frauds with the mantle of your respectability… you are as deeply implicated in them to-day as though your name were Tweed, O'Brien, or Oakey Hall."[32]

Tilden never answered Greeley's charge. He'd pick his own day and his own way to make known his feelings about Bill Tweed and Oakey Hall.

◎ ◎ ◎ ◎ ◎

Next came Tweed, ushered into the committee's private room moments after Sam Tilden had left. The contrast could not have been sharper. Unlike Tilden's cold personality, Tweed lit up the room. Big and boisterous, he knew how to lavish the congressmen with humor, look them in the eye, slap shoulders, shake hands, crack a joke, share a confidence, poke fun at his own girth. Tweed dressed sharply these days—he'd grown wealthy since the war. But his black suit, gold watch chain, and stiff collar only accentuated his most prominent new physical feature, a bulging stomach. Good food had become his favorite vice. "I was never drunk in my life," he'd tell a newspaper writer later. "I have never smoked a cigar nor chewed a piece of tobacco. I never liked whiskey. Being a man of large body, I am fond of eating."[33]

Tweed too had come to the committee this morning to declare his innocence. He sat down at the table, filled the large leather chair with his 300 pounds, and swore to tell the truth. It took little prompting to start him talking:

"State your official position," Congressman Kerr asked at the outset as the others looked on.[34]

"I am deputy street commissioner, member of the board of supervisors, and State senator," Tweed answered, ticking off his official titles as a clerk taking longhand notes struggled to keep up. And more: "I was chairman of the general committee at Tammany Hall."

"State whether your identification with the party machinery is extensive or limited."

"It is very extensive," Tweed said with some pride. "I have that reputation, and I think it is pretty well deserved."

Tweed had every reason to crow at the outcome in 1868. He and his Tammany crowd didn't really care who sat in the White House as president. Washington, D.C. was far away and Horatio Seymour was Tilden's friend, not Tweed's. Instead, Tweed that year had accomplished a masterstroke: He'd taken Tammany's two most popular figures, mayor John Hoffman and district attorney A. Oakey Hall—the same two who had impressed the public by prosecuting draft rioters five years earlier—and installed them as his new hand-picked New York governor and New York city mayor, respectively. Both owed their jobs squarely to Tweed. Their newly-won control of the Albany governor's mansion would give Tammany a veto over the state legislature that in turn would tighten its grip on the city.

This latest voting scandal and congressional probe only heightened

Key Democratic-Tammany candidates in New York, 1868:

- For president: former governor *Horatio Seymour* (against Republican Ulysses Grant)—defeated;
- For governor: New York mayor *John T. Hoffman*—victorious;
- For seat on the New York Supreme Court: incumbent *George Bernard*—victorious;
- For county board of supervisors: incumbent *William M. Tweed*—victorious.
- For mayor of New York City (to fill the seat vacated by John Hoffman on becoming governor): district attorney *A. Oakey Hall.* (Elected in a separate contest in December.)—victorious.

Tweed's stature in a city that respected bare-knuckle toughness. The fact that he'd led Tammany's campaign, used illegal tactics that worked, and gotten away with it, all made him a person to reckon with. He could be excused for looking like a cat who had just eaten a canary.

Things had changed in New York since the Civil War: Tweed no longer worried about his control of Tammany; he'd remade the club in his own image. For starters, he'd given it a new Hall—a three-story "Wigwam" on Union Square opened just that summer with arching windows, marble inlays, and red brickwork elegant enough to outshine even the nearby New York Academy of Music. Its concert room seated 5,000 people under a 35-foot high ceiling with cut-glass chandeliers, galleries, and private boxes; it was surrounded by smoking salons, promenade lobbies, a library, and a life-size statue of a Tammany brave. The building had cost an eye-popping $300,000—a staggering sum paid entirely by Tammany friends—and had received instant respectability that July when Democrats chose it to house their 1868 National Convention. Already, designers were refitting its main hall into a musical concert theater to compete with Booth's, Wallack's, Pike's, and all the city's best.

At the same time, Tweed had reorganized Tammany's power structure. He'd made Tammany's general committee a rubber stamp* and lodged true

* Tweed had increased the committee's size from 21 to 150 members, making it too bulky for routine decisions while creating more patronage slots for him to fill, and he decentralized the process for choosing local nominees to local ward committees whose memberships he strictly controlled. Tweed had also eclipsed the other political clubs; Mozart Hall now routinely rubber-stamped Tammany's choices for key positions.

Tammany Hall on the south side of Union Square.

control in a tiny circle consisting of himself, mayor Hoffman, comptroller Richard Connolly, and Peter Barr Sweeny, the city chamberlain and long-time Tammany strategist. People called this foursome the "lunch club" because they'd started meeting years earlier for strictly social lunches and, over time, had formed a political pact. They still ate together most days in a private City Hall room or at Wingate's restaurant across the street—Tweed made a point not to miss his meal and a good glass of wine at noontime—but now they used the time to plot strategy and divide patronage while enjoying each other's company.[35]

Most newspapers still ignored Tweed. They often confused him with Peter Sweeny as Tammany's real power,[36] but behind the scenes Tweed ran the organization with a firm gavel. As Deputy Street Commissioner alone Tweed commanded over 500 jobs, more than any other department. "[S]anguine, active, and exuberant, social, jovial, and shrewd" was how a newspaper writer described him around this time—a good politician who knew how to keep friends.[37]

Rubbing elbows at City Hall, riding about town in his private carriage, or holding court at his Duane Street office, Tweed showed every sign of wealth. The year before, his wife Mary Jane had made him a father for the tenth time with a new baby son, George, and they were preparing to move uptown to a new house on Fifth Avenue and 43rd street.[38] As a father, Tweed had begun grooming his eldest son, 22-year-old William Jr., by giving him a city patronage job—assistant to State Supreme Court Justice Albert Cardozo. For his next-eldest, Richard, he'd rented out the popular six-story Metropolitan Hotel on Prince Street, one of New York's largest with 400 rooms, hot and cold running water, and steam heat, and set his son up as manager. Increasingly, though, Tweed had become an absentee husband. He spent his nights huddled with Tammany cronies or sharing laughs at his private clubs—mostly the Americus where he was president.[39] Mary Jane seemed to resent this treatment, especially carrying a final child in middle age. She apparently left Tweed for months in 1866 during the pregnancy and moved into their second home, a large estate—two houses on forty acres—that Tweed had purchased in Greenwich, Connecticut where his Americus Club kept its lodge and where he now docked his two steam-powered yachts—the *William M. Tweed* and the *Mary Jane Tweed.*

Tweed made his money from many sources, not the least of it from graft like the usual 15 percent he and his circle skimmed from city contracts through the board of supervisors. These days, contractors now came to Tweed and agreed to pay up to 35 percent on all bills to win city business. Tweed would split these gains with his lunch club friends Richard Connolly, the city comptroller who controlled access to the treasury, and Peter Sweeny.[40] Tweed easily brushed away charges of graft that occasionally arose, either pointing to their lack of evidence or painting them as political hot air.* But it seemed an open secret, a grimy fact about New York City. Its government was corrupt, like its streets were dirty, its traffic clogged, its alleys dotted with brothels and pickpockets—the cost of living in a big city.

Tweed owned a growing real estate portfolio: Just a few months earlier he'd purchased the entire west side of what later would be called Columbus Circle and often bought vacant lots just before major city improvements were

* In 1866 and 1868, the New York Citizens Association led by Peter Cooper had complained of overspending on the County Courthouse being constructed near City Hall. Begun in 1858 with a projected cost of $250,000, outlays by the close of 1868 already approached $3.2 million with an annual payroll of $280,000. Several days of hearings, however, uncovered no evidence of wrongdoing. Similarly, an 1866 probe into Street Department abuses found little evidence and led to the removal of Commissioner Charles Cornell, but not his Deputy, Tweed.

announced. Neighbors delighted when Tweed planted his stake on their block, guaranteeing imminent upgrades: "They [Tweed and company] are well paid and paid in advance," William Martin of the West Side Association put it. "They were supported in the last election by many taxpayers, on the avowed ground… that the great public works on this Island would be vigorously pushed forward, even without our help."[41]

Tweed owned the New-York Printing Company along with a group that included James B. Taylor, a principal stockholder of the *New-York Times*, and used his power to make it the exclusive printer for New York County. In 1868 alone, it had provided 105,000 blank citizenship forms to the courts for naturalizing immigrants before Election Day—part of the election scandal.[42]

In 1867, Tweed also began spending large amounts of time upstate in Albany—150 miles north up the Hudson River—winning a seat in the state senate which met usually from January to April. Mary Jane joined him at first but she found Albany too snowbound and isolated and soon stopped, leaving Tweed to cavort with his cronies. In his first year there, Tweed engineered the selection of a new Assembly Speaker,[43] giving him enormous leverage. Here too he found graft: "I found it was impossible to do anything [in Albany] without paying for it," Tweed explained later; he came ready to play the game.*[44] He made himself a central player in the Erie Railway War—the high-stakes contest between Jay Gould and Cornelius Vanderbilt for control of that rundown line. The battle had shifted from Wall Street to the state capitol when Jay Gould sought legislation to validate some $10 million worth of watered stock he'd issued in the company—a step that even George Barnard called "legalizing counterfeit money."[45] The Gould-Vanderbilt face-off in Albany spawned a titanic orgy of bribes;[46] legislators who normally earned $300 annual salaries bid the two sides against each other and demanded pay-offs of $5,000 or more for a single vote. Tweed originally backed Vanderbilt but ultimately sided with Gould and his partner, Jim Fisk.

Gould, having won the war, repaid the debt by giving Tweed and Peter Sweeney seats on the Erie Railway corporate board, a position whose perks included a cornucopia of inside stock–trading tips. This expanded Tweed's "Ring" to include one of America's richest and most aggressive corporate powers.

---

* Around this time, the state assembly was dominated by the so-called Black Horse Cavalry, a loosely-organized group of about twenty members who'd band together to extort bribes, but there is no indication Tweed, a senator, had a direct connection with them.

Rumors also started around this time about Tweed's keeping a mistress, a "small blond" woman he hid away in Albany or at the Americus Club lodge in Greenwich, far from the eyes of Mary Jane or the New York press, but it always remained just talk. If any mistress actually did exist, he kept her well hidden, as a Victorian-era gentleman would. Her identity never came out.[47]

For Tweed, the 1868 election had presented a rare opportunity. He had ambitious plans, topped by trying to install John Hoffman in the governor's mansion in Albany. And he faced towering obstacles: The huge popularity of General Grant that would assure a large upstate Republican turnout, U.S. marshal Robert Murray's crackdown on immigrant voters, and now the collapse of Horatio Seymour's presidential bid in October. Tammany would have to fight even to protect its own base in New York City.[48] As the battle approached, the "Temporary Headquarters of the Democratic General Committee" became the "Office of William M. Tweed. No. 237 Broadway."[49]

To win the governorship for Hoffman, he'd need a huge majority in New York City to offset an upstate Republican surge, and Tweed knew exactly where to find the votes—the large enclaves of Irish and German immigrants, Tammany's core supporters. The problem, however, was that most immigrants who'd come to New York since the 1850s had avoided becoming citizens. During the war, when citizenship meant conscription into Lincoln's army to face rebel cannon on Virginia battlefields, naturalizations had frozen to a trickle—barely 3,000 a year from 1861 though 1863. Now, in 1868, some fifty to seventy thousand foreign-born Tammany warriors in New York City urgently needed to swear their oaths and get their papers before Election Day.

All that fall, Tweed pressed his organization to get the job done. In October, the New York Supreme Court alone cranked out more than 1,600 naturalizations each day, in addition to hundreds more from the Superior Court and the Court of Common Pleas.[50] When Marshal Robert Murray began his crackdown in mid-October, it signaled a new danger: that Republicans would use the scandal as a pretext to challenge all immigrant votes at the polls, legitimate or not—potentially thousands of ballots.[51] Murray had begun hiring dozens of assistant marshals and Republican Governor Reuben Fenton had placed the state militia on alert. "Challenge! Sharp challenging will be necessary at every poll," shouted the partisan *Evening Post* in a typical call to arms, "do not be deterred by threats."[52]

The Tammany machine, a juggernaut with its backbone in the local wards and neighborhoods, worked best in this type of pinch. Each of the city's

340 election districts—about fifteen in each of its twenty-two wards—contained about four hundred eligible voters and each had its own Tammany captain and its own local ten-member committee assigned to visit every single Democrat. The party provided each with $1,000 in cash for Election Day "walking around" money. Three citywide committees oversaw the effort and were responsible for challenging Republicans at the polls.[53] Asked once if he'd ever directed anyone to falsify election returns, Tweed could swear that he didn't have to: "More in the nature of a request than a direction."[54]

Instead or giving orders, Tweed's Tammany gave its braves something to fight for: the chance for a patronage job, respectability, and advancement. "Is not the pending contest pre-eminently one of capitol against labor, of money against popular rights, and of political power against the struggling interests of the masses?" a Tammany circular argued that year during the campaign. It appealed to fear as well: if Republicans win, it threatened, "[t]heir next step will be to bring the Southern negro North to vote down and compete against the white laborer"[55]—a lingering raw nerve from the Civil War even though most black citizens had left New York after the bloody 1863 riots.* Tammany also backed the Irish nationalist Fenians and the anti-Spanish Cuban independence movement, both being causes to raise the dander of many immigrant partisans.

In the final days before voting, Oakey Hall, the district attorney who also acted as Tammany's own in-house counsel, began pressing the legal case: that any immigrant with citizenship papers carrying a valid stamp from a New York court MUST be allowed to register and vote with no questions asked. Then, to fight the U.S. marshals on the street, Tammany created its own instant platoon of bullies: James "Jimmy" O'Brien, New York's 27-year old, Irish-born sheriff elected on Tammany's ticket the year before, took the initiative to hire between 1,500 and 2,000 deputies, a force almost as large as the city's 2,200-man Metropolitan Police. "I feared there would be some trouble, and I thought it would be no harm to have these men as assistant police," O'Brien later told the congressional investigators.[56] "I ordered them to arrest any one who interfered with the voting"[57]—that is, anyone who got in the way of Tammany's immigrants and repeaters.

* Black men were eligible to vote in New York State in 1868 if they paid property taxes of $250 or more—a requirement not applicable to whites. After the 1863 riots, the city's black population had dropped to just 1.39 percent, just 12,600 people out of about 942,000, in 1870.

Finally, on Election Day eve, John Hoffman, the mayor and Tammany's candidate for governor, lowered the final gauntlet: "Unscrupulous, designing, and dangerous men, political partisans, are resorting to extraordinary means" to disrupt the election, he charged in a formal City Hall proclamation. They were being led by the U.S. marshal, "a violent political partisan," with "swarms of special deputies" aiming to intimidate foreign-born citizens. Hoffman offered rewards of $1,000 each for the arrest of anyone "intimidating, obstructing, or defrauding any voter in the exercise of his right as an elector," a call to arms for Jimmy O'Brien and his bruisers.[58]

On Election Day, the Tammany legions came to work: "[N]ext to the Roman army under Caesar, the organization of Tammany Hall was the most thoroughly disciplined body that the world has ever seen," Peter Sweeny boasted a few months later. "We had good discipline."[59] Starting at daybreak, Tammany's legions came out by the thousands: gangs of repeaters, O'Brien's deputies, Tammany's vote inspectors, all in orchestrated attack.

O'Brien landed the first punches. First thing that morning, his deputies began arresting Republican vote-watchers. They started with James Dennis, an uptown inspector who apparently had a list of one hundred and fifty 'repeaters' who intended to vote and whom he intended to challenge. The deputies stopped him at his house, handcuffed him and dragged him off to Ludlow Street Jail. They arrested at least two more inspectors and then circulated to polling places around town, bullying any others who challenged a Tammany ballot. Then came swarms of repeaters; some deputies actually escorted them from poll to poll to prevent interference. At Spring and Varrick Streets, for instance, one Tammany deputy pulled a revolver on a policeman trying to arrest him for fighting; the officer too pulled a gun and for several moments each threatened to shoot the other until finally the deputy backed down.[60]

After sundown, when the polls closed, Tammany's inspectors played havoc with the count, giving its backroom fixers time to manufacture whatever numbers they needed. In the Thirteenth ward, for instance, just as the ballot box was being opened, a group identified only as "ruffians" reportedly "turned off the gas, leaving the room in darkness" and "before the lights could be procured many of the tickets were removed and others mixed with those lying on the table." In other wards, Democratic counters allegedly haggled for hours on technicalities or insisted on reading every name on every identical ticket, all to delay the counts.[61]

Robert Murray, the U.S. marshal, made his own arrests that day, he and his men carting off dozens of Tammany braves for trying to cast illegal votes, many with fake citizenship papers. But he couldn't hold them long in jail; Tammany sent squads of lawyers to friendly judges who quickly began to free them. George Barnard of the state Supreme Court issued one *habeas corpus writ* that released twenty-seven with a single flash of his pen.

Tweed himself spent election night celebrating at the Metropolitan Hotel. When the dust settled, they'd won John Hoffman the governorship by more than 47,000 votes, making a mockery of Horatio Seymour's mere 10,000-vote statewide margin over Grant. Tweed himself won reelection as county supervisor, and Barnard as supreme court judge, both by huge margins. Even a Republican stalwart like E.L. Godkin, editor of *The Nation*—a rapidly anti-Tammany journal—found the spectacle irresistible: "I want very much to show 'the unterrified' in their glory to two English friends tonight at Tammany Hall," he wrote to Manton Marble during the day, "& write to ask whether you could kindly put me in the way of getting three tickets" to the celebration.[62]

Tweed could be especially satisfied with his new front man. John Hoffman, the new governor, a Union College graduate who'd been popular as mayor, independent, and apparently honest. "He was not approachable with money," Tweed himself would later claim, both with pride and lament.[63] Come 1872, four years from now, Hoffman would be a strong challenger for the White House against Ulysses Grant. Using Tammany ballot-box tactics coast to coast, how could they loose? Tweed himself stood to become a national power.*

Now, as he sat before the congressional investigating committee in the federal courthouse on Chambers Street answering questions about the alleged election frauds, Tweed could be gracious. A former congressman himself, he knew how to talk turkey with the committee. Confronted with specific charges of fraud, he claimed ignorance. "O, I hear rumors on every subject," he shrugged. "Everything you have asked me there have been rumors about, of course. I have heard them in the general rumble of city politics and city conversation." He had nothing to say about the Tilden letter; asked if he

---

* Under this vision, Tweed could take a seat in the U.S. Senate and become the force in a Hoffman presidency, similar to what New York Republican leader Thurlow Weed had attempted with William Seward in 1860 and what U.S. Senator Mark Hanna (R-Ohio) would accomplish with president William McKinley in 1896.

knew about Benjamin Rosenberg and illegal citizenship papers, he said simply: "No sir; I do not."[64]

The congressmen accepted Tweed's word at face value, just as they'd done with Samuel Tilden earlier that morning. Tweed charmed them: "I was born in New York and have lived here all my life, and have as many friends among republicans as among democrats," he recounted. He joked about the money he'd personally sunk into the campaign: "Perhaps I contributed entirely about $10,000... I subscribed $5,000 to the State committee and the rest went out in driblets after that."[65] Asked if he had city street employees drawing salaries but doing no actual work—political "sinecures"—he hardly bothered to deny it: "I don't suppose that I have been through the [street department] building more than twice a year; but I know that when I send for them during business hours I usually find them."[66]

In the end, Tammany Hall itself recognized the biggest winner in the episode. On March 5, 1869, it unanimously elected Tweed its new Grand Sachem—taking the seat vacated by John Hoffman, the new governor—making Tweed simultaneously both its symbolic and its actual chief, a leader of whom they could say "no one really in need ever turned away from him empty handed."[67] As for the voting itself and the forged letter from Samuel Tilden, Tweed only years later would suggest he knew more than he'd let on in his easy denials to the congressmen that day. "The ballots didn't make the outcome. The counters did," he'd say cryptically.[68]

The congressional committee issued its final report on the 1868 New York voting in February 1869. By then, its members had heard from 417 witnesses—a dizzying parade of thugs, policemen, and backroom fixers—and the drama in the federal courthouse on Chambers Street had degenerated into strong-arm tactics and finger pointing. Jimmy O'Brien sent his deputy sheriffs one day in early January to arrest seven witnesses waiting in the lobby to testify and drag them off to a nearby police station; the next day, Metropolitan police officers came too, this time to eject the deputy sheriffs and post guards at the committee's meeting room until Democrats insisted that they too leave.

In its conclusion, the committee found the 1868 election to have been grossly manipulated. "The frauds were the result of a systematic plan of gigantic proportions, stealthily prearranged and boldly executed, not merely by bands of degraded desperadoes, but with the direct sanction, approval, or aid of many prominent officials and citizens of New York," it claimed, and was "aided by an immense, corrupt, and corrupting official patronage and power, which not only encouraged, but shielded and protected, the guilty principals and their aiders and abetters [sic.]."[69] Of the 156,054 votes cast in New York City that year, the committee estimated that 50,000 had been fake or illegal, the product of repeat voting, illegal naturalizations, or fictitious counts. The total votes cast in New York City that year had exceeded the number of possible voters—actual human beings of voting age and gender—by more than 8 percent.[70]

Hoffman's election as governor was a fraud, they charged, as was Seymour's carrying of the state.

But beneath these splashy headlines, the investigation produced few specifics: It recommended no prosecutions and proposed only a handful of generic reforms such as stripping New York courts of their power to grant citizenships and passing a constitutional amendment allowing Congress to regulate the appointment of presidential electors.[71] The *New York Herald* dismissed the whole effort as "a hifalutin and long-winded peroration of a bitter partisan character" with "no direct evidence of such extensive frauds."[72] The *New York World* labeled it simply "A Stock of Stale Slanders."[73]

Other than Benjamin Rosenberg—caught red-handed selling fake citizenship papers to the U.S. marshal—no one was ever convicted of a crime for the 1868 voting scandal. In New York City, Judge Barnard convened a grand jury to pursue violations of local laws, but the jury—which included eleven Tammany members out of twenty jurors—discovered none.[74] The fraud charges, it concluded, were "manifestly unfounded … except those which ordinarily arise in any excited political contest, and which are comparatively trivial."[75]

For Tammany it looked like a clean getaway: griping by the losers but no serious challenge to the result and no lasting mud on its skirts. In fact, in the celebrating, only one small cloud appeared to block the sunshine and cast a shadow on the scene: Shortly after Election Day, a small cartoon appeared on a back page of *Harper's Weekly*, the popular illustrated magazine. "A respectable screen covers a multitude of thieves," its caption read. It showed the figure of John Hoffman, looking handsome and smug with his signature handlebar mustache, "Our Mayor," a proud smirk on his face, drawn onto a large stand-up screen placed in a position to block the sight behind it of several

"*A Respectable Screen Covers a Multitude of Thieves.*"
Harper's Weekly, *October 10, 1868.*

grubby-looking men taking fistfuls of cash from a box labeled "city treasury." Over the men hung a sign that read: "Thou shalt steal as much as thou canst. The Ring."

Tweed himself probably saw the cartoon and may have snickered at the satire. He would have noticed the signature in small neat letters at the bottom corner: "*Th. Nast.*" But it wouldn't have bothered him. None of the "Ring" figures in the cartoon had a recognizable face and the drawing gave no details—it made only a vague charge. Still, Tweed had to wonder: Did this "*Th. Nast*" really know anything? Probably not. Hearsay aside, Tweed knew he kept his secrets carefully. And it was just a cartoon. What difference could it make?

• 4 •
SPOILS

"I think ... that a great injustice has been done me. I have been charged with breaking the pledge I made... I deny that, during the whole course of my life, I have ever broken any pledge made by me to either friend or foe. Whatever else there might be in my conduct to censure or find fault with, I HAVE ALWAYS KEPT MY WORD....

—TWEED, to a private caucus of so-called Young Democrat rivals in the state legislature in Albany. *New York Sun*, March 26, 1870.

"Tweed was not an honest politician, but a level one—Kelly is honest but not level."

—S. FOSTER DEWEY, Tweed's secretary, on Tweed's death, comparing Tweed to his Tammany successor "Honest John" Kelly, April 12, 1878.[1]

On New Year's Day, January 1, 1869, Abraham Oakey Hall swore the oath to become New York City's new mayor. He now took the place of former mayor John T. Hoffman—who'd left for Albany to become the state's new governor—at the daily "lunch club" at City Hall. The lunch group now included Hall, city chamberlain Peter Sweeny, comptroller Richard Connolly, and Tweed wearing his many hats—state senator, deputy street commissioner, and boss of Tammany. These four men now controlled almost every key lever of power in New York City, with a tightening grip on the state government in Albany:

City Hall, through the mayor;

The city and county treasuries, through Connolly as comptroller;

The law, through Tammany judges like George Barnard, sheriff O'Brien, and a friendly police board;

Wall Street, through Jay Gould, Jim Fisk, and the Erie Railway;

The state legislature, through Tweed as senator and Hoffman as governor;

The newspapers, through advertising, flattery, and ownership.

They could reward friends with jobs and contracts and punish enemies with a cold shoulder, and they had backers by the thousands, people ready to trust them and do their bidding. They'd proven they could always win elections and they'd grown very rich.

The reign of the Tweed Ring at its height of power, started here.

NEW YORKERS WAKING UP on the first day of the Tweed era in 1869 would notice one immediate difference in their noisy city—a flamboyant new mayor. "Elegant Oakey," that's what his friends called him for his dapper suits and comic airs. He rarely had enemies; everyone liked him, even men he'd sent to prison. Witty and urbane, he often signed his name "OK" and wore his pretensions on his sleeve. He wrote literary essays for local journals and dramas for the New York stage. "I've been called the king of the Bohemians," he once quipped, "and I'm jolly proud of that title."[2] Skinny with narrow eyes, pince-nez glasses, and full beard, he proudly traced his ancestry to Coll Okey, an Englishman hanged in 1662 for his role in the execution of King Charles I—a favorite point with Irish voters. Born in Albany, raised in New Orleans, educated at Harvard Law School, Hall had won elections as New York's district attorney consistently since 1853—first as a Whig, then a Republican, then a Mozart Hall Democrat, then a Tammany Hall Democrat.

He lived with his wife Katherine "Kate" Louise Barnes Hall—daughter of marble magnate Joseph Barnes—in a large brownstone on West 42nd Street across from the Croton Reservoir* with their son and five teenage daughters. Oakey joined every club—he traded gourmet tips with the Manhattan Club's famous chef, led dialogues on literature at the Lotus Club, and easily made "the list," New York's earliest Social Register. He'd joined Tammany during the Civil War, drawn as much by ambition as by distaste for that uncouth Republican backwoodsman Abe Lincoln in the White House. He'd signed the Tammany membership log with a flourish: "Whilst Council fires hold out to burn, The vilest sinner may return. OK."[3]

As district attorney, Hall craved the limelight. He took credit for argu-

* The Croton Reservoir, a fortress-like structure covering the site of today's Bryant Park and the New York Public Library, opened in 1842 and operated for most of the century. Its high walls gave one of the best views of the city. An engineering marvel of its time, it connected to the Croton Aqueduct bringing water into the city from the Croton Dam in upstate New York 41 miles away.

A. Oakey Hall.

ing 10,000 cases before juries and sent legions of criminals to jail—from Civil War draft rioters to murderers and pickpockets to gang members and political crooks. But he was equally famous for the 10,000 other indictments he'd chosen to ignore, mostly liquor law violations. "Somehow or other the press of business in my office has been so great that I have never yet found time to prosecute a man for taking a drink after 12 o'clock at night," he once quipped.[4] Saloonkeepers loved him. "Few persons have as many *tried* friends as I have," he bragged after one election victory with a trademark pun, "and *tried* friends are always magnanimous."[5]

In November 1868, after John Hoffman's election as New York's new governor had left the mayor's office vacant, Tammany decided to nominate "the strongest man in our organization," as Peter Sweeny put it.[6] Sam Tilden's Manhattan Club crowd had raised its own challenger—John Kelly, the former sheriff and Tammany Sachem—but Kelly withdrew late in the race for health reasons.[7] Oakey Hall, facing a Republican, won 75,054 votes out of some 96,000 cast—a whopping 80 percent.

"It will be refreshing to have for Mayor of New York a strictly upright, honorable, capable man, and at the same time one who writes drama or a farce with equal success, acts a part as well as most professionals on the stage, conducts the most difficult cases on the calendar, sings a good song, composes poetry by the yard, makes an effective stump speech, responds to a toast with remarkable eloquence and taste, mixes a lobster salad as well as Delmonico's head cook, smokes the best cigar in New York, respects old age, and admires youth, as poets and orators invariably do,"[8] the *New York Herald* pronounced shortly after the election—words Hall probably wrote himself, having long ago charmed *Herald* publisher James Gordon Bennett, Jr. Said the *Herald* of the mayor: "He calls a spade a spade and Horace Greeley a humbug."[9]

Tweed, the hard-nosed pragmatist, grumbled at "lightheaded" Oakey Hall. "Hall's all right," he once said of the mayor, "all he needs is ballast. Politics are too deep for him. They are for me and I can wade long after Oakey had to float."[10] But Tweed recognized in Hall the perfect public face for his machine. Oakey Hall stood for progress. In an April letter to the newspapers that year, he ridiculed the backward, chaotic "old" New York, "a Metropolis without ... boulevards, and without museums, lyceums, free libraries and zoological gardens" cherished by "some rich old men who cannot realize that New York is no longer a series of straggling villages" along Manhattan Island.*[11] He pushed to pave sidewalks with Nicolson concrete instead of the traditional wooden planks or dirt, despite complaints over the $5 per square yard cost, and drew a line with city aldermen "not to give approval to schemes for wooden pavement unless property-holders in rather quiet side streets should petition for them."[12]

Hall became ubiquitous, attending public events at the drop of a hat, from the dedication of a new statue of railroad magnate Cornelius Vanderbilt to every sort of funeral, even of political enemies like ex-Mayor James Harper and *New-York Times* founder Henry Raymond. Manton Marble's *New York World* called him "our eccentric but talented Mayor" who "says and writes more bright things and commits more stupid blunders than any politicians we know of." During a quarrel over how to treat loose animals causing havoc in New York's muddy, clogged streets, another local paper quipped: "Mayor Hall does not intend incurring even the displeasure of the dogs."[13]

Tweed, too, increasingly enjoyed the public display in this new era: As Tammany's Grand Sachem, he now presided over the club's arcane rituals with pomp and ceremony. At Tammany's annual July 4 gala that year, he led the traditional grand procession draping his large body in "glittering regalia and bearing a silver war hatchet, the Tammany saint's symbol in his hand," as one reporter described it. His Indians and Sachems, themselves decked out in colored shoulder sashes and gold medals, followed in double file. He led the crowd in booming cheers as he mounted the podium wearing a silly-looking red, white and blue "liberty cap" and holding a staff.[14]

---

* Hall's vision included "our river fronts ... patterned after the Thames embankments; the Park could be converted into a plaza; Fifth-avenue, from Washington-square to the Central Park, might be covered with concrete in order to afford a safe and comparatively noiseless carriage thoroughfare; our wretched cobblestone pavements could be covered with concrete; Sixth-avenue would be cut through from Minetta-lane to West Broadway; First and Second avenues might be opened to Chatham-square; suspension bridges could be constructed over the channels each side of Blackwell's [Roosevelt Island] with a center arch resting on the Island, so as to allow railway trains and teams from Long Island entrance into the City [today's 59th Street Bridge]; the sidewalks of Fulton-street adjoining St. Paul's Church could be thrown into the roadway for vehicular relief, and Ann-street opened."

Tweed loved costumes. At his Americus Club lodge on Greenwich's Indian Harbor where his Tammany friends flocked on summer weekends, he enforced a strict dress code: blue cloth navy pantaloons with gold cord down the seams; blue sack coat of the navy cut; white cloth vest cut low, and navy cap.[15] In January, he led the dancers at the club's annual ball at the Academy of Music.

His political events, too, became carnivals. That August, he called a mass meeting to protest American inaction against British oppression in Ireland and Spanish oppression in Cuba. Thousands of immigrants came pouring out of slum neighborhoods to flood Tammany Hall and fill Union Square with picnic lunches and pails of beer. A green Irish flag waved over a wooden stage and sounds of fiddles and tin whistles filled the air with songs like "*Garry Owen*" and "*Patrick's Day*." Tweed greeted them and blushed at the applause, but as usual handed off the speech-making to "our worthy mayor" Oakey Hall who happily entertained the crowd. Shouting out his speech from the platform, he mocked President Grant for lounging in his "smoking room" as "the American eagle sits supinely in the White House and smokes cigars." When a voice in the crowd shouted back "The General is looking for a crown," Oakey Hall stopped his speech, paused a moment, then observed: "Ah, as they say in the streets of London, the smallest change for a sovereign is half a crown"—winning a round of laughs.[16]

In August, Tweed invited a boatload of charity children—260 teenage boys from pauper schools on Hart and Randall Islands—to spend a sunny afternoon on his forty-acre Greenwich, Connecticut estate, Tweed's "country seat" as some called it. He sent a band, the "Tweed Blues," to welcome the boys arriving by boat at the Americus Club pier at Indian Harbor and then greeted them at his home, standing side-by-side with his 18-year-old daughter Josephine. After a few speeches, he served them a banquet under what reporters called a "spacious circular pavilion" erected on the wide green lawns, though the charity boys had to fight for food with the swarm of news reporters Tweed had invited to witness his good deed. "I never saw so many persons claiming to represent the newspaper profession," one of them wrote.[17]

These were gravy days. Tweed had grown rich, and bolder in showing it. He held court each morning at his Duane Street office, dispensing liquor, cigars, and favors amid the elegant finery of mahogany furniture, cut flowers, and glass dividers. Passersby described his new home on Fifth Avenue at 43rd Street as "a palatial mansion, with a brownstone front, an aristocratic flight of stone steps, and a front door buried in gorgeous moldings and carvings of mahogany and rosewood." Inside, Tweed served champagne and dollar cigars in "rich parlors [kept] warm with luxurious gaslights, which danced within their figured shades."[18] He rode about town in a barouche carriage with a four-horse team and traveled the state's rail lines in a private Wagner parlor car, playing fifty-cent-ante draw poker with political friends along the way. At the train stations, he avoided pesky job seekers and favor-askers by using his own private entrance.

His wife Mary Jane and their eight children seemed mostly to disappear from his public life these days, except his two oldest sons, 24 year-old William Jr. whom he'd now made an assistant city district attorney, and 22-year-old Richard whom he'd installed as manager of the Metropolitan Hotel. Tweed planned soon to renovate the hotel into a showplace. He still ate well, but his extravagance raised eyebrows: "That's Tweed. Drinks wine at 1 o'clock in the afternoon," one neighborhood steakhouse owner grumbled. "He'll come to a bad end. Never knew a man who drank champagne in the daytime who didn't."[19]

In Albany at the state legislature, Senator Tweed began using his parliamentary muscle to build a unique record as city champion: He sponsored bills to charter the Metropolitan Museum of Art and the New York Stock Exchange, to support Presbyterian and Mount Sinai Hospitals and the Shepard's Fold orphanage, and to open new streets in crowded Manhattan—extending Lexington Avenue[20] and widening Broadway from 34th to 49th Street. Critics charged graft, but Tweed as usual shrugged off the complaints for lack of proof.[21] He made his suite at Albany's Delavan House one of the capitol's finest private apartments; he fitted its seven spacious rooms with cut-glass decanters, steel-engraved wall hangings, rose-decorated porcelain cuspidors, and lushly carpeted floors. Tweed had a penchant for flowers and canaries; they decorated all his rooms.[22] He kept a walnut sideboard cabinet always stocked with whiskey, champagne, and cigars to woo the constant stream of visiting politicos, newsmen, and lobbyists.

For his Irish and German immigrant backers, Tweed used his chairmanship of the legislature's Charitable and Religious Societies Committee to win direct public subsidies for Catholic parochial schools—violating the traditional rule against public funding of religious institutions.[23] He hid the provision in the back pages of the annual Tax Levy, a long, complex bill that contained the city's overall budget and tax base and was loaded with pork for districts throughout the state; for upstate Protestants to get their own special favors, they'd have to give Tweed his. Tweed's victory won him cheers from immigrant wards where it greatly expanded classrooms at a time when public schools barely met the need, but drew protest from Protestants and opponents of church-state meddling. "Papal conspiracy," some Republicans cried. "Another raid on public schools," echoed the *New-York Times*, arguing that "no Catholic parent will be permitted to send his child to public schools of the State on pain of excommunication."[24] Tweed stuck to his guns, though. He enlarged the state's annual charity appropriation bill, a vehicle used to provide state funding for social needs through private charities, religious and non-religious alike, from orphanages to hospitals to "homes for the friendless" at a time when government services simply didn't exist. During his three years as chairman, from 1869 to 1871, the number of charities benefiting under it would grow from 68 to 106 and funding itself would top $2.2 million, a six-fold jump over prior levels, including creation of the Manhattan Eye and Ear Hospital.[25]

This came on top of Tweed's own private charity: lumps of coal at Christmas, food at Thanksgiving, and city jobs by the hundreds for poor breadwinners.

Tweed had his finger in every pie. "Do not forget to put through our fishery law," Robert B. Roosevelt, uncle of future president Theodore Roosevelt and then a New York's Fisheries Commissioner, wrote him during the 1870 session.[26] A *New-York Times* reporter identified Tweed by 1869 as master of patronage even on the rich upstate New York canal system: "He appears to take to responsibilities (especially when patronage is to be dispensed) as a duck does to water."[27]

Around this time, Tweed also hitched his star to the proposed new Brooklyn Bridge, a bold plan to construct the longest suspension span ever attempted to that time. Tweed joined the bridge company's Executive Committee that August; earlier, he claims, he'd helped get the project started by aiding organizers in handing out $65,000 in bribes to New York aldermen—he took none of the money himself—to win their approval for a $1.5 million bond issue, then he paid $8,400 for 420 shares of company stock which would soon swell in value. Tweed had lived most of his life on streets near the East River; he'd seen the bustling city of Brooklyn across the way and knew the river as a swirling, turbulent, bad-tempered barrier where boats and barges frequently collided or sank trying to navigate its treacherous tidal currents.

For Tweed, the bridge offered not just "a well-paying dividend stock" but a political jackpot as well. It would take years to build, cost millions of dollars, and employ thousands of workers; "we expected to get the employment of a great many laborers," he'd later explain, "and an expenditure of the money for the different articles required to build the bridge."[28]

Money flowed to Tweed from all directions. For instance, he had great success helping his Erie Railway Company friends Jay Gould and Jim Fisk terrorize Wall Street. Two of his judges—Barnard and Cardozo, both of the state supreme court—issued injunctions at Jay Gould's command that struck like lightning bolts through the financial world.*[29] With rarely any appeal to Albany or to the federal courts under narrow nineteenth century rules, they stood as absolute mandates. Tweed found a kindred spirit in Jim Fisk and they became fast friends. "Jubilee Jim," a big, playful, outgoing character, had raised himself from poverty in rural Vermont and now savored his role as Wall Street buccaneer. Fisk spent his money producing lavish *opera bouffe* performances in his Grand Opera House, covering himself in diamond pins, and openly supporting his mistress, actress Josie Mansfield, in a New York townhouse. He made her parlor a salon for his closest friends; Judge Barnard reputedly issued one of his injunctions there and Tweed himself enjoyed sharing laughs there with Jim and Josie over oysters and champagne. The "playboy side of Fisk ... appealed to Tweed," Denis Tilden Lynch explained. "[Tweed] was accustomed to associating with men always on their dignity, pretended or natural, and the change amused him."[30]

Tweed's New-York Printing Company had grown to over 2,000 employees, making it one of the largest such firm in the country based on its city business. His system of forcing contractors to pad their bills with kickbacks had grown dramatically—these days, they gladly paid gratuities to Tweed and friends of up to 35 percent or more for city business. The city comptroller, Richard Connolly, one of Tweed's "lunch club" buddies, controlled all disbursements of money from the local treasuries and haggled over every penny. Comptrollers stood for election and Connolly had held the post since 1866.

---

* For instance, when Gould and Fisk's corner of the New York gold market collapsed on "Black Friday," September 24, 1869, Cardozo issued an order handing them control of the Gold Exchange Bank, which held millions of dollars of frozen transactions, and ordered the receiver to pay Gould's brokers and nobody else's. In a final round of the Erie Railway war, Barnard named Gould himself the company's receiver to silence protesting stockholders. In another case, Barnard named Tweed's son, William Jr., as temporary receiver of the Union Pacific Railroad, soon to be embroiled in the *Credit Mobilier* scandal.

Richard Connolly.

Long known inside Tammany as "Slippery Dick" for having more than once sandbagged his friends in backroom rumbles, Connolly often wore a stovepipe hat that exaggerated his tall physique. With gold-rimmed spectacles and a clean-shaven face, he had two assets that Tweed appreciated. He was popular: "He was a powerful man in his ward and district, being from Cork, [Ireland]," Tweed would explain years later. Connolly had worked his way up the Tammany ladder from "hurrah boy" to ward leader to county clerk to state senator and had learned bookkeeping managing the New York Custom House's Statistics Bureau and as cashier in New York's Bank of North America, making him popular with the rank-and-file braves. "We could not get along without Connolly, and annexed him [into the ring] for the vote he controlled."[31]

He also knew graft: His predecessor as comptroller, Matthew Brennan, another popular Irishman, had been a shade too honest. When Tammany dumped him for reelection in 1866 and Brennan asked why, Tweed reputedly blurted out: "why, because you won't make money yourself nor let others make any. That's why!"[32]

Now as comptroller, Connolly held a tight leash on the city till, often taunting political foes by refusing to pay their bills. Even Tweed had to beg like everyone else to get Connolly to cooperate. "The bills of the *Democrat* [a newspaper belonging to Tweed's friend Brick Pomeroy] certainly come under the head of 'Arrearages,'" Tweed wrote to Connolly in mid-1870. "The time has come to redeem *my word*. I ask you as a personal favor to me to pay their Bills and when you call on me to reciprocate you will find me as ever ready."[33] The quibbling sometimes drove Tweed to distraction: "Dear Dick: For God's sake pay ___'s bill," he wrote after hearing of one argument. "He tells me your people ask 20 per cent. The whole d__d thing isn't but $1,100. If you don't pay it, I will."[34]

For his friends, though, Connolly kept the money flowing: claims from favorite contractors like builder John Keyser, furniture-supplier James Ingersoll, stationer E. Jones, among others, had gravy enough for everyone. One list of vouchers from this period listed over $3.3 million in claims with no corresponding records showing any city department receiving any of the supposedly delivered goods.[35] The wealth trickled down to dozens of Tammany men in local wards and neighborhoods—jobs, contracts, deals, pay-offs. New silk top-hats became the rage, and people starting calling newly-rich politicos the "shiny hat brigade."

By late 1869, Tweed's grip had become so firm that he could engineer Oakey Hall's re-election as mayor literally on a whim. Arguably, Hall didn't have to run at all in 1869, and no mayoral contest had been announced. Mayors served two-year terms on New York City in the mid-1800s. But Hall had taken the office midway through John Hoffman's unfinished term in 1868, raising a legal question. Fearing that some unscrupulous Republican might exploit the issue by putting up a last-minute candidate and collaring a friendly judge to issue an order declaring him the winner, Tweed decided not to take chances. Without even telling the candidate, he directed New York's police the afternoon before Election Day to distribute boxes to all the polling stations in the city for collecting ballots for mayor. Not surprisingly, voters had only one ballot to choose from, Tammany's.

The mayor himself grumbled to newspaper friends on hearing the decision—especially about his being left in the dark. "Mr. Hall knew nothing of this arrangement until he saw it announced in the morning papers," the *New York World* explained on his behalf.[36] Hall found the ballots "a most unexpected discovery," echoed the *New York Herald*, and it "would have been against his wishes had he been consulted."

Remarkably, nobody objected. The vote stood. The final tally: 66,000 for Hall versus 151 for everyone else.

Tweed's Democrats that autumn also won an outright majority in both chambers of the state legislature in Albany, a slim four votes in the Senate and sixteen in the Assembly. It wasn't much, but enough to open the door in 1870 on what Tweed expected to be his crowning achievement: a new governing structure for New York City. Friends and foes alike would call it "the Tweed charter"—it would mark the height of his regime and the start of its downfall.

❁ ❁ ❁ ❁ ❁

Since the mid-1850s, the state government in Albany, dominated by rural "hayseeds," had intruded deeply into New York City affairs. By 1870, Albany controlled the city's police force, school board, fire department, docks, and even the city budget—all from a distance of more than a hundred miles away up the Hudson River. Plans to improve urban life, whether by widening Broadway, expanding the Croton Reservoir, developing Central Park, or fixing dilapidated streets or sewage pipes—let alone Tammany's political designs—sat frustrated as upstate legislators blocked them or demanded pay-offs. New Yorkers almost universally hated this interference: the one cause that united every faction in Gotham was Home Rule.

Peter B. Sweeny.

In Albany, Tweed chaired the state legislature's Committee on Municipal Affairs and set right to work when it convened in January 1870. He too wanted home rule, but suited to his own special needs. To draft a plan, he turned to his other stalwart "lunch club" friend, Peter B. Sweeny, the so-called "Brains" of the Ring.

Sweeny, dark-haired, stocky, with heavy mustache and narrow eyes, hated the public spotlight. Son of a New York Irish saloonkeeper, educated at St. Peter's Roman Catholic School and Columbia College, a lawyer and Tammany insider since the 1850s, Sweeny had won election as district attorney in 1857—his only elected office—only to resign midway through his first trial after getting stage-fright in front of the jury. He avoided public speaking and rarely met with reporters. This secretiveness gave Sweeny a "mysterious glamour around his name," one observer wrote; others described it as sinister.[37] "I am not, and never claimed to be a leader," Sweeny told a newsman in 1869. "I am simply a passenger in the ship, with the privilege of going ashore if I do not like its management or its course."[38] But Tammany insiders long had respected his brilliance as tactician and negotiator. Described as "a man of education, widely read and of real ability," Sweeny traveled frequently to Europe and, though a bachelor, was rumored to have a French paramour.*

Sweeny had made a public splash in 1866 on being appointed City Chamberlain, responsible for managing the city's bank accounts. On taking the post, he'd announced that from now on, he'd refuse to keep for himself the interest accrued on city accounts, long considered the job's richest perquisite worth up to a million dollars over four or five years. "As a taxpayer… I am not willing to receive a great or any sum of money against the public sense of right, however legally justifiable," he told the newspapers, settling instead for a $10,000 salary and startling reformers who'd always assumed him corrupt. The *New York Herald* called it "a self-denial and a sublime courage never before equaled," though on closer look the altruism wore thin.[39] Sweeny had reportedly paid $60,000 in party contributions for the job and he knew that the practice of keeping interest payments would likely soon be abolished by the legislature; he stood to gain more from a showy public display.[40]

Next, Sweeny showed his tactical genius again. During sessions of the legislature, Sweeny kept a room in Albany's Delavan House just down the hall from Tweed's so the two could talk constantly. He worked there steadily through January and February. After a few weeks, he'd produced a draft charter that legal scholar Charles O'Conor would call "an almost perfect document … under which to administer the affairs of a municipality" unless a "band of thieves [could] place at each checking point one of the members of their own clique."[41] This would be Tweed's charter.

On its face, it had all the markings of Home Rule; it gave the mayor the power to run the city, eliminated hated Albany interference, and moved municipal powers back home to Manhattan. But the finer print, its subtle web of clauses and sub-clauses, did something more. Within New York, it created effectively a four-person oligopoly: the mayor, the comptroller, the commissioner of parks, and the commissioner of public works, a post combining the old streets department and the Croton Reservoir, intended for Tweed. These four officials would form a board of apportionment that would

---

* There's a story that when Sweeny and Connolly both were young upstarts at Tammany, Connolly fretted over Sweeny's dour, aloof manner, and decided to teach him charm. One night, he sat Sweeny down and spent hours in a room practicing how to slap shoulders, shake hands, and grin until their hands ached and faces twitched. "Now, if you'll only do that when you go out among the lads you'll be a grand success," Connolly had told Sweeny when they'd finished. "You can talk, but unless you smile, even when you're condemning your bitterest enemy, it will not have all the effect it should." Sweeny tried, but soon reverted to his natural gloomy form.

approve all city spending, fix budgets, and even control judgeships. The city's elected aldermen, who traditionally controlled the purse, would formally be stripped of this power. The system seemed designed perfectly for Tweed and Connolly to continue their bill-padding and to spend money on whatever they chose.

What's more, to assure that the right people filled these posts—Tweed, Connolly, and Sweeny—the charter made Oakey Hall's appointment power absolute by eliminating the aldermen's traditional authority to confirm nominees. Once in place, no future mayor could fire them; they'd hold their jobs for terms of six to eight years and could be impeached only by special action of all six judges of Common Pleas. And if anything happened to Hall in the meantime, if he left office or was replaced, his appointment function would fall not to an acting mayor but, rather, to the comptroller, Connolly, and nobody else.

Public Works, Tweed's department, would direct the lion's share of patronage—the hundreds of laborers who built and fixed the streets and reservoirs—followed by the Parks Department, intended for Sweeny.

Not surprisingly, resistance to this charter was passionate and intense. The resistance came not from Republicans or Upstaters, though. It came instead from within Tweed's own Tammany club, from rivals who felt excluded from all the gravy. They called themselves "Young Democrats," and from the start their leaders included Jimmy O'Brien, the county sheriff who just a year before had patrolled the ballot boxes with hundreds of deputies to help Tweed win his 1868 electoral triumph. O'Brien, eighteen years younger than Tweed, would always deny having any personal gripe against the Boss; instead, for O'Brien, the split had begun in an argument over money, Connolly's refusal to pay some of his vouchers for running the sheriff's office—possibly full of graft themselves.

O'Brien and his insurgents called themselves "reformers" but their goal soon became transparent: power. At first, it looked like they could settle the whole affair with a simple back-room deal. For weeks, the rebels met secretly with Tweed and hammered out a detailed compromise to divide city offices and commission seats under the charter. "All this was agreed to," an unnamed "prominent Democratic office holder" told the *New York Sun* at the height of the contest, "and everybody was satisfied. But each man was afraid to trust his comrade." O'Brien's rebels worried particularly about Oakey Hall who, as mayor, would have the power to make appointments and easily could renege on the deal. "He is a notorious liar," one of them called the usually popular mayor. "He never told the truth but once, and then it was by accident and he took off his coat and ran a mile and a half to cover it with a lie."[42]

Before signing onto any final compromise, five insurgent Senators insisted on meeting with Tweed and the mayor face to face and swearing an oath. Tweed agreed; he invited them all to his Fifth Avenue mansion one night in early March and had each man literally put his hand on a large family Bible placed on a wooden table and promise to keep his word. Then, having made peace, Tweed feasted them all with lobster and champagne.

But the deal lasted barely twenty-four hours; it collapsed when O'Brien's insurgents demanded more and Tweed refused to let them have it. "[T]he greediness of the Young Democrats made Tweed break his word," the same source told the *Sun*.[43] "They were young, they were unscrupulous, they were very hungry," journalist Charles Wingate wrote of the Young Democrats.[44] A showdown became unavoidable.

Charges of foul play flew back and forth across the capitol in Albany: Tweed claimed that his enemies were buying votes at $7,000 to $10,000 apiece to kill his charter. Later, Tweed admitted that he himself entered the bribery contest with a flourish, doling out a fortune in pay-offs.[45] Then as now, the Albany legislature was divided into two chambers, the Assembly and the Senate. To handle the Assembly members, Tweed turned to experienced lobbyist A.D. Barber whose business was "to walk up and down the hill and talk to people," as Tweed put it later.[46] He didn't remember exactly how much money he gave Barber to distribute among the legislators, but it was certainly a lot, totaling "hundreds of thousands" of dollars.

For the state senators, Tweed handled things himself. He invited several for personal talks in his Delavan House suite—which had a private rear exit for members to come and go unseen—and ultimately claimed to pay a total of $200,000 in cash, to be divided $40,000 apiece among five Republicans. To other senators, he gave jobs, or jobs to their friends, or help in their businesses. He later made Barber himself a deputy collector of assessments paying a salary of over $10,000 per year[47] and sent checks for $67,250 in 1869 and 1870 to Democratic senator Michael Norton. Norton appreciated the favor enough to send Tweed a Clarence carriage and team as a gift, with a note reading "My greatest wish is that you may live long and enjoy it!"[48]

One newspaperman reputedly barged into Tweed's Delavan House suite just as he was sorting out cash for the senators; he promptly demanded a

$40,000 cut for himself to keep quiet and Tweed apparently had no choice but to pay.[49]

The contest grew close. Each side declared "war to the knife" and the rebels appealed for help to anyone in Tammany whose toes Tweed had stepped on during his rise to power. As their strength grew, so did their ambition; perhaps they could topple Tweed altogether, not just in Albany but at Tammany itself. The fight shifted back and forth between Albany and New York City. Its climax came one night in late March when O'Brien's insurgents finally thought they had enough support to face Tweed directly in his own Wigwam. They demanded a meeting of Tammany's general committee to settle things; Tweed agreed and set the date for Monday night, March 28, at 7:30 pm. A few days before the meeting, Tweed muddied the waters by resigning his post as deputy street commissioner and circulating a rumor he'd been fired.[50] When the Young Democrats gathered at nearby Irving Hall before the confrontation to find their courage in a few shots of whiskey, they counted 174 Tammany committeemen, a majority, under their tent.

Tweed, too, spent the day making plans. "He sat in his [Duane Street] private office calm, collected, and cool," wrote a newspaperman who'd come by to watch, "and received each visitor with a smile and thanks."[51] Behind closed doors, he railed at his ingrate enemies: "They've killed me dead, they think," he told one supporter, "perhaps they have, but I'm Tweed now and I'll be bound if I don't show that I mean to kick the lid off the coffin pretty lively."[52] To another: "It has become a personal fight against me, and I would rather lose my life than lose a fight."[53]

He waited until after sunset to spring his trap: When the Young Democrats arrived at Tammany Hall that night for the meeting, they found themselves locked out, standing in the street with no place to go. Tweed, flexing his muscle as Tammany's Grand Sachem, had shut them out. He'd called his friend Henry Smith, commissioner of New York's Metropolitan Police, and told him that a riot might occur at Tammany that night. Smith had responded by sending over 800 police officers to the neighborhood, blocking all entrances to the Tammany building as well as the nearby Bryant's Minstrel Hall. By 7:30 pm that night, an estimated 5,000 people jammed the streets around Tammany and Union Square, standing outside in a cold driving rain, including as many friends of the Boss as enemies. Police refused to let anyone inside Tammany without a ticket signed personally by Tweed. When a reporter found Tweed that night "calmly reposing in the house of one of his most trusted friends" and asked him about the police raid, Tweed must have worn a delicious grin. He knew nothing, he claimed. "It astonished me."[54]

The Young Democrats' found their meeting cancelled and, by the next morning, their votes had vanished, scared away by the shifting fortunes.

Meanwhile, Tweed struck behind their backs in Albany. While O'Brien and his friends were still crying in their beer, Tweed had his own friends in Albany introduce the Sweeny-drafted charter in the legislature and rush it through the assembly. It passed 116 to 5; he'd cut a deal with Republicans allowing them to pass an election reform bill[55] along with the charter and promising them a share of the spoils—a handful of patronage jobs.

By April 4, he'd won his triumph and reached his height of respectability. The city stood with him, the champion of Home Rule. Eighty-seven leading citizens signed a petition supporting Tweed's charter, including merchant kings Moses Taylor, C.L.Tiffany, William Vermilye, and Morton, Bliss, and Company, the banking firm of Levi P. Morton, future vice president of the United States.[56] Even Peter Cooper, the 81-year-old merchant and philanthropist widely considered New York's most distinguished citizen whose money had launched Cooper Union—the city's showplace institute for science and art—and whose factories had built America's first working steam engine, had grown cozy with Tweed. He and Nathaniel Sands of the Citizens Association—once the sharpest critics of local corruption—both had confided in Samuel Tilden that month that they now considered Tweed safe. "They were convinced that the [Tammany] Ring had become conservative," Tilden wrote, "that they were not ambitious of more wealth, and that they were on the side of the taxpayers."[57]

On the eve of his charter's final vote in the legislature, Tweed called together all the key players for a formal public hearing of his Committee on Municipal Affairs.[58] All the respectables came. "The Committee is met to hear the advocates and the opponents to the charter," Tweed announced, holding the gavel as chairman. The committee met in Tweed's suite at the Delavan House; hundreds of city politicians jammed into every corner, aldermen, sheriff's deputies, police, clerks, and department lobbyists squeezing in among the porcelain cuspidors and walnut liquor cabinets. All the newspapers sent reporters. Only the Young Democrats, humiliated by the Tammany lockout, conspicuously stayed away.

For two-and-a-half hours, Tweed presided with aplomb—over his committee, his legislature, his charter, his hotel suite. Half a dozen city leaders came to speak, and Tweed welcomed them all. "We shall be happy to hear gentlemen representing interests in the city," he announced.[59]

He started by calling his lead witness, Horace Greeley, the "Sage of Chappaqua" and firebrand publisher of the *New York Tribune* who a year earlier had blasted Tammany's strong-arm ballot-box tactics. Now, Greeley appeared in a rumpled black suit on behalf of the Union League Club and stood before Tweed in amiable deference. He spoke for nearly an hour, his trademark white hat and coat folded under his chair, "not as fidgety as usual," a reporter noted, "the general tone of his remarks were rather favorable than otherwise to the Charter."[60] Greeley offered a few suggestions to amend it, but stressed that they were not meant "in any fractious spirit. Nor do [the Union League members] desire to be understood as enemies of the charter reform," he explained, "they regard this document as embodying many excellent advances to reform, we are not here to ask you to reject it; we ask you to improve it."

Tweed answered each of Greeley's points as he raised them, and the old man seemed satisfied. To his plea to leave the Central Park Commission unaffected, Tweed said: "We don't desire to change it." On Greeley's opposition to state spending for sectarian schools, Tweed replied: "I have seen clergymen of various denominations, and we shall arrange that in a different manner." On Greeley's complaint against any person holding multiple city jobs, Tweed demurred: "We thought that more a matter of ordinance than of State law."

Greeley's biggest gripe still seemed to be last year's voting frauds: "I don't care if any archangel were to make a charter for the city of New York, and then you were to elect by ballot-box stuffers, it would not be possible to have an honest government," he told the panel, and was glad to hear of the separate election bill moving through the legislature, backed by Tweed.[61]

His issues addressed, Greeley, the dean of New York journalists, thanked Tweed politely for his "courtesy in giving us this hearing" and the "care and deliberation" behind the document. Then he sat down.*[62]

* The *Evening Post*, a Charter opponent, would blast Greeley for his weak performance: "his sympathies were with Tweed rather than the citizens whose spokesman he was," he was "wavering and uncertain... simply a fraud, a dishonorable disservice of a clearly implied duty, a gross breach of trust." The *New York Herald* would report that Greeley, addressing Republicans the night after his testimony, confused them with "the shambling manner in which he argued now for and now against the bill." The *Tribune* replied: "Happily, there are a good many persons... who know these aspersions to be groundless, malignant, and ridiculous."

Next came Joseph Daly of the Citizens Association who "forcibly but briefly" backed the charter,[63] followed by R.F. Andrews of the Republican Union Committee who too was "highly laudatory."[64] It seemed an amiable feast all around. Finally, as the hour drew late, Tweed called one last witness who'd asked for a special chance to address the group: Samuel J. Tilden.[65]

Tilden, stiff and formal in his high-collar suit, couldn't have felt comfortable in the cozy roomful of back-slapping politicos. In fact, it doubtless was an awkward moment: He and Tweed personally had barely seen each other since the 1868 election scandals, but neither made any secret of their mutual aversion. For weeks, Tilden had talked up a storm against Tweed's charter. He denied backing O'Brien and his Young Democrat revolt but passed them advice through a third party, *New York World* publisher Manton Marble.[66] He made no secret of meeting with like-minded "reformers," mostly newspaper editors—Greeley, Marble, Charles Nordhoff of the *Evening Post*, and Jackson Schultz of the Union League. To Denis Tilden Lynch, it was "inconceivable that Tilden, early in the spring of 1870, was not advising Tweed's enemies" and Tweed certainly knew it.[67]

Still, Tweed had little fear of Sam Tilden. Tilden came across as an arrogant elitist who always did things halfway; when pushed, he usually backed down. The prior summer, when Tweed was attacking August Belmont—one of Tilden's closest Manhattan Club friends—Tilden had refused to help Belmont even by signing a letter vouching for Belmont's campaign work, leaving Belmont stunned at his supposed friend's "more than ungentlemanly conduct."[68] In February, Tilden had helped found a new New York City Bar Association and given a rousing call to "restore both the judiciary and *the bar* … as it formerly was, an *honorable and elevated* calling." This was a thinly veiled dig at Tweed's judges Barnard and Cardozo,[69] but soon afterwards Tilden wrote Cardozo a long pleading letter asking special leniency for one of his own clients, Russell Sage, the notorious stock speculator who'd been convicted of usury.[70] Tilden had opposed Tweed's friend Jim Fisk in his litigation against the Union Pacific Railroad but continued to accept legal retainers from Fisk's Erie Railway partner Jay Gould. Gould, in turn, complained about Tilden's wishy-washy representation: "I paid you a retainer for Erie R.R. Co. $10,000…. I wish to ask you whether, in view of the foregoing, we are not justified in being surprised to find you against us *without notice*? Please reply and oblige."[71] Tilden had answered Gould in a long letter claiming that the

$10,000 retainer was for a single arbitration and arranged "without any agency of mine, and the subsequent payment of it was purely voluntary on your part."[72] He never returned the money.

Even Sweeny, in a rare newspaper interview that autumn, had dismissed Tilden as irrelevant. "He don't stand in the way of any one down here."[73]

Now, Tweed as chairman, presiding over his legislative committee in his own hotel suite, put aside whatever irritation he had and called on Tilden to speak. As Tilden's flat, nasal voice began to fill the air in the stuffy room, though, Tweed soon found it grating and his patience grew thin.

"At the request of several gentlemen for whom I entertain a high respect, I have come back here [to Albany] to make some observations… I come here, sir, to aid no party of men, nor to injure any party of men," Tilden began, typically washing his hands of the recent head-knocking between Tweed and the insurgents, placing himself above the fray. "Nothing on earth would induce me to enter upon a career in city politics. I have quite as much in my present avocation as I am able to attend to, perhaps more." Then, oddly, Tilden looked squarely at Tweed who sat just a few feet away across the cloth-covered witness table. "And let me say here that if I know my own heart I have no feeling of unkindness to any human being. To you, Mr. Chairman—"

"I am sick of the discussion of this question," Tweed snapped,[74] his voice unmistakably sharp as it carried to every corner of the room. Tweed stopped himself; he managed to hold his tongue through the rest of Tilden's testimony, but his face apparently wore every sign of contempt.[75]

"I am unconscious of ever having done an unkind act or entertained an unkind feeling," Tilden went on with his well-practiced calm. "I simply desire to submit a few suggestions for your consideration."

Once he began it, Tilden's critique of Tweed's charter, which he now presented, pinpointed the core paradox in Sweeny's draft: that it lodged power in a small circle of unaccountable, non-removable department heads. Under it, "you have a Mayor without any executive power" since he'd have given it away to the bureau heads whom he could no longer remove, "you have a Legislature without legislative power; you have elections without any power in the people to affect the Government for the period during which these officers are appointed."

Tilden stated his piece: "It is in the stagnation of bureaus and commissions that evils and abuses exist," he said, summing it up. His words had clearly presented the problem, but he'd failed to make an impression on the legislators and made no visible effort to press his point.[76] When he finished, he gathered his papers and left the room. One friend noticed how his face had turned "ashy white" from "repressed rage."[77] Within a few hours, Tilden had disappeared from Albany, not staying to lobby privately on the issue. Another observer found his timid performance "typical of the timorous, cringing attitude of foremost Democrats."[78]

Years later, after the scandals had broken and Tweed was destroyed, Tilden would boast about how he'd bravely come to Tweed's own lion's den that day in Albany and told the truth to Tweed's face, unmasking his charter as a fraud. For now, though, he simply walked away. "I felt more scorn than I ever remember to have felt for the pusillanimity which characterized the hour.... An intenser [sic.] animosity than was excited against me in the men who grasped an irresponsible despotism over this city, cannot be imagined," he'd say later. "None of the Ring ever came near me."[79] After the session, Tilden told his friend Henry Richmond that Tweed "would close his career in jail or in exile."[80]

Reaching his Gramercy Park home in New York City that night, Tilden scribbled a note to Manton Marble at the *New York World*: "As to myself don't mention my name in the paper till I see you."[81] "No one was more thoroughly cowed than Tilden" that day, a Marble biographer concluded.[82]

The next morning,[83] Tweed came early to the state capitol. The New York Legislature in 1870 met in the old Capitol Building, a dignified, two-story, granite-columned structure sitting in the southwest corner of Albany's Washington Park. The senate chamber was arranged so that all 32 senators sat facing each other, their desks forming a circle beneath half a dozen small gas-lit chandeliers. Spectators stood behind them outside an iron rail. With Tweed's charter the order of business, the building swarmed with people. In the Senate Chamber, they stood "piled twenty deep and with open eyes and mouths took in the whole exciting scene." Tweed, as the bill's sponsor, would manage the debate; one newsman scribbled a description of him at his hour of triumph: "Tweed's good natured face flushed like the rising sun against the white pillar before which he sits while the discussion is progressing. He was as watchful as a cat before a mousehole, ready for a spring the moment any motion was made hostile to the vitality of his measure."[84]

By 5 o'clock that day they'd finished. The senators passed Tweed's charter by a margin of 30 to 2 with no amendments.* All the Republicans supported it, pointing to what they called a good compromise in also winning enactment of the election reform law that day. Governor Hoffman—Tweed's candidate in 1868—signed the charter within the afternoon and Tweed made a point to take the pen, ink, and blotter that Hoffman used for the event to keep as souvenirs.

Telegraphs flashed the news downstate and the response was electric. Tweed had promised home rule and he'd delivered it. A few voices complained: Horace Greeley's *Tribune* claimed that the new law "surrenders the City to the rule of Tweed and Sweeny for a number of ensuing years. We believe our friends in the legislature have made a mistake."[85] But the large majority disagreed. To James Gordon Bennett Jr., Tweed had shown "it takes a general to lead an army."[86] Hundreds of local Tammany-ites gathered to celebrate at East Broadway and Canal Street—a triangle they now called Tweed Plaza**—complete with balloons, fireworks, Chinese lanterns and "good tunes" from Fink's Washington Band.

With the ink barely dry on the charter, Oakey Hall put his own pen to paper and exercised his new power as mayor to make appointments: twenty-odd police and fire commissioners, health officials, and dock and park board members in an initial set. He made a point to include high-profile Republicans in the mix: Judge Henry Hilton to the Public Parks Board and police commissioner Henry Smith—who'd helped Tweed crush the Young Democrats a few weeks earlier—to the new Police Board. Tammany had grown skilled at placing Republicans in a handful of visible city posts to create a veneer of fairness. Even Chester Alan Arthur, future Republican president of the United States, held a job as counsel to New York's city tax commission at $10,000 per year during this period, one of about eighty "Tweed Republicans" in Tammany-controlled slots.[87]

But the two most important names stood out: William M. Tweed as Com-

---

* One historian, professor Leo Hershkowitz, points to this vote as evidence that Tweed's bribery of the legislature for the charter was only a myth. "Historians have universally held in their fairy tales that passage was the result of bribery. Yet at the time there was no such suspicion.... Even though later a desperate confused Tweed 'admitted' to his own use of bribery, the buying of votes was really not necessary.... It was not bribery that carried the charter but political maneuvering and expediency. With a vote of 116 to 5 and 30 to 2, was bribery necessary?"

** "Tweed Plaza" is today called "Strauss Square" at the southern tip of Seward Park on the lower East Side, renamed in 1931 for businessman-philanthropist Nathan Strauss, a one-time owner of retailers Macy's and Abraham and Strauss who also created a system for pasteurizing milk for delivery in New York City.

missioner of Public Works and Peter B. Sweeny to head the Public Parks Board.[88] The mayor's letter to Tweed virtually gushed: "I beg you to take [it] so that you will not deny me the pleasure & the public the justice of hearing your affirmative answer. I shall ask you to take it untrammeled and I feel already assured that in your hands the [Public Works] Department will augment the glory of the City & your fame." He signed it: "With cordial regards, Believe me, Your obliged friend and ob[edient] S[erva]nt. A. Oakey Hall."[89] The *Albany Argus* was hardly less effusive: "Senator Tweed is to take charge of the bureau of Public Works. A man of comprehensive plans and of indomitable energy, Senator Tweed will make his administration of this department notable in the history of the city. He will be to New York what [Baron George] Haussman has been to Paris."[90]

Peter Cooper, New York's most respected merchant, also gave Tweed a compliment on the occasion, an invitation to appear at the annual commencement ceremony at Cooper Union Institute: "It would give me great pleasure to have you on the platform," he wrote."[91]

* * * * *

Sometime in mid-April, about a week after the charter became law, the four met again behind closed doors in Albany, this time in Peter Sweeny's room at the Delavan House: Sweeny, Oakey Hall, Connolly, and Tweed. The City Hall "lunch club," soon this group would be branded for posterity as "the Tweed Ring."

They'd come to Albany because the legislature was preparing to take up the Tax Levy bill, which set the city's annual budget for the coming year, and they planned to use it to tie up loose ends. Tweed and Sweeny had become masters of hiding little kickers in the tedious, arcane package. This year, two items topped their list: extending aid to parochial schools despite opposition from upstate Republicans—crucial to their immigrant friends—and perfecting their control of the city government. This last part included making the comptroller an appointive office to guarantee Connolly his place for five more years and allow him to avoid a threatened election contest, formally stripping the city's aldermen of their financial oversight powers, and closing down the old county Board of Supervisors.

At the last minute, they decided to add one more. Tweed remembered watching Oakey Hall draft the idea on paper as they sat around Sweeny's hotel suite that day. It involved a chance to make money—a great deal of it.

The old Board of Supervisors, which they planned to abolish in the legislation, had collected a pile of unpaid bills over the years: vouchers from city contractors that the supervisors had never approved, either because of poor documentation or because they'd just fallen through the cracks. Taken together, they amounted to millions of dollars. Why not pay them now, all at once, and clear the books, someone suggested. And while they were at it, they could collect the normal bill-padding percentages on the whole amount.

It seemed easy. To implement the idea, they'd simply create a special *ad interim* Board of Audit consisting of three people: Hall as the mayor, Connolly as comptroller, and Tweed as president of the old Board of Supervisors. These three would audit "all liabilities against the County of New York incurred previous to the passage of this act," according to Hall's draft, and pay them.

At least at first, their purpose was more than simply to pocket graft. As Tweed explained it later, they wanted "to reimburse ... those who had advanced the moneys for the passage of the charter." The legislative war in Albany had cost them a fortune, hundreds of thousands of dollars in bribes to key legislators. At its height, messengers literally had carried bags of cash from the city to Albany by train.[92] To pay for it, Tweed had taken a collection from all his friends who stood to gain—the lunch club, top city bureaucrats, his Erie Railway cronies Jay Gould and Jim Fisk, and major city contractors. Plasterer Andrew Garvey and furniture maker James H. Ingersoll, for instance, each claimed to have paid $50,000 into the pool; furnisher-plumber John Keyser and Oakey Hall $25,000 each.[93] The "Republican Legislature had to be bought, and, as I understood it, Mr. Tweed had to pay the money, and I thought it right and proper for him to reimburse himself," as Tweed's clerk E.A. Woodward explained later. It was only fair.[94]

But the sheer size of the potential pot quickly dwarfed any such rationale. Money became a purpose in itself, four rich men seeing an easy chance to get much richer. Tweed's testimony given years later is the only direct account of the meeting.[95] Oakey Hall would deny all of it, claiming he'd never been part of any such scam, that he himself had been a victim of fraud. Sweeny and Connolly would keep their mouths shut about it till they died.

But according to Tweed, it went this way: every one of the old Supervisors' bills would be padded by 50 percent and each of the four—Tweed, Connolly, Sweeny, and Hall—would receive an equal share of 10 percent. The final ten-percent share would go to the bookkeepers—James Watson, the county auditor who worked for Connolly, and E.A. Woodward, the supervisors' clerk who worked for Tweed—who'd prepare the paperwork and keep things secret. Tweed considered Watson "a very confidential man" who "had my confidence to the utmost degree"; Woodward had been doing his bidding for over a decade.[96] He trusted them both completely.

The Albany legislature passed the Tax Levy bill on April 26 and, about a week later, the wheels started turning. Records showed that the new *ad interim* Board of Audit—Hall, Tweed, and Connolly—met only once, in Connolly's office on May 5, 1870, and transacted only one item of business—adopting a resolution proposed by the mayor:

> *That the County Auditor [Watson] collect from the.... Board of Supervisors all bills and liabilities against the county, incurred prior to April 26, 1870, ... and that the evidence of the same be the authorization for the same by the said Board.... on certificate of clerk or president, and that thereupon the said County Auditor annex the voucher to the appropriate blanks for our signature and action as directed by the section aforesaid and payment.*"[97]

The dense legal language made a simple point: Once Watson had collected them and Tweed had signed them, the old bills stood. They'd never need to "audit" anything.

Watson started promptly. All through May, he and Woodward, the two bookkeepers, scampered about City Hall collecting the old bills—some 190 items altogether going back to 1868, many claiming costs for work on the new County Courthouse recently opened on Chambers Street. The Courthouse, the largest local government building besides City Hall itself, had taken more than ten years to build and was a show-stopper: a four-story "Anglo-Italianate" marble temple with a unique octagonal, three-story rotunda topped by a stained-glass skylight, decked with cast-iron stairways, tile floors, painted ceilings, interior columns, and exquisite detail. Its 120,000 square feet now housed the Comptroller's Office, the sheriff's and district attorney's rooms, and every major local court. Originally budgeted at $250,000 in 1858, its cost already had topped $3.2 million by 1869 amid repeated charges of graft, though none ever proven.[98]

Other bills covered a potpourri of odds and ends: legal services, carpets, carpentry work, plumbing, plastering, furniture, stationery, and safes. The claimants ranged from the *New York Daily News* for advertising to Oakey Hall himself for running his old district attorney office. Together, they added up to a staggering sum: $6,312,541.37 (or more than $120 million in modern dollars).

The bookkeepers assembled the paperwork and then began walking it around to collect signatures, first to Tweed, then to Connolly, then to the mayor. Tweed remembered clearly how he'd done it: "Woodward brought me over a batch of bills on which I wrote my name, 'Wm. M. Tweed, Ch., Chairman.' " There were "quite a number of them, and I certified 'approved and correct;' some of those I wrote those words over myself."[99]

But before the paper-passing could finish and the bills be paid, they began to quarrel. Connolly complained; he wanted a bigger cut. As Tweed explained it in his own words: "Watson came to see me, and said that Connolly wasn't satisfied with the ten per cent; he wanted twenty. I asked him what was the reason of that. He said that Connolly said that he had to take all the responsibility and the risk, and the thing couldn't be done without him. I said: 'It couldn't be done without me either." Tweed and his auditor batted the problem around for a few moments; finally, Tweed agreed to change the deal, but only on his terms: "Give Connolly twenty, and you must give me twenty-five, and give Mr. Sweeny ten percent," he said.

When Watson explained that the new numbers didn't add up, Tweed quickly concocted a solution: shortchange the odd man out: "see [Oakey] Hall and tell him that expenses are 'so heavy we can't afford to give him but five.'"[100]

With the new deal in place, money began to flow. All through June and July 1870, a complex web of warrants, checks, and vouchers began working its way through the New York financial system. The city issued 190 warrants (authorizations for payment) based on the Tax Levy provision totaling $6.3 million and, of this, the overwhelming bulk—$5.7 million—landed in three bank accounts: John Ingersoll, the furniture-maker, Andrew J. Garvey, the plasterer, and Woodward, Tweed's own clerk. In fact, most of the other contractors apparently took their city checks and simply signed them over to Woodward, who deposited them in his own bank account with the notation "E.A.W." One contractor, plumber John Keyser, later complained that he'd never even seen his checks at all, that Woodward had simply taken them and forged his endorsements. "Watson, at that time, told the tradesmen who had bills against the city that I would manage the matter," Woodward explained later, and they all cooperated smartly. Of the large amounts that ended up in Ingersoll and Garvey's back accounts, they too transferred large sums to Woodward, who ended up with about $3.6 million, or about 65 percent of the total.

Of this, Woodward then deposited $932,858.50—26 percent—into the Broadway Bank checking account of William M. Tweed.[101] In addition, the city issued eleven warrants as part of the process totaling $384,395.19 to the New-York Printing Company—Tweed's company—which in turn issued a check the same day for $104,333.64, deposited the day after that by Tweed, bringing his grand total to $1,037,192.14.[102]

A much more convoluted trail connected Sweeny and Hall to the Tax Levy vouchers. Woodward would claim later that after paying Tweed and keeping some for himself, he transferred the rest of the money back to Watson. "[Watson] told me that he had to pay it to the Comptroller [Connolly]," he explained later, "and give some to the Chamberlain's office [Sweeny]."[103] In fact, a large amount of money ended up with James M. Sweeny, Peter B. Sweeny's brother—Tweed alone wrote him checks for $75,000 in June and July. During those months James paid his brother a total of $228,120 through two different banks, both in cash and securities. In one case, he deposited $10,000 to pay for his brother's stock in the Mutual Gas Company; in another, he paid $4,200 for his brother's shares of the New York Bridge Company; in another, he paid $74,900 for his shares of the Cleveland and Pittsburgh Rail Road.[104] The connection to Oakey Hall was even more indirect: On June 7, attorney Hugh Smith—who'd received funds from Watson—purchased 1005 shares of stock in the Suspension Bridge and Erie Junction RRG. Five months later, he transferred 173 shares to James M. Sweeny and 162 shares to an account labeled "blank." Then, the next day, Tweed transferred 162 shares to Hall.[105]

On the surface, not a penny looked out of place on the city's books. Each scrap of paper, each check, voucher, and deposit standing alone looked well in order. The pattern of cash flows emerged only after piecing together records from dozens of accounts in dozens of banks covering hundreds of transactions. As it stood, Tweed and the others could easily deny having gotten a cent. In fact, over a century later, for Oakey Hall in particular, it's still not clear whether any of the proceeds from the Tax Levy ever reached his pocket.

Still, he'd drafted the law, offered the motion, made the appointments, and signed the warrants. Whether he did it for money, for vanity, for Tweed's promise of the New York governorship, for loyalty to his friends, or out of sheer stupidity, may never be known.

Of all the cash collected by Woodward in his bank account traceable to the city vouchers—a cool $3.6 million—a full 24 percent ultimately would be tracked to Tweed, 7 percent each to Woodward and Watson, and 10 percent to Peter Sweeny. Their actual spoils likely were even more: Andrew Garvey, the plasterer, for instance, later claimed that out of $1,177,413.72 paid to him under the Tax Levy, only $264,660 actually represented work for the city or county. Of the rest, he paid $880,000 to Woodward, about $60,000 represented his contribution to Tweed's pool for bribing the state legislature, and the rest mostly covered personal favors for the Ring: construction and plastering work on Connolly's private home at 130 Fifth Avenue, $60,000 on Tweed's house in Greenwich, and $13,000 on Woodward's.[106]

In June 1870, Tweed, wealthy to start with, now had money to burn; he sent a check for $96,300 to Smith, Gould, Martin and Company—Jay Gould's brokerage house—apparently simply to invest.[107]

The financial impact of all this—the bill-padding games on top of the bloated city pay-rolls, street widenings, and park improvements, a torrent of frauds building over time into a huge unseen bulk—began to weigh on the local economy. Taxes for New York property owners stayed low; they paid only two percent of their property's assessed value in taxes, a level capped by law. By some measures, their burden was less than that of taxpayers in Boston, Chicago, Philadelphia, or Cincinnati.* Many tax bills went uncollected: $907,158.86 in 1870 alone.[108]

Instead, though, the city borrowed. In the single year from January 1869 to January 1870, New York city and county's total debt rose from $36.3 million to over $48 million; by January 1871, it would top $73 million—primarily in the form of bonds issued by Connolly under dozens of separate accounts and sold to banks, savings and trust companies, and a growing portion placed by private bankers to overseas investors in Europe.[109] The house of Seligman alone underwrote $2 million of city bonds at 72 percent of face

* Total 1870 taxes (city, county, and school) *pre capita* in New York were $29.08, compared with $36 in Boston and $30 in Chicago; for that same year, a calculated theoretical ratio of New York taxes to real estate values was 1 to 65, compared with 1 to 40 for Boston, 1 to 54 for Philadelphia, and 1 to 30 for Cincinnati.

value in 1869, sold through offices in New York, Frankfurt, and Paris. The House of Rothschild in London and Frankfurt and Discounts Gesellschaft in Berlin took up a $3 million issue in April 1870. In 1871, the Rothschild's secretly brought outright $15 million of 6 percent thirty year bonds through their American agent August Belmont.[110]

Nobody seemed to get hurt and nobody was the wiser. The banks and Europeans kept buying the bonds, which they considered safe American investments compared to the railroad stocks being manipulated on Wall Street.

And no one would find out. In January 1870 Connolly, as comptroller, failed to issue his annual report on city finances and would continue to deny requests to see his books for as long as he could get away with it.

• PART II •

Critics

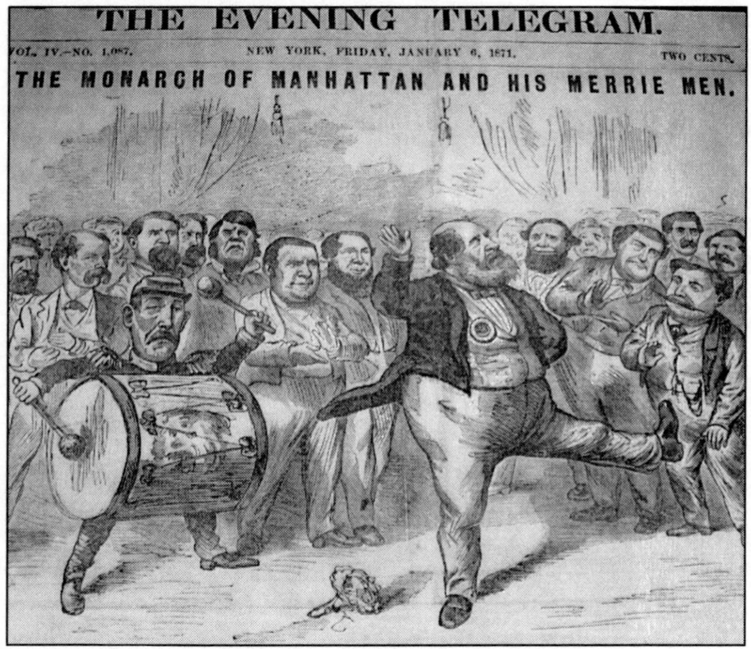

Tweed and friends at their height of power, celebrating in an annual ball at the Academy of Music.

5
PARK ROW

GEORGE JONES, a quiet, serious man with thick spectacles and a lush dark beard who often ate lunch at his desk alone, had seen *The New-York Times* prosper since he'd co-founded it with Henry Raymond twenty years earlier. Under Jones's watch, the newspaper's share value had risen from $1,000 to $11,000 and Jones had heard purchase offers of up to a million dollars—more than ten times the paper's original value. From the start, Jones had always managed the paper's money while Raymond, his brilliant journalist friend, managed its content. Now, in 1870, the *Times* boasted the newest and showiest of the large newspaper buildings crowded side-by-side into the neighborhood called Printing House Square. Its five-story structure on Beekman Street and Park Row sported Hoe cylinder presses, marble floors, wood paneling, plate glass, and ceiling frescoes. Jones, from his corner office on the top floor, could look out over a panorama; on clear days, he easily saw City Hall, the spire of Trinity Church, acres of city rooftops, and even the blue Hudson River beyond.

Some older competitors, the *Herald*, the *World* and the *Tribune*, sold more newspapers, but the *Times* held its own in circulation while printing more news on larger pages than any other journal in the city.

But George Jones struggled under a burden these days. Henry Raymond, his friend and partner, had died suddenly the prior June at just 49 years old, placing the whole responsibility now on Jones. For eighteen years, Raymond had shaped the *New-York Times*, conceiving it as an independent journal with Whig-Republican leanings and wide, objective coverage. His death had come as a shock. Jones had been sick that spring and spent the prior winter in Florida to avoid the cold northern winter. "My doctor says peremptorily I must not leave before the 1st of May," he'd written to Raymond.[1] Jones knew little to nothing about editing a newspaper. He made "suggestions" on hiring writers or managers, but that was Raymond's affair.[2] It was Jones' business to make sure the *Times* had plenty of high-quality paper in stock, that its employees got paid, and its owners made a profit. What's more, Raymond had died under curious circumstances: A servant had found him lying unconscious in the doorway of his house on West 9th Street well past midnight; whispers had it that Raymond had spent the evening with a well-known actress named Rose Eytinge.[3] He died before dawn. Tongues now wagged all over town, not just about Raymond's death but also about whether his mild-mannered partner Jones had the stomach to run the paper.

Henry Raymond had been more than a newspaper editor; he was a leading public figure. In an age when publishers felt no hesitation about pursuing political careers, Raymond had served terms in the U.S. Congress, as lieutenant governor of New York State, and speaker of the state legislature, all while editing the *Times*. It was George Jones who'd urged Raymond finally to stop in 1864 and devote himself full time to news. Raymond had learned his journalism under Horace Greeley, first as Greeley's assistant on his *New-Yorker* magazine, then writing editorials for Greeley's *New York Tribune* in the 1840s.

Jones felt the absence sharply. Almost 60 years old, he enjoyed a comfortable life, hobnobbing with wealthy friends at the Union League Club or sitting in with Sarah, his wife of thirty-three years, and their grown children. A son of Welsh Baptists, born in a farmhouse in Poultney, Vermont, Jones had come to New York City in the 1830s and learned about newspapers in the business office at Greeley's *Tribune*. It was there that he met young Henry Raymond and the two found a common spark: the idea of starting a journal of their own. Jones had moved upstate to Albany in the 1840s and made money in banking until Henry Raymond, now a state legislator, approached him again with the idea: "[W]ill you start that paper with me?" Raymond asked. Jones hesitated at first until Raymond explained the new economics of New York City print in the early 1850s. It had become profitable; the *Tribune* itself had cleared $60,000 in 1850, he said, even under Horace Greeley's sloppy management. Certainly, they could do better.

It was Jones who pulled together the circle of Whig investors who fronted the money to get things started, including $25,000 from Jones's own pocket. Now, twenty years later, he put up a brave front. Shortly after his partner's funeral, his old mentor Greeley had dropped by his house—Jones was sick in bed at the time—and asked what Jones planned to do with the newspaper. When Greeley suggested he'd like to buy it, Jones refused. "I shall never sell the Times as long as I am on the top of the ground, and I don't want to hear anything more about it," he said.[4] But Jones also recognized realities. He knew how newspapers made money, not how they were written. Without Henry Raymond, he'd need a strong editor to survive, and Raymond's own son Henry Warner was far too young to take charge —still a student at Yale when his father died.

A few days after the funeral, Jones called together the newspaper's executive committee: himself, New York businessman James B. Taylor, and Brooklyn tycoon Leonard Jerome. They decided to offer the editorship to John Bigelow, a well-known local figure, former American minister to France and past editor of William Cullen Bryant's *Evening Post*. Bigelow accepted, but he soon found himself over his head and lasted only six months. In August 1869, Bigelow committed a fatal journalistic sin, allowing himself to be tricked by Wall Street speculator Jay Gould over Gould's scheme to corner the New York gold market. Gould, through an intermediary, had submitted to Bigelow a phony editorial claiming to represent President Grant's "Fiscal Policy"—suspiciously friendly to higher gold prices. Without checking the source, Bigelow had sent it to the typesetters. Only a last-minute catch by *Times* financial writer Caleb Norvell, who smelled a rat and made a few surgical edits, saved the paper from major embarrassment when the gold corner collapsed in scandal on Black Friday.

After Bigelow came George Shepherd, a strait-laced *Times* editorial writer who resisted the promotion to editor-in-chief. He too threw in the towel after a few months. Only then, in early 1870, did Jones finally find himself a new chief editor he could really trust, a terse writer with a tough competitive edge, an ear for controversy, and a sense of American politics like his own, even if he was thoroughly British.

Louis Jennings, thirty-three years old, tall and trim with crisp mustache, was born in London and trained in the rough-and-tumble English tabloid press, from local country papers in Derbyshire and Manchester to London's *Morning Chronicle* and *Saturday Review* to finally its flagship, the *London Times*. Since the mid-1860s, the *London Times* had featured Jennings as its premier foreign correspondent. In 1864, it had sent him to India, from which Jennings sent a stream of graphic cables that stunned sedate readers. On arriving in Calcutta, he described how "it takes a steamer three days to get out to sea, the passengers homeward bound feeble and ill, being pent up in close cabins all that time in a river filled with corpses." His stories on India's gory

Juggernaut saturnalia festival, complete with self-immolations and people trampled to death by immense crowds, caused a political furor.[5] After the Civil War, the *London Times* sent him to America to tour the defeated South and explain the turmoil of post-war Reconstruction. Here, Jennings became friends with Henry Raymond; for a time, he lived in Raymond's New York City home on West 9th Street and they shared a boardinghouse in Washington, D.C., as well.

Raymond saw talent in the young Britisher and began courting him for his own newspaper. When Jennings returned to England in 1867 after his last American assignment, Raymond urged him to write columns for the *New-York Times* giving a London perspective on world events and made him a regular *Times* contributor. When Raymond visited Europe in 1868 with his 18-year-old daughter Mary, he made a point to cultivate his new friend: "I have seen a good deal of Jennings," he reported to George Jones from London in July 1868. "He would like very much to come to NY again and join us again, but he makes too much money here. He is sought by all the papers here and can easily make 10 guineas a day by writing by the article.... I don't believe less than £2000 a year would tempt him to quit here and come over to our side of the water. But I am satisfied that he would be worth that to us if we could afford to pay it. He is living very nicely here and seems to be in every way comfortable."[6]

Jennings, though, was ready to jump. He'd grown enamored with America and turned sour on the *London Times*, his old employer, after its years of promising him promotions that never materialized. Raymond's sudden death had shocked him. "He was the most lovable man I ever knew, and his high principle and conscientiousness could not but make an impression on all who lived with him," Jennings wrote to Jones from Piccadilly in June 1869.[7] Jennings had acquired a special tie to New York City in 1867. He had married a local actress, Madeline Louise Henriques, lead player at New York's Wallack's Theater. Now, Louise's second pregnancy had left her ill and longing to see her family. Late that year, Jennings accepted George Jones's offer to leave London and join his newspaper as a staff writer. With wife and baby daughter, Jennings returned to America—she to pick up her acting career on Wallack's stage, he to the editorial rooms at the *New-York Times*.

Jennings made his mark quickly. On November 25, 1869, a new scandal hit Gotham: Daniel McFarland, a jealous, divorced husband, had taken a gun and shot Albert Richardson, a contributor and stockholder of Horace Greeley's *New York Tribune* who had been having an affair with McFarland's former wife. The shooting had taken place in the *Tribune*'s own office; afterwards, Mrs. McFarland had rushed to Richardson's side and married him on his deathbed. Louis Jennings saw good copy in the gory sex-murder tragedy and had no hesitation about using it to embarrass the *Times*'s Park Row rival, Greeley and the *Tribune*. Newspaper wars made good business, and he convinced George Jones that the story would boost circulation.

Louis J. Jennings, Jones's choice as the Times' *new managing editor in 1870.*

Jennings, on the attack, wielded what even his friends called "the most abusive pen known to post-bellum journalism."[8] In this case, he saw the story's target not in the murder itself, but the moral depravity of Horace Greeley's newspaper—a journal that in past years had touted free love, socialism, women's suffrage, Fourierism, and a host of other free-thinking causes. His jabs so irritated Greeley that the *Tribune* responded with its own attacks against the *Times*; but instead of targeting Jennings, a mere writer, the *Tribune* blasted thin-skinned George Shepherd, still the *Times*' chief editor. Shepherd wanted no part of the free-for-all and promptly resigned. George Jones, impressed with his new prodigy's spunk and aggressiveness, gave him the helm.

⁂

Some time in 1870, Jones and Jennings began discussing a possible new crusade for the paper that could rattle New York to its core and perhaps make them a bundle of money—a campaign against the biggest fish in local politics, the boss of Tammany Hall.

Just what bee in his bonnet got George Jones started on Tweed at that precise moment is far from clear. Jones had known the Tammany crowd for years. Oakey Hall had marched as a pall-bearer at Henry Raymond's funeral just a few months earlier, had written articles for the newspaper in the 1850s, and remained friendly with many on the staff. Jones knew Bill Tweed as a friendly, outgoing man. But there was more: Every day, he and Jennings walked past City Hall and the new County Courthouse and saw the newly-rich politicians going in and out, the "shiny hat brigade" and well-heeled contractors brimming with arrogance and wealth. Jones bristled at Tweed's friends Jay Gould and Jim Fisk, the Erie Railway stock manipulators, people with no respect for honest moneymaking. Everyone assumed that Tammany Hall was corrupt; stealing from the city treasury had been common knowledge for decades even if no one could prove it. And Tammany's bully tactics at the ballot box alone demanded that somebody punch them back. Jones' *New-York Times* was an unabashed Republican newspaper, independent in name but partisan and pro-reform; it stood for everything that Tweed was against.

But Jones also knew the reasons that most newspapers went easy on Tweed. Tweed had an easy, back-slapping way with newsmen: "jolly, genial, and off-handed Tweed" was how a *New York Sun* reporter put it, someone who'd invite you into his office with a hearty "Come boys, let us take a drink all around," quick to break out the glasses and cigars, or to give a newsman a few dollars for a favor.[9]

As recently as April, the *New-York Times* had backed Tweed solidly. After all, the *Times* had demanded home rule for New York City and it joined the praises when Tweed had delivered his new charter. "Senator Tweed is in a fair way to distinguish himself as a reformer," it had crowed. "Having gone so far as the champion of the new Election bill and charter, he seems to have no idea of turning back… he had put the people of Manhattan Island under great obligations."[10] And more: "Democrats who were successful in the recent struggle"—Tweed and his circle—"have thus far, in the main, fulfilled the various promises they were reported to have made." When Oakey Hall announced Tweed's appointment as new Commissioner of Public Works that month, Jones's newspaper had no complaint. It called Hall's choices "far above the average in point of personal fitness, and should be satisfactory."[11]

Jones and Jennings also knew the darker side about how Tweed's crowd kept reporters on a leash: that summer, the *Evening Free Press* had broken the usual silence by pointing a finger at D. George Wallis, a senior editor at the *New York Herald*, as holding three sinecure positions at City Hall paying him a salary of $15,000 per year.[12] Many newspapers and editors depended on Tammany subsidies; the *Albany Argus*, for one, received $80,500 in printing contracts from the city in 1869 and another $176,600 in 1870.[13] Altogether, from January 1869 through September 16, 1871, $2.7 million in city dollars had flowed from the public's coffers to the press, a financial pillar without which many on Printing House Square would crumble.[14]

The *New-York Times* too had played the game. It happily had accepted an

1867 designation as official outlet for "necessary legal advertisements of the city."[15] As a result, it saw its paychecks from City Hall jump to over $21,000 and $29,000 in 1868 and 1869, up from a mere $3,887 the year before.[16][17]

Leading New York newspapers

	Circulation	City advertising*	Annual gross receipts, 1869
Herald	100,000	$31,837	$801,327
World	26,000	$80,675	$689,040
Tribune	—	—	$514,207
Times	25,000	$33,400	$445,211
Harper's Weekly & Bazaar	—	$444,934	—
News	40,000	$305,422	$269,000
Sun	100,000	$43,326	$186,707
Mercury (weekly)	50,000	$117,046	$151,907
Express	8,000	$101,304	$99,472
Democrat	5,000	$184,547	$77,265
Irish American	—	$59,177	$43,298
Commercial Advertiser	8,000	$74,622	$41,050
Leader (weekly)	—	$41,001	$24,702
Atlas (weekly)	—	$68,936	$22,766
Transcript	—	$533,578	—
Star	9,000	$241,945	—
Citizen	—	$67,046	—
Metropolitan Record	—	$66,515	—
Real Estate Record	—	$44,688	—

* For January 1869 through May 1871.

George Jones had seen first hand how Tammany could sting him with these favors. To get his bills paid, Jones had to go begging to the comptroller, "Slippery Dick" Connolly, the most arrogant of the bunch. Just recently, in July 1868, Connolly had refused to pay the *Times* for an advertising bill of $13,764. In his letter denying the claim, Connolly almost boasted of his political motive. He pointed to Reuben Fenton, then the Republican governor, who had refused to sign that year's Tax Levy bill that provided the funding for paying such claims. Fenton had balked at the overbroad power it gave Connolly to pick and choose which bills to pay. To win him over, Connolly said he'd promised to pay none, that "I would not exercise the power," and only after that did Fenton sign the bill. "I shall not enter upon any argument to justify my action," Connolly now lectured George Jones. "I considered the greater good of the greater number."[18]

For Jennings, raised in London, Tammany abuses fed his native British prejudice against the Irish. He'd written a manuscript in 1865 before joining the *New-York Times* that detailed how he felt Irish immigrants had corrupted New York City life far worse than Germans or other Europeans. Citing the Civil War draft riots, he argued that Irishmen would never amount to much in America, pointing to the "serious evil that hordes of Irish who land here [are] utterly ignorant and forlorn."[19]

Perhaps Jones had gotten the idea from one of his competitors: Thomas Nast, the star illustrator at *Harper's Weekly*: While most newspapers had praised Tweed and his charter, Nast had openly ridiculed it: His cartoon that week—titled "Senator Tweed in a New Role"—showed the overweight, bearded Boss dressed in women's clothes as the distraught Queen in Shakespeare's *Hamlet*, wearing a Tammany crown and cradling in his arms the new charter. Behind him lay an awkwardly discarded corpse labeled "O'Brien Democracy" with a sword driven into its belly; in the distance are Indian braves with tomahawks are fighting over a box labeled "New York City Treasury and Fat Offices." Hamlet confronts the Tweed-Queen: "While rank corruption mining all within, Infects unseen. Confess yourself to heaven. Repent what's past; avoid what is to come," to which Tweed responds: "Oh, Hamlet! thou hast cleft my heart in twain."[20]

Nast had drawn a handful of other early Tammany cartoons, but most put Tweed in the background.[21] They'd won a few chuckles, but hadn't made much impact. It's not unlikely that Fletcher Harper, Nast's publisher, had sat down with George Jones about this time to suggest they join forces. Harper had once owned a large financial stake in the *New-York Times* in the 1850s and been a business partner with Jones at the time. If *Harper's* and the *Times* worked together, Nast's cartoons backed up by Jennings' sharp prose and the *Times*' fact-finding resources—reporters and money—perhaps they could shake things up. Nast had no actual evidence against Tweed, but that hadn't stopped him from basing his attacks on common knowledge. Besides, make a stink, and the evidence will come forward.

Taking on Tweed could be a great opportunity, but the idea also carried enormous risk. Boss Tweed was no Horace Greeley; he knew how to fight back. And George Jones had plenty to lose: For one thing, he barely controlled his own newspaper. Of the 100 shares of stock in the *New-York Times* company, Jones in 1870 owned only about 30. Henry Raymond's family held 34 and had voiced no opinion on whether they planned to keep it. The rest of the shares were scattered among half a dozen investors: board members James Taylor and Leonard Jerome, upstate businessman E.B. Morgan, and others. Would they back Jones in a war with Tammany, especially if it affected their bank accounts?

Large advertisers too might pull out, loyal to Tweed or afraid of losing city business. And James B. Taylor, a 10-percent owner of the newspaper and a respected voice on its board of directors, was part owner of Tweed's New-York Printing Company and always spoke well of the Boss.

Two things fell into place during that summer of 1870, however, that eased the decision. James Taylor died on August 22, removing the one pro-Tweed face from the *Times*' management. Then, in September, a new political season began. The Republicans decided to nominate a dynamic young candidate to challenge John Hoffman for the governorship: Stewart Woodford, a former Lieutenant Governor and popular stump speaker. Late that month, Democrats would gather in Rochester for their own annual political convention—a session promising to be dominated by Tweed. It presented the perfect chance for a trial balloon.

All through September, Jennings prepared. News from Europe dominated the front pages that month. The Franco-Prussian war was turning disastrous for France, with the fall of its Emperor, Napoleon III, the defeat of its army at Sedan, and the imminent siege of Paris. But on September 20, just as Prussian troops crossed the Seine and planted batteries on the Heights of Clamart to begin their bombardment of Paris, the *Times* opened up its own new fall offensive. Whether it was civic duty, personal pique, or financial opportunity that tipped the balance, George Jones now chose to be bold. He gave Jennings the go-ahead to unleash his pen. Jennings, having no actual evidence to work with, took a page from Nast and opened his barrage with a dose of ridicule:[22]

> *"We should like to have a treatise from Mr. Tweed on the art of growing rich in as many years as can be counted by the fingers of one hand. It would be instructive to young men, both as an example and a warning. Most of us have to work very hard for a subsistence, and think ourselves lucky if, in the far vista of years, there is reasonable prospect of comfort and*

independence. The expenses of living do not decrease, and money accumulates slowly.

"But under the blessed institution of Tammany, the laws which govern ordinary human affairs are powerless. You begin with nothing, and in five or ten years you can boast of your ten millions.

"How is it done? We wish Mr. Tweed, or Mr. Sweeny, or some of their friends would tell us. The general public say there is foul play somewhere. They are under the impression that monstrous abuses of their funds, corrupt bargains with railroad sharpers, outrageous plots to swindle the general community, account for the vast fortunes heaped up by men who spring up like mushrooms."

In the days following, Jennings would hit again and again. In his columns, Tweed soon became "King," "Dictator," blackmailer, and thief. Later, the *Times* would ask for information, for Connolly to open his books.

Imagine what they could do if they ever came across actual proof.

⊚ ⊚ ⊚ ⊚ ⊚

Samuel Tilden saw nothing to be embarrassed for after Rochester at first. His Democrats had held their annual convention there on September 20 with all the usual ceremony. Two thousands delegates and spectators had jammed Corinthian Hall, its podium decorated with red, white, and blue flags and banners. In some ways, the convention had been the party's best in years: "Perfect Harmony and Splendid Enthusiasm," the *New York World* had pronounced.[23] Every vote had been unanimous. At its climax, when delegates chose John Hoffman as their candidate for another term as governor, "the whole convention rose and gave cheer after cheer, while simultaneously the salvos of the guns were heard from outside," as one reporter described the scene. "A salute was fired from a full battery."[24]

Afterwards, Democratic clubs sounded 100-gun salutes in small towns all across the state.

But Tilden had also seen a seamier side in Rochester and soon realized he'd have to pay a price: At every step, utterly in command, calling every shot, deciding every issue and every logistical detail, was the highly visible corpulent form of the Boss of Tammany.

Tweed. Ever since his victory that April on his new city charter, Tweed's stature had soared, and with it, Tilden had seen ever more backhanded slaps.

Late that April, when Tammany had held its annual election for Sachems in its opulent new meeting room, Tweed had humiliated Tilden in front of the whole tribe by placing Tilden's name on a slate of malcontents—mostly O'Brien rebels—which Tweed then had his members promptly reject by an overwhelming vote of 242 to 23; Tilden had known nothing of it until reading it in the newspapers.[25] And more: friends told Tilden that Tweed had threatened to Lieutenant Governor Allen Beach, one of Tilden's upstate allies, that he planned to boot Tilden from the state party leadership at first opportunity.[26]

Now, in Rochester, Tilden saw Tweed throw his weight around again. Rather than complain, Tilden had bowed and played along. The night before the convention, Peter Sweeny had summoned him to his hotel room where Sweeny, "as a matter of form," told him what Tammany's decisions would be for the next day. Tilden swallowed it all. He even went along with helping Tweed in his vendetta against O'Brien's Young Democrats—Tweed had been systematically purging them from Tammany and city offices since April—by now blocking a group of them from coming to lodge a protest on the convention floor. Shortly before the convention, the O'Brien friends had visited Tilden and asked him for tickets, hoping to win delegate seats through a formal credentials challenge. Tilden had put them off by saying the "arrangements" hadn't been worked out yet. When they came back the next morning, Tilden told them the New York seats had already been given away to Tammany men; the best he could offer were passes to the gallery as "spectators." The O'Brien-ites declined—"unless they could be admitted as contesting delegates he did not want the tickets," one of them told a reporter.[27] Rumor had it that Tilden's own extra set of 500 tickets that he kept secretly hidden in his hotel room just for such emergencies had disappeared during the night, possibly stolen.[28]

When the convention opened the next morning, Tilden continued to play along: As state party chairman, he gaveled the hall to order, delivered a scholarly speech on world affairs—the growing threat of "centralization" in Europe—and supported each Tweed decision. When one sympathetic delegate rose to object to excluding the O'Brien Young Democrats, Tilden, standing on the podium, kept his mouth shut as the chair announced the absence of any contesting delegates and ruled the point out of order. Later in the day, Tilden watched from the podium as the convention delegates "called out" Tweed himself and insisted he give a speech: Tweed, shouting to be heard, "assured [the convention] that the City of New York would give from 55,000 to 65,000 majority for the ticket nominated here to-day." The crowd cheered; everyone knew Tweed would deliver the goods.[29]

As a final indignity, Tilden watched helplessly as the convention hall itself was terrorized that day by a band of about twenty bruisers, "roughs and thieves" according to the press, who'd arrived on a special overnight train from Manhattan. Somehow, each of the thugs had gotten a ticket to the convention hall—rumor had it that these were the tickets stolen from Tilden's hotel room the night before. Tammany denied any connection to the intruders, but people began calling them "Tweed's lambs" and whispered that Tweed had brought them along as extra muscle just in case O'Brien's Young Democrats tried anything. Before the day was over, more than a dozen reports of pocket picking and fighting had reached local police, including one from the Mayor of Rochester. Sam Tilden himself, as he was leaving the podium after the convention's final gavel, looked down to see one of the toughs sticking his hand into Tilden's own pocket to steal his watch.

Outsiders gasped: "The audience was put to sleep at the outset by Tilden's speech, and most of them did not wake again till the affair was all over," the *New-York Times* reported.[30] "Tammany is supreme. … Mr. Tweed nodded, and they obeyed…. Mr. Tweed lifted his little finger and promised a big majority—and that was the only speech that possessed significance …. All else was dry and barren."[31]

Tilden probably had enjoyed reading the *New-York Times*' initial attacks on Tweed a few days earlier—perhaps seeing a helping hand in his quiet resistance to the Boss. He'd known George Jones for years, part of the small circle of New York elite gentlemen at the Union League and other clubs. But he just as probably jumped out of his chair on seeing the *Times*' next installment in its anti-Tammany tirade. Its title made the point perfectly: "Mr. Tilden as the Slave of the 'Ring'":[32]

> "*Mr. Samuel J. Tilden … is as much disgusted with the City Government as any of us, and probably knows more of its horrors than most of us…. He knows how they cheat, and lie, and steal, and he knows that they rely for the perpetuation of their power on the fidelity and exertions of jail-birds,—and on the perpetration of frauds, such as, until lately, only jail-birds were guilty of. We venture to assert that he is disgusted with these monstrous abuses; that he would not venture to defend the rule now exer-*

cised in this City by the Tammany General Committee in any private room...

Nevertheless, Mr. Tilden—such as we see and know of him, was one of the most prominent performers in the late farce at Rochester. He is Chairman of the State Committee ... [but] is only a sham,... an ornamental subordinate, and that whatever he does has been done subject to the approbation of William M. Tweed. So far from being disgusted with his position, he seemed to delight in it...."

Tilden must have shuddered. He, Samuel Tilden, had a national reputation to protect. Within a few hours, Tilden, back in New York City, apparently raced across town to buttonhole Manton Marble, his Manhattan Club friend and publisher of the partisan-Democrat *New York World*. Marble gladly agreed to help; he'd happily respond for his friend. Newspaper wars made good business. The next morning, the *World* counter-punched with a column that Tilden may have written himself. Pointing to the *New-York Times*' own recent support of Boss Tweed's charter and its praise of his appointment as commissioner of Public Works, it asked an obvious question: "Will the [*Times*] tell us what those officers [Tweed and company] have done [since April] to forfeit its confidence?" Then, menacingly, it suggested a sinister secret: "[The *Times*] dares not avow the real motive of its attacks," it said. "Why does the journal so soon stultify itself? We could easily state the reason, and may do so at no distant day."[33]

What dirty laundry had the *New York World* gathered in its files to fling against the *New-York Times* in the next round of the battle? Readers would have to buy tomorrow's paper to find out.

If Tilden thought he'd escaped the storm, though, he was wrong. Not only did the *Times* hit back a few days later, but so did such elite New York friends as E.L. Godkin, publisher of *The Nation*. "We hope [Mr. Tilden] has a realizing sense of the company he keeps, when he opens conventions for Mr. Tweed, Mr. Hall, and Mr. Sweeny," Godkin wrote in late September. These men were "wretched thieves and swindlers," and Tilden was one of them.[34]

Sam Tilden, sitting in his Gramercy Park townhouse, recognized the obvious fact: So long as Tweed ruled the roost, he had no hope for a political future. Tweed would never let him become governor; he'd already given the job to Hoffman and probably promised it to Oakey Hall after that. If a seat opened up in the United States Senate, Tweed probably would give it to Peter

Sweeny or perhaps take it himself. Meanwhile, Tilden's reputation suffered. And if Tweed fell, he could bring the entire Party crashing down with him—including Tilden and his Swallowtails.

Tweed had to go. Someone had to take him down, but at the right time and in the right way, skillfully, with the proper hands on the weapon. Meanwhile, Tilden saw the Boss grow only more popular: Clubs in his honor popped up all over town.

At rallies and parades, his backers wore bright red shirts in honor of the Big Six Firemen who'd launched Tweed's political career almost twenty years earlier. Tweed had become more than a political leader; he'd become a cult, and each day he gathered more converts.[35]

Tilden saw it all: For now, though, he could only wait.

6
WHITEWASH

"I have been about as much abused as any man in public life; but I have never yet been charged with being deficient in common sense."

—TWEED, in a letter to police justice Edward Shandley, president of the Tweed Testimonial Association, declining the erection of a statue in his honor in New York City, March 13, 1871.

"MILDLY STARTLED"—that's how a *New-York Times* historian described Tweed's reaction to first seeing the newspaper's attacks on him beginning in late September 1870.[1] Most likely, it bothered him not at all. "King Tweed is our master, and men like Fisk, Jr. compose his Court." Irritation aside, Tweed probably delighted reading such plaudits while sipping tea in his Fifth Avenue mansion or reposing at his Duane Street lair, sharing a laugh with friends. By ascribing him so much power, the *Times* was building him up more than knocking him down. "The firman [edict] of an Eastern potentate does not carry more authority with it than the orders of the lord paramount of New-York," the *Times* railed day after day.[2] "From your lips to God's ears," Tweed could have mumbled over his noontime glass of wine.

Tweed could dismiss the attacks themselves as vague and political, typical for Republican insults in an election campaign. Besides, he knew his core backers, immigrants and poor workingmen: few if any read the *New-York Times*. Many couldn't read at all and those who did preferred friendly, Democratic-leaning papers like the *Sun* or the *Herald*—the city's two largest in circulation—or the *Leader*. The *Times* was just one lonely voice, a grouchy, squeaky wheel. Certainly Tweed learned quickly from his friend Dick Connolly, the city comptroller, that the *Times* had an axe to grind: Connolly's refusal to pay their $13,764 city advertising bill—sour grapes in anyone's book.

He probably cringed at the *Times*' personal slurs. "Mr. Tweed passes his Sundays drinking punch in a stable," charged one *Times* piece, quoting an old *New York World* story from back during the Young Democrat revolt. "Mr.

Tweed was worth less than nothing when he took to the trade of politics, for he was bankrupt [while now] he is rich enough to own a gorgeous home in town and a sumptuous seat in the country, a stud of horses, and a set of palatial stables."[3] Other attacks read like back-handed compliments: "Tweed and Fisk are bold, out-spoken rogues, whose very audacity almost makes one admire them."[4]

Friends urged Tweed to fight back but he refused. Why give them attention? "No man can answer newspaper attacks and stop with the reply," he told one friendly group that fall.[5] How had Tweed grown so rich, the *Times* asked? He had answers he could have given—such as pointing to his many business ties. Tweed held stock or directorships these days in a dozen profitable local firms: the New York Mutual Insurance Company, the New York Gas Light Company, the Guardian Savings Bank, the Bowling Green Railway Company, the National Broadway Bank, and the Third Avenue Railway Company, on top of his mainstays, the Erie Railway, the New-York Printing Company, the New York Transcript, and the Tenth National Bank—plus his multiple government salaries.[6] No law at the time stopped a public man from making money on the side: United States senators from Daniel Webster to Roscoe Conkling all had earned top-dollar legal fees while serving in office. And if Tweed had stepped on toes getting rich, he had good company: Cornelius Vanderbilt, Jay Gould, and Daniel Drew—Wall Street's richest players—all prided themselves as feared, ruthless manipulators ready to cut throats or corners.

As for corruption, why should Tweed be embarrassed? He knew the *Times* had not a scrap of evidence on his "percentages" from the Tax Levy or other thefts; he knew his bookkeepers hid the trail well. But even if *The Times* did, what of it? New York had been corrupt for generations. At the height of Civil War as Union boys were dying on Virginia battlefields, Tweed had seen "respectable" city merchants scramble like pigs at feeding to sell the army shoddy uniforms, defective weapons, and diseased food for exorbitant profits.* With post-war prosperity came even more corruption and it was President Ulysses Grant in Washington—a Republican—who wore the darkest black eye. Scandal had hit Grant's presidency in its very first year, 1869, with the Black

* None less than Brooks Brothers Clothiers supplied 12,000 sets of uniforms early in the war using "shoddy"—ground up rags—that fell apart after a few days. George Opdyke, the Republican wartime mayor, supplied 4,884 blankets to the army and, even while in office, sold over 1,000 carbines for $25 apiece, an estimated $10 above cost. Federal investigations abounded.[7]

Friday gold corner; Congressional hearings had revealed bribes from speculators Jay Gould and Jim Fisk reaching senior officials including the president's own brother-in-law and sister. Graft among Reconstruction carpetbaggers in the South, land speculators in the West, whiskey rings, postal rings, Indian supply rings, and railroad rings all festered like boils waiting to explode during the next few years.

If Tweed and his Tammany crowd had taken their share when opportunity knocked, why should they be scapegoats? In their own eyes, they doubtless saw themselves at least as giving something back: a voice for the poor and immigrants, improvements to the city, and jobs for their friends.

Pressed to justify its charges, the *Times* virtually admitted in late September it had no direct case against Tweed. "Why Attack Mr. Tweed?" it explained in an editorial, "We single out Mr. Tweed for the present, because he is the prime mover in the audacious faction which are now trying hard to ruin this City, and are making their own fortunes in the process. One at a time is a very good rule. 'After the master, the valets'... We look upon Mr. Tweed as the incarnation of all the vice in the City Government."[8]

Tweed boasted of being a take-charge man: "I am always in the habit of going to the front, and not in the habit of putting dummies forward," he'd blurted out earlier that year while confronting political enemies in Albany.[9] Now, seeing himself smeared, Tweed saw opportunity, a chance to consolidate power and silence his critics once and for all. An important election was coming up in 1870; his two leading protégés, Governor John Hoffman and Mayor Oakey Hall, both would stand for reelection in November. A big win for Hoffman could set the stage for Hoffman's run at the White House in 1872, catapulting Tweed to the national stage. He could defeat his attackers where it counted most, at the ballot box.

Already by mid-October, the *Times* attacks had produced a backlash among New York's working poor: Tweed's supporters throughout the city had rallied to him. Late that month, Republicans handed him another weapon: Fearing Tammany would use its now-famous repeaters and crooked counters to cheat them out of a fair vote, they'd appealed to President Grant's White House in Washington, D.C. They pointed to Tammany's control of the police and sheriff's office and recent evidence that the city had added more than 1,300 names to its payroll in September—"ruffians" to use on Election Day.[10] Grant agreed to intervene; on October 25 he ordered thousands of federal troops to march on Gotham: the Eighth U.S. Infantry to occupy harbor forts and two warships, the U.S.S. *Guerriere* and the U.S.S. *Narragansett*, to drop anchor in the rivers. He also ordered General Shaler, commander of the state militia, to prepare his soldiers to support U.S. marshals at the ballot box.

Gunboat politics! cried Democrats. Radical intimidation! Washington was treating New York no better than defeated Southern confederate cities like Richmond or New Orleans. No self-respecting New Yorker could tolerate the insult.

Finally, late that month, the *Times* too made a mistake; it lodged a specific charge giving Tweed something solid to knock down. "Where is Connolly's Report?" the *Times* demanded on October 21. "The Comptroller, Mr. Richard Connolly by name, alias 'Slippery Dick,'" had failed to issue his annual financial statement, it claimed. Something must be rotten in those books—specifically involving city bonds. He "*dare* not publish any statement of accounts. *There is an immense deficiency in his department—amounting, it is reported, to between four and five millions of dollars*, every dollar of which belongs to the public," the *Times* warned.[11] "[W]e charge them [Tweed, Connolly, and Sweeny] with intentionally keeping the public in ignorance of the amount of City revenue bonds issued" and manipulating them "much as James Fisk, Jr. treats Erie stock* .... In other words, in this matter of City bonds, the 'Ring' are acting dishonestly. Twist the words as much as you please, and the gravity of the charge is unaltered."[12]

Truth or not didn't matter. The law required the city to publish a full fiscal report in newspapers two months before each election and Connolly had ignored the rule, but that was beside the point. If he and Tweed could humiliate the *Times* on this concrete charge, they could blunt its entire campaign. They talked it over and quickly decided what to do: If the *Times* wanted the city's books examined, then so be it, they'd give them what they wanted. But rather than let the *Times*, a biased partisan, examine them, they'd pick their own judges: a special committee of six eminently respectable citizens, bluebloods with impeccable reputations, to study the records and make a report.

Within barely two days of the *Times*' attack, Connolly announced a new Committee of Investigation, its members comprising a virtual "Who's Who"

---

* In a famous incident at the height of the 1868 war with Vanderbilt for control of the Erie Railway, Fisk and Jay Gould had used a basement printing press to produce $10 million of secretly-authorized stock and sprang it on the market without warning to drown Vanderbilt's raid—producing rounds of angry legal counterattacks.

of the city's financial elite. As chairman, he named John Jacob Astor III, grandson and heir of the legendary fur trader who became New York's largest landowner and died in 1848 the richest man in America. Next came Moses Taylor, ship-owner, importer, president of City Bank, director of the city's gas light system, partner of Cyrus Field in the transatlantic cable, and owner of a $40 million fortune. Taylor also had been part of an underwriting consortium that sold city bonds overseas. After Taylor came Marshall O. Roberts, steamship magnate, part owner of the *New York Sun* and leader of the West Side Association whose Fifth Avenue mansion housed an art collection alone worth over $750,000. The three other members, George K. Sistaire, Edward Schell, and E.D. Brown, each had sterling business credentials, paid heavy taxes, and boasted financial expertise.

As Connolly organized the new committee, Tweed attacked publicly. A week before Election Day, Tammany held its usual pre-election rally that, this year, ballooned into a dazzling spectacle. A crowd estimated at between 40,000 and 100,000 people ignored a driving rain to jam the streets around Tammany Hall and shout their affection for the Boss—a remarkable turnout. They arrived dramatically: tens of thousands marched in formation from rallying points in each of the city's 22 wards, "mile after mile of men" flooding the streets carrying lighted torches in their hands, singing, chanting, and laughing while converging on Union Square at 14th Street which itself was transformed into a fantasy of light and sound, a vast landscape of banners, fireworks, and gas jets matched by the deafening roar of cheering voices, brass bands, and exploding roman candles. Swarms of people wore bright red shirts, symbols of the "Big Six" Americus volunteer fire company that had launched Tweed's career. Local clubs carried silk banners with names sewn in bright colored letters, red, green, purple, and orange: the "Young Men's William M. Tweed Club", the "Seventh Ward William M. Tweed Association," the "Fifteenth Ward William M. Tweed Club," along with banners for "Democratic Repeaters" and a large streamer reading: "John T. Hoffman: For Governor, 1870; For President, 1872."

On the platform, faces shining in the bright calcium light, stood Democratic leaders of every faction. Tweed's red-bearded head towered over the other celebrities: August Belmont of the national committee, 1864 presidential nominee General George B. McClellan, former governor Horatio Seymour, and even Sam Tilden keeping to himself in a corner. Weeks of *New-York Times* attacks, gunboat interference, and the hint of a national ticket had produced stunning unity among Democrats. Tweed took the podium and looked out over a sea of torch-lit faces cheering back at him. "I need not say that we are pleased to see so many of you here tonight," he roared, shouting to be heard, "who think with us the time has arrived at length when the great City of New-York must ... struggle for the overthrow of that despotic sway under which we have groaned for the past eleven years." They cheered again, then sang, then shouted. Tweed gave them defiance as thousands strained to hear through the rain and noise. Then he appealed to their intelligence. Tweed had a message tonight: discipline. He'd reached a watershed moment. He knew this time his machine could win a clean, fair contest by a landslide that would silence critics for years to come.

"We of New York, those who were born here upon the soil, and those who were not born here but have sworn allegiance to the country, feel that to be respected we must unite [and] as one voice denounce and frown down any attempts at mob violence," he argued, and saw heads by the hundreds nod in agreement. "We know our rights, we know our power, and we have over ourselves entire control, and hope that no act of violence will mar that day."[13] The crowd cheered again. They understood the point: Come Election Day, Tammany's rank and file must do nothing to tarnish victory or give soldiers an excuse to interfere. Instead of the usual ballot box roughhousing, they must show the city their very best manners.

After his speech, Tweed made another gesture. He turned to a former rival standing beside him on the platform—August Belmont, the national party chairman with the thick mutton chop whiskers and former agent of the Rothschild banking firm whom Tweed had attacked just months earlier—and named him the meeting's honorary chairman. Belmont still privately detested Tweed over the earlier incident; he called Tweed's crowd "canaille," French for riffraff from the Italian word for pack of dogs.[14] But he recognized the time to bury the hatchet and graciously accepted Tweed's peace offer. He avoided mentioning Tweed by name in his speech but did the next best thing: he endorsed Tweed's vision. "Every Democratic vote... will help towards the election of our Presidential candidate in 1872," Belmont declared, "and I for one hope to see our ticket then headed by the same name honored today—that of John T. Hoffman." The square erupted in cheers from thousands of voices.[15]

Surprisingly, the night's most popular speaker was no politician at all but rather Jim Fisk, the pugnacious "Prince Erie" who spent his days manipulating Wall Street and producing operas. "I ... have never in my life spoken at a political meeting before, have never voted the Democratic ticket," Fisk told the crowd, strutting back and forth on the platform. "After to-night there is no question of doubt but that I shall be a Democrat [and] there is no necessity for asking me for my influence with the 25,000 men [Erie Railway employees] under me." His spunk won the crowd: "I am not afraid of soldiers," he bellowed. "I don't think but what, if I find an opportunity, I shall vote three times a day."[16]

On Election Day, Tweed's army followed orders: They came, voted and kept calm; no violence occurred at the polls. Federal troops and marshals stood sentry but had little to do. Tammany produced a stunning outcome: Oakey Hall won reelection as mayor by 24,645 votes and John Hoffman's statewide majority for governor topped 52,000—all with few complaints of fraud.* Hoffman was on his way to the White House and Tammany could boast of facing down Ulysses Grant's soldiers: The *New York World* congratulated the mayor's "cool judgment, perfect self-possession, skill, and tact" for winning a "bloodless victory" over the federal army.[17]

To the extent the vote had been a referendum on Tweed, he'd won hands down; the *New-York Times* stood repudiated.

Even more important, just before Election Day, John Jacob Astor and his committee had issued their report. They found the city's finances sound and gave Tweed and Connolly an unqualified clean bill of health: "we ... certify the account books of the department are faithfully kept, that we have personally examined the securities of the department and sinking fund and found them correct. We have come to the conclusion and certify that the financial affairs of the city under the charge of the Comptroller are administered in a correct and faithful manner." Following Connolly's policies, they said, the city could pay its debts within twelve years.[18]

Astor and the others had spent only six hours actually looking at the ledgers and accounts, had seen only material Connolly had shown them, and hadn't looked behind any of the entries. Still, their blessing cast a shadow far beyond any single Election Day. "These names [Astor and the others] represent the foremost financial interest of their time, and no group of men could

---

* One exception was the Sixth Ward, the Five Points neighborhood, where only 153 registered voters cast ballots at 5 Mott Street, but Democratic inspectors announced 275 votes for Hoffman versus 5 for his opponent, despite Republican poll watchers who swore seeing at least 30 of their voters cast ballots.

have been selected more likely to command the confidence of the people of New York," conceded even the *New-York Times'* own reporter John Foord.[19] How could anyone credibly accuse Tweed or Connolly of financial foul play after this endorsement? Tammany's mouthpieces used it immediately to slam critics: a "full and fearless vindication," the *World* called it. "No one ever questioned that [the books] were [honestly kept] save such unscrupulous and incompetent libelers [sic]" as the *Tribune*, the *New-York Times*, and other "imbecilities."[20]

Critics might shout "whitewash," but who would believe them? Much later, they'd charge that Astor and his six committeemen had been tricked, threatened, or bribed with tax breaks to issue the report—not likely, given their wealth and experience. Marshall Roberts later would apologize publicly, claiming he'd been manipulated, his certificate "used as a cover and a shield by those who were robbing the city" and took "much blame… for having so readily fallen into the trap."[21] For now, they'd settled the issue. Connolly and Tweed were honest men.

◎ ◎ ◎ ◎ ◎

Jimmy O'Brien had suffered dearly at Tammany Hall for his rebellion. Ever since Tweed had crushed his Young Democrat insurgency in April, O'Brien had been slapped down at every turn: He'd lost his seat on Tammany's general committee, been excluded from the state convention, and publicly rebuked. Stout, outgoing, with square shoulders, a round, clean-shaven face, dark hair and friendly grin, O'Brien loved a good fight. In September that year, instead of sulking or begging forgiveness, he'd taken another poke at Tammany, publicly throwing his weight behind Thomas Ledbeth, the anti-Tammany candidate running for mayor against Oakey Hall backed by Young Democrats and Republicans, and he invested in an anti-Tammany newspaper called the *Evening Free Press*. Both failed miserably.

O'Brien and Tweed had always liked each other personally. O'Brien as a young Tammany upstart in the mid-1860s had looked up to Tweed, befriended him and called him "Paps." Tweed, in turn, had backed O'Brien in his bid for sheriff in 1867 despite criticism from older rivals. "Jimmy, I think as much of you as if you were you were one of my own family," O'Brien recalled Tweed's telling him once at City Hall, coming up and putting his arm around him at the height of the Young Democrat revolt, offering to make him rich if he dropped the fight.[22] But sentiment carried no weight now; O'Brien had strayed and Tammany had no room for traitors. "We shall cut off their supplies," one Tweed crony had told the *New York Sun* at the height of the contest. "Thousands of O'Brien roughs now hold sinecures [no-show jobs] in this city. They will never be allowed to draw another cent from the city treasury."[23]

James "Jimmy" O'Brien.

Late that year, Tammany had stripped O'Brien of his nomination for another term as sheriff. Then, when O'Brien had submitted two claims for sheriff's office expenses, totaling over $350,000—supposedly for "supplies to county jail, carrying prisoners to State Prison and other duties devolving on the sheriff," separate from O'Brien's own generous fees—Connolly called them excessive and refused to pay.[24] True or not, fair or not, O'Brien felt the pinch.

O'Brien had learned politics on the tough streets of the 21st ward (today's East Side between 26th and 40th Streets): Born in the Irish midlands, his family had settled in New York when he was a child. As a teenager, he'd worked manual jobs. Once, he'd spent two weeks at the Blackwell's Island prison for participating in a political riot: He was working in a stone-yard on 29th Street and "Our boss was at the time a candidate for some office, and a squad of us went down one evening to attend a primary election in his interest. On our way back there was some little disturbance, and some potatoes thrown, something of that kind," he explained later, though more likely it was bricks, broken windows and bloodied faces that prompted city prosecutors to put him behind bars. "None of us had any money or friends.... I had nobody to defend me."[25]

Later, O'Brien had shown a charm and political knack; he joined Tammany Hall and, at just 23 years old, he won an alderman's seat in 1864. He founded a neighborhood club—the Jackson on 32d Street and Second Avenue—and became a local power, the man to see in the 21st ward for political favors. In 1867, Tammany had nominated him for county sheriff, a plum job famous for making men rich, and he won a close race. O'Brien had proved his worth in 1868 by tipping the balance for Tammany on Election Day, ordering his hundreds of deputy sheriffs to arrest Republican voting inspectors and even raiding the lobby of the Congressional investigating committee to bully witnesses.

Now, having rebelled and failed, he needed to mend fences or leave politics forever, and, at 29 years old, he considered himself far too young to end his career. O'Brien used every ounce of his Irish charm to win his way back to the Wigwam. He took his punishment humbly: "I can hardly get a street sweeper appointed now," he told a reporter asking about patronage.[26] He stood first in line to join the Tweed testimonial association and used Oakey Hall's annual New Year's Day reception at City Hall to come and grovel: "You've been a kind friend to me, Mr. Hall," he said, buttonholing the mayor in front of a knot of reporters. "You have never been struck dead for lying; you have never turned one of my friends out of office; you have ever spoken in the highest terms of me behind my back, and slandered me to my face; you have loved me like a brother, and have done everything you could for me." Oakey Hall loved the oration; by one account, "Tears as big as black walnuts rolled down [the mayor's] face."[27] But for burying the hatchet with his former friends, the effort accomplished nothing.

Then one day in mid 1870, Jimmy O'Brien got a break: A neighborhood friend, a fellow named Bill Copeland, came to see him. O'Brien had done a favor for Copeland once and now, Copeland said, perhaps he could return it. Back in January that year, before his rupture with Tweed, O'Brien had used his Tammany pull to win Copeland a city job: Copeland was an accountant by trade, and O'Brien had visited Dick Connolly personally to ask him to hire his friend in the Comptroller's Office.*[28] "[A] smooth, smiling fellow, bright, clever, and quick," O'Brien described Copeland.[29] Connolly agreed to take him in; after all, he'd always liked O'Brien—a fellow native Irishmen transplanted in New York City—and sometimes they rubbed elbows together at O'Brien's haunt, the Jackson Club.[30] Why not do a friend a favor?

All went well at first. Connolly hired Bill Copeland and gave him a desk in the auditing department under bookkeeper Stephen Lynes, an assistant to county auditor James Watson. The Comptroller's Office was a showpiece: It occupied a large, high-ceilinged chamber on the top floor of the fancy new

* Twenty years later sitting on a veranda in Saratoga talking with a reporter, O'Brien would dramatize his demand on Connolly to hire Copeland: "Connolly was in a terrible flutter. Perspiration rolled down his face in streams. He didn't want to give the place and he didn't want to antagonize me." But since Copeland joined Connolly's office in January 1870 before the revolt had grown bitter, the story is probably malarky.

County Courthouse on Chambers Street. Its interior looked like a bank lobby with marble floors and brass chandeliers, divided by mahogany-and-glass walls into rooms and cubicles with teller windows for clerks to serve merchants doing business with the city. Connolly had given his own son a plum job there as an assistant to city auditor W.A. Herring.

People in the office liked Copeland; they described him as "a seemingly inoffensive fellow and a skilled accountant, who performed his duties... to the satisfaction of his superiors."[31]

Now, months later, Copeland had come back to O'Brien with a problem. He seemed troubled. Copeland had seen things in Connolly's office that bothered him, he said, and he did not know what to do. O'Brien had been his patron; now he needed advice. "I told Mr. O'Brien about them, because he was the only friend I had in public life," Copeland remembered. "I would have come to the mayor had I known him."[32] But for now, Copeland did not know Oakey Hall and he didn't trust Connolly, Watson, or Lynes enough to confront them.

Copeland's desk at the Comptroller's Office was in a room next to Watson's but separated by a wall lined on both sides with wooden cabinets. These cabinets each held pigeonholes for filing records. "I could not hear anything going on there," he said.[33] Copeland had been assigned the tedious job of taking vouchers on claims after they had been paid and filing them away in the right pigeonhole. Watson and Lynes normally kept the closets unlocked during business hours: "every person in the office had access to those pigeonholes," Copeland explained.[34] Watson himself kept the most private, sensitive records in a desk drawer in his private office, but even these normally weren't locked. Stephen Lynes, the bookkeeper, would review them regularly to record in his ledger books. Watson, Lynes, and the other clerks were responsible for keeping meticulous track of city spending; Lynes himself recorded every disbursement of city money in a ledger, no matter how big or small, and only gave his approval to pay money from the treasury after checking the voucher to assure it had all the required signatures. Lynes countersigned every warrant and obtained a receipt from every contractor who received a check. One ledger, called "County Liabilities," Lynes kept personally and never allowed it to leave the room.

Copeland learned the system over time and, after a while, began to notice odd things about vouchers he was filing, particularly bills from large city contractors involving the new County Courthouse itself. For one thing, he said, many of the vouchers, despite having the needed signatures—Tweed's, Connolly's, and the mayor's—had never been sworn to by the contractor as required by city rules. They contained no affidavit or supporting document to prove the claim. And some claims on their face seemed ridiculously large: "it was utterly impossible that the furniture, cabinet-work, and fittings itemized as having been furnished to the County Court-house [could have been used by] any dozen buildings"[35]—awnings costing $18,000, carpets enough to cover miles of hallway, plaster enough for acres of buildings, expensive repairs to structures that were brand new.

Sometimes he saw the contractors themselves—men like plasterer John Garvey—come to the office along with Tweed's clerk from the Board of Supervisors, E.W. Woodward, to meet privately with Watson carrying large envelopes. He may have noticed the envelopes bulged with money, checks or cash.[36]

Copeland tried to examine the vouchers, he said, but spying under his supervisors' noses made him uneasy. One time he'd begun copying items from Lynes' "County Liabilities" book but had to stop when Lynes saw him, abruptly came over and took it away; Watson and Connolly would be "very angry if he found out that anyone but him" had touched these particular records, Lynes told him.[37]

What should he do? Copeland asked. He'd never been in such a pinch. If something illegal was going on, whom could he talk to?

Jimmy O'Brien listened closely. He knew the city fraud game; he'd attacked it in his anti-Tammany speeches while dirtying his own fingers all the while. His recent claim of $350,000 in dubious sheriff's expenses had been one attempt at loot; according to Tweed, there'd been others. O'Brien all during his years as sheriff had had an arrangement with a friendly county supervisor to present padded bills, pocket the difference, and pay the supervisor a bonus for getting them approved.[38] Still, nobody ever seemed to have proof of foul play; the grafters always hid the trail. Vague charges had languished for years and the recent Astor committee had made Connolly untouchable—despite the *New-York Times* and its daily lambastes. Hard evidence could be worth a fortune. In fact, O'Brien could count the value in dollars and cents. He still had a following in New York City; he'd given donations to the right charities and kept his name afloat with local clubs, a political base for the future. With solid proof of Tammany fraud, records taken straight from the Comptroller's Office, he'd have enormous leverage, either to settle his financial claims against the city, win back his place at Tammany, or perhaps fight them all if they refused him.

After listening to his friend Copeland, O'Brien gave him the advice he'd asked for: First thing, he said, Copeland must say nothing about his suspicions, it must be their secret alone. Instead, he should start copying. Anything in Connolly's records that looked out of place, wrong, or incriminating, he must copy with as much detail as possible. The job might take days, weeks, or months, but would be worth his while. Then, O'Brien told his friend, Copeland must bring the copied records back to him. He, Jimmy O'Brien, would know what to do with them. Copeland would take the up front risk; after that he wouldn't have to worry.

New Year's Day, 1871, found Bill Tweed, Boss of Tammany Hall, basking in glory, the toast of New York City: fresh from a major election victory, hero of Home Rule, rich, powerful, and popular. Everyone he met called him friend; strangers rushed up to give him gifts. He arrived at the mayor's annual City Hall New Year's reception and received the loudest ovation: "The applause was deafening and long continued—cheer upon cheer ringing from the throats of the Great Almoner's admirers," a newsman wrote, "while [Tweed] stood with outstretched right arm, vainly endeavoring to" talk to supporters.[39]

On Christmas Eve, some "friends" had given him a diamond shirt-front pin weighing ten and a half carats, valued at $15,000, said to be "more closely approximate [to] a calcium light in brightness."[40] Tweed wore it "like a planet in his shirt front," one admirer said.[41] At the Americus Club Ball at the Academy of Music that week, he danced and laughed: "Boss Tweed had a bouquet, a $15,000 diamond, a ripping good time, partners by the score, a superb supper, and more attention than anybody else," wrote a society reporter for *The Star*. He "did all the [dance] figures as he should, and made a hit with his double shuffle. His partners—thirty of 'em—expressed their unbounded satisfaction with his efforts to please them, and all the boys cried out amen." Tweed's Americus club mates indulged his penchant for showy outfits: they wore "blue uniforms, liberally upholstered with gold trimming."[42] The *Evening Telegram* dubbed him "The Monarch of Manhattan and his Merrie Men" and covered its front page with a drawing of Tweed dancing an Irish jig to a drummer's beat, his large body lighter than air as famous admirers looked on.[43] A few days later, *The Star* carried drawings of him at another party clog dancing side by side with Oakey Hall.[44]

After all, Tweed's city was booming: manufacturing concerns up from 4,400 to 7,600 in a decade, factory jobs up from 90,000 to 130,000, stock prices up on Wall Street, numbers of bankers and brokers up from 170 to 1,800 and rents near City Hall up almost 1,000 percent since the War, and property values up all over town.[45] Property owners saw values rising high and taxes staying low; not surprisingly, both the East Side and the West Side owners associations smiled on Tammany.

Tweed had much to enjoy: his new thoroughbred horse Alderney Bull, his new farm in Westchester County, and his arrival at the pinnacle. Early in December, the *New York Sun*, apparently as a hoax, had suggested that New Yorkers collect money to erect a bronze statue of Tweed in a public park—perhaps Tweed Plaza at Broadway and Canal Street—to be finished on time for Tweed's birthday the next April. Joke or not, self-proclaimed friends quickly formed a "Tweed Testimonial Association" that within weeks raised over $10,000 for the project from city officials and contractors—even from former Young Democrats like Jimmy O'Brien. Rumor had it that Tweed had originated the idea himself to see which "friends" would contribute the most money. Fawning newspapers tripped over themselves to suggest designs.

Oakey Hall too luxuriated these days in his profile as the city's most flamboyant mayor. Friends called him Mayor "O'Hall" after he wore a bright emerald-green suit on Saint Patrick's Day, or Mayor "Von Hall" for officiating at German beer festivals. His clothes often made bigger splashes than his speeches: "The Mayor was dressed in a blue swallow-tail coat, with brass shamrock buttons, white vest, black doe-skins, and calfskin boots," read a clipping from one appearance that year. "While speaking he kept his hands under his coat-tail, and appeared as he usually does in public."[46] Hall enjoyed trading *bon mots* with literati: "Here [in New York City] you enjoy extensive freedom—freedom in newspaper abuse; freedom to gamble in Wall Street; freedom in marriage; freedom in divorce; free lager; free fights; free love!" he told the city's New England Society late in 1870, sparking a grumpy reply from Horace Greeley in the *Tribune*: "New York must be delivered from the thralldom of the Hall family. It is wearied of Tammany Hall, Mozart Hall, all the political halls, Oakey Hall, and alcohol."[47]

"[Hall's] first message as Mayor, in point of perspicuity and attractiveness, might have been written by Thackeray," a friend quipped.[48]

Critics ridiculed the mayor as a puppet of sinister Tammany wire-pullers: "Mr. Peter B. Sweeny is said to have remarked of Mayor Hall that 'he is a useful man; he is always ready to make a speech, and will make any sort of speech we tell him to,'" the *Evening Free Press* reported.[49] But Oakey Hall regarded all press as good press and walked the extra mile for ink.

Peter Sweeny, for his part, focused his energies these days on his new role as Czar of Central Park—already a New York showpiece though only part-finished. Sweeny had cosmopolitan tastes; during his yearly trips to France he'd met novelist Victor Hugo, Paris city planner Baron Haussmann, and artist Jean Corot.[50] Applying his continental airs to New York, he began spending money at a wild pace; he doubled city park expenses from an average $250,000 per year before to over $550,000 in 1870 and almost $400,000 in the first ten months of 1871 while collecting piles of unpaid bills.[51] "The greatest fault which Mr. Sweeny can find in the old [Park] Commission is one inexplicable to a member of the City Ring—that they did not provide comfortable offices for themselves. This, of course, he will immediately correct," the *Times* chided.[52] In a famous encounter, Sweeny cracked down on Professor Waterhouse Hawkins, a renowned geologist hired to make plaster models of dinosaur skeletons for the city's new Paleontological Museum of Animals, including a "Hadrosaur"—similar to an exhibit at London's Crystal Palace. Sweeny and fellow board member Henry Hilton decided to stop him, apparently incredulous that prehistoric creatures ever existed. They ordered workmen to barge into Hawkins' office, smash his models with hammers, bury them in the park, and destroy his scientific notes. In his Park Commission report that year, Sweeny dismissed the museum itself as designed for animals "alleged to be of the pre-Adamite period" and blocked its $300,000 cost as excessive for "a science which, however interesting, is yet so imperfect." He claimed the museum would block line-of-sight park views for nearby homeowners.[53] While at it, he reputedly also ordered a whale skeleton donated by Peter Cooper painted white to look more authentic.

Long time park patrons gasped. Andrew Haskell Green, the respected, visionary leader of the Central Park Commission since its 1857 inception, who'd guided its design and was kept on the board when Sweeny took control, now refused to attend meetings for fear of being connected to scandal.[54] Sweeny's spending and patronage, graft notwithstanding, was making Green's own ambitious plans now a possibility, but it rubbed against Green's ethic of frugal penny-pinching and long-term planning.[55]

During the holiday season, Tweed made a show of giving lavish gifts to charity and using friendly newspapers to trumpet his generosity. This year, his bounty overflowed. In December 1870, he gave $1,000 to each of the city's aldermen to buy coal for poor families in their districts. He listed charities totaling $163,591 that year, a stupendous jump from $3,100 in 1869 and less than a thousand in 1868, and he pressed Tammany to practice the same largesse. In late January, Tammany contributed $15,000 to the Fenians, the radical Irish nationalists whose American followers had launched an abortive raid on British-ruled Canada and whose prisoners had recently been freed from English jails.[56] The prior summer, when drought had caused water levels at the Croton Aqueduct to fall and threaten city supplies, Tweed had paid $25,000 of his own money to buy property adding over 50 million gallons to the system, though he planned to turn a nice profit by selling the property to the city later at good value.[57]

He made his most conspicuous gift that year to his old neighborhood: When approached to join a subscription to buy Christmas dinners and winter food for poor families in the 7th Ward—the lower East Side between Grand and Catherine Streets along the East River, the neighborhood where Tweed grew up—he took pen in hand and wrote $5,000 as his contribution. "Oh, Boss, put another naught to it," an official reputedly joked; Tweed added another digit, making the total $50,000.[58] This time, though, when Tammany trumpeted the story through friendly newspapers, Tweed was startled to find his gesture thrown back in his face—by his tiresome enemy, the *New-York Times*. "Some Stolen Money Returned," the *Times* headlined, ridiculing it as "Tweed's Bogus Gift." "When a man can plunder the public at the rate of $75,000 or $80,000 a day, it does not cost him much to give a few odd thousand dollars to the 'poor.'"[59]

Months after the Astor committee, Tweed saw the *Times* still pummeling him day after day. Though usually he hid the irritation behind his easy-going manner, the constant harping had worn on him. When a *New York Herald* reporter cornered Tweed in Albany at a post-New Year's reception in January 1871 and asked about the $50,000 donation, Tweed bristled: "That donation, as you call it,... has already given me a good deal of trouble. I don't want to talk about it at all. I would rather nothing were published about it."[60] He shifted in his chair as the reporter pressed him on the point, winding his watch chain, crossing his legs, and clearing his throat. "You see, my private affairs of late have kept me a great deal busier than during previous years," he

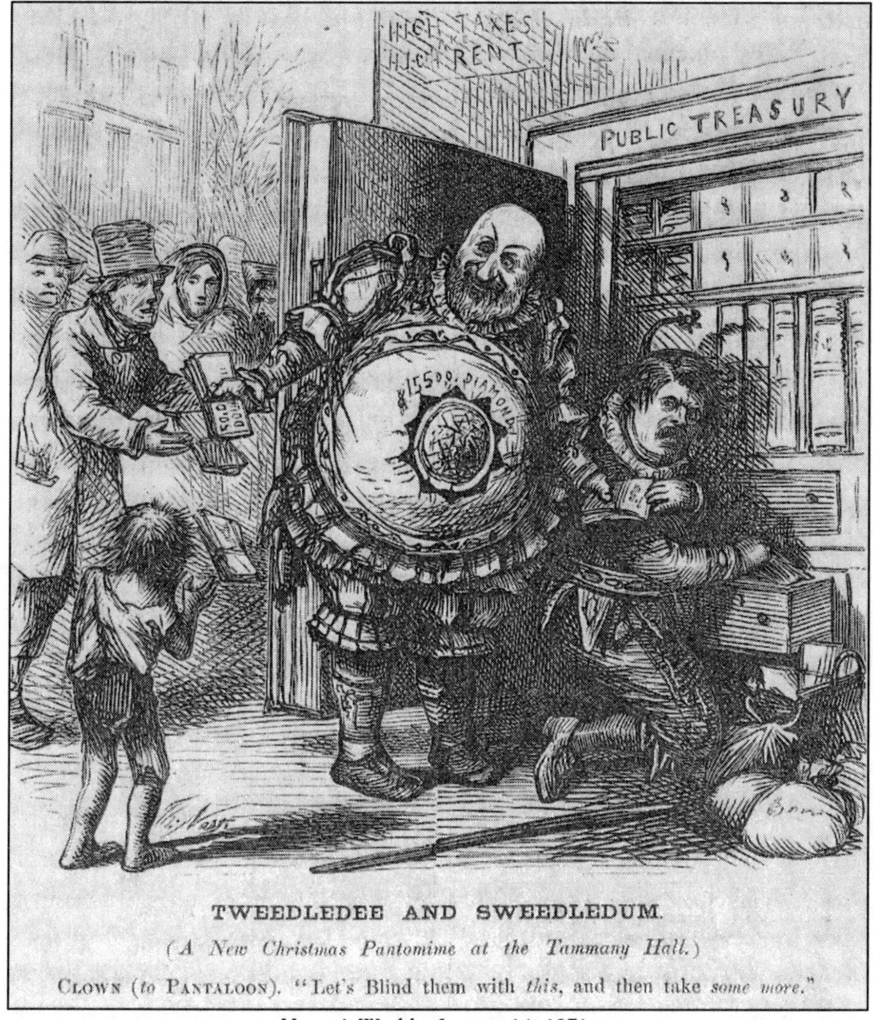

TWEEDLEDEE AND SWEEDLEDUM.

(A New Christmas Pantomime at the Tammany Hall.)

CLOWN (*to* PANTALOON). "Let's Blind them with *this*, and then take *some more*."

Harper's Weekly, *January 14, 1871.*

explained. When the reporter asked Tweed if he'd given the charity simply for "political effect," Tweed looked at him as though he were either about to laugh in his face or kick him out of the room. "Now, I tell you what it is," he said, "if I want to spend $50,000 for political capital, I know how to do it as well as the next man. What I don't know in that way isn't worth knowing; and you can rest assured that I wouldn't use $50,000 as a charitable donation if I wanted to make $50,000 worth of political capitol out of it."

The newsman scribbled furiously in his notebook as Tweed kept on: "Yes, sir, I have been roughly abused," he said. "I know that a public man's lot is a hard one. He's got to stand abuse; and I am not thin-skinned in the least. I don't personally care a snap, one way or the other, for either abuse or praise. But when a man is abused even when he is doing what no person of good heart can call a bad act, and he has a family and children he loves, the case is changed entirely. He cares for them, and knows they feel hurt by the abuse which he himself can outlive and outlive happily. But a man's family is dear to him."

Tweed finally got up. "A man's family is dear to him," he said to himself, and walked away.[61]

The next week, Tweed made a decision. He felt abused again, this time by another source: He saw the latest drawing in *Harper's Weekly* by Thomas Nast. To Tweed, these Nast cartoons, still barely a handful, had become even more annoying than the *New-York Times* attacks. The latest, called "Tweedledee and Sweedledum," showed Tweed and Sweeny dressed as clowns named "Clown" and "Pantaloon," with Tweed's character wearing a diamond big as a grapefruit lying atop his bulging stomach. The cartoon showed Tweed happily handing out fistfuls of cash from a vault labeled "Public Treasury" to poor men, women, and children while plotting to keep most for himself. "Let's blind them with this," Clown (Sweeny) says to Pantaloon (Tweed), cash in hand, "and then take some more."

Tweed must have noticed how people responded to the cartoon. They laughed—at him! The drawing on its face said nothing. It presented no evidence, no specific charge. It was just an image, a joke, a crude smear, but it made him look ridiculous and weak. How could he answer such a thing?

"That's the last straw," Tweed is reported to have snapped on seeing that cartoon in mid-January 1871. "I'll show those d__d publishers a new trick!"[62] He called together his brain trust. It was time to put the press in its place.

7
FATE

IT TOOK WILLIAM COPELAND several months to finish copying the suspicious records he'd seen at his job in the Comptroller's Office. Coming to work each day at the County Courthouse, walking up the cast-iron stairs beneath the painted ceilings, sometimes passing Dick Connolly, the tall, imposing comptroller himself, in the hallway, he worked secretly. He waited until his supervisors James Watson and Stephen Lynes couldn't see him. He'd take ledger books down from the shelves and find private corners away from the teller windows or glass dividers to do his pencil work. Finally, by late 1870, Copeland had copied a voluminous treasure trove of information, thousands of ledger entries from the County Liabilities book, each reflecting a city outlay he considered odd. To avoid mistakes, he'd stopped trying to separate suspicious entries and began copying entire pages, ultimately entire books. For each transaction, he recorded the amount, the payee, and the stated purpose. He made no effort to look behind any specific outlay, to confirm its accuracy or legitimacy; he'd taken a big enough risk just in copying the records. The numbers, he hoped, would speak for themselves.

Copeland now took his package—three copies of the hand-written ledgers—and brought them to Jimmy O'Brien, his friend and mentor. O'Brien took them gladly and sent Copeland on his way; whether he paid Copeland money for the job is unclear.[1] O'Brien seemed to recognize fully the import of his new possession; he handled it delicately, like nitroglycerine liable to explode in his hands. He gave it for safe keeping to a city judge, but by January 1871 he'd taken it back. He kept one copy in a safe, the second at his home, and the third with a private secretary. He decided first to use the ledgers to confront Connolly and Tweed over the money they still owed him, the $350,000 in sheriff's office expenses that O'Brien had claimed in mid-1870 and Connolly had denied him as excessive.

Some time around mid-January 1871, O'Brien prepared a new bill for his $350,000 claim and submitted it to the city Board of Apportionment, a new body created under the 1870 charter consisting of the mayor, Connolly as comptroller, Tweed as director of public works, and Sweeny as parks commissioner—the Tammany Ring in full glory. This time, O'Brien included a note threatening to print certain documents he held if they denied him his money.

Tweed, Sweeny, and Connolly met to talk it over one day[2] and apparently they couldn't believe O'Brien's cheek in making the outrageous demand. They started to bicker; the meeting "is said not to have been harmonious," one reporter heard.[3] First thing, they recognized the obvious; they had a traitor in their camp. Within weeks, Connolly had identified Bill Copeland as the culprit and fired him from his job in the Comptroller's Office for "political reasons," as Copeland would put it.[4] As to O'Brien's direct threat, they split. Tweed and Connolly argued to pay him the money, even though they considered the former sheriff's claim bogus and exorbitant: "very much in excess of any we paid prior to that time," Tweed would explain. Tweed had no desire to spark another internal Tammany war like the previous year's Young Democrat revolt: "I wanted to stop O'Brien's tongue; he was running around talking."[5] But Peter Sweeny balked, appalled at the naked blackmail: "Sweeny not unwisely insisted that O'Brien's greed was insatiable," journalist Charles Wingate wrote soon after these events, "and [insisted] that an issue might as well be made with him then as at any other time."[6] They argued, but Sweeny stood firm.

When the meeting broke up, Sweeny and Connolly walked away and left Tweed the job of seeing O'Brien and giving him the bad news. Hoping a personal touch, a cigar and a slap on the back, might smooth things over, Tweed invited O'Brien to his private office at the Public Works Department across the street from City Hall. "Mr. O'Brien wasn't against me at that time," he said later. "I was with him, had been his friend in every way, and he professed to be friendly to me."[7] O'Brien, too, claimed he had nothing against Tweed personally: "Tweed had done me a favor once," he insisted, "when I was running for sheriff [in 1867, four years earlier] he saved me a great deal of expense and treated me very honorably in certain ways. The inspectors of election were against me, but [Tweed] wouldn't allow them to cheat me."[8] But the appeal failed. On hearing he wouldn't get his money, O'Brien lost his sentimentality, threw a tantrum, and stormed out.

Still hoping to avoid a rift, Tweed insisted that Connolly and Sweeny regroup that same afternoon and reconsider the issue. They haggled it over at length, until after 5 pm that day. Finally, Sweeny relented. They agreed to send James Watson, the county auditor and all-purpose go-between for the Tweed Ring, to go see O'Brien, talk to him, calm him down and maybe reach a deal to buy back his ledgers. Watson, after all, had been Bill Copeland's supervisor in the Comptroller's Office; it was his ledgers that had been pilfered. That made it his responsibility. Watson dutifully followed orders and immediately set about to arrange a meeting. He sent messages to O'Brien asking for a time and place. "[Watson] wanted me to take dinner with him and Connolly and Tweed," O'Brien recalled years later, but he decided to play hard to get. "I refused. But he kept after me." Soon, they made a date. "He asked me to luncheon one day when we were both on the road," O'Brien recalled, while they were enjoying their favorite pastime, riding their fast horses through Central Park.[9]

James Watson loved horses. When he wasn't keeping the books or managing financial deals for Tweed and Connolly, he indulged his favorite passion: racing thoroughbreds. Watson's private stable at 42nd Street just behind his Madison Avenue home housed some of the city's fastest: "*Charlie Green*," the quickest, had set a public record of 2 minutes, 31½ seconds per mile; two of his stable mates, "*Fred*" and "*Loleto*," each had clocked miles under 2:40 and another, "*Dan*," was acknowledged to have a 2:30 gait but hadn't been officially timed. "*Loleto*" alone had cost $8,000 when Watson purchased him a year earlier.[10]

Watson looked younger than his 45 years and could afford fast horses, along with the stable full of carriages, sleighs, harnesses, saddles, and leather gear that went with them. He'd done well working for Tweed; he'd invested heavily in stocks and real estate and had assembled a portfolio worth almost $600,000.[11] Friends described him as "fully cosmopolitan" despite his Scottish birth and limited education. He belonged to half a dozen clubs including the Blossom, the Jefferson, and the Americus and had raised himself professionally by hard work: Imprisoned in the late 1850s in the Ludlow Street Jail, then the city's debtor's prison, for having fled to California with unpaid bills, Watson had earned his freedom by winning the warden's trust and becoming his jailhouse record-keeper. Afterwards, he'd won a series of jobs from then-sheriff John Kelly and did well enough to be made county auditor by then-comptroller Matthew Brennan in 1863. Since 1866, he'd earned the trust of his newest bosses, Dick Connolly and Tweed.[12]

After dining with his wife and two teenage children on Tuesday, January 24, 1871, Watson bundled himself in furs and stepped outside into the crisp, cold air; it was a perfect day for sledding. He hitched his sleigh to two horses and climbed onto the wooden front seat along with his coachman Sylvanus Townsend. He took the reigns himself and snapped the whip; his horses bolted forward, pulling them out onto snow-covered Madison Avenue. They rode north, then turned to the fast roads around Yorkville on Central Park's east side, thrilling at the speed and wind. They entered the park and followed twisting lanes along steep wooded hills and boulders, occasionally racing other horses, passing shanties where poor families camped by fires, then reached the wild spaces beyond the park and finally the small town of Harlem at the northern edge of Manhattan Island. Here, they stopped the sled, hitched the horses, and stepped into Harry Berthold's clubhouse for a glass of champagne by the hot fire.

Watson and his coachman didn't stay long at Berthold's; night was falling. There was "too rough a crowd upon the road," Watson later explained, and the road itself had turned rutty. He wanted to travel home in daylight. After a few moments by the fire, he and Townsend bundled up again in their furs and headed back out for the drive south.

They hadn't gotten far, coming down Harlem Lane with Townsend at the reins, when something happened: Reaching 138th Street, still far above the park, Watson heard a whinny. A horse from the opposite direction had panicked and dashed suddenly across the road, coming directly at them. Townsend yanked hard on the reigns, trying to turn, but the sled's tracks had gotten stuck in ruts in the snow and wouldn't budge. The oncoming horse slammed its massive body into the space between Watson's own two-horse team, breaking the neck-harness holding them together and knocking one horse to the ground. The loose horse reared his legs in the air over the sled's dashboard. One hoof smashed Watson in the forehead; the other stamped down on the wooden seat sending the coachman, Townsend, flying in the air and crashing down on the frozen street.

Townsend, unharmed, quickly lifted himself from the snow and, looking back, saw Watson lying unconscious on the sled. He raced back to help. Watson soon regained his senses enough to climb down under his own power.

Able to walk and having come just a short distance, he had Townsend help him on foot back up the road north to Berthold's clubhouse. Here they found a police officer named Frazier who dressed the wound on Watson's forehead and, seeing he was all right, took him home. Police later arrested the driver of the other carriage, a Charles Clifton, but released him after Watson declined to file a formal complaint.

At first, Watson seemed fine. Fully conscious, he was able to walk up the steps to his Madison Avenue home that night and his wound healed nicely the next few days. Then he fell ill, bedridden and feverish. Tweed heard the news in Albany and immediately made plans to return to New York; meanwhile, he sent friends to Watson's house to help the family and to watch. Doctors soon confessed they could do nothing; just a week after the accident, Watson fell unconscious and died in bed at five o'clock in the morning.

Watson had been a popular fellow. Clerks at the Comptroller's Office held a vigil and his funeral drew hundreds of friends. The parade from his Madison Avenue home to the 34th Street pier for the ride to Brooklyn's Cypress Hills Cemetery included dozens of city officials. Tweed, the mayor, Sweeny and Connolly all acted as pall bearers.

Connolly had the strangest response to Watson's death, seeming both panicked and relieved. Friends saw him dancing at a formal ball that night. Over the next few days, he began shifting people in his office. Watson had handled the Ring's finances: divided the "percentages," prepared the bogus paperwork, distributed the money, and kept secrets that could send them all to jail. Could he trust anyone else to do what he did, to know what he knew? Connolly quickly promoted bookkeeper Stephen Lynes to the role of county auditor and, to take Lynes' spot, he hired a new bookkeeper named Matthew O'Rourke. O'Rourke, a former newsman who wrote on military affairs, seemed trustworthy, but Connolly didn't rest easy. What exactly he did or how much he actually understood of Watson's operation isn't clear, but James Ingeresoll, a city contractor and Tammany Sachem, heard Connolly tell him around this time: "I did a big day's work yesterday… I got hold of Watson's book containing the list of payments to us. I tell you, I soon put it out of the way."[13]

❂ ❂ ❂ ❂ ❂

Whether James Watson had been *en route* to see Jimmy O'Brien that January afternoon when the panicked horse collided with his sled on the Harlem

Road is unclear.[14] What is clear, though, is that he and O'Brien never connected. After Watson died, the former sheriff's talks with Tweed broke down. His outstanding claim of $350,000 in sheriff's expenses was never settled.

Instead, weeks passed and Jimmy O'Brien stewed. He puzzled over what to do with the secret ledgers his friend Bill Copeland had copied from the Comptroller's Office. Should he try again to reach terms with Tweed? Or should he find another use for them, something more dramatic? He hid the books and bided time. When a reporter cornered him in January at a New Year's reception and asked him about Tammany's future, he answered with curious fatalism: "[Tammany] is the real power," he said, pointing to France's Napoleon III, recently vanquished by Prussian armies under Otto von Bismarck. "However, we cannot tell what a few months may bring forth. No one could foresee the sudden dissolution of the Napoleonic dynasty, which was a greater power, and a few short months since it crumbled into dust."[15]

8

I PLEDGE MYSELF TO PERSEVERE…

GEORGE JONES COULD BARELY leave his home on West 37th Street these days without getting cross looks and cold shoulders—from his club friends at the Union League, his fellow newsmen on Park Row, or city workers he passed on Broadway or Chambers Street. Even his own *New-York Times* staff, the clerks, writers, and typesetters, seemed to doubt him. He didn't mind the small slights, like not being invited to the mayor's City Hall New Year's reception. Jones' newspaper's fight with Tammany had dragged on for almost six months and, so far, he'd taken a public beating. Despite months of bluster, he'd failed to prove his case against Tweed and been embarrassed by the Astor committee's blessing of Tweed's finances—a direct rebuke of the *Times*. Other than Fletcher Harper and his young *Harper's Weekly* artist Tom Nast, Jones counted no allies in the New York press. The other large newspapers held their noses at him; even Horace Greeley, smelling a possible run at the White House in 1872, had turned quiet over Tweed and Tammany.

"Is it a hopeless fight?" Jones' *Times* had asked editorially in mid-January 1871. "Even those who are anxious to see us continue the struggle profess to be in very low spirits concerning the probable result."[1]

George Jones had gambled heavily on this contest and now saw failure staring back at him, even the prospect of losing control of his newspaper before having the chance to finish. In January, he received a letter from Henry Raymond's widow, still a 34-percent owner, asking for an accounting. Already, Jones had had to deny two published reports of Tweed's muscling him out of the *Times*, one in the *Rochester Chronicle* that Tweed had purchased "all the stock" and another in the *Philadelphia Ledger* that Tweed had cornered the shares of recently-deceased director James B. Taylor, both flatly wrong.[2]

One *Times* shareholder, Leonard Jerome, a member of the *Times*' executive committee, had joint real estate holdings with Tweed, and other directors would desert Jones the minute they saw red ink on the bottom line.[3]

Around this time, one of his reporters overheard a conversation at City Hall among some Tammany men saying: "I think the deal with Mrs. Raymond will go through." Jones could only guess what Tweed was plotting against him.

Instead of retreating, Jones had responded to each setback with a new attack. When John Jacob Astor's committee had blessed Connolly's financial books just before Election Day 1870, the *Times* blasted them as "fools" and "white washers" who "went like sheep to Mr. Connolly and were shorn," their committee "a disgraceful fraud," people who knew it was impossible to judge the city's books based on just a few hours' study, making them complicit in any thefts.[4] As a result, Astor, Moses Taylor, Marshall Roberts, and their highbrow friends now joined Tweed and Tammany in treating George Jones as a social pariah, someone to snub at clubs and restaurants. Who really ran the *Times*, people asked, conservative George Jones or his hothead British editor Louis Jennings?

Jones probably knew much more about Tweed's financial doings than he'd been able to print so far. The *Times* later would acknowledge having seen figures from Connolly's account books as early as November 1870.[5] But without hard evidence—actual documents and witnesses to vouch for authenticity—it meant nothing, hearsay at best. Printing detailed charges without proof could subject Jones to severe legal penalties—libel actions placing him in jail and his newspaper under the sheriff's control.[6] Libel laws in the 1800s frequently were used to put newspapermen behind bars; in December 1868, for instance, Jim Fisk had convinced a friendly New York judge to jail *Springfield Republican* publisher Samuel Bowles, visiting New York on Christmas holiday, after Bowles' newspaper had truthfully disclosed Fisk's adultery with Josie Mansfield and identified his wife, Lucy, in Boston.

Jones directed his editor Jennings and his staff of newsmen to keep digging, hoping for something to break their way: evidence to come forward, an insider to leak his story, an incriminating scrap of paper to emerge. Readers now expected a daily anti-Tammany slam in each morning's *New-York Times* to enjoy with breakfast. To wage the daily fight, Jennings brought in reinforcements in the form of 26-year-old John Foord, a recently hired reporter, British like himself, born in Perthshire, Scotland, and trained in the London press. In October 1870, fresh on the job, Foord had painstakingly assembled a list of 1,300 sinecures—people drawing salaries with no visible work—on the city payroll: "the rowdies and vagabonds of New-York, the sneak-thieves and the shoulder-hitters," he called them in an article headlined "Tweed's Lambs."[7]

Over the next few months, Jennings and Foord looked under every stone: They traced personal real estate transactions by Tweed and his Tammany cronies searching for patterns. In March, they found one: county auditor James Watson, a few months before his sledding death in January 1871, had purchased the Broadway Hotel on Broadway at 42d Street (today's Times Square), putting down $82,500 in cash and a $100,000 mortgage, just before Tweed had pushed through the Albany legislature a bill to widen the street at that spot. Watson immediately had won a city compensation award of $150,000, a huge windfall publicly listed as going to the property's prior owner, a Mr. Putnam, who actually had been offered only $50,000.[8] "Fraud," shouted the *Times*, in fact "stupendous frauds." The story charged that Watson actually held the property for Tammany higher-ups and planned to receive kickbacks from affected neighbors on the block. "It is now known that the Tweedites were to make four to five millions out of the job!" But the article gave no details on how.[9]

A few weeks later, they shouted fraud again: "Another Street Job"—this time, an extension of Madison Avenue from 19th to 23rd Street with "Tweed & Company Cramming Their Pockets." The story pointed to land Tweed had purchased nearby on 21st Street just on time to benefit from the work.[10] "Whenever large quantities of property are being bought by members of the Ring," the *Times* claimed, "it may be set down as an axiom in our municipal economy that improvements or the construction of public works will soon take place."[11]

When things got slow, Jennings stretched to find daily attacks: Once, he sent a reporter walking across City Hall park to the city's tax office to ask how much Tweed and Sweeny each paid in local property taxes; when an official refused to answer for privacy reasons, the paper concluded: "No Proof That The Ring Pay Taxes."[12] Other times, he resorted to name-calling: He quoted the proverb "although every Democrat is not a horse-thief, it is quite certain that every horse-thief is a Democrat"[13] and ran descriptions of Tweed himself as a "coarse and illiterate man."[14] Jennings saved his worst venom for so-called "Tweed Republicans," prominent Republican officials who gave cover to Tammany Hall by holding high-profile jobs under Tweed. Jennings called them "Republican Traitors" or "Wolves in Sheep's Clothing" and named names—Henry Smith and Benjamin Mannierre of the Police Board, for instance, who "With Mr. Tweed's chains clanking upon their wrists, they could scarcely be expected to show a spark of manliness."[15]

Jennings exploited what had become the comic scandal over the movement to built a bronze statue in the city in Tweed's honor. The original joke had grown into a public furor. "Has Tweed gone mad, that he thus challenges public attention to his life and acts?" the *Evening Post* asked.[16] Tweed himself had finally squelched the idea in a mid-March letter to organizers: "Statues are not erected to living men," he conceded, recognizing the political damage. "I claim to be a live man, and hope (Divine Providence permitting) to survive in all my vigor, politically and physically, some years to come.... I hardly know which is more absurd, the original proposition or the grave comments of others, based upon the idea that I have given the movement countenance."[17]

Jennings and Foord produced dozens of articles during those months of early 1871, but instead of converts they'd won only a few sneers. Why, people asked, was it that only foreigners—British-born Jennings and Foord and German-born Thomas Nast at *Harper's Weekly*—who complained about Bill Tweed? George Jones recognized that Tammany money stood behind much of the sniping from the other newspapers. Manton Marble's *New York World*, for instance, had openly opposed Tweed until its advertising revenue from the city fell to $7,588 in 1869, its lowest level in ten years. In 1870, after Marble came to terms with Peter Sweeny, the *World*'s balance sheet had recovered miraculously; its city revenue exploded to $43,527, giving it its second most profitable year ever.[18]

Even worse was the *New York Sun*, Jones' Park Row neighbor, the paper that had first suggested the Tweed statue and whose part-owner Marshal Roberts had been a member of the Astor committee. That February, the *Sun* issued the ugliest slur yet at Jones and his staff:[19]

> "*The decline of the New-York Times in everything that entitles a newspaper to respect and confidence, has been rapid and complete. Its present editor, who was dismissed from the London Times for improper conduct and untruthful writings, has sunk into a tedious monotony of slander and disregard of truth, and black-guard vituperation....*

"Let the Times change its course, send off Jennings, and get some gentleman and scholar in his place, and become again an able and high-toned paper. Thus it may escape from ruin. Otherwise it is doomed."

Sun publisher Charles Dana knew perfectly well the charge against Jennings was false, but that didn't matter. Even William Cullen Bryant's *Evening Post*—a staunch Republican journal—had now changed its tune and abruptly let go its editor Charles Nordhoff after Nordhoff had ridiculed the Tweed statue. The *Evening Post* now called Jones and *Harper's Weekly* "dishonest and disingenuous partisans" whose views counted for little "with honest and intelligent men."[20]

All this made George Jones' blood hot, but he didn't reach full boil until mid-March 1871 when he picked up a competitor's newspaper one morning and saw a column about himself that was not only untrue but malicious: "We are informed that negotiations are in progress for the sale of the *New-York Times* to a company, in which Mr. Peter Cooper, Moses Taylor, Cyrus W. Field, A. Oakey Hall, James Fisk, Jr., Jay Gould, Peter B. Sweeny, and William M. Tweed"—a line-up of New York's wealthiest men, all recent targets of *Times* attacks—"are to be the principal stockholders. The present managers of the establishment will leave as soon as the purchase is concluded." The new owners planned to throw Jones and Jennings to the wolves. And worse, the story fingered Jones himself as instigating the sale: "We learn, also, that the first overtures for this transaction were made by George Jones, through a third party, to Mr. Sweeny, about six months ago, but that the plan has not been entertained until recently."[21]

Jones had to control his temper. If true, this threat could signal disaster; the combination of millionaires and Tammany sharpers could destroy him. Jones knew he could never compete with the likes of Jay Gould and Cyrus Field over pure money. He began to see connections with other rumors he'd heard—that Tweed's friends recently had contacted small *Times* shareholders offering to buy them out for huge profits. Should this new combination get control of even a single share of *New-York Times* stock, it could file a lawsuit and run to one of Tweed's pet judges on the state Supreme Court, like George Barnard or Albert Cardozo, to get an injunction putting the newspaper in receivership—just as Gould and Fisk had done to the Erie Railway, the Union Pacific, the Albany-Susquehana, the Gold Exchange Bank, and a half-dozen others, naming one of their friends as receiver.[22] Even the hint of a stock raid, or of Jones' showing the "white feather" as they put it, could scare off advertisers, shareholders, and news sources, crippling the paper.

"[A]s soon as the Hon. A. O'Hall has completed his term as mayor," the article went on, "he will become the editor [of the *Times*], and then the political character of the concern will doubtless be changed." Jones knew that the *Times* under Elegant Oakey's control would be a Tammany pawn with no more credibility than the *Leader*, the *Star*, or the *World.*

Forewarned was forearmed. Politicians had tried to silence newspapers in America from the days of John Peter Zenger to John Adams' "Alien and Sedition" acts.* To keep his newspaper and fight off this new threat of Boss Tweed wielding the power of cash back by crooked judges, George Jones would need to keep his nerve. Fortunately for him, he still had a powerful weapon in this fight, the newspaper itself. Now he would have to learn how to use it.

Thomas Nast still preferred to work at home on his *Harper's Weekly* drawings, though success had given him the money to move north out of the city with Sarah and the children to a house in Harlem at 24 West 125th Street. He rode the train down to the city and Franklin Square only occasionally to see his publisher and deliver his latest works. It was here he heard the news, probably from Fletcher Harper directly: Tammany had found a way to blackmail Harper's company. Fletcher and his brothers took the threat seriously and had called a meeting to discuss it. At issue was whether to silence Nast and the *Weekly's* campaign against Tweed. The cost had grown too high.

The actual threat involved textbooks that Harper produced and sold to New York City schools, normally tens of thousands each year comprising a major source of income for the company. Harper had learned that the Board of Education had decided to reject any future books from the company and to throw out all Harper books it currently had in stock. These existing textbooks included standards like *Willson's Reader* and *Frenon's Arithmetic*; the

* Zenger, a German-born printer, was found not guilty by a New York jury in 1735 after being tried for sedition against New York's royal governor William Cosby, the first major test of press freedom in the American colonies. The "Sedition Act," adopted in July 1789, defined treasonable activity to include "any false, scandalous, and malicious writing" and was used to prosecute editors including Benjamin Franklin Bache of *the Philadelphia Democrat-Republican Aurora* and grandson of Benjamin Franklin. After the law expired in 1801, President Thomas Jefferson pardoned all those convicted under it and Congress reimbursed all penalties paid.

city would replace them with new books ordered from the New-York Printing Company, Tweed's firm.

James Harper, oldest of the four brothers who'd founded the company in the 1820s, had died in March 1869; now, of the remaining three, Fletcher feared he might be alone in wanting to resist the pressure. His older brothers, 76-year-old John and 70-year-old Joseph Wesley, sympathized, but they had a business to run, hundreds of employees to pay, and could not afford to lose their largest single customer. If City Hall boycotted Harper's textbooks, others might join them. The financial impact on the company if several large customers abandoned them in sympathy with City Hall could be devastating. Harper estimated the value of the existing textbooks alone at $50,000.

Nast's friends had warned him this could happen. "They will kill off your work," his cousin James Parton had cautioned months earlier. "You come out once a week—they will attack you daily. They will print their lies in large type, and when any contradiction is necessary it will be lost in an obscure corner."[23] Nast probably didn't believe it; he had a national reputation and made good money. Ulysses Grant himself had praised him for his role in the 1868 political campaign: "Two things elected me [as president]," Grant had said, "The sword of Sheridan and the pencil of Thomas Nast."[24] Nast had recently sold a single drawing for $350, the largest amount ever paid for such a work, and he had well-paying contracts to illustrate editions of *Humty Dumty* and *Dame Europa's School* for a British publisher.[25] News clippings guessed his personal wealth at the time at $75,000, a huge sum for a mere newspaperman or illustrator.[26] Nast wasn't shy about promoting his work: "Please see my picture *exhibited* again tonight [at the] seventh regiment armory," he'd telegraphed to *Tribune* editor John Russell Young to guarantee publicity for one particular show.[27]

But Tammany was a different animal altogether; Nast began to hear rumors about himself circulated around town—that he'd fled Germany to avoid military service, for instance, despite his being only six years old on reaching America.

Nast had always thrown himself into crusades. When he rode with Garibaldi on his "march of conquest" across Italy back in 1860, young Tommy had become a shameless follower of the "liberator," dressing like the soldiers in red shirt, Garibaldian hat and bandana, joining their marches and sharing their confidence. He'd followed Garibaldi on his triumphant entry into Naples and drew the hero's portrait, both on Garibaldi's handing the newly united country to King Victor Emmanuel and then on departing humbly to his home in Caprera, the small island near Sandinia.

Later, back in New York when he'd briefly re-joined *Leslie's Illustrated*, Nast had participated in *Leslie's* crusade against polluted "swill milk" sold in the city from diseased cows. He drew pictures of infected barns and sick animals and saw his publisher at *Leslie's* stand firm when angry dairymen threatened his life. This experience, plus the Civil War, had taught Nast to see political issues as stark moral choices, questions of wrong versus right, evil versus good.

For Nast, lampooning Tammany Hall had begun almost by reflex. City corruption was a natural target. People saw it all around them: police officers demanding payoffs from gambling dens or brothels, repeaters on Election Day, ward politicians with fat bankrolls. Nobody doubted that thieves haunted City Hall. In late 1869, at the height of a campaign by Tweed to depose August Belmont as national Democratic chairman, Nast had penciled a cartoon of Belmont as "The Democratic Scapegoat"—complete with horns and hooves—loaded down with sacks labeled "Sins of the Democrats." Tweed had appeared only as a face in the background, Nast's first depiction of the Boss.[28] A few months later in mid-1870, Nast portrayed Peter Sweeny as Tammany's villain-in-chief in a cartoon called "Greek Slave;" it showed Sweeny, whip in hand, bullying an Irishman chained to a pillory marked "Tammany," fed rum and whiskey and led by "slave drivers" to the ballot box.[29]

Over the next few months, as Tweed emerged as the dominant personality in city politics, Nast found him an irresistible subject: the easiest to draw of the Tammany crowd with his big belly, big nose, and silly grin. Just before the 1870 election, he moved Tweed into the foreground. One cartoon, "The Power Behind the Throne," showed Governor John Hoffman still the frontman sitting as monarch but with Tweed at his shoulder wielding a sword of "power." Another drawing, called "Our Modern Falstaff," showed jolly fat Tweed dressed like a clown while reviewing his brigade of Irish "repeaters," Hoffman reduced to merely a midget at Tweed's side.[30] In April, he made Tweed a Napoleon on the battlefield: "Emperor Tweed" leading his political troops through the a "Baptism of Fire" with "Political Reform" bombs exploding overhead.[31]

Nast and *Harper's* had not a shred of evidence against the Boss. Instead, they pointed to the "universal conviction" that Tammany was corrupt, a fact "familiar to every citizen" and "universally understood."[32] Nast used symbols

Nast's typical Irishman, being corralled by Peter Sweeny to back the Tammany line. Harper's Weekly, *April 16, 1870.*

to exploit his readers' prejudice: against the showy rich, against immigrants, against politicians. He sprinkled his Tweed drawings with recurring features: Tweed's big diamond, the brute Irishman—always with a threatening look, dirty clothes, a battered hat, over-sized skull, and whiskey bottle—and the Tammany tiger.

His anti-immigrant, anti-Catholic slant fit comfortably at *Harper's*. James Harper, the eldest founding brother, had been elected mayor of New York City in 1844 heading an anti-immigrant movement called the American Republican Party—a forerunner of the Know-Nothings. The Harper company itself had then recently published the American edition of *The Awful Disclo-*

sures of Maria Monk, or The Hidden Secret of a Nun's Life in a Convent Exposed, alleging wide sexual misconduct in Catholic institutions.*[33] Fletcher Harper and his brothers had come of age cringing at what they saw as an immigrant horde invading their city, congregating in filthy neighborhoods, speaking gibberish foreign tongues, practicing their strange "Popish" religion, and corrupting their politics—let alone their rising as a treasonous bloody mob against the draft at the height of their country's peril during the Civil War.

Nast apparently did not know his Tammany targets personally. At first, he drew his pictures of Tweed and Sweeny from photographs. By one account, he happened to pass Oakey Hall on the street one day about that time and Hall stopped to be polite: "I have not seen your 'handwriting on the wall' of late," the mayor said, referring to a recent Nast cartoon. Nast reputedly looked back without smiling, said "You will see more of it, presently," and walked on.[34] Once that spring he supposedly passed Tweed as well driving in Central Park; Nast smiled and tipped his hat as Tweed simply nodded and went on.[35]

When the three Harper brothers finally met privately at Franklin Square, the conversation apparently turned harsh, the two older brothers, John and Joseph Wesley, arguing loudly against Nast's anti-Tweed cartoons. Their hard-edged young illustrator was costing them money, they argued, and over what? A campaign heavy on smear and light on evidence? Fletcher Harper listened to the bluster and is credited with a heroically brief response: "Gentlemen, you know where I live. When you are ready to continue the fight against these scoundrels, send for me. Meanwhile, I shall find a way to do it alone." [36] His stubbornness won the day; his brothers agreed to let him continue. Tom Nast was delighted and responded typically by producing two new cartoons taking the fight to the next level: The first, titled "The New Board of Education," showed the inside of a city schoolroom under the new regime, with "Brains" Sweeny tossing Harper textbooks out the window, fat diamond-studded Tweed cajoling a student, and Oakey Hall writing the day's lesson on the chalkboard for the children to master: "Hoffman will be our next president; Sweed is an honest man; Tweeny is an angel; Hall is a friend of the poor."[37]

The second cartoon, "Under The Thumb," published a few weeks later,

* Harper lasted one term as mayor, recognized for having started the first New York police organization—the "Day and Night Watch"—and raising controversy by banning sale of alcohol on July 4 and shutting saloons on Sunday. Harper had tried to hide its fingerprints on the *Maria Monk* book by publishing it through a subsidiary called Howe and Bates, named for two of its employees.

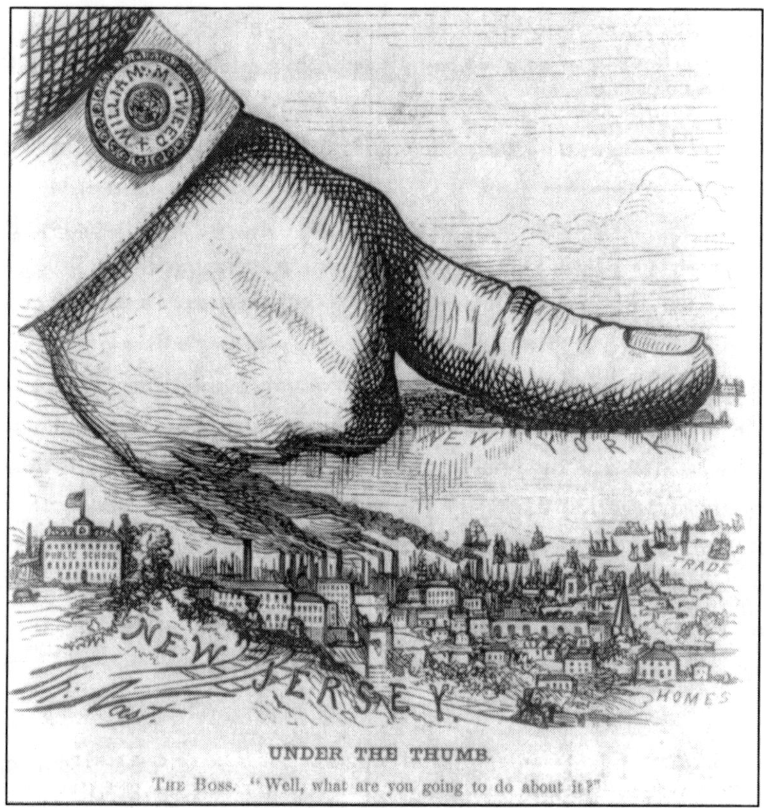

Harper's Weekly, *June 10, 1871.*

showed a giant hand placing down its huge thumb over the island of Manhattan, totally smothering the city, as surrounding suburbs remain peacefully undisturbed. A cufflink on its wrist says "William M. Tweed." The caption reads: "The Boss: 'Well, what are you going to do about it?'"[38] There is no evidence that Tweed ever said these words; Nast apparently made it up. But repeated again and again by Nast, the *New-York Times*, and a chorus of echoes, it became accepted as fact, Tweed's most famous saying, tarred on him as a rallying point to drive him from power.*

◎ ◎ ◎ ◎ ◎

* The *New-York Times'* editorial for July 1, 1871 similarly read: "People cry out in outrage. The Ring too have heard it, and what do they do? Thrusting their hands into their pockets filled with money filched from the people they have defrauded and then have the gall and arrogance to ask, 'Well! What are you going to do about it.'" Note that Tweed himself is not even identified as the speaker in this version.

George Jones made a decision. He refused to yield the *New-York Times* to anyone—certainly not to Tweed and his band—and refused to drop his fight. He had already climbed too far out on this limb. He'd lost dozens of friends, placed his fortune at risk, and subjected himself to insults and intimidation. A stranger had followed him on dark streets for several nights that spring. This most recent threat to steal his newspaper only stiffened his spine. Pride, stubbornness, greed, and duty all pointed him in the same direction, forward.

Jones recognized that until he could purchase a direct controlling interest in the *Times* company and prevent any shares from falling under Tweed's control, he remained vulnerable. He'd already had one near miss: following a tip, he'd found Tweed's agents already talking with Henry Raymond's widow to buy her shares and he'd had to plead urgently to prevent the sale.[39]

Now, putting pen to paper in his corner office at the *New-York Times* building, Jones laid out his position bluntly. He probably turned to his editor Jennings to help sharpen his words. First things first, Jones had to settle any doubt that he controlled the newspaper and would not allow any corporate scheme from interfering with his policy. The message had to reach both his own friends, reporters, and shareholders as well as Tweed and the public:[40]

> *"It is my duty to say that the assertion that I ever offered to dispose of my property in The Times to Mr. Sweeny, or anybody connected with him, or that I ever entered into negotiations for that purpose, or am ever likely to do so, directly or indirectly, is a fabrication from beginning to end....*
>
> *"But, believing that the course which The Times is pursuing is that which the interests of the great body of the public demand, ... no money that could be offered should induce me to dispose of a single share of my property to the Tammany faction, or to any man associated with it, or, indeed, to any person or party whatever, until this struggle is fought out. I have the same confidence in the integrity and firmness of my fellow-proprietors....*
>
> *"Rather than prove false to the public in the present crisis, I would, if necessity by any possibility arose, immediately start another journal to denounce those frauds upon the people, which are so great a scandal to the city, and I should carry with me in this renewal of our present labors the colleagues who have already stood by me through a long and arduous contest.*
>
> *"I pledge myself to persevere in the present contest, under all and any*

circumstances that may arise... even though the 'Ring' and its friends offered me for my interest in the property as many millions of dollars as they annually plunder from the city funds, it would not change my purpose."

In an era before newspapers developed the custom of attaching "by-lines" to columns, Jones ended by signing his name. No one must doubt who stood behind this pledge. In the next weeks, little would change at the *New-York Times*; the daily anti-Tammany attacks would continue, though Jennings would use more space to cite the other newspapers supporting the *Times*' stance. He had to look far for friends: the *Alta California*, the *Boston Advertiser*, the *Cleveland Daily Herald*, the *Indiana Evening News* and, of all the papers in New York City, only one, *Harper's Weekly*.

One promising sign reached him, though. Jones had heard a rumor: Someone in New York City was shopping secret information about the Ring, financial accounts of some sort. Maybe they'd come to him.

•9•
THE WEDDING

"If [your enemies] give any annoyance, laugh at them. The man who smiles on his adversary gets the best of the fight. [I] recommend the same remedy and believe it would be equally effective if applied to the men now trying to disunite and mislead the Democracy."

—TWEED, in a pre-election speech to democrats in the Fifth Ward (today's "Tribeca" neighborhood), November 5, 1870.

BOSS TWEED LOOKED THE PROUDEST of fathers and the best of hosts on May 31, 1871, dressed in his black evening formal suit, diamond flashing on his chest, as he stood in church to give his eldest daughter, Mary Amelia, away in marriage to 25-year-old Arthur Ambrose Maginnis of New Orleans. Tweed made the wedding magnificent in every way. Carriages clogged the streets around Trinity Chapel on West 25th Street as the hour approached. Inside the jammed church, well-wishers rose to their feet as the wedding party began its procession, the ladies "aglow with rich silks and satins and flashing with diamonds" with a "confusion of white arms and shoulders, elegant laces and valuable jewelry."[1] Richard Tweed, the bride's brother, led the wedding march, walking arm in arm with Maggie Maginnis, the groom's sister, followed by Frank Tweed with Josephine Tweed. Mary Jane Tweed, the bride's mother, marched with her new son-in-law wearing a gown of "salmon-colored silk, elegantly trimmed with deep *point aiguille* lace," a reporter noted.

Tweed escorted his daughter down the aisle as the organ rose in Mendelssohn's Wedding March played by popular pianist E.A. Gilbert. She wore "white corded silk, décolleté, with demi-sleeves, and immense court train" with orange blossoms at her waist and, on her bosom, "a brooch of immense diamonds, and long pendants, set with three large solitaire diamonds, sparkled in her ears."[2] Reverend Joseph Price, who twenty-seven years earlier had conducted Tweed's own marriage to Mary Jane Skaden at the old church on Chrystie Street, presided now again for Tweed's daughter.

William Tweed, Jr.

Tweed and his family had blossomed into New York celebrities that spring. A sailing sloop, the "*General Tweed*" named for oldest son William Jr., raced the fastest yachts in New York harbor, and a racehorse, the "*Richard* M. *Tweed*," named for his next-eldest son, won contests at the Fleetwood Park Track. William Jr. had grown into a skinny, side-whiskered, good-natured 25-year-old who enjoyed his growing fame. Beyond being an assistant district attorney, a commissioner of street openings, and a state militia general on Governor Hoffman's staff, he'd recently been appointed receiver of the Commonwealth Fire Insurance Company, a major legal case covered in the newspapers.[3] Showing political flair even his father would envy, William Jr. broke tradition that summer by making himself chief sponsor of the Excelsior Guards, the first all-black militia regiment to march in a city July Fourth parade since the ugly 1863 draft riots and welcomed them to loud cheers outside the Blossom Club on Fifth Avenue.[4]

Tweed's son Richard, too, had begun making his mark. As the 23-year-old manager of the Metropolitan Hotel—which his father rented for $90,000 per year from retail king A.T. Stewart—he'd launched a costly renovation of the hotel's 400 guestrooms with new furniture, new carpets, new lace curtains, all paid for by the Boss. A grand opening banquet promised to be a social highlight of the summer.

Tweed himself gloried as the city's grand benefactor, Santa Claus with a diamond pin. In the weeks before the wedding, he'd showered New York with largesse. In April, as Public Works commissioner, he'd awarded contracts for $800,000 in city improvements: paving roads from Water to Hudson to Hoboken Streets, installing sewers on Second, Third, and Tenth Avenues, and one throughout Harlem costing $433,000 alone, and grading land to lay streets in the unsettled regions north of Central Park—all steps to transform clogged, chaotic Manhattan into a livable city. The *New-York Times* cried foul on the street contracts, but few people believed the charges.[5] Merchants largely applauded: "from Boulevards and cross-streets are laid out and improved in the highest style of Tammany Art—opened, regulated, curbed, guttered and sewered, gas and water mains laid, with miles and miles of Telford-McAdam pavement, streets and avenues brilliantly lighted by fancy lamp-posts," cited the *Real Estate Record and Builder's Guide*.[6] Tweed that year also laid plans for a grand new engineering feat—the viaduct railroad, which would provide intra-city transit by running trains on two forty-foot high masonry bridges that would be built for $40 million each and run the entire length of Manhattan—a plan greater even than the Brooklyn Bridge and bolder than the fledgling schemes for elevated subways.

Oakey Hall, in his annual mayor's report issued that June, proposed spending $20 million over the coming three years to "improve the waterfront, repave streets, finish boulevards, supply [repair] defects in sewage and drainage, and widen, cut, and extend streets"—extravagance to some, but progress to most.[7]

Rather than pay higher taxes for all this, the city simply sold more bonds, mostly to investors in Europe. "It is quite generally understood ... that the Rothschilds are to advance a sufficient sum of money through [August] Belmont as their agent in this country to purchase all the indebtedness of New York City," chided a rare critic.[8] It seemed like a great free ride, especially for the banks and brokerage houses making huge commissions on the bond sales. Tweed economics—borrow, spend, and keep some for yourself—made sense to New Yorkers. Even the poor benefited. In May, Tweed sat with his fellow Apportionment Board members Peter Sweeny, Dick Connolly, and the mayor to accept applications for charitable donations, money Tweed had won from the Albany legislature. The Five Points Mission, the Ladies Union Relief Association, the New York Eye and Ear Infirmary, the Association for Deaf Mutes, the Saint Joseph's Asylum, and a dozen others all came forward.[9]

Few New Yorkers noticed the cracks forming in the system. But overseas, foreign investors, particularly European bankers who held the city and county bonds, had seen the recent attacks in the *New-York Times* and begun to worry about their investments. In April, the respected Berlin journal *Zeitschrift fur Kapital und Reute* had sent shudders through German fiscal circles by arguing that only the reputations of bond underwriters Rothschild and Discounts Gesellschaft made it still trust the financial soundness of New York securities.[10] Credit continued to flow, but cautiously.

Tweed didn't mind letting his family tug him around to buy yachts, horses, or expensive weddings. "[O]rdinarily very determined and courageous, [Tweed] is a great coward on the water, and disliked yachting parties," despite his owning two large boats himself, a newspaper said of him. Tweed is "very susceptible to the influence of women and can be wheeled by them into doing many things he would not otherwise undertake," it went on, though "the women in Tweed's case are his relatives and not improper characters."[11] Two years earlier, when Tweed had married off his second-eldest daughter, Elizabeth, to Arthur Maginnis' younger brother John Henry, the city barely took notice. This time, in 1871, at his height of fame, every newspaper sent a reporter to the wedding and spectators thronged the streets around Trinity Chapel to gawk at celebrities.

After the church service, Tweed led the guests back to his Fifth Avenue home for the season's most elegant reception. A blue and white awning covered the sidewalk in front of the entrance as carriages arrived. Inside, the bride, groom, and parents greeted friends under bouquets of japonicas, roses, and white tuberoses; flowers and more flowers, "all from my own place at Greenwich," Tweed bragged to a *New York Sun* reporter. Flowers from his greenhouses decorated the parlors, stairways, and arches, forming scarlet letters M. [for Maginnis] and T. [for Tweed] in one room and a huge harp of green and white with baskets of roses in another. A band played promenades and dances. "A magnificent supper was also spread and wine flowed with profusion," a newsman wrote.[12] Delmonico's restaurant served dinner—a meal so elegant it took its kitchen two days to prepare. Guests included a dazzling roster of city officials.

As the night wore on and dancers swooned, guests began gravitating toward an upstairs room to gawk at a stunning sight: the wedding gifts set out on a display table, silver, gold, diamonds, pearls, and plate settings filling an entire chamber, including forty silver sets, one with over 240 pieces. One reporter described "a cross of eleven diamonds, pea size" from a state senator, "diamonds as big as filberts" from a judge, "a pin of sixty diamonds, representing a sickle and sheaves of wheat" from a city contractor, "bronzes, thread lace, Cashmere shawls, rare pictures, everything that could be conceived of which is rich and costly."[13] Another reporter, this one from the *New York Herald*, pegged the gifts' total value at "over $700,000," causing even this normally friendly newspaper to gasp: "Seven hundred thousand dollars! What a testimony of the loyalty, the royalty, and the abounding East Indian resources of Tammany Hall!"[14]

Descriptions would dominate newspaper reports for days. The *New-York Times* jumped on the extravagance for a new round of attacks, deriding the bride's trousseau as "the most costly design" and her dress "the richest ever produced, and fit for a Princess" at $4,000. The wedding, coming on top of the hubbub over the statue, Tweed's shirt-front diamond pin, and his ostentatious charities, all pounded in day after day by the *New-York Times* and in Thomas Nast's cartoons, began to change the city's image in Tweed to a shallow caricature—rich, flagrant, and arrogant.

Of his close friends, only one had declined an invitation to the wedding: Oakey Hall, the mayor and his wife apparently sent no present and gave no excuse for staying away.* More than the others, Hall seemed to sense a rising unease in the city, though blinded by his own glibness. Addressing a meeting that summer when Chinese exclusion became the topic, he quipped, "on such a hot night as this, it is well to consider the coolie question."[15]

Jimmy O'Brien too stayed away from the Tweed wedding. By June, he still had not decided what to do with the explosive transcripts of city accounts he'd had copied by his friend Copeland. Months had passed since Tweed and Sweeny had rejected his payoff demands. Lacking any better idea, he waited. "These figures were my protection, they were the ammunition which I depended on to make my defense against their attack," he explained.[16] He found himself isolated. Most of his fellow Young Democrat insurgents had made peace with Tweed, some selling their friendship for healthy amounts: Michael Norton and Henry Genet, two anti-Tweed legislators in early 1870, had since received checks totaling $10,000 and $30,000, respectively, from Tweed.[17] "There wasn't one of them who hadn't been bought," O'Brien commiserated.[18]

Perhaps he still hoped to force Tweed's friends to relent on his $350,000 claim for sheriff's expenses—a lot of money to hold his attention—but personal friction made that increasingly unlikely. "O'Brien hated Sweeny, and Sweeny detested O'Brien," journalist Charles Wingate reported, "while Sweeny was vindictive and malignant, O'Brien was hot-tempered and revengeful."[19] O'Brien went out of his way to aggravate the wound. He continued to visit Tweed and taunted the older man with blackmail over the secret ledgers, pushing the Boss to lend him money; he took checks of $6,000

* Hall family descendants long after the scandal pointed to this event to show that the mayor and his wife kept social distance from Tweed, that she in particular refused 'to have Tweed or any of those Tammany politicians in the house."[20]

each in November 1870 and May 1871 and signed a thirty-day promissory note for a $12,000 loan on May 1. But when the note came due in early June, he refused to pay—essentially picking Tweed's pocket for $12,000.[21] He claims he saw Tweed a final time that spring in Tweed's office and that Tweed had begged him to relent: "You can have anything you want. I will have your father nominated for Sheriff, and I will see that he is elected. I will make you a rich man for the rest of your life." When O'Brien asked Tweed how he'd pay for it, he recalled Tweed's blurting "What the ___ do you care... as long as you get the money."[22]

During these same months, O'Brien claims he flirted with newspaper editors about selling his story and printing his evidence, but could never close a deal. "I didn't want to be mangled or distorted," he explained, and found most editors to be pawns of the hydra-headed Tammany machine: "[I]mmediately after I had dealings with them the members of the ring would come around me or send for me and make all sorts of offers," he recalled, the editors having leaked his advances back to Tweed and Sweeny. "I couldn't get the papers to touch the documents. I had them seven months before they were published." O'Brien claims that he went to see George Jones at the *New-York Times* during this period. "At all events, I think you will find him honest in his dealings with you," Hugh Hastings, editor of New York's *Commercial Advertiser* newspaper, had told him. But that meeting too apparently amounted to noting. "I didn't let him have the papers for over two months," O'Brien would say later.[23] But Jones at least had kept his secret.

Jimmy O'Brien seemed frozen in indecision. He knew that once he let go of the Copeland ledgers, he'd have no control over whatever damage they'd cause his former friends or himself. Perhaps a lingering spark of friendship still made him reluctant to burn a final bridge back to Tweed and Tammany. Besides, George Jones' *New-York Times* was a Republican newspaper and O'Brien still considered himself a loyal Democrat.

George Jones, meanwhile, finally got lucky. Early in July 1871, a few weeks after the showy Tweed wedding, he looked up from his desk to see a stranger come to see him in his top-floor corner office of the *New-York Times*. O'Brien, it turned out, was not the only person in town with secret numbers from the county Comptroller's Office.

Jones and his editor Louis Jennings had taken their fill of abuse from Tweed and his crowd by then. Jones' stern pledge in March had scared away raids on the company stock but recently they'd heard a new threat: City lawyers were asking questions about the land the *Times'* had purchased in 1857 to construct its new building, the Old Brick Presbyterian Church property on Park Row. Rumor had it they hoped to find a flaw in the legal title, a basis to shut the paper down or evict it from its building.

Jennings, meanwhile, found himself increasingly the target of strong-arm tactics: tough-looking strangers following him on the street making vague threats. Late one night when he was working alone in the *Times* building, a hard-faced man had burst into his office and threatened to "cut [Jennings'] heart out."[24]

To every anti-Tammany attack they launched in the *Times*, a Tammany mouthpiece would respond with flowers and bells: "There is not another municipal government in the world which combined so much character, capacity, experience and energy as are to be found in the city government of New York, under the new charter," Manton Marble's *New York World* crowed in mid-June, for instance. "The ten most capable men in the National Administration at Washington would be no match in ability and sagacity for the best ten in the New York City government, although General Grant has the whole country to select from."[25]

By early July, George Jones had been waging his campaign for almost ten months. His mysterious visitor couldn't have come at a better time. He introduced himself as Matthew O'Rourke, a bookkeeper who'd worked for Richard Connolly in the Comptroller's Office starting shortly after James Watson's death in January. He'd seen things that he claimed shocked him. A former military reporter, O'Rourke had noticed large claims under the heading "Armories and Drill Rooms"—half a million dollars for non-existent repairs, exorbitant rents for rooms that were nothing but stable lofts or saloons, and shabby bookkeeping, large sums being directed to a single contractor, furniture-maker James Ingersoll, despite the fact the other companies had filed the claims.

Jones quickly sent for Jennings, who joined them. Did O'Rourke have evidence to support his story? Certainly. Before resigning the job on May 19, he'd made a point to copy several suspicious entries from the city's ledger books, about two-dozen altogether.[26] He'd tried to tell his story to other newspapers, but none would listen. Finally, he'd visited professor Dexter Hawkins, whom the *Times* had hired to conduct an analysis of the city's published financial reports a few days earlier, and Hawkins suggested he see George Jones.[27]

Jones had been waiting for months for a moment like this. It had taken that long for the first concrete, usable piece of evidence to emerge, a disgruntled city employee willing to speak out and armed with first-hand details. Certainly he was interested in O'Rourke's story. He asked O'Rourke to help Jennings and Foord write up the material.

On July 8, 1871, the *New-York Times* launched a new phase in its campaign against Tweed and Tammany. Under the headline "More Ring Villainy: Gigantic Frauds in the Rental of Armories," it presented O'Rourke's story. It cited "Reliable and incontrovertible evidence [from] a good and trustworthy source" backed by figures "transcribed literally from books in the Controller's office. If Controller Connolly can prove them to be inaccurate he is heartily welcome to do so."[28]

The numbers, printed in tables, painted an eye-catching picture: $85,500 spent in rent for national guard drill rooms so unfit for use—small, filthy, or dilapidated—that they were never occupied. Each was listed with its street address so readers could see the buildings for themselves. Then it listed a dozen obvious overcharges, such as the city's renting the top floor of Tammany Hall for $36,000 per year when comparable space could be had for a tenth the price. Jennings' prose made other examples laughable, such as one stable loft rented for $24,000 per year for soldiers' drilling where "the ammonia generated in the stables is most injurious to arms, equipment and clothing, and the effluvia arising therefrom are often so offensive as to render the upper part of the buildings unfit for human occupancy."

"Who is responsible for these frauds?" the *Times* demanded. It listed its full cast of villains: Mayor Hall and Controller Connolly "who pass upon these claims and sign checks for their payment—knowing them to be fraudulent," Tweed and Sweeny who "pocket their share of the proceeds," and even the clerks like Stephen C. Lynes "whose agency in these matters is as palpable as it is shameful."

The story delivered a solid punch, but not more. Jennings could exploit it by repeating the details in subsequent days, but O'Rourke's leak had provided fuel for just a single day. Connolly and Tweed easily could minimize it. Even if O'Rourke's embarrassing numbers were true, they reflected a mere pittance, a tiny fraction of the city's total business, exceptions that proved the rule. Besides, as all New York society knew, John Jacob Astor's blue-ribbon committee had already decided the issue: Tweed and Connolly were social pillars who ran an honest, thriving city.

• PART III •

Revolt

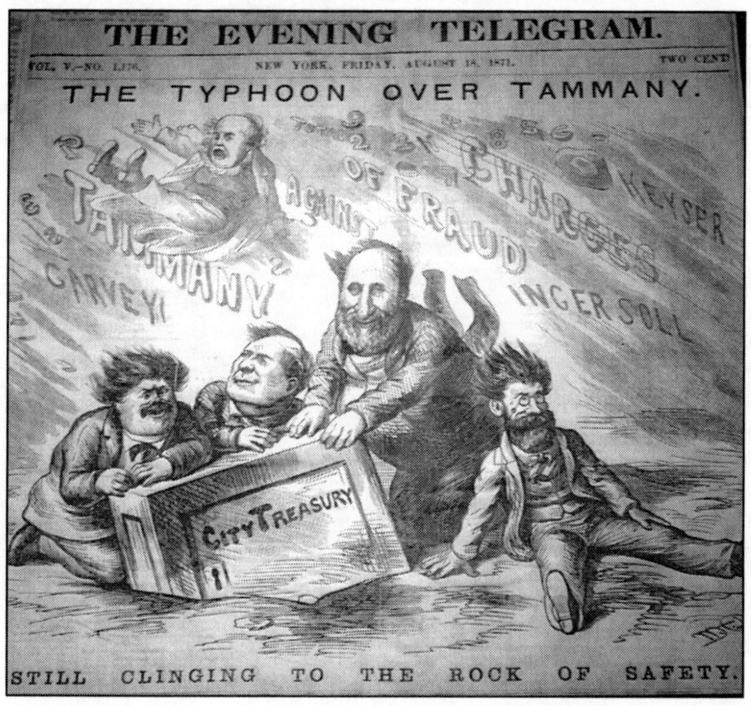

• 10 •

JULY

"[W]e find [the wealthy uptown landowners]are supported by the newspapers. But we know the virtue of a $50 bill when it is wisely employed, and the echo that it will produce.... But no matter, all the clamor of the newspapers is produced by the almighty dollar. However, the noise is of little importance; there is not one of them scarcely worth reading, and the most of them are never read at all."

—TWEED as a young alderman, complaining about biased newspaper coverage in a contest over a traffic right-of-way. December 29, 1852.[1]

SUMMER SOON TURNED BLOODY that year in New York City. Hundreds of quarrymen—gangs of unskilled workers who dug ditches, smashed boulders and piled gravel for new streets being laid near the East River around Yorkville (today's upper East Side) left their jobs in May and went on strike. They demanded better pay, $2.25 per day, and threatened to beat the tar out of any worker who refused to join them. The strikers marched *en masse* down First Avenue carrying clubs, iron pipes and axes, drawing a crowd of two thousand people to the streets. Club-wielding police rushed to the scene to avert a riot. The first day stayed peaceful; on the next, strikers chose to fight. They battled police around Central Park and beat senseless one gang-member on 76th Street who refused to quit work. The third day, a few striking "shovelmen" returned to their old jobs, but the "rockmen" refused and kept up the daily agitation. For two weeks they paraded and bullied other workers as the pay issue festered. A handful of construction sites began paying the higher wage, but most stood firm.

After that, the strike collapsed in confusion, violence threatening to return any time.[2]

All that Spring, New York had been riveted to terrifying news from Europe: France, recently defeated by Prussian armies under Otto Von Bismarck, had sunk into anarchy. Frenchmen had elected a new government to make peace, but dissidents in Paris rebelled. They declared their own republic under the worker-led Paris Commune that attracted support from Karl Marx and socialists worldwide. Already starved after months of Prussian siege, the Paris Communards defied French national troops sent to crush them. In a bloody three-month siege, they burned buildings and murdered the Archbishop of Paris whom they'd held hostage. When French soldiers re-took the city, they arrested 38,000 alleged radicals and killed an estimated 20,000 in an effort to destroy the Commune movement; they still held about 7,500 for deportation—ultimately to France's penal colony on New Caledonia in the Pacific.

Images of Paris street violence plastered across the pages of New York's illustrated journals like *Harper's Weekly* and *Leslie's Illustrated* evoked chilling memories of the city's own draft riots eight years earlier. New York's elite had little trouble seeing Paris' bloody Communards in their own Irish laboring class that had already risen once in revolt.

Now, that summer, it threatened to rise again. Early in July, New York's Loyal Order of Orange—representing immigrant Irish Protestants from Ulster in the country's North—announced plans for their annual parade on Orange Day, July 12, a landmark anniversary in religious conflict. It marked the 1690 Battle of the Boyne where Protestant King William defeated English Catholic King James II midway between Dublin and Belfast, setting the stage for centuries of Irish internal strife. Each year, New York's Orangemen celebrated the 1690 Protestant victory by marching down Eighth Avenue carrying Ulster and Orange flags, singing "Boyne Water," then enjoying family picnics in the city parks. Irish Catholics, who vastly outnumbered Orangemen in New York City, took it as a religious insult and had attacked Orange parades repeatedly since the 1820s. Violence the year before, in 1870, had been the worst ever, with five people killed and hundreds wounded in fights and rock-throwing, but the city had refused to prosecute rioters.

Now, in 1871, Catholics and Protestants planned to fight their battle again, this time on a bigger scale. The Orangemen demanded safety and appealed to City Hall to protect their parade; Irish Catholics vowed to stop them dead in their tracks and expected city police to stand aside.

When the Orangemen's request for a parade permit reached City Hall in early July, the mayor, Oakey Hall, wanted no part of it. He huddled with Tweed and Connolly and all three agreed: Religion aside—Hall and Tweed being Protestants and Connolly an Irish-born Catholic—each recognized the danger of wide bloodshed as well as the political bonus of siding with their own Tammany Catholic constituents. At the mayor's direction, police superintendent James Kelso issued General Order Number 57 to ban the parade. Blaming "foreign feuds" for inciting the conflict in the first place, it instructed police "to prevent the formation or progression of the public street procession of the 12th instant [Orange Day, and to] keep all the streets cleared from groups and assemblages."[3] There would be no Orange march that year.

Barely had the ink dried, though, when protests erupted: Protestants denounced Kelso's order as a cowardly surrender to a Catholic mob and suppression of free speech. Orangemen had as much right to march in America as anyone else, they argued. Merchants at Wall Street's Produce Exchange posted a pro-parade petition and backers waited in line for two hours to sign it. Religious loyalties split the city: Two leading Catholics, Archbishop John McClosky and activist Jeremiah O'Donovan Rossa, applauded Kelso's order while Protestant Wall Street merchants and Republican newspapers denounced it.[4]

Refusing to be denied their rights, Protestant leaders decided to take their case to Albany, the state capitol, and Governor John Hoffman, who recently had returned from his summer holiday in Newport, Rhode Island. Hearing their pleas, Hoffman saw a bigger stake in the contest than mere religion or free speech: hanging in the balance could be his own ambition to become president of the United States. He decided to intervene.

Ever since Tammany had put Hoffman in the governor's mansion in 1868, he'd been preparing to run against President Ulysses Grant in 1872, the centerpiece of Tweed's own ambition for national status. Hoffman, a handsome German with handlebar mustache and thick dark hair, had won six straight election victories—including two as governor and two as mayor—and remained popular with a wide range of Democrats. Things looked promising: Tammany had plenty of money to spend on winning him the party's nomination, and Hoffman had begun counting Washington leaders using as conduits New York Congressmen S.S. Cox and Fernando Wood.[5] He saw only one shadow on his prospects—his own sponsor, Tammany Hall, and its reputation for corruption. He saw comments like the one from the *Cincinnati Commercial*: "the [Tammany] 'Ring' … will be a principal agency in destroying his chances," its name "ruinous in a national campaign."[6] The *London Times*' Philadelphia correspondent likewise reported: "[Hoffman's] subserviency to the 'Erie Ring' [Tweed, Fisk and Gould] of New York [is a] blur upon his fame that may yet cost him the Presidency."[7]

Hoffman already had irritated Tweed that year by flouting his independence. A reporter told of seeing Tweed barge into the governor's Albany office, angry over Hoffman's plan to veto one of Tweed's bills in the state legislature, causing the governor to shoot back: "Senator Tweed, I propose to be governor of the State of New York one term, and to accept no dictation during it."[8]

Now Hoffman saw another chance to be his own man. On Tuesday afternoon, July 11, less than twenty-four hours before the planned march, he ordered a special train to rush him to Manhattan. Reaching the city at 9 pm, he spoke quickly with Tweed, Connolly, and Mayor Hall; then he met with police officials. Shortly after midnight, he announced his decision: The mayor had been wrong. Free speech must prevail. The Orangemen must be allowed their parade. "I hereby give notice that any and all bodies of men desiring to assemble and march in peaceable procession in this city tomorrow, the 12th inst., will be permitted to do so," the governor proclaimed. "A military and police escort will be furnished to any body of men desiring it...."[9] He, the governor, personally would spend Orange Day at police headquarters making sure things went smoothly.

Oakey Hall, embarrassed at being overruled, made no effort to hide his quarrel with the governor. "I may ... conform my action to that of my superior in office," he grumbled to a newsman the next morning, "[but] I still preserve my belief that the original order was proper."[10]

Orange Day came, Wednesday, July 12. At midday, thousands of Catholic Irish workmen left their jobs on the city's docks, streets, and construction sites—ditch diggers, pipe layers, longshoremen, veterans of the May quarry strikes, reinforced by hundreds of jobless thugs, women, and street children. They flocked downtown under a hot sun and congregated along the parade route on Eighth Avenue. Skirmishes erupted long before the actual march: a group of Irishmen attacked the city armory on Avenue A to loot for guns; police raided the Hibernian Hall on Houston Street where rifles were being handed out, and fifty policemen took positions around the Harper building at Franklin Square.

At 2 pm, the parade itself began, fewer than two hundred Orangemen surrounded by five hundred blue-uniformed policemen reinforced by five National Guard regiments: federal troops under General Pleasanton and state militia under General Shaler. Armed soldiers on horseback led the procession down Eighth Avenue; mobs of Catholics, mostly women and children, screamed at them from sidewalks and windows, heaping trash and abuse on soldiers and marchers alike. Anger on both sides was aggravated by the glaring heat that worsened during the day. When the parade reached 26th Street, the mounted soldiers at the lead found a dense mob blocking their way. They plowed forward, pushing people back as stones and bricks showered them from nearby rooftops. At 25th Street, the crowd forced them to a complete stop. The horse-borne soldiers charged the crowd again, and again were greeted by rocks, garbage, and insults.

Then a gunshot rang out, fired by a hidden sniper or a nervous soldier, it wasn't clear which. More shots followed. Without orders, a regiment of militiamen raised rifles and shot into the crowd; other militia units fired a second volley, then a third. Clouds of acrid smoke filled the air, blinding soldiers and rioters alike. In the melee, a young girl in an orange dress died instantly from a bullet shattering her brain. Several militiamen fell from bullet wounds; rioters grabbed the body of one soldier to stamp and kick. The shooting lasted only a few minutes. "The sight which was disclosed when the smoke cleared away was heart-rending and terrible in the extreme," police inspector George Walling recalled. "Dozens of bodies—men, women, and children even—lay upon the ground; the shrieks and groans of the wounded rang out above the noise of the vast mob, now madly trampling upon the weaker of the fugitives in the wild rush to reach a place of safety."*[11]

After the encounter, the parade continued from 25th Street downtown to Cooper Union, a band playing the Star Spangled Banner as soldiers and Orangemen walked sullenly along the way. Back on Eighth Avenue, at least 38 people lay dead, including three national guardsmen, with some counts putting the fatalities at almost 130—a toll rivaling the 105 killed in the July 1863 draft riots.[12] Dozens of police, militiamen, and rioters lay injured or dying in the street.

Conservative New Yorkers celebrated the harsh military response as a great victory. Law had triumphed over chaos, free speech over rabble. "Ex-

* In the panic, James Fisk, who among other things had a money-bought rank of colonel in the Seventh Regiment, climbed down from his horse, ran to a saloon on Eighth Avenue, climbed a fence and hid in a hotel on 23rd Street, then changed into civilian clothes, rode a tugboat across the Hudson, and reached Long Branch for a stiff drink by the ocean beach.

celsior," headlined the *New York Herald.*[13] The rioters had been scattered: "They did not even fight with the courage of religious bigots," one newspaper bragged, but "hid behind chimneys, prowled in ambush in cellars and doorways, [and] skulked behind innocent men, women, and children who had gathered along the sidewalks to look at the procession."[14] Irish Catholics especially seethed with anger, feeling betrayed, stamped on by bigoted Protestant-leaning soldiers, their national pride crushed in blood.

But both sides, Protestants and Catholics alike, agreed on the chief villains: Tammany Hall. They blamed the mayor, the governor, and Tweed for their "criminal weakness and vacillation," as the *Tribune* put it, for causing the debacle.[15] Why hadn't Tammany pressured its Irish patrons to avoid trouble, Protestants asked. Oakey Hall, the mayor, became the principal target: he'd seen the storm coming and "instead of reefing down close and endeavoring to weather the gale like a man, he delayed action until the wind split his sails," one observer wrote.[16] A newspaper suggested writing an epitaph on the graves of Wednesday's dead: "Murdered by the Criminal Management of A. Oakey Hall."[17]

After the riot, Governor Hoffman hid behind closed doors at the Clarendon Hotel and quickly left town to Newport, Rhode Island, "by order of his physician," an aide claimed, saying he needed "absolute quiet and undisturbed repose."[18] Tweed, Sweeny, Connolly, and Hall each refused to see newspapermen or appear on the street that day, fueling bitter ridicule of them as cowards, rich men hiding in their mansions.

Only Oakey Hall, of all the Tammany crowd, finally showed himself. He arrived at City Hall the next morning looking tired but indignant behind his usual *pince nez* glasses and clipped beard. He'd been right all along, he told a *New York Herald* reporter in his office. "There were three regiments of soldiers guarding a hundred and sixty Orangemen, flanked by five hundred policemen," he explained; without his original order blocking the march, there would have been 5,000 marchers facing 20,000 rioters and many more dead. "I am New York's housekeeper," he argued. "I must not allow lives to be taken unnecessarily.... I am bound to keep the peace." He dismissed the uproar against his opposition to the march as "a mistaken idea of public liberty being attacked." As for the anger: "the people [will] vindicate me," he said. "I have waited for vindication many times before."[19]

Friends later described Hall that day as hardly the usual "Elegant Oakey" but rather a man having "wept bitter tears over the ingratitude of his fellow citizens," insisting "he had not the blood or the stain of the wounded on his head."*[20]

John Hoffman, who'd staked his future on intruding into the affair and allowing the march, now also found himself crippled politically. Catholics saw blood on his hands. "The Irish element are permanently disaffected toward you," Peter Sweeny told the governor by letter, trying to console him. Hoffman's chances of ever becoming President of the United States had vanished in a hail of gunfire. "But your position is a great deal more comfortable than you would occupy as a defeated candidate for the Presidency," Sweeny wrote, "I think the Republican Press have made such a bugbear of the Tammany Ring that the people would not be likely to elect as President a man supposed to be in sympathy with them."[21]

Tweed himself tried to avoid the whole mess. Having left Manhattan altogether after the riot, sailing his yacht across Long Island Sound to his Greenwich country seat, he returned the next day to find his office jammed with panicked callers. He tried to put the best face on disaster. "It was an unfortunate business from beginning to end," he told people, dismissing the whole affair as if it were an impersonal force of nature like a hurricane or a blizzard, "one of those remarkable fiascoes for which it was impossible to tell who was to blame."[22]

Eight years earlier, Tweed and his circle had used the Civil War draft riots to demonstrate Tammany's ability to deliver effective government to a fractured city. Now he seemed adrift. His two leading public faces, Hoffman and Hall—both of whom had made their names prosecuting draft rioters in 1863—now stood humiliated, the city angry and bloodied. Tammany had failed to manage what New York's elite saw as the smoldering slum class of immigrants—its implicit social contract with them since the war. Still, his instinct that summer, rather than grappling with the problem, was to spend his free time in Greenwich, enjoying the breezes from Long Island Sound and the chumminess of his Americus Club lodge.

"[The Irish] want more money, and less work, and fewer Protestants, and cheaper whiskey," pronounced E.L. Godkin in *The Nation*, voicing widespread fears now reduced to raw bigotry. To his circle, the time had come to crack

* It didn't help that Hall was quoted blaming the Orangemen for the riot: "I still believe that the Orange procession to be a mischievously contrived one, intended to break the peace for the sake of ulterior effect in exciting the religious passions of the people.... What would police do with ten men who should march down Broadway with a banner on which was inscribed 'Death to the Pope,' 'Down with the religious harlot,' &c."

down on the rabble and its most visible symbol besides the Church itself—Tammany Hall.

❂ ❂ ❂ ❂ ❂

One who saw bloodshed and shared the anger from Orange Day was a young reserve soldier with the Seventh Regiment called up that day to march down Eighth Avenue when the militia made its stand: *Harper's Weekly* illustrator Thomas Nast.[23]

❂ ❂ ❂ ❂ ❂

Lewis Jennings reveled in work these days after the Orange riot, his team of reporters, copywriters, and typesetters spending endless hours at the *New-York Times* editorial rooms as news erupted around them. Jennings had not batted an eyelash at leading the newspaper attacks against Tammany Hall after the massacre—another blast in his ten-month campaign against Boss Tweed. He'd happily joined the chorus of jeers against the mayor: "A correspondent wishes to know whether the initials 'A.O.H.' stand for A. Oakey Hall or 'Ancient Order of Hibernians,'" he asked in an unsigned *Times* article that week, "The public has arrived at the conclusion that the owner of the initials is 'An Odious Humbug.'"[24]

Six days after the riot, the city remained in shock. The *Times*, like every other newspaper, consumed its front pages in the maudlin aftermath: funerals for rioters and slain national guardsmen, the discovery of more dead as bodies turned up during the week, the witnesses—rioters, guardsmen, and police alike—coming forward to give detailed accounts of their roles in the battle. Jennings printed it all with relish, more flames for the fire.

In the ten days since September 8 when the *Times* had printed its expose of exorbitant city spending on empty and decrepit armories using numbers filched by Matthew O'Rourke from Comptroller Connolly's own account books, City Hall had found ways to strike back. Jennings increasingly had felt their strong-arm tactics. "I was arrested two or three times a day as the [Tammany] fight grew brisk," he would write in a later memoir, "but the magistrates, albeit in the 'Ring,' never refused bail; and there were gentlemen of the city who stood ready day and night to give bail for me to the extent of five million dollars, had so much been wanted."[25]

Now, on Tuesday, July 18, Jennings again worked late at his desk in the *Times* building on Park Row. He remembered it being especially hot that night as he clipped through his routine of assembling the next morning's paper, editing columns of typeset print, flourishing his pen to sharpen a rhetorical slant or cut a few excess words, barking orders to clerks or reporters, keeping an eye on the clock for the next deadline. Then, at one point, he looked up to see a man standing in his office doorway. Jennings recognized him instantly, but chose not to say a word. As he watched, the man entered the room uninvited.

"Hot night," Jimmy O'Brien said.[26]

"Warm," Jennings replied. He noticed that O'Brien was holding a large envelope under his arm.

Jennings had no reason to be friendly to O'Brien, the former sheriff and long-time Tammany hack; he allowed a long silence to hang between them. O'Brien was the last man he'd trust on that hot summer night. O'Brien's stormy relations with Tweed had been a public soap opera for over a year, and his loyalties shifted like the wind. One day O'Brien touted himself a true-blue reformer, the next day he reverted back into a corrupt hack groveling for his share of graft like all the rest. Jennings certainly knew the rumors that O'Brien had been flirting with newspaper editors about secret ledger books he claimed to have gotten from Connolly's office. His own publisher George Jones at the *New-York Times* had probably told him about O'Brien's come-ons. But so far O'Brien had failed to deliver anything to anyone.

For all Jennings knew, the former sheriff had made his peace with Tweed, taken his cash, and now come over at Tweed's behest to rough up his office.

"You and Tom Nast have had a tough fight," O'Brien said finally.

"Still have."

"I said *had*." With that, O'Brien walked over to Jennings, laid the envelope on his desk, and thumped it with his fist. "Here's the proof to back up all *The Times* has charged.... They're copied right out of the city ledgers." Then he left without saying another word.*[27]

---

* Jennings told this story to the *London World* in 1887, though there are other versions of O'Brien's dramatic leak to the *Times*. Wingate, writing in 1875, reported that O'Brien came to the *Times* building that night, but handed the package to Jones, not Jennings, and said: "These are all the figures: you can do with them just what you please," then left with no further explanation. *Harper's Weekly*, in an 1890 profile of Jones, described O'Brien as bringing his evidence to Jones; on learning later that the *Times* planned to publish it, "he took away the papers, but brought them back in a few weeks, and told Mr. Jones to go ahead" without asking for conditions or compensation. O'Brien himself gave several versions. In the earliest, he claimed Copeland had made the delivery, not him. Years later, in 1891, he'd expand his own role but mix up the chronology, claiming he gave the papers to Jones in Saratoga with Samuel Tilden present, a meeting which did not occur until mid-August that summer, weeks after the disclosures.

Alone again in his office, Jennings studied the envelope, opened it and, seeing what was inside, he immediately got up from his desk and headed out to find George Jones. Reaching Jones' office on the top floor, Jennings showed him the envelope and they quickly called in John Foord, the young *Times* reporter who'd been working the Tweed story for months. The next several hours that night, they all studied the reams of handwritten notes and numbers, pages of ledgers that O'Brien had crammed into his envelope. It took them time to appreciate its full import. After ten months of waiting, the evidence they needed had finally dropped from the sky. Whatever information George Jones had perhaps *seen* eight months earlier about the inner doings of the Tweed ring and Connolly's financial accounts, he now *held*, along with a witness to vouch for it.

Time was wasting; they'd just been handed the scoop of the century.

❂ ❂ ❂ ❂ ❂

Jimmy O'Brien had gone to at least one other newspaper that week after the Orange riot before handing his secret ledgers books to the *New-York Times*. The *New York Sun*, just down the block on Park Row, had turned him away, possibly because its publisher Charles Dana had been out of the building and the managing editor on duty hadn't wanted to take responsibility.[28]

Twenty years later, after all the hoopla, O'Brien would still be bragging about the night he gave his damning evidence to the *Times*. With each telling, he'd expand his own role in toppling the Tweed Ring. By the time he laid it out for a newsman in Saratoga in 1891 sitting on the veranda of the Grand Union Hotel, drink in hand and a red geranium flower in his lapel, he'd have made himself the central character. He'd describe how George Jones was "very much frightened" and how he, Jimmy O'Brien, had stiffened his backbone. "[Jones] couldn't believe the steals were so gigantic," he'd say, and "he had to depend entirely on my word. He had no means of verifying any of the documents." O'Brien would tell how he himself had masterminded the entire *New-York Times* campaign, meeting Jones in Saratoga months earlier to lay out the plan: "Now… you have got an opportunity to make a name and a fortune, but you have got to go in boldly and without hesitation and you have got to startle the public into a realization of what those papers mean by immediately calling all those men in the ring thieves and robbers. Then produce these documents to prove the truth of your assertions."[29]

But all the bragging would come later. For now, with Tweed still paramount in New York City and the *Times* still gasping in its fight, O'Brien receded back into the shadows to wait for the fireworks.

❁ ❁ ❁ ❁ ❁

Thomas Nast returned home to his small house in Harlem after marching with the Seventh Regiment guards and set immediately to work. Whatever passion had driven Nast in creating his Tweed cartoons so far, the experience of carrying a rifle on Orange Day, seeing bloodshed and perhaps even firing his own round into the mob, compounded it. Sleeping barely four hours a night, virtually ignoring his wife Sarah and their three small children, Nast began producing a torrent of art; each *Harper's Weekly* edition through July and August would contain multiple cartoons, full-page illustrations, and satires from his pencil. Immediately after the riot, he sat down and drew a dazzling two-page, multi-paneled homage to the battle on Eighth Avenue, captioned "Something that Wouldn't Blow Over,—July 11 and July 12, 1871." From his pencil flowed images of heroic guards and police facing horrific hordes of Irish brutes with torches, clubs, and pistols attacking women and civilians, the "Colored Orphan Asylum" burning in the background—a throwback to July 1863. Around this, he drew a half-dozen smaller panels each containing a separate cartoon hammering the same theme: blood on the hands of Tammany. One showed Tweed, Connolly, Sweeny and Hall all cowering on their knees behind the woman's skirts of Lady Liberty as she leads militiamen and police rallying to protect the American flag, a battle scene as vivid as any from the Civil War; another showed the four as "Slaves of the Greeks," sitting glumly on the pavement as two ape-like Irishmen hold them as petty captives.[30]

For the same issue, Nast penciled a cartoon ridiculing Oakey Hall by turning him into a horse, "The Mare," sick with "The New Horse Plague." "Mare" Hall stood in a stable as Tweed (diamond as usual) and Sweeny (dark presence at Tweed's side as usual) look on.[31] In Nast's mind's eye, the images all seemed to merge now in a powerful creative surge: He had enemies to knock down—Tweed, Tammany, the Irish—and the new disclosures in the *New-York Times* of graft-ridden city spending gave his work urgency.

Readers began snatching up newsstand copies of the *Weekly* as much to laugh at Nast's latest satire as to gasp at the illustrations of the Orange riot and its aftermath. Pictures more than words became their staple.

❁ ❁ ❁ ❁ ❁

A panel from Nast's epic portrayal of the Battle of Eighth Avenue, Harper's Weekly, *July 29, 1871.*

George Jones, after ten months of shadow-boxing with Tammany Hall, had grown wary. Before giving his editor Louis Jennings final approval to unleash his final grand assault against Tweed, he wanted to tie up one last loose end. Jones still fretted over his Achilles heel: the 34 shares of *New-York Times* company stock still owned by Henry Raymond's widow and the threat that Tweed still might use it to steal his newspaper once the fight began.

In early July, George Jones found his answer in E.B. Morgan, an old friend from Albany who'd made his fortune on the Wells Fargo stagecoach company and had retired in upstate New York. Morgan had been an original investor in the *New-York Times* twenty years earlier and he and Jones had kept in touch over the years. Hearing from Jones about the recent threats from Tammany Hall, "The old Colonel [Morgan] was angry right down to his woolen socks," a *Times* assistant recalled.[32] Morgan, happy to help and rich enough to do it, rushed down to New York City and within a few days handed Mrs. Raymond a $370,000 payment to buy her entire stake in the company at $11,000 per share—a growth of more than 1,000 percent from its original value.

"The shares in the *New-York Times* attached to the Raymond estate, representing about one third of the property, were yesterday purchased by Mr. E.B. Morgan, of Aurora, Cayuga County [in upstate New York]," Jones announced publicly on July 19. He and Morgan now directly held eighty-two percent of the *Times*, a solid enough hold to scare away any back-room suitor.[33] That done, he now gave Jennings the signal to strike.

For a full day after receiving his surprise visit from Jimmy O'Brien and his envelope stuffed with hand-copied city account records, Louis Jennings had pawed through the material. He and his writing team, John Foord and Matthew O'Rourke—the original source of the armory data whom Jennings had now hired onto the newspaper's staff—spent hours dissecting the vast array of data. O'Brien's envelope had contained entire ledger accounts hand-copied by his friend William Copeland. O'Rourke and Foord scoured the mass of numbers looking for patterns, using O'Rourke's own stolen numbers as well as public financial reports on city and county debt to fill gaps. Fitting together the story piece by piece, they worked in secret. Jennings had no intention of risking last-minute foul play by tipping his hand, asking Tweed, Connolly, or Hall for comments or verifying the ledgers with the city.

Beyond security, Jennings and his team faced a daunting challenge as writers: how to explain the sheer mountain of complexity, three years' worth of detailed account records with hundreds of entries, in a way to convey its meaning while grabbing attention. Their strongest weapon appeared to be the raw numbers themselves—numbingly detailed but intimate and personal. With work, they realized, they could turn the dry account books into a voyeuristic sensation, a visual image as stark as anything from the pencil of Nast.

Jennings approached the job as if staging a drama for his wife, the actress at Wallack's theater. His would be a three-act play, starting with curtain raisers designed to build suspense. He began with foreshadow: On Wednesday,

July 20, he alerted the city that a great secret would soon be revealed: "Tomorrow morning we shall publish a still more important document, also compiled from Connolly's own books," he warned in an editorial titled "Two Thieves." "We shall prove … that the public are robbed of several millions a year under the armory accounts alone." But even this was mere appetizer: "Our article tomorrow, though of great import, will be exceeded in interest by a true copy which we shall shortly publish of the money paid on warrants… for the new Court-house."[34]

Each day that week, he banged the drum: On Thursday, the *Times* carried new accusations about city spending on armories: focusing on the $941,453.86 paid for "repairs" during a nine-month period, all going to four contractors. "[T]hey charged the money to the city, and divided the money among themselves, and this, we say was robbery," it claimed. Oakey Hall and Connolly, who signed and approved the payments, were "the chief thieves."*[35]

Then on Friday, he alerted the city again; more secrets were coming. "Will It 'Blow Over?'" he asked in an editorial. He described Connolly's office, where the city's accounts were kept, as being "guarded … with fixed bayonets." What awful secrets must it hold? "We have however, not yet begun to tell the story."[36]

"[Mayor] Hall goes about assuring every body who will listen him that he is 'used to newspaper attacks,'" the *Times* said. On Saturday would come the biggest attack of all.

---

* The *Times* explained the system as working like this: "A man does some work for the City authorities and charges $5,000 for it. When he presents his bill, one of Connolly's agents says to him, 'We can't pay this, but make the amount $55,000 and you shall have your money at once.' A warrant is drawn for $55,000, and endorsed by the presenter of the bill over to [the Ring's agent]. He then received five $1,000 bills, and the Ring pockets the $50,000." New-York Times, July 21, 1871. The proportions are exaggerated, but otherwise it is consistent with what Tweed himself would describe years later.

• 11 •
DISCLOSURE

"THE SECRET ACCOUNTS.

"Proofs of Undoubted Frauds Brought to Light.
"Warrants Signed by Hall and Connolly Under False Pretenses.
"The Account of Ingersoll and Company."

"The following accounts, copied with scrupulous fidelity from Controller Connolly's books, require little explanation...."

—FRONT PAGE HEADLINE, three columns wide, the first banner in the *New-York Times*' history. *New-York Times*, Saturday, July 22, 1871

Nothing like it had ever appeared before in an American newspaper. "THE SECRET ACCOUNTS," screamed the headline. Underneath it, covering fully half the front page, appeared a simple list of ledger entries, bare, naked, unadorned—136 line items altogether, exact to the penny, totaling $5,663,646.83.[1] Each line alone looked innocuous: "Sept. 28—Paid for repairs to County Offices and Buildings, July 2, 1869... $48,798.62" or "May 27—Paid for Cabinetwork Furnished in County Court-House, Aug. 23, 1869... $125,830." Together, they painted a stunning portrait—geysers of cash flying out from the city treasury, amounts impossibly large for their stated purpose. They raised an obvious question: Where had all the money gone? The implicit answer: fraud, waste, and God-knows-what. "The following accounts, copied with scrupulous fidelity from Controller Connolly's books require little explanation. They purport to show the amount paid during 1869 and 1870 for repairs and furniture for the New Court-House," read a brief headnote.

The new Courthouse, which housed the Comptroller's Office, they would make Tweed's signature building.

Not only were the amounts exorbitant, but the *Times* showed how all the money eventually went to a single account, "Ingersoll and Company," even

The New-York Times.

VOL. XX......NO. 6189. NEW-YORK, SATURDAY, JULY 22, 1871. PRICE FOUR CENTS.

THE SECRET ACCOUNTS.

Proofs of Undoubted Frauds Brought to Light.

Warrants Signed by Hall and Connolly Under False Pretenses.

THE ACCOUNT OF INGERSOLL & CO.

The following accounts, copied with scrupulous fidelity from Controller CONNOLLY's books, require little explanation. They purport to show the amount paid during 1869 and 1870, for repairs and furniture for the New Court-house. It will be seen that the warrants are drawn in different names, but they were all indorsed to "INGERSOLL & CO."—otherwise, J. H. INGERSOLL, the agent of the Ring. Each warrant was signed by Controller CONNOLLY and Mayor HALL. What amount of money was actually paid to the persons in whose favor the warrants were *nominally* drawn, we have no means of knowing. On the face of these accounts, however, it is clear that the bulk of the money somehow or other got back to the Ring, or each warrant would not have been indorsed over to its agent.

We undertake to prove whenever we are afforded the opportunity, that the following account is copied literally from the Controller's books, and forms a part of the documents to which the public is entitled to have access.

The dates given for the work done are obviously fraudulent. For example: On July 2, 1869, a warrant was drawn for furniture supplied for County Courts and offices, from Oct. 18 to Nov. 23, 1868, for $42,560 64. On July 16—*fourteen days* afterward—another warrant was drawn for $94,038 13 for furniture supplied to the same offices from Nov. 7 to Dec. 31. That is to say, the bill was fully paid by the *first* of these two warrants down to Nov. 23. And yet a fortnight afterward another warrant was drawn paying the bill over again from Nov. 7. It is obvious that the fictitious dates were not remembered by the City authorities when these warrants were drawn. Many similar cases will be observed in the figures given below.

It will be seen that on one day furniture is supposed to have been supplied to the amount of $129,469 48—at least a warrant for that sum was signed by HALL and CONNOLLY in favor of C. D. BOLLAR & Co., and indorsed by INGERSOLL & Co.

1869. INGERSOLL & CO. 1869.

Date of Warrant.	Character of Work. Date on Which Work was Supposed to be Done.	Amount Drawn.
July 2	—Paid for Furniture in County Courts and Offices from Oct. 18 to Nov. 23, 1868	$42,530 64
July 16	—Paid for Furniture in County Offices from Nov. 7 to Dec. 31, 1868	94,038 13
Aug. 4	—Paid for Furniture in County Offices July 19, 1868	58,306 73
Sept. 7	—Paid for Furniture in County Offices Aug. 30, 1868	60,334 71
Sept. 8	—Paid for Furniture in County Courts and Offices Sept. 28, 1868	42,901 47
Oct. 23	—Paid for Iron Railing, Cases, Stairs, &c., Check in name of M. W. Davis, indorsed by Ingersoll & Co., July 28, '68	58,201 16
Oct. 23	—Paid for Carpets, &c., in Co. Courts and Offices, Check in name of J. A. Smith, indorsed by Ingersoll & Co., Aug. 19, '68	27,154 56
Oct. 28	—Paid for Furniture in County Courts and Offices Dec. 28, 1868	26,032 11
Nov. 5	—Paid for Carpets, &c., in Co. Courts and Offices, Check in name of J. A. Smith, indorsed by Ingersoll & Co., April 6, '68	36,432 10
Nov. 12	—Paid for Carpets, &c., in Co. Courts and Offices, Check in name of J. A. Smith, indorsed by Ingersoll & Co., Jan. 26, '68	22,817 13
Nov. 16	—Paid for Carpets, &c., in Co. Courts and Offices, Check in name of J. A. Smith, indorsed by Ingersoll & Co., July 29, '68	23,155 20
Nov. 19	—Paid for Furniture, &c., in County Courts and Offices, Oct. 18, 1868	10,494 61
Nov. 24	—Paid for Furniture, &c., in Co. Courts and Offices, Check in name of C. D. Bollar & Co., in'd. by Ingersoll & Co., Aug. 17, '68	32,926 81
Dec. 3	—Paid for Furniture, &c., in Co. Courts and Offices, Check in name of C. D. Bollar & Co., in'd. by Ingersoll & Co., Nov. 9, '68	22,082 36
June 8	—Paid for Furniture, &c., in Co. Courts and Offices, Check in name of C. D. Bollar & Co., in'd. by Ingersoll & Co., May 8, '69	129,469 48
June 15	—Paid for Carpets, &c., in New Court-House, Check in name of J. A. Smith, indorsed by Ingersoll & Co., April 16, 1869	72,006 97
June 8	—Paid for Furniture, &c., in New Court-House to April 5, 1869	93,923 40
Dec. 16	—Paid for Furniture, &c., in County Court-rooms and Offices, April 26, 1866	54,243 57

June 30	—Paid for Carpets Furnished in Armories and Drill-rooms, March 16, 1870	37,438 87
July 26	—Paid for Carpets Furnished in County Court-house, April 17, 1870	72,819 81

GEORGE S. MILLER—*Checks Indorsed by Ingersoll & Co.*

Jan. 17	—Paid for Carpenter-work in Court-rooms and Offices, Aug. 19, 1868, to Sept. 11, 1868	$30,391 44
Jan. 17	—Paid for Repairs and Alterations in County Buildings, June 7, 1868	22,005 83
Jan. 24	—Paid for Repairs and Alterations in County Offices, Aug. 5, 1868	26,952 99
Jan. 28	—Paid for Repairs and Alterations in County Offices, Sept. 25, 1868	25,366 49
Mar. 21	—Paid for Repairs and Alterations in County Offices, May 13, 1869	20,235 00
April 8	—Paid for Repairs and Alterations in County Offices, Aug. 7, 1869	18,965 69
April 8	—Paid for Repairs and Alterations in County Offices, July 23, 1869	22,494 74
April 8	—Paid for Repairs and Alterations in County Offices, June 10, 1869	21,418 99
May 7	—Paid for Carpenter-work in Court-house, May 13, 1869	42,128 47
May 13	—Paid for Carpenter-work in Court-house, Sept. 29, 1869	38,903 32
May 21	—Paid for Carpenter-work in Court-house, Dec. 15, 1869	34,390 66
May 28	—Paid for Repairs in County Buildings and Offices, Aug. 31, 1869	39,361 21
June 3	—Paid for Repairs in County Buildings and Offices, Sept. 22, 1869	37,326 02
June 6	—Paid for Repairs in County Buildings and Offices, Dec. 18, 1869	32,381 73
June 9	—Paid for Repairs in County Buildings and Offices, Oct. 25, 1869	35,663 82
June 10	—Paid for Fitting up New Court-house, Jan. 12, 1870	44,474 30
June 17	—Paid for Repairs in County Buildings and Offices, Jan. 25, 1870	45,786 21
June 20	—Paid for Carpenter-work in Court-house, Feb. 9, 1870	40,965 41
June 27	—Paid for Repairs in County Buildings and Offices, March 29, 1870	44,874 59
June 30	—Paid for Repairs in Armories and Drill-rooms, Aug. 8, 1869	40,549 24
June 30	—Paid for Repairs in Armories and Drill-rooms, Sept. 8, 1869	35,748 79
July 8	—Paid for Repairs in Armories and Drill-rooms, Feb. 10, 1870	29,317 58
July 8	—Paid for Repairs in Armories and Drill-rooms, March 2, 1870	46,947 22
July 26	—Paid for Repairs in Armories and Drill-rooms, March 21, 1870	49,251 31
Aug. 9	—Paid for Repairs in County Buildings, April 19, 1870	40,507 49
Aug. 12	—Paid for Repairs in Armories and Drill-rooms, April 2, 1870	46,839 49
Aug. 12	—Paid for Repairs in Carpenter-work in Court-house, March 23, 1870	46,243 45
Mar. 14	—Paid for Repairs in Armories and Drill-rooms to Nov. 13, 1869	38,184 28
Mar. 31	—Paid for Repairs and Carpenter-work in Armories and Drill-rooms, July 6 to July 31, 1869	45,268 04
April 16	—Paid for Repairs and Alterations in Armories and Drill-rooms, Aug. 3 to Aug. 13, 1869	25,949 28
April 16	—Paid for Repairs and Alterations in Armories and Drill-rooms	8,147 86

A. G. MILLER—*Checks Indorsed by Ingersoll & Co.*

June 24	—Paid for Cabinet-work in Court-house, Jan. 9, 1870	$43,086 30
June 27	—Paid for Cabinet-work in County Buildings and Offices, March 29, 1870	55,163 22
June 30	—Paid for Cabinet-work in County Court-house, April 2, 1870	59,922 01
Aug. 1	—Paid for Cabinet-work in County Court-house, Oct. 8, 1869	62,537 68
Aug. 9	—Paid for Cabinet-work in Armories and Drill-rooms, April 16, 1870	77,949 86
Mar. 28	—Paid for Repairs in Armories and Drill-rooms, Aug. 28, 1869	43,742 45
Mar. 31	—Paid for Repairs in Armories and Drill-rooms, Oct. 20, 1869	38,818 84
April 16	—Paid for Fitting up Armories and Drill-rooms, Oct. 2, 1869	23,612 10
	Grand Total	**$5,663,646 83**

WASHINGTON.

Clearing up a Muddle in the Revenue Department—Lively Work in the Pension Bureau—Imports at Australia—Immigration at New-York—Kuklux Investigation—National Bank Circulation.

Special Dispatch to the New-York Times.

WASHINGTON, July 21.—It will be remembered that over a year ago Congress tried to give an expression of its will concerning the reduction of a part of the income tax, but failed to find language to convey its purpose successfully in regard to the payment of certain income taxes for the last five months

Kuklux organizations in that State. A telegram was read in the Committee from a citizen of Macon, that he telegraphed on the 11th of July he was ready to report, but received the next day a telegram from the Sergeant-at-Arms of the Senate, telling him he need not come, as the Committee had not time for more witnesses. The Sergeant-at-Arms being out of town could not explain, but at the instance of the Democratic members this Georgian and six or more others were summoned by telegraph to appear before the Committee.

NATIONAL BANK CIRCULATION.

The total circulation issued to the national banks to date is $318,686,396. The act of July 12, 1870, authorized the issue of $54,000,000 addi-

principally mares, with the new disease. There were only six cases now under treatment.

The stables of the Second-avenue line were next overhauled. Mr. SHAW reported that they were now quite free of the disease, not having had a case for two weeks. They had lost eleven horses out of 135 stricken down with the malady. The stables were in pretty good condition, but there were no signs of bedding, and apparently the poor beasts, after toiling over sixteen miles every day, had nothing but the hard and damp boards to lie on at night. The stock consisted of 750 horses. Daily feed, ten pounds—half oats and half corn. The hospital had some twenty patients in, under the homeopathy treatment.

The stables of the Third-avenue line were visited. In them were 1,806 horses. In an extra stable were a number of "green horses," which the hard work of the road had crippled. In the hospital were several bad cases, the poor creatures being covered with blisters, and scars arising therefrom. Two or three appeared in a dying state. There were no signs of bedding in

AFFAIRS IN EUROPE.

Mr. Gladstone's Sensational Flank Movement Against the Lords.

The Constitution Declared to be Violently Wrenched.

Parliament Brought into Contempt Before the People.

German Troops Ordered to be Withdrawn from Amiens and Rouen.

Formation of a Spanish Cabinet by Marshal Serrano.

Tumultuous Scene on the Adjournment of the Cortes.

GREAT BRITAIN.

The London Journals on the Recent Act of the Government—The Queen's Warrant Laid on the Table of the House of Commons—The New Castle Strikers.

LONDON, July 21.—The *Times* says the act of the Ministers abolishing the system of purchase of army commissions by royal warrant is a violent wrench of the Constitution, and a wanton setting aside of the will of the House of Lords. The *Times* regrets that this grave issue has been raised, but expresses the hope that the Lords will in their future action think of the effect upon the officers of the army rather than the indignity to their own privileges. The *Daily News* approves the conduct of the Government in making themselves the exponents of the popular will, and recommends that the Lords pass the bill abolishing the purchase of Army commissions. The *Telegraph* is exultant over the action of the Ministry, and says that Mr. GLADSTONE will be the more popular for vindicating the dignity of the House of Commons, in securing the harvest of its laborious session, and for reorganizing the defenses of the country and guarding the interests of the Army. The *Post* says the course of the Government has been somewhat unconstitutional, bringing, it believes, Parliament into contempt before the people. The *Standard* asserts that Mr. GLADSTONE has though the warrants had named a dozen different companies as payees. "Ingersoll & Company," it turned out, belonged to James H. Ingersoll, a longtime family friend of Tweed, one-time business partner with Tweed's brother Richard, and son of a one-time partner of Tweed's father. "What amount of money was actually paid to the persons in whose favor the warrants were *nominally* drawn, we have no means of knowing. On the face of the accounts, however, it is clear that the bulk of the money somehow or other got back to the Ring,"—How? It didn't say.—"or each warrant would have been endorsed over to its agent."

Saturday's blast was the first installment, the next two coming on Monday and Wednesday, July 24, and 26. Each followed the same pattern: the huge front page layout of ledger entries showing payments to contractors too impossibly large to be real.

Monday's list covered warrants for payments to Andrew Garvey for "plastering and repairs"—$2,870,464.06 total over two years, "copied verbatim from the Comptroller's books—the books entitled the 'Register of Warrants' and the 'Book of Vouchers'" as if citing volumes of scripture. In an editorial, Jennings dubbed Garvey the "Prince of Plasterers" and ridiculed his claims as reflecting "repairs" to the new courthouse just recently opened. He pinpointed items showing $126,578 received by two contractors for four days' work and concluded with another mystery: "How much money these persons actually received ... they might be forced to testify under oath, but are probably not willing to inform us."

Wednesday revealed payments to Keyser & Company, plumbers and gasfitters—totaling over $1.2 million in two years. "We have seen what a good thing it is to be appointed furniture-dealer, or carpenter, or plasterer, or plumber, under the City authorities," Jennings wrote.[2] He asked how carpenters could be paid hundreds of thousands of dollars on a courthouse "chiefly constructed of marble and iron—there is very little woodwork in it." He highlighted $170,727.60 paid to Ingersoll to supply chairs to armories which, at $5 each, would buy "314,145 chairs, and if placed in a straight row these chairs would have reached over 85,363 feet, or about 17 miles.... Even at $25 each they could stretch from the City Hall Park to Forty-second-street." And then came the $2,817,469.19 paid for cabinets and furniture, enough to furnish "nearly three hundred homes on Fifth avenue, from Washington-square to Thirtieth street, on both sides of the street."[3]

"[S]crutinize them, analyze them, test them thoroughly," the *Times* told its readers. And in fact, readers began snatching up its 4-penny newsstand copies. Politics aside, the Secret Accounts made good theatre. The ledgers, authentically raw and bare, tantalized the eye, like stealing a glance at a stranger's diary, peering into a neighbor's window, or happening to see a friend's bank balance—things hidden made glaringly public. Even the name "Secret Accounts" evoked mystery. The ledgers raised endless questions. "Observe—we are only quoting County accounts. The City accounts *reveal fraud of still greater magnitude*: but we speak now only of what we can prove," the *Times* explained; "We will not… analyze these figures today. They speak for themselves."

Jennings used his editorials to point a special accusing finger at the city blue-bloods who'd embarrassed the *Times* by giving Tweed's finances their blessing back in November: "Did John Jacob Astor, Moses Taylor and Marshall O. Roberts see the accounts now published on our front page when they signed their certificate?" he asked. "If they did see them, what right had they to certify that the Comptroller's accounts were all right?"

Each day that week, Jennings and his writers pounded their message, repeating highlights over and again. They listed a carpenter named George S. Miller, for instance, as receiving nine warrants in a single month for work on the courthouse totaling $360,751.61. "Is not this Miller the luckiest carpenter that ever lived?" They listed purchased carpets for the courthouse and county buildings totaling $565,731.34; at $5 per yard, that was "money enough for carpets in the new Courthouse alone to have covered the whole City Park three times over."[4] A strip a foot wide "would go nearly from New-York to New Haven, or half way to Albany, or four times from the Battery to Yonkers, or from Albany to Oswego."[5] They pointed to another $636,079.05 for work supposedly done on Sundays when the buildings were closed. On Friday that week, Jennings dramatized the fake names they found in the account books by sending one reporter to the Comptroller's Office asking "Who is A.G. Miller?" and another to downtown rug-dealers looking for a "J.A. Smith"[6]—names that Ingersoll himself later would admit to be fictional—and turning their wild-goose chases into comic front-page copy.

Who was the "Company" in Ingersoll and Company, he asked? The answer, by implication, was Tweed.*[7]

* Ingersoll later acknowledged that he'd separated himself from his earlier firm, Ingersoll, Watson, & Company, and gone into business for himself when his partners refused to pay kickbacks to city officials. There was no "Company"—Ingersoll had no factories; he simply purchased the goods he later sold to the city and kept the difference.

Harper's Weekly, August 19, 1871.

Capping the week, on Saturday, July 29, the *Times* issued a pamphlet called "*How New York Is Governed: Frauds of the Tammany Democrats*" that contained a full set of the Secret Accounts, all the ledgers they'd printed on the front page covering over $12 million in city payouts. New Yorkers grabbed them as fast as they came off the presses. Trucks and mail wagons lined up at the *Times* building from early morning until late that night carrying bundles to newsstands throughout the city. The pamphlet's initial print run of 220,000 copies—the largest ever yet for the *Times*—sold out within hours. For the entire next week, George Jones directed the *Times*' Hoe steam presses to work overtime cranking out more; ultimately they sold over 500,000 copies, including a German-language edition, this too a first in the newspaper's history.

The word was out; the charges had been made. Now, the question on everyone's lips was: What would Tweed say?

⊛ ⊛ ⊛ ⊛ ⊛

One night about this time, a messenger interrupted George Jones while he was working at his desk in his corner office at the *New-York Times*. A tenant in the building, a lawyer who rented office space, needed to see him urgently.

Jones got up from his desk and walked over to the lawyer's office, but on opening the door he found a surprise. Instead of his tenant, waiting there to meet him was Richard Connolly, the tall Irishman with the sharp eye, clean-shaven face, and stovepipe hat whom Jones' newspaper for months had been calling "Slippery Dick," chief swindler of the Tammany Ring. "I don't want to see this man," Jones said; he quickly turned to leave.[8]

Jones could guess what Connolly wanted—another trick to steal his newspaper, intimidate his employees, or insult him with bribes. Jones claims that he'd already been buttonholed earlier that month by a Tammany agent offering to buy his stake in the newspaper "at any valuation that might be put on it," he said. "This offer was made in cash, to be paid at once."[9]

"For God's sake! Let me say one word to you," Connolly's blurted out. "For God's sake, try and stop these attacks! You can have anything you want. If five millions [of dollars] are needed, you shall have it in five minutes."[10]

George Jones stood at the door; if he savored this moment, he didn't show it. The sheer size of the offer—equal to about $100 million in modern dollars—apparently caught him breathless. He remembered answering wryly: "I don't think the devil will ever make a higher bid for me than that."

"Why, with that sum you could go to Europe and live like a prince."

"Yes," Jones said, "but I should know that I was a rascal. I cannot consider your offer or any not to publish the facts in my possession."*

As a young boy in rural Vermont, George Jones' childhood friend Horace Greeley had once convinced him to skip church on a Sunday for a "loafing expedition" in the woods. When Jones came home later that day, his father, a strict Baptist, confronted him. "I have been over the hills with Greeley studying nature," Jones remembered telling his father, who wasn't amused. "Indeed!" his father said, "well, then, come into the wood-shed and we will have another lesson in the study of nature." Jones' father had died a few years later, but young George recalled the "lesson" he learned in the woodshed that day. As a 70-year-old man, he would still point to it as a key event in his life.[11]

Now, fifty years later, these roles seemed reversed. Horace Greeley, now the venerable publisher of the *New York Tribune* who knew the power of scan-

* This story, first told by Wingate in 1875 and expanded on by *Harper's Weekly* in 1890, is presumably Jones' account. Like many pieces of Tweed lore, it has no known corroboration—not surprising for an attempted bribe with only two people in the room and one, Connolly, never telling his story publicly. Neither account cited sources, though one of Connolly's lawyers, Samuel Courtney, did have an office in the building. Given the story's obvious anti-Connolly slant, a grain of salt is needed: The core facts might be true, but embroidery along the way is apparent.

dal to sell newspapers and once observed "[t]he public run instinctively to a dog fight,"[12] now counseled caution: "We have scrupulously refrained from the intemperate style of attack in which the *Times* has of late profusely indulged because words thus lose their force and because we did not have proofs to warrant charges which nevertheless we have often believed to be true," Greeley wrote in the *Tribune*.[13] "We do not indorse it neither do we discredit [the *Times*' charges]. We are not in possession of facts that would warrant us in making such charges... If it be justified by facts Messrs. Hall and Connolly ought now to be cutting stone in a state prison."[14]

Others of Jones's old friends in New York journalism likewise took a balanced view of the Tammany affair: "We may remark that a little more moderation in epithet would not detract from the *Times's* case," E.L. Godkin, himself a former *Times* editorial writer who'd known George Jones as the quiet financier of earlier days, wrote in *The Nation*. "The bladder with beans in it, as well as the lash, is audible after some of its strokes."[15]

Just two years after inheriting the paper from Henry Raymond, conservative, serious George Jones had not only survived as owner of the *New-York Times* but had produced the most ground-breaking, controversial story of his era. After seeing Connolly that day, he went back to work and never said a word of it in his newspaper until years later.

• 12 •
PANIC

"Compare A. Oakey Hall and William M. Tweed with General Grant and Tom Murphy [Grant's New York customs collector]! A. Oakey Hall is a gentleman who never takes a bribe. Not so with General Grant. They (the Grant officeholders) all take bribes—they are rotten with corruption....

"Grant will not appoint a man to office without a bribe. Not so with William M. Tweed and A. Oakey Hall. Grant appointed an illegitimate son of [Mormon polygamist leader] Brigham Young to West Point—appointed a young man who does not know who his father is.... It is bad taste for such men to accuse our Democratic city authorities of thievery, when they are all such thieves themselves."

—JAMES LYNCH, New York assistant district attorney, addressing a pro-Tweed rally shortly after the *Times*'s Secret Accounts story. *New York Sun*, August 8, 1871.

A FEW DAYS AFTER the *Times* finished running its Secret Accounts expose, the local Citizens Association for the Twelfth and Nineteenth Wards (today's upper East Side and Harlem, sparsely-settled areas in 1871) called a public meeting to denounce the Tammany frauds. Dozens of neighborhood people came to the group's new building on Third Avenue at 86th Street to hear speeches and pass resolutions. Respectable gentlemen in suits and top hats filled the front rows; workmen with muddy pants and torn shirts crowded the back. When the chairman called for order, though, he quickly discovered that most of the crowd, especially the workmen, took the wrong side—they'd come to blast the newspapers, not the politicians. They hissed and groaned and started making a ruckus.

As the first few speakers demanded reform and called on Mayor Hall to quit, cheers for the *New-York Times* became mixed with cheers for the Tammany Bosses. A pro-Tweed man mounted the podium and denounced the *Times*' charges as "buncombe." Another leader demanded order but the squad of club-toting policemen brought for protection stood aside as the room degenerated into pushing and shouting, hooting and hollering, the speeches lost in the free-for-all. "Curses and indecent language followed," one newsman wrote.[1]

The Secret Accounts had stirred the city's passions—and a copy of the *Times' "How New York is Governed"* sat on most every Manhattan kitchen table—but feelings differed as day and night over what they meant.

"[A]ccusations are not proof," fumed James Gordon Bennett's *New York Herald*, one of George Jones' neighbors on Park Row. "If the city's credit will be destroyed… [a] great scandal will work a great injury."[2] Manton Marble's *World* dismissed the whole expose as "a reckless attempt to shake and undermine the city credit, block the wheels of municipal machinery, and introduce a reign of anarchy."[3] For every supporter like U.S. Senator Roscoe Conkling who called the *Times'* stories "the most brilliant dashing foray seen in the American press in my memory,"[4] another saw them as demagoguery, character assassination, and politics.

Only in one place in New York did the message meet a unified response: on Wall Street. The city's elite class of merchants and speculators who ran the Stock Exchange, the Gold Exchange, the Produce Exchange, and the hundreds of banks, brokerages, and retail houses, the capitalists who enjoyed the city's finest luxuries, dinners at Delmonico's, cigars at the Union League or Manhattan Club, musicals at Booth's theater or the Grand Opera House, all recognized their immediate stake in the affair. As property owners and taxpayers, they'd been cheated. And worse, if the *New-York Times* stories proved true and if Tammany mismanagement were to cause the city's fiscal house of cards to collapse, they stood to lose millions.

All through the Tweed years, New York banks and brokers had bought oceans of city debt, bonds and stock issued by Connolly's Comptroller Office. Now, the city had bonds coming out its ears: Croton Aqueduct Bonds, Central Park Improvements Bonds, four classes of County Court House stock, Bonds for Repayment of Taxes, Assessment Fund Stock, Park Improvement Bonds, Street Improvement Bonds, to name a few. Total city and county debt had exploded from $36.3 million in January 1869 to over $97 million by the summer of 1871; at that rate it would reach the billions in another few years.[5] Interest payments alone approached $10 million per year.

If credit dried up and the city defaulted on its debt, the impact on New York's wealthy would be devastating. Beyond wiping out their bulging bond portfolios, it would cripple their standing in Europe—still a principal source of capital for American finance. British and German investors had been burned before by American investments, particularly railroad stocks whipsawed by Wall Street manipulators. Many had purchased New York bonds as a safe haven and, if this too became a lawless frontier, their money might flee the country altogether.

In fact, as the *New-York Times* had printed its disclosures that summer, bankers had begun cutting off credit to the city. In late July, the city put $40,000 in bonds up at auction one day and failed to receive a single bid. A few days later, fears spread that a major Savings Bank might buckle because it held millions in city debt that depositors now distrusted.[6] The respected *Commercial and Financial Chronicle* warned of a panic and, in Europe, the Berlin Stock Exchange banned New York city and county bonds from its official trading list. Worse still, the city had looming in its future an interest payment of $2.7 million due on its securities on November 1, just three months away. If its agents, Seligman, Belmont, and the rest, could no longer raise money in world markets, meeting it would be impossible.[7]

"They distrust our securities in London," one unnamed broker told the *Tribune* just days after the Secret Accounts appeared.[8] New York stock exchange president Henry Clews warned of catastrophe: "[I]f our local government cannot be reformed, the credit of the metropolis will be gone and ... the standing of every large [banking and brokerage] house will be more or less affected."[9]

Not surprisingly, an "insurrection of the capitalists" quickly organized itself in the financial neighborhoods. Some 1,000 merchants rushed to sign a petition refusing to pay any more property taxes until city officials gave a full account of their spending and another group filed a lawsuit to block the Broadway widening job.[10] "[W]e want to know where the money goes," an unnamed banker explained.[11]

Suddenly, the free ride of Tweed economics had taken a frightening turn. By mid-August, calls went out for city leaders to convene publicly at the Academy of Music on September 4—after wealthy men had returned from their summer holidays—to consider their options.[12] Politics was one thing, but trifling with the flow of international money could not be tolerated.

◎ ◎ ◎ ◎ ◎

The Honorable A. Oakey Hall tried to act as if things were normal after Orange Day 1871, going about his usual duties: As mayor, he laid the cornerstone at Turner's Hall on July 17 and kept all his City Hall appointments; he even tried his hand at humor: "Shocking levity," he wrote in the *Leader*, "the lightship at Savannah has gone astray. Counts at Newport are at a discount."[13] But behind the scenes, he quivered at the unfolding disaster. With Tweed mostly off enjoying the sea breezes at Greenwich and Sweeny unreachable at his summer retreat by Lake Mahopac in upstate New York, Hall found himself alone in New York as the Ring's public voice against the avalanche of charges from the *New-York Times*.

As a first step, Oakey Hall met privately with Connolly, the comptroller, and they brought in some of the large city contractors fingered by the *Times* in its Secret Accounts expose, but the session sank into finger-pointing. Within hours, John Keyser, one of the major contractors, told reporters he planned to publish his own expose of his city dealings and "indicate where the fraud really was."[14] Others, including plasterer Andrew Garvey, iron merchant Barger, and stationer Edmund Jones, feared that some malcontent might sue to block their getting paid on legitimate work they'd done for the city. Garvey remembered bumping into the mayor scurrying across the rotunda of the Courthouse that week and telling him his concern. "Is there any danger of [their] tying up our property," he asked.

"Who is going to do it?" Hall responded,* dismissing the threat as nonsense. Instead, he suggested that Garvey and the others themselves file lawsuits against the city to demand their pay.[15]

Garvey especially bristled at the public humiliation he'd taken over the disclosures. "Prince of Plasterers?" "Look at that wall, gentlemen," he told a group of friends while leading them through the new Courthouse's rotunda one day, pointing to the ceiling like a proud Michelangelo. "Garvey the plasterer. My God! Do they call that plastering? See that inimitable wall, those *bas reliefs*, those figures, those frescoes, those gorgeous paintings—Justice with the sword and blind as a bat—and this fine imitation of bronze, showing the law books laid out. … Not in the Vatican in Rome, the Tuileries in Paris, anywhere in Europe can anything be found like it," he insisted. "I earned my money for this work, and I'll keep it."[16]

Even without the contractors' help, Oakey Hall and Richard Connolly decided to defend themselves by producing their own account of city spend-

* This remark from Hall, testified to by Garvey in 1872 and later embroidered by Tilden into "Who is going to sue?" would become a staple of Tweed lore, a supposed sign of the Ring's disdain for the coming storm.

ing, a step required by law in any event, to demonstrate that the *Times*' "secrets" were only routine public information. But the process would take at least ten days to complete.

This wasn't enough for Oakey Hall, though. The mayor decided it would be a mistake to sit silently in the face of accusations. He considered himself among the city's top *literati*, an accomplished author, playwright, and poet; they didn't call him "Elegant Oakey" for nothing. Facing the worst crisis of his career, he decided to take pen in hand and turn the tide. The same Saturday morning as readers awoke to the *New-York Times*' opening salvo in its Secret Accounts expose, they also saw in the *Leader*—Tammany's own tabloid newspaper—a long, rambling column written by the mayor. At its heart, it made a simple point: He, the mayor, as a gentleman, had been badly mistreated, all because *New-York Times* publisher George Jones was trying to squeeze him for money.

Casting himself in the third person, Hall recounted his long personal tie to the newspaper. "[H]e [the mayor] had been a twenty-year friend of the living proprietor of the *Times* [George Jones], equally long an intimate associate with the deceased partner [Henry Raymond], and one of the latter's pall bearers, [he'd] once been regarded as a valued correspondent of the paper,… had penned, at the request of its editors, through a long series of years, literary criticisms and editorial paragraphs [and] had received pleasant and often undeserved praise in its columns for oratory and published volumes."[17]

Now, he lamented, all this had changed—all because George Jones, the publisher, was sore over a $13,761 advertising bill that the city had refused to pay the year before. Up until then, the *Times* had accepted over $94,000 in city and county advertising during the 1860s and rarely complained about Tammany abuse, but "During the summer of 1870 the city authorities withdrew advertising from the *Times*. Immediately its tone toward them changed." After that, "he, the once-be-praised Mayor, began, … to grow daily into a monster."[18] The problem was greed: not Oakey Hall's or Boss Tweed's, but George Jones'.

Not satisfied with his handiwork, the mayor felt compelled to weigh in again a few days later. This time he wrote a "To the Public" letter flatly denying any wrongdoing on his part. He'd never received any money from the exorbitant contractor bills listed in the *Times* Secret Accounts: "I know that none of my friends will believe this… but feel amused at a falsehood too absurd to grow indignant over, especially when the malice of Mr. Jones … has been so succinct."[19] If Jones knew otherwise, "why does he not publish an affidavit of the fact?" Hall, in fact, was not a wealthy man by Tweed standards; his law partner Augustus Brown estimated the mayor's total assets as barely $70,000, mostly tied up in his residence on 42nd Street—not the millions of Tweed, Connolly, or Sweeny. His salary as mayor was just $7,000 and, if he did receive graft, it was invisible even to his closest friends.[20]

As for his approving of the exorbitant pay-outs, the mayor argued he was innocent here as well: His signatures on the warrants were mere "ministerial" acts. The issue remained personal: "the malice of Mr. Jones" hiding behind "his mask of public spirit."[21]

To each of his broadsides, he saw the *Times* throw the same answer back in his face: "*Are the figures we are publishing accurate or not?*"[22]

By the end of the week, as the *Times* was flooding the city with copies of its "*How New York is Governed*" pamphlets, Oakey Hall went about town with a pained look. His friends asked him questions: Was any of it true? Had he been duped? Could he explain the embarrassing payouts? His answer, his own account of city spending, would take at least two more weeks to prepare. Meanwhile, his literary blasts had embarrassed him: "The defense set up by the mayor has startled the public even more than the broad accusations of *The Times*," Horace Greeley grumbled in the *Tribune*. "It indicated an unconsciousness of official responsibility that borders on the sublime."[23]

That Saturday, the mayor escorted his wife, Kate, and their two eldest daughters to the city piers on South Street to see them off by steamer across the Atlantic for a summer holiday in Europe. For the ride home to 42nd Street, he invited a *New-York Times* reporter to share his carriage. Along the way, clip-clopping through lower Manhattan's crowded alleys, he talked incessantly, trying to defend himself to his worst accuser. The charges were "unjust and false," he insisted; he, Tweed, and Connolly all were being victimized and his report of city finances would prove it. When asked if he planned to go to Europe himself, Hall turned indignant: "I shall remain at my post, and let my enemies see that I am invulnerable to their malicious attacks."[24]

But as the reporter pressed him on the political fallout of the back-to-back debacles, the Orange riots and the *Times* disclosures—his terrible month of July—Oakey Hall finally lost his patience. "My dear Sir," he said, apparently raising his voice, "you may rest assured that neither one nor the other will exercise the slightest influence! .... We [the Democratic Party] have the state [legislature and governor's mansion] now, and we are determined to keep

N.Y. TREASURY
"STOP THIEF!"
"They no sooner heard the cry, than, guessing how the matter stood, they issued forth with great promptitude; and, shouting 'Stop Thief!' too, joined in the pursuit like Good Citizens."

Nast's depiction of panic among The Ring following the New York Times *disclosures.*
Harper's Weekly, *October 7, 1871.*

it. By the time the election for Governor takes place [in November] the charges of corruption against us, even if there was anything in them, will all be forgotten."[25]

Back at the *New-York Times* office on Park Row, Louis Jennings would take these words and twist them, but only slightly: the mayor's prediction that the charges "will all be forgotten" became "It will all blow over"—a phrase that Nast already had been using in his cartoons and that Nast and Jennings now planted squarely in Hall's mouth. They soon made it common knowledge: "Being interviewed, [Hall] took the line that 'even if there was anything in it, it would blow over before the next election,'" *The Nation*, for instance, reported the next week.[26] Oakey Hall could talk all he wanted, but his message could only be what the *Times* and Nast said it was.

❁ ❁ ❁ ❁ ❁

By mid-August, *Harper's Weekly* could brag that its own star trouble-maker, Thomas Nast, had become "The most cordially hated man in New York at the present day—hated by men whose friendship would be a dishonor."[27] Nast's anti-Tweed cartoons had become a sensation—bigger even that his Civil War drawings—and Nast himself was developing a personal fame unknown in journalism then except for Horace Greeley and a handful of other publishers. *New-York Times* articles carried no by-lines; even the most devoted reader of the Secret Accounts would never see the names Jennings or Foord identified as authors. But Nast, his neatly scribbled "*Th. Nast*" at the bottom corner of each cartoon passed around by people in local shops, factories, or saloons, posted in store windows or on bulletin boards, or argued over at corner clubs, became as widely-known as Tweed, Sweeny, or anyone else in New York.

Nast relished his celebrity, the hate mail as much as the compliments. One letter to him that summer contained a picture of him with a thread tied around its neck like a noose. Police Captain Ira Garland posted guards around Nast's house on 124th Street; when city officials removed Garland from his post, Nast moved with Sarah and the children temporarily across the river to Morristown, New Jersey.[28] His pictures had made not just the names but the *faces* of Tweed, Sweeny, Hall and Connolly as well-known to New Yorkers as their own neighbors', more familiar even than those of President Grant or the best-known actors or actresses. "Every stroke of his pencil cut like a scimitar. His caricatures... are admirable in their grotesque fidelity," *Harpers Weekly* wrote of its own prodigy, "so marked that if you catch only the glimpse of an eye-glass, the tip of a nose, or a straggly bit of hair, you know it stands for Hall, or Tweed, or Sweeny, or Connolly."[29]

The pictures gave New Yorkers a rare chance to laugh at their stodgy city fathers knocked off their pedestals. When the *Times* blasted John Jacob Astor and his blue-blood friends for having failed to notice frauds during their examination of city books months earlier, Nast drew these well-heeled respectables—Astor, Marshall O. Roberts and Moses Taylor—as "Three Blind Mice" scurrying across a kitchen floor, their tails of "prestige" cut by a carving knife labeled "Sharp Editorials."[30] When Horace Greeley refused to attack Tweed or Oakey Hall as sharply as the *Times* had, Nast ridiculed the world-famous *Tribune* publisher by showing him in rumpled coat and puzzled face standing crying over the sick horse, "Mare" Hall as Tweed and Sweeny look on and Connolly fans himself with one marked "City Fan cost $10,000." The caption read "Not a Bailable Case"—a poke at Greeley's own recent bail bond for former Confederate president Jefferson Davis.[31]

Readers began to expect a barrage of weekly Nast anti-Tammany slams just as they expected a daily blast from the *New-York Times*. In late August,

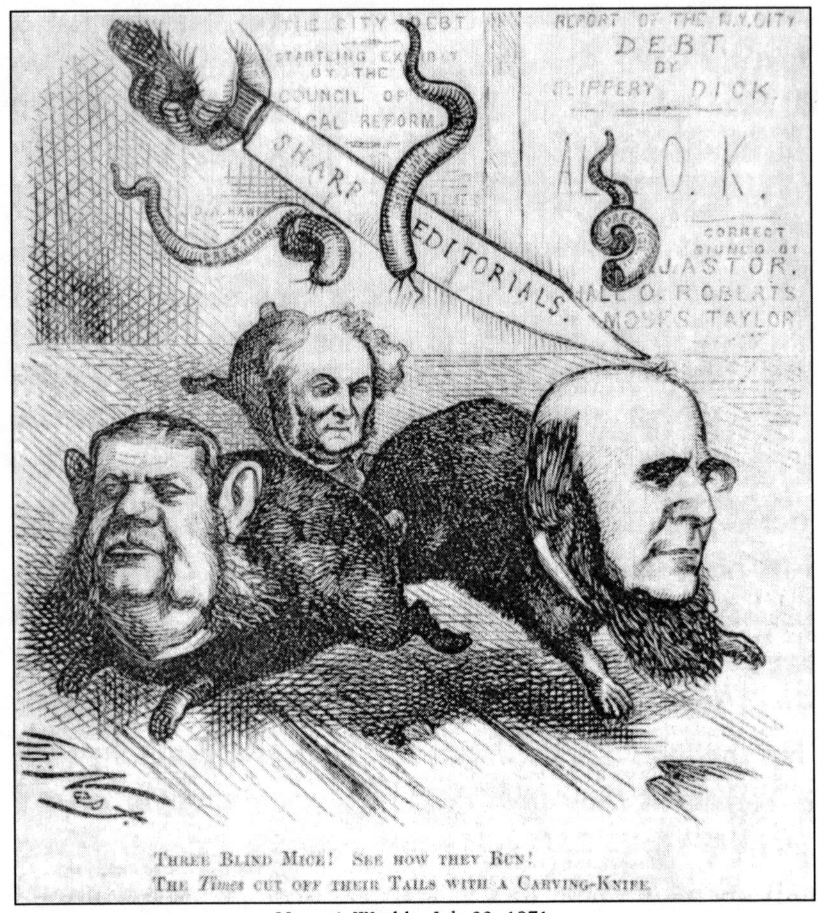

THREE BLIND MICE! SEE HOW THEY RUN!
THE *Times* CUT OFF THEIR TAILS WITH A CARVING-KNIFE.

Harper's Weekly, *July 22, 1871.*

Nast climaxed his assault with a full-page spread titled "The Rich Growing Richer, The Poor Growing Poorer." Its bottom half showed a poor family in a squalid, dark basement paying exorbitant rent while, on top, Tweed, Sweeny and Hall lived like kings, sipping wine on the lawns of country estates, Connolly on a "bed of roses." A page later, readers saw drawings of the actual country homes of Tweed in Greenwich, Connecticut; Keyser, Ingersoll and Woodward in rural Norwalk; and the Americus Club lodge on placid Indian Harbor.

When his victims squirmed, they made themselves only more ridiculous. Oakey Hall labeled Nast the "Nast-y artist of Harper's Hell Weekly—A Journal of Devilization,"[32] and he banned sales of *Harper's Weekly* at city-licensed newsstands. Fletcher Harper spoiled to make a fight over the issue: "I used to walk down to the office [on] mornings with my grandfather," Harper's grandson John Harper recalled, "and I distinctly remember how anxiously he would inquire of the newsdealers on the day of publication if the *Weekly* had been suppressed as yet; and he always seemed to be greatly disappointed when he learned that the Ring had failed to carry out its threat."[33]

Tammany may have tried to buy Nast's silence around this time, but they never got far. Nast claims they approached him twice, first through a lawyer friend and then through an officer of the Broadway National Bank who visited Nast at his home on a Sunday. In his own version of the story, Nast described this second encounter as a comic drama much like a scene from one of his cartoons:*

> *"I hear you have been made an offer to go abroad for art study," the bank official says in Nast's account.*
>
> *"Yes, but I can't go. I haven't time."*
>
> *"But they will pay you for the time. I have reason to believe you could get a hundred thousand dollars for the trip." Nast playing along: "Do you think I could get two hundred thousand?"*
>
> *"Well possibly. I believe from what I have heard in the bank that you might get it." Then ominously: "You have a great talent; but you need study and you need rest. Besides, this ring business will get you into trouble. They own all the judges and jurors and can get you locked up for libel. My advice is to take the money and get away."*
>
> *"Don't you think I could get five hundred to make that trip?" Nast asks.*
>
> *The bank official hesitates: "You can. You can get five hundred thousand dollars in gold to drop this Ring business and get out of the country."*
>
> *Nast, in his account, then laughs: "Well, I don't think I'll do it. I made up my mind not long ago to put some of those fellows behind the bars, and I'm going to put them there."*
>
> *"Only be careful, Mr. Nast, that you do not first put yourself in a coffin."*[34]

Almost lost in the cacophony were complaints from Catholics and Irish leaders over Nast's constant ugly stereotyping of immigrants and the Church.

---

* Professor Hershkowitz rightly points out that, given the lack of corroboration, Nast's talent for self-promotion, and his liberty in making up Tweed quotes, this story deserves extra skepticism. "A million? Nast could have been bought for the proverbial mess of pottage. He was not the most respected individual," he wrote.[35]

Harper's Weekly, *September 30, 1871.*

The journal *Irish People* protested his putting a rum bottle in every Irishman's pocket and *Catholic World* objected to his dressing Tammany figures as priests and bishops. When the *New-York Times* reprinted a *Harper's Weekly* anti-Catholic column, an offended reader highlighted the bigotry of connecting Tammany corruption with religion: Tweed, Sweeny, and Connolly "as individuals [are] corrupt and criminal, … not as Democrats, even, much less as Roman Catholics, that they are on trial."[36] But if any of these groups expected an apology, they were barking up the wrong tree. *Harper's Weekly* instead blasted what it called the "astounding insolence" both of *Catholic World* and the Pope himself, citing a recent Vatican pronouncement that secular governments exercised rights "only by the permission of the superior authority, and that authority can only be expressed through the Church"—suggesting Church supremacy over law.[37]

Nast gave his own sharp response: a full-page illustration called "The American River Ganges" showing a group of young school-children huddled in fear on the banks of a river as dozens of crocodile-like creatures crawl from the water, mouths agape, teeth bared, ready to strike. But on closer look, the reptiles actually are Catholic priests and bishops, their hats and vestments transformed into scales and jaws. In the distance, Tammany Hall is seen as St.

Peter's Cathedral from the Vatican, a "political Roman Catholic School" at its side, a public school in ruins, and Tweed himself leaning over the riverbank smiling at the spectacle.[38]

All the while, Nast's anti-Tweed cartoons were making Fletcher Harper and his septuagenarian brothers a bundle of money: *Harper's Weekly* circulation had tripled by August 1871 to 300,000; every newsstand window drew crowds of giggling readers when the new weeks' issue arrived for sale.

❂ ❂ ❂ ❂ ❂

Where was Tweed all this time as crisis after crisis gripped his city—the Orange riot, the *Times* Secret Accounts, the freeze in city credit, the citizen denunciations, the Nast cartoons? When in town, he avoided reporters and public meetings. Mostly, he enjoyed the summer social season in Greenwich. If he cringed at the attacks privately, he didn't show it publicly. By every outward appearance, he seemed unattached, unconcerned, and unembarrassed.

Harper's Weekly boasted that summer that Tweed had snapped at seeing some of the Nast cartoons, saying he "doesn't care a straw for what is written about him, the great majority of his constituency being unable to read, [but] these [Nast] illustrations, the meaning of which everyone can take in at a glance, play mischief with his feelings."*[39] Tweed was also quoted as telling a friend "if the people got used to seeing [me] in [prison] stripes, they would soon put [me] in them."[40] But he kept any such reaction well hidden. His public silence infuriated many; diarist George Templeton Strong took it as an admission of guilt "*pro confesso*."[41] Asked in mid-August whether he'd stolen money from the city, Tweed answered "This is not a question one gentleman ought to put to another."[43]

Instead, as OakeyHall wrestled with the crisis back home, Tweed led the festivities for the July gala christening of the new Americus Club lodge house on Greenwich's Indian Harbor—a festival of back-slapping, cigars, and fancy nautical costumes. Tweed had sunk more than $118,000 of his own personal money into the club between June 1870 and July 1871 to help finance its new building—its 225 cuspidors, barber chair, upholstered tapestries and divans, smoking rooms, dining halls, and moorings for yachts and sailing sloops.[44] As club president, he'd arranged for it to rent the small island he

* This quote too took a life of its own. It morphed into "Let's stop them d__d pictures... I don't care so much what the papers write about me—my constituents can't read; but d__d it, they can see pictures." Or "But they have eyes and they can see as well as other folks."[42]

owned nearby in Long Island Sound called Tweed Island, accessible from the lodge by a naphtha-powered launch. He brought Tammany political friends out for weekends to enjoy sailing, sipping champagne, and slurping oysters on cool summer nights.

Back in New York, his name appeared publicly only in connection with his latest business deals. In addition to the new Viaduct Railroad, newspapers carried accounts of Tweed's joining a well-heeled group of humanitarians putting up $35 million to rescue thousands of Paris Commune prisoners still being held for deportation by the French government. His new Lower California Company, whose directors included national figures like Illinois U.S. Senator John Logan and local celebrities like August Belmont and former New York governor John Griswold, offered to colonize the French prisoners on the American west coast, giving each man fifty acres if France paid for food and transport.[45]

Late in August, New York society flocked to join Tweed's two oldest sons Richard and William Jr. for the gala opening of the Metropolitan Hotel, which Tweed had spent over $450,000 on renovating that summer, in addition to the $90,000 he paid in annual rent for the building.[46] Over a thousand invited guests came to gawk at the hotel's elegant improvements: its 400 rooms each held new gold and walnut furniture, Turkish-styled walnut bedsteads, Royal Wilton and Axminster carpets covering buffed hardwood floors in the bridal suite, ballrooms, and corner suites, walls covered with blue and satin lace curtains. Afterward, the two brothers stood side-by-side, both in dark suits and diamond pins, as the hotel opened its grand ballroom for a luscious feast from the kitchen of *chef de cuisine* M. Ludin: *saumon froid a la ravigote*, *pate froid de Gibier aux truffes*, *petits poulet rogis*, *jambon de Virginie*, capped by Irish harp, champagne, ice cream *napolitaine*, and coffee *a la Francaise*.

But as Tweed and his sons enjoyed their high-profile parties, Oakey Hall and Richard Connolly, their honors the mayor and comptroller, grappled with the unfolding disaster: When the mayor appealed to New York's business leaders early in August for help in addressing the credit crisis sparked by the *Times*' exposes—asking that a "large and influential committee of well-known and upright citizens" be chosen to take a neutral look at the city books[47]—Wall Street abruptly slapped him down. Its top citizens wanted no part of it, having seen their friends John Jacob Astor, Moses Taylor, and Marshall O. Roberts played as dupes, vilified by the *New-York Times* and ridiculed by

Thomas Nast. Instead, they demanded the city make a full, clear statement of its finances before they'd lift a finger.[48]

When Hall and Connolly did finally produce their financial report on August 23, it started only more squabbling. Again, the mayor asked business leaders to join him in reviewing the numbers and, this time, they agreed, but demanded a larger role and named eight leading financiers to join the project who insisted on getting a full chance to study the details.[49]

Meanwhile, Oakey Hall kept irritating the wound with his constant nibbling attacks at his accusers. He still couldn't get George Jones' personal affront off his mind. "The gross attacks of a partisan journal upon the credit of the city should be answered," he wrote in a circular for the City Council.[50] He asked city employees not to eat their lunches at the popular cafeteria in the basement of the *New-York Times* building on Park Row, just across the street from City Hall. At the same time, he pressured conductors on city trains to prevent sales of the *Times* on local newsstands, forcing George Jones to appeal directly to New York Central Railroad owner William H. Vanderbilt who pressured to prevent any "discrimination against any respectable journal on our trains."[51]

Hall raised the biggest stink of all by announcing plans to evict the *Times* from its own office building. The Old Brick Church property—the lot on Park Row that the *Times* had purchased back in 1857 for erecting its current structure—actually had once belonged to the city, the mayor argued, and its sale to the newspaper had been illegal. Speaking through the *Sunday Mercury*, he announced plans to ask the state Supreme Court to seize the newspaper, put it under control of a receiver, eject it from the building, and demand it pay six years' back rent. "The litigation promises to cover a very long period, and a number of Republicans have volunteered to raise a fund to aid the owners of the *Times*," the *Sunday Mercury* reported."[52] A few days later, city aldermen met and voted to initiate formal proceedings to recover the property.

All this agitation by the mayor brought the expected result: Louis Jennings at the *Times* launched his own wave of new late-August attacks. Using the same front-page banner format of the original Secret Accounts, he presented a list of eye-catching items from Oakey Hall's own latest financial report: more money for vacant armories, $27,200 for safes at the new Courthouse, $82,184 in advertising payments to twenty-three newspapers, and the more serious ticking time bomb: $3.3 million in interest paid on the city's growing pile of bonds. A separate column pin-pointed cost overruns on the new County Courthouse: budgets of $6.4 million between 1852 through 1871 for the building had been dwarfed by actual payouts in 1869 and 1870 of $6.9 million, plus line items of $7,500 for thermometers and $175,000 for carpets. "Property owners may well be alarmed at the new exhibit we now place before them," he charged.[53]

On August 21, Oakey Hall sued the paper for libel.

All through August, Hall and Connolly appealed to Tweed and Sweeny to please come home and help put out the fire, but weeks went by without the four getting together. Sweeny, from his summer house upstate, made a special point to stay away, prompting whispers of a falling-out within the Ring.

Sweeny returned to New York City for one weekend that summer and used the chance secretly to begin digging graves for his friends, quietly contacting allies to deny any connection with the frauds, blame Connolly and Tweed for the debacle, and even going so far as to plant stories in friendly newspapers that Connolly should resign so he, Sweeny, the post-scandal survivor, could take his place.*[54]

Why didn't Tweed speak up or take control? Was he too busy relaxing to appreciate the danger? Or had he grown so accustomed to power that he considered himself untouchable? Did he see this as just another political attack that inevitably would do just as Jennings and Nast said: blow over?

Legally, Tweed had little reason to panic: So far, the *Times* had failed to make a case against him. Its Secret Account stories had shown the city's being gouged by inflated bills and himself, the mayor, and Connolly being perhaps negligent or sloppy in approving them, but no evidence to date actually connected any of the misspent money to Tweed personally. Where did it go, they asked? Without a clear answer, reformers or prosecutors couldn't lay a finger on any of them.

Nast himself laid out the legal ambiguity in perhaps his most famous *Harper's Weekly* cartoons from that summer. "Two Great Questions," he'd titled it. First: "Who is Ingersoll's Co?" In answer, it showed a giant Tweed

---

* One newspaper that played along was the *Evening Post*: "It is no secret that the most influential of the Democratic leaders desire that Mr. Peter B. Sweeny be the new Controller," it reported. "They say that Sweeny personally commands more of the public confidence … than any other man whom Mayor Hall would be asked to appoint; that he is not implicated in any of the frauds of 'the Ring;' that his administration of the office would be independent, energetic, and thorough, his reports full and unreserved," so on, so on.

WHO STOLE THE PEOPLE'S MONEY? — DO TELL. N.Y. TIMES.
'TWAS HIM.
TAMMANY RING

Harper's Weekly, *August 19, 1871.*

(with giant diamond) and all his Tammany hangers-on crouched hiding behind him like pygmies. Second: "Who stole the people's money?" For this, Nast drew all the members of the Ring—Tweed, Sweeny, Connolly, Hall, the contractors and the Irishmen—all standing in a circle, each pointing to the person on his right, saying "Twas him."[55]

The clever caricatures couldn't help but produce a chuckle. "You have never done anything more trenchantly witty than the 'Co.' of Ingersoll… and the "Twas him!'" Nast's editor George W. Curtis wrote him that week. "My wife and I laughed continuously over them. They were prodigiously good."[56]

Tweed certainly didn't laughed, but he recognized the point: Millions had been stolen—but by whom? Until a specific person could be proven guilty, all remained innocent. Still, he and Connolly took precautions. On August 16, Tweed executed deeds transferring at least seven parcels of real estate to his son Richard—including the "circle property" (today's Columbus Circle), his farm at Fort Washington, and his home on Fifth Avenue and 43rd Street—to shield them from creditors, though he didn't actually file the deeds; he simply held on to them. About the same time, Mary Connolly, Connolly's wife, transferred ownership of $500,000 in United States treasury bonds from her own name to that of her son-in-law Joel Fithian.[57]

All the while, the drumbeat grew. On August 28, the German Democratic Union met and passed a series of anti-Tweed resolutions;[58] on September 2, the City Council of Political Reform met to raise money for waging court fights against the Ring.[59] Even among its friends, Tammany's prospects had soured. "They are since July public enemies," *New York World* managing editor David Croly privately told his publisher Manton Marble. "The *World* blundered terribly in supporting them." He quoted a source who'd spoken with the mayor as saying "no honest defense of the city of the present state of city finances is possible [and] any defense of the Ring can only bring shame and confusion on its defenders when the facts come out."[60]

In a few days, New York's wealthy elitists would return from their summer holidays for their mass meeting. A feeling of imminence hung in the air. The moment was ripe for *coup d'etat* ; it waited only for a qualified plotter to come along.

• 13 •
TILDEN

"I think a spasm of virtue will run through the body politic. Business is dull."

—HORATIO SEYMOUR, writing to Tilden
from upstate New York, August 12, 1871.

"Sam Tilden wants to overthrow Tammany Hall. He wants to drive me out of politics. He wants to stop the pickings, starve out the boys, and run the government of the city as if 'twas a blanked little country store up in New Lebanon... He wants to get a crowd of canting reformers in the Legislature, who will talk about the centrifugal force of the Government...; and then, when he gets everything all fixed to suit him, he wants to go to the United States Senate."

—TWEED, responding privately in 1869 to the question:
"What does Tilden want?"[1]

SAMUEL TILDEN SPENT JULY at home in New York that year minding his business while enjoying his Gramercy Park townhouse, horse-riding in Central Park, and dinners at the Manhattan Club. He tended his railroad clients from his law office on Wall Street, a third story suite with three large rooms and plenty of sunshine. Its library held over 4,000 books and its walls held portraits of political heroes like General George B. McClellan and former Governor Horatio Seymour. Tilden delighted passing time there. He mostly avoided politics these days; he presided as state party chairman but stayed away from the Tweed-dominated state legislature. He had better things to do.

Like everyone around him, Tilden took time between concerts, dinner parties, and office work in July to follow the dramatic Secret Account disclosures in the *New-York Times*. He read the banner headlines, talked them over with friends and heard the reactions around town. He claimed to doubt the *Times*' charges at first; the articles made a strong case for theft—a "moral conviction of gross frauds," as he put it—but the numbers seemed far-fetched. He'd always assumed Tweed corrupt, but never expected the scale to be so large.[2]

Early that August, Tilden left Manhattan for a short vacation and brought a stack of the *Times* articles along to study. Traveling north by train, he reached New Lebanon, the tiny upstate hamlet at the base of the Berkshire Mountains where he'd spent his boyhood and where his two brothers still lived; here, Tilden took the time to read the articles more closely. What he saw alarmed him, the political fallout especially. As he saw it, the Tammany scandal threatened to sink not just Tweed's circle but the entire state Party, and Tilden with it. "I think you had better note the tone of the 30 or 40 extracts which the *Times* daily publishes from journals of all parts of the United States [showing that] the evils and abuses in the local government of the city of New York are general characteristics of the Democratic party," he wrote his friend and *Albany Argus* publisher William Cassidy that week.[3] One particular *Times* column must have made him gasp: "Where are the Honest Democrats?" it asked, naming Tilden specifically as shamefully silent.[4] He began hearing nervous calls from friends across the state. "Is it not a good time to dismember the New York ring?" Judge Samuel Church wrote him from Albion, a small town in western New York near Lake Ontario.[5]

After a few days in New Lebanon, Tilden left his family and visited Albany where he met former Congressman Francis Kernan returning from the seashore. Together, he and Kernan traveled up the Mohawk River to Utica and visited former Governor Horatio Seymour at his farm. On his way back, Tilden stopped at Saratoga to enjoy the horse racing and social hobnobbing; here he ran into George Jones of the *New-York Times*—himself taking a few days off for a summer break. Tilden described Jones as looking exhausted from his Tammany fight. "I told him I should appear in the field at the proper time," Tilden said. Jimmy O'Brien too apparently came to Saratoga that week and bent Tilden's ear.[6]

By the time Tilden returned to New York City on August 10, all these talks had brought him to a decision: Tweed had to be toppled. He became strident in his private conversations. "We have to face the question, whether we will fall with the wrongdoers or whether we will separate from them and take our chances of possible defeat now, with resurrection hereafter," he wrote Rochester newspaper publisher William Purcell, telling him his *Rochester Union and Advertiser* must "begin at once prudently to disavow and denounce the wrongdoers, and educate our people."[7] Tilden buttonholed *New York World* managing editor David Croly and told him his newspaper must abandon its defense of Tweed.[8] He got encouragement for this tough talk: A "financial gentleman" representing angry Wall Street investors came to see him one night and explained the financial impact of the crisis, and Horatio Seymour wrote him letters from upstate Utica laying out the scandal's wider political dimension. "When the public mind is turned to the question of frauds, etc. etc., … there will be a call for the books at Washington [President Grant's scandals] as well as in the city of New York," Seymour explained. "We can lose nothing by stirring up questions of frauds."[9]

All this talk was private, though. Publicly, Tilden remained invisible. He made no speeches, gave no interviews, and refused to reveal his plans even to close friends like Manton Marble and August Belmont. Secrecy, he decided, was essential for any plan to work. He began to weigh options: Statewide elections were scheduled for November that presented a chance to break Tweed's hold on the Albany legislature and, with it, perhaps to overturn his city charter. Tilden also visited lawyer Charles O'Conor to discuss whether the state government in Albany might have grounds to sue Tweed for stolen funds.

But Tilden knew these steps were only window dressing. His lawyer's eye had caught the fatal flaw in the *New-York Times*' case against Tweed. The Secret Accounts demonstrated that *someone* had robbed the city, but they failed to show *who*. Without a direct link connecting the crime to a specific person, he'd never be able to bring legal action against anyone.[10] Tweed could hide behind Connolly, Connolly behind Garvey or Ingersoll, the contractors behind Oakey Hall—just as in Thomas Nast's cartoon, each man pointing to the next and saying "'Twas him." They'd all walk free.

To transform the Secret Accounts into a rock-solid legal case against a specific villain meant solving a puzzle, the kind that set Tilden's mind aglow.

Ever since childhood, young Sammy Tilden had loved games and puzzles, especially involving numbers. He'd shown his brilliance many times: As a young lawyer in 1855, Tilden had once represented a political friend named Azariah Flagg who claimed he'd been cheated out of his election as New York City's comptroller by a Know-Nothing candidate with a razor-thin margin of 179 votes. The case looked hopeless. It all boiled down to a certified return from a single election district that gave Flagg a 316 to 186 majority: Lawyers for the Know-Nothings produced a stable of witnesses—two voting inspectors, an election clerk, and others who'd claimed to see the actual count—all of whom swore that these numbers had been reversed by a clerical error and that Flagg's opponent had actually won the majority, tipping the race his way.

Tilden knew they were lying, but he couldn't accuse all these men of perjury without proof and the tally sheets showing the number of "regular" votes cast had conveniently disappeared. These "regular" votes—ballots cast for a full slate of candidates for each of the contested positions—could have helped him reconstruct the lost tally sheets; without them, he had nothing.

Rather than giving up, though, Tilden spent two nights thinking about the issue. Pieces of the puzzle dangled before him: Could he not reconstruct the missing tally sheets based on what he *did* know: the total number of "regular" ballots, the number of "split" ballots (those where a voter deleted one or more names from the slate), and the number of votes cast for each candidate in each of the eleven *un*contested races? Counting backward from the *other* races, perhaps he could fill in the gaps. For instance, if Samuel Allen, the candidate for street commissioner, had received 215 "regular" votes on the same slate as Flagg in a given ward, than Flagg must have received the same 215 votes.

Tilden asked a Columbia College mathematics professor named Henry J. Anderson to help him devise a formula using the evidence at hand. By the time the trial reconvened, Tilden had finished the job. Standing to address the jury, he startled the packed courtroom: "I propose now, gentlemen, to submit this case to a process as certain as a geometrical demonstration. *I propose to evoke from the grave that lost tally.*"[11] How? "If, by a violent blow, I should break out the corner of this table, split a piece off, the fractured and abraded fibers of the wood would be left in forms so peculiar that, though all human ingenuity might be employed to fashion a piece that would fit in its place… it could not be done. So it is with truth. It is consistent with itself."[12] Tilden then handed out a vote tally sheet he'd reconstructed using his mathematical process and explained the logic step by step—adding Flagg's share of each of the other candidates' "regular" tallies, then calculating his remaining "split" votes. He'd won the case before calling a single witness; the jury deliberated less than fifteen minutes before declaring Flagg the winner.

Now, in 1871, Sam Tilden again saw a puzzle dancing before him, a mass of numbers begging for a pattern: the *New-York Times*' Secret Accounts. This puzzle too must have an answer, a key to trace stolen city funds through the maze of vouchers, warrants and bank accounts directly to the personal pockets of Tweed and friends—proof that would put them all behind bars. To find it, he'd need more information: data from the inner sanctum of city finance, the Comptroller's Office in the new courthouse on Chambers Street. Richard Connolly, the comptroller, would be the key.

Tilden shared his thoughts with no one. If his secretiveness irritated his friends, so be it. "Tilden is very positive in his views, but rather shrinks from what he has got to do," one insider grumbled. "He has no sympathy for the Ring but sees its power. He is bitterly hostile to the whole gang."[13] Sam Tilden wasn't looking to make friends or headlines in the late summer of 1871. He was looking to take down Tweed, to lunge without warning, aiming straight at the heart.

⁂

In early September came the long awaited mass meeting of city "respectables" to protest the Tammany Ring and George Jones, the night's most-honored guest, had to marvel at his good fortune. After almost a full year leading his *New-York Times* in its lonely fight against Tammany Hall, being harassed, ostracized, and threatened, he found himself tonight the center of attention.

The turnout for the anti-Tammany meeting far surpassed anything its organizers had hoped for. Thousands came, forcing them to change the venue from the Academy of Music to the much larger Cooper Union at Third Avenue and Astor Place. Half an hour before its scheduled start, swarms of men in suit jackets, some wearing top hats, women with bonnets and parasols, and merchants in swallowtail coats—a well dressed, respectable crowd—crammed into the Cooper Union's Great Hall, the same room where Abraham Lincoln had delivered his famous speech in 1860. They filled its every corner, clogged the hallways and haggled over tickets, clamoring to get inside. Carriages jammed nearby streets and overflow crowds flooded the sidewalk; a separate platform with speakers had to be improvised on the street to accommodate them. More than a hundred police officers came to keep order.

Inside the hall, beneath its high ceilings, glass chandeliers, and calcium lights, hundreds of chairs crowded the stage for special guests. These included dozens of speakers and over two hundred honorary "vice presidents," and a special place for George Jones of the *New-York Times*. *Times* reporters circulated through the room, preparing to cover the paper's front page with the story.

By the time the meeting started, Jones sat on stage surrounded by a tightly-packed throng of people, cheering, shouting, waving handkerchiefs, many stopping to shake his hand, pat his back, and congratulate him. They'd finally joined his crusade. His sense of vindication must have been profound. His worst enemies these days were fellow Park Row publishers jealous of his success: "The *Times* rolls itself up like a porcupine and shoots out its venomous little quills alike at friend and foe," Horace Greeley grumbled in the *Tribune*;[14] James Gordon Bennett Jr.'s *Herald* called the *Times* a "political guerilla" with "English cockney proclivities."[15]

Tonight, Jones could laugh at the insults. People were buying his newspaper. *New-York Times* circulation had jumped by 40 percent to almost 50,000 copies per day in the two years since Jones had taken over, mostly due to excitement over the Tweed Ring exposures.[16] His city was listening to him.

Respectable old-time New Yorkers dominated the platform: 79-year-old James Brown, founder of Brown Brothers' New York bank (today's Brown Brothers Harriman & Co.),* opened the rally and handed the chairman's gavel to 67-year-old William F. Havemeyer, retired sugar merchant, banker, and New York mayor during the 1840s. Behind them sat a startling coalition of city elite: Congressman Robert Roosevelt (the future president's uncle), German publisher Oswald Ottenderfer, piano maker Theodore Steinway, and a parade of Wall Street chiefains: stock exchange president Henry Clews, bankers Henry Stebbins, Abraham Kuhn, and Joseph Seligman, broker W.R. Vermilye, among many others. All three leading members of the earlier "whitewash" committee—John Jacob Astor, Marshall O. Roberts, and Moses Taylor, now fully chastised by the *Times* and Thomas Nast—sat onstage along with Peter Cooper, all come to make their amends.

Jimmy O'Brien, now happily acknowledging his role as the *Times*' secret source for its dramatic expose, also came to take a bow.

For the next several hours, speakers took the podium to demand reform while blasting the villains Tweed, Connolly, and Oakey Hall. Corruption must be stopped and frauds punished. "A deadly disease is consuming [the city's] vitals," Havemeyer roared from the platform. New York was "a great whale stranded upon a coast and devoured piecemeal by sharks," repeated

* Old James Brown held the special distinction of having led the group of New York bankers who'd faced down Jay Gould and Jim Fisk on their abortive corner of the New York gold market; Brown personally had stood on the Gold Exchange floor and sold $5 million in gold to Fisk's broker Albert Speyers at the market's peak of $162, minutes before Washington intervened by announcing gold sales from the local sub-treasury, prompting the corner's collapse on Black Friday, September 24, 1869.

Judge James Emott. They recounted the Tammany scandals, the huge debt, the outrageous vouchers, the brazen thefts, citing all the details from the *New-York Times'* front pages. The rhetoric brought the crowd repeatedly to its feet. The new courthouse "has cost you seven millions of dollars—not for building it, but for furnishing, repairing and decorating it," Emott said to roars of laughter.[17] Fists rose in the air as Tweed, Connolly, and Oakey Hall were described as living in "vast estates, of magnificent mansions, of stables that might rival those of the most luxurious of the Roman Emperors, of steam yachts, of picture-galleries and jewels of almost fabulous value"—all paid for with money "stolen" from the city.

Mere allegations? No, they shouted. The Tammany villains stood convicted by their silence. "What are the answers that these men have made [to these] charges?" Emott asked. "They plead guilty," a voice said. They'd issued "contemptuous denials… flippant evasions [and] studied concealment," yelled another. They'd "laughed a hollow laugh, and smiled a false smile, and shrugged their coward shoulders…. as these things were told," lawyer Edwards Pierrepont roared.

Havemeyer, the former mayor, ended his own speech by taunting the crowd with Tweed's own mythical quote: "I now ask you in conclusion—WHAT ARE YOU GOING TO DO ABOUT IT?" The angry voices in Cooper Union Hall that night gave a chilling response: "Send them all to Sing Sing!" yelled some; "Hang them!" shouted others—both drawing "immense applause" according to reporters. Without reform, Tammany would face "the yells of an infuriated mob, the fire and rapine and slaughter, the noise of musketry and cannon," Edwards Pierrepont declared. Havemeyer's response to his own question was hardly more gentle: "To eradicate these evils will require the use of the cautery and the knife."

Nobody in the room blanched at the talk of physical violence. It had already come from the most respectable source: E.L. Godkin's *The Nation* that still pointed to "the ignorant Irish voting element" as root cause of the scandal.[18] Godkin had demanded a "vigilance committee" for Tweed, literally a lynch mob, noting that "the Anglo-Saxon race has never consented long to stand still and be robbed."[19] Pressed to explain himself, Godkin wrote: "in our opinion, Hall, Connolly, Tweed, Barnard and all the class to which they belong… fear no penalty… except a violent death."[20]

Tonight in Cooper Union Hall, though, the well-mannered horde of angry respectables hadn't yet reached the point of finding a rope and a sturdy tree limb. After listening to the speeches, they calmly passed resolutions calling for repeal of the Tweed charter, the resignations of Tweed, Connolly and Hall, and the creation of a blue-ribbon panel to try to recover stolen funds: the Committee of Seventy. George Jones appeared satisfied; all that night he heard his *New-York Times* repeatedly cheered, quoted, and cited as leader of the cause. He understood the anger: New Yorkers felt that they had been played for suckers. And didn't like it.[21]

Not everyone in the city was impressed by the Cooper Union affair. Even some reformers found its pomposity and one-sidedness offensive. "Saints Lashing Sinners," the *New York Sun* called it in its next morning's headline, dismissing it as so much chest thumping.[22] Of all the names connected to it, the most conspicuously absent was that of Samuel J. Tilden. The morning after the meeting, the *New York World* used Tilden as its example in blasting it as partisan and stacked: other Democrats should have "followed the example of Mr. Tilden," it said, "and kept away from this Custom-house meeting."[23]

Two days later, the reformers drew first blood. They marched into the state Supreme Court chambers on Duane Street on Wednesday morning, September 6, and filed a lawsuit to stop the city government in its tracks. They demanded a legal injunction barring the city or county from raising, borrowing, or spending any money unless approved by a new, reformed board of apportionment. The order would also forbid the city from paying a penny more to the New-York Printing Company, the New York Transcript Association, and the Manufacturer Stationers Company, all companies connected to Tweed. As its defendants, the suit named the now-famous "Tweed Ring" foursome: Tweed, Connolly, Sweeny, and the mayor.

Just as eye-catching was the judge they asked to issue the order: George G. Barnard, Tweed's most loyal pawn on the bench.

Barnard, 42 years old, owed his career to Tweed as much as anyone in New York City: Born in Poughkeepsie, educated in Union College, Barnard had left home for California in 1848 to make his fortune among the original gold miners but returned broke to Manhattan in 1856 to stake his claim in politics. Here, he joined Tammany and befriended "Paps" Tweed. When the job of recorder (judge of the General Sessions court) came open in 1857,

Barnard wanted it and asked the Wigwam for its nomination. By one account, he first had to face a rival named Doyle backed by local Tammany strongman Isaiah Rynders. Tweed chaired the meeting the night Tammany chose its slate that year and enjoyed telling the story of how he used his gavel to hand Barnard his victory: "I saw, as the roll proceeded, that Doyle had the majority of delegates. So I said to the secretary: 'Have a motion made to dispense with calling the roll!' It was done. 'All in favor of Mr. Barnard as the nominee of this body say aye. Carried! The meeting is adjourned!' Well, there was a riot and I was driven into one corner. Isaiah Rynders had a pistol as long as my arm drawn and cocked. Said he: 'I'll pay you for this.' I was scared but I didn't say so. 'I'm not afraid of a whole ward of you fighting villains,' said I, and we got out of it."*[24]

With Tweed's support, Barnard won his race for recorder in 1857, then won a seat as state Supreme Court justice in 1861. He always found ways to repay the Boss, be it by naturalizing thousands of Irish immigrants before Election Day in 1868 or by issuing injunctions for Tweed's friends Jim Fisk and Jay Gould. During the bitterly-fought 1868 Erie Railway War between Gould and Commodore Cornelius Vanderbilt, Barnard had loyally matched his judicial decrees to Tweed's shifting alliances, issuing injunctions first for one side and then the other. "I was the best friend he ever had" Tweed said of Barnard. "I risked my life to get [his judgeship] for him."[25]

More recently, though, the two had drifted. Barnard seemed increasingly impressed by his own power. He'd won his last citywide election to the bench by 60,000 votes. "[Y]ou had to waste much time with him, coax him, and make him believe that he was a great man—pat him on the back," Tweed grumbled.[26] Barnard himself complained how "from 1868, and including the granting of the injunction against him, I did not in those years speak six words with Mr. Tweed."[27]

Instead, Barnard fell under the spell of Jim Fisk, Prince of the Erie Railway Company, and Fisk's mistress, Josie Mansfield. He became a regular at

---

* This oft-quoted Tweed legend, a story Tweed himself told from jail twenty years after the fact, doesn't quite match the facts. A contemporary account of Barnard's 1857 nomination contest at Tammany shows no Doyle in the race and Barnard winning a clean plurality on the first ballot. Tweed probably confused the incident with one involving John Hoffman's nomination for recorder in 1860. In that contest, Hoffman had trailed after the first ballot; then, during the second, a scuffle broke out. According to one account, "a handful of tickets were snatched away by some party, it being understood that Mr. Hoffman was then in the majority." A few minutes later, Tweed gaveled Hoffman the winner by acclamation. Still, even if wrong on details, Tweed's story probably had seeds of truth from Barnard's early career.

Josie's dinner table and was accused of signing judicial orders in her parlor, though he insisted "I never called at her house except I went there in a party of gentlemen composed to two or more."[28] Hanging around with Fisk and Josie, Barnard suddenly had money to burn. Asked how he happened to be carrying $600 in cash (about $12,000 modern dollars) to pay Fisk once for an off-the-cuff favor, he said: "Why, I presume I got it out of my safe, or else I carried it in my pocket; I'm no pauper." He happily accepted a three thousand dollar loan once from Gould, new dining room chairs from Fisk, and plenty of smaller favors.[29]

Dark-haired, with a crisp mustache and brusque manner, Barnard now found himself appealed to by the reformers. Friends found it incredible. There were whispers: "Do you think Judge Barnard would grant an injunction against those who made him?"[30] The reformers evidently had reason to think so.

Their first day did not bode well. The reform lawyers arrived at Barnard's courtroom promptly at 10 am but a clerk announced that Barnard was home in bed, too sick to come to court. A reporter raced over to Barnard's house on West 24th Street and found him "suffering from the convenient and aristocratic disease, the gout, and his foot … so swollen that he could not stand."[31] Barnard had good reason for cold feet that day; he faced a political crossfire of epic proportions. By granting the injunction, he'd forever burn his bridges with Tweed and Tammany. But if Tweed's machine were going to sink regardless, why should he, George Barnard, sink with it? By aiding the reformers and giving them their injunction, he could make himself an instant hero. Who knew what opportunities might come his way?

By the next morning, Barnard had made his choice. He arrived promptly in his chambers and called on the reformers to make their case. Barnard had a reputation for making caustic remarks from the bench: When a lawyer in a divorce case once announced that he'd brought the wife to appear in court before him, Barnard had joked "What of it; do you think that I can tell whether a woman will commit adultery [just] by looking at her?"[32] This morning, though, as lawyers for the reformers walked him through their argument, he kept his mouth shut. He asked no questions about glaring legal gaps in the case: whether the plaintiff had technical standing to sue, for instance. At the end, he raised just one concern: "[I]f the court should grant your injunction, it would have the intention and effect of stopping the operations of the city government—of stopping the payment of the laborers who work upon the streets, on the public parks, and roads, and prevent them from receiving any money whatever."[33]

If workingmen were going to suffer in the crossfire, Barnard wanted his own hands clean. "We have endeavored not to put it so," said Judge Barrett, one of the lawyers, though the injunction's plain language said the opposite. Still, the answer was enough to satisfy the judge.

"You are entitled to your order," Barnard announced. Cheers erupted in the room, but these were quickly silenced. The injunction was temporary, Barnard explained; he'd schedule arguments to continue in his courtroom the next week before making it permanent.

Within minutes, the city exploded in gasps. George Barnard, the ultimate lapdog, had bitten the hand that fed him. Speculation abounded about whether there'd been a fix: "Knowing Barnard as we do, this summary action ... can be explained only on the theory that he had been promised the Democratic nomination for Governor," Denis Tilden Lynch concluded. "There was only one man capable of making good such a promise. This was Tilden."[34]

There is no evidence actually connecting Tilden to the episode. Tweed, following events from across town, saw a different implication. His friends were abandoning him: first Jimmy O'Brien and now Barnard. It was the beginning of the end. "We owe to Barnard all our troubles," he'd say much later looking back on these days.[35]

* * * * *

Tweed, tanned and fat in his dark suit and diamond pin after his summer spent indulging in the comforts of Greenwich, hardly looked the relaxed gentleman that morning. On the contrary, a reporter described him as "fatigued and worn."[36] He closed the door to his inner sanctum, his private office on Duane Street three blocks from City Hall. Inside, he looked around the polished mahogany table beneath gas chandeliers, fresh-cut flowers, and mahogany liquor cabinets to see three dour faces staring back at him: Sweeny, Connolly, and Oakey Hall. How many hundreds of hours had Tweed spent closeted in meetings with these three men over the years? By now, he'd known each for almost twenty years. He knew their wives and families, their bank accounts, their personal quirks and habits—the mayor's silly puns and tinny laugh, Sweeny's brooding silences, Connolly's Irish malarkey. Their unique partnership had come far since the City Hall "lunch club." Now they shared a dark moment. After weeks of ridicule, vilification, and attacks, they faced ruin. As newspapermen clamored in the hallway and lawyers harassed them with writs and demands, Tweed doubtless skipped the glad-handing, brandy and cigars and got down to business.

He still called this foursome by its formal legal name, the City Board of Apportionment, but everyone else in town had another: "the Tweed Ring," notorious swindlers of Tammany Hall.

Tweed had pulled his circle together several times that week.[37] Now, the morning after Barnard's injunction, they met again. Tweed had had no trouble recognizing treachery in Barnard's decree: "That fellow was seized with the idea he would become Governor of New York," he'd say later.[38] Within his own inner circle, it was Connolly who felt the strain most directly. As comptroller, Connolly ran the city's finances and Barnard's order had made his job a nightmare. By its terms, Barnard had effectively rendered the city bankrupt. For years, Connolly had financed New York's operations with debt, bonds and securities. He kept virtually no cash in the treasury. Since Barnard had now forbidden him from raising or borrowing a penny more, he couldn't issue a single check or warrant. He had no cash to back them up. As a result, construction on city projects stopped, contractors went begging for payment, and thousands of employees, laborers who worked in the streets, the parks, and the stone quarries, all feared losing their pay.

Angry gangs of workmen already roamed the streets. Tweed himself had faced over fifty callers that morning at his Public Works Department office clamoring for appointments.

A newspaperman catching Connolly that morning at his office described the big Irishman as "fatigued and careworn." Asked about the injunction, Connolly had ducked the question. "I have no opinion to give," he'd said. "In fact I know nothing about it. I don't believe it will amount to anything."[39] With legal charges leveled against them in Barnard's courtroom, Tweed and Connolly both had hired lawyers that week,[40] and Connolly was barraged with requests for records from the new citizens' investigating committee.

The pressure made Tweed a prisoner in his own town. He couldn't hide; reporters hounded his every step. He picked up newspapers each morning and saw himself portrayed as a criminal and scoundrel. He couldn't walk down the street or enter a restaurant without strangers recognizing him from the Thomas Nast cartoons. They laughed behind his back and sometimes to his face. Friends kept their distance, embarrassed to be seen with him in public.

Since returning from his summer retreat, Tweed's private meetings with

Sweeny, Connolly, and Hall had degenerated into fruitless melodrama with Sweeny and Hall openly warring against Connolly. They'd all read the *New-York Times* charges and heard the clamoring for their scalps. Someone had to be sacrificed to satisfy the reformers, Sweeny argued, and the mayor agreed. They pointed their fingers directly across the table: Connolly, as comptroller, was the one most directly connected to the now-discredited city vouchers. Why not him?

Connolly didn't balk at first. By one account, he'd actually agreed weeks earlier to give up his seat. "When the damaging evidences of the frauds were first [printed in the *Times*], Connolly thought he would have to resign and did actually send in his resignation," an anonymous insider told the *New York Tribune* that week, but the mayor had refused to accept it.[41] After that, though, his attitude hardened. Why should he be the scapegoat? When Sweeny pressed him again to quit, he refused flatly. "Gentlemen, to resign would be to confess myself guilty of a crime. I am guilty of no crime," sources quoted him as saying.[42]

Tweed must have resented Sweeny's holier-than-thou sanctimony. Sweeny, having hid for months in his upstate retreat at Lake Mahopac, had barely returned to New York before jumping at the chance to leave again the week before to attend the State Democratic committee meeting in Albany and rub elbows with the state chairman, Sam Tilden of all people. Sweeny left footprints all over town of his backroom flirting with reformers: At the Cooper Union reform meeting, as speakers from the podium blasted Tweed, Hall, and Connolly, they barely mentioned Sweeny's name at all. Calls from the crowd of "how about Sweeny" or "tell us about Sweeny" went ignored. When Judge Barrett, a reform lawyer, was asked about the rumored Sweeny-Tweed rift, he happily stoked the fire by vouching for Sweeny's honesty: "Mr. Sweeny was not greedy for wealth," he said, but only for political advancement.[43] Newspapers openly speculated that Sweeny, after forcing out Connolly and Tweed, planned to keep power for himself and take credit for "purifying" Tammany Hall. Tweed couldn't have missed seeing the articles.

Oakey Hall too now used his long-time friendship with *New York Herald* publisher James Gordon Bennett Jr. to plant self-serving stories at Tweed's expense: "If William M. Tweed and Richard B. Connolly have made enormous fortunes within two or three years the same cannot be said of Mayor Hall," the *Herald* argued in an editorial that week. "It is generally understood, we believe, that Mayor Hall is not a rich man, though he derives a handsome salary from his legitimate business as a lawyer."[44] But at least the mayor still kept a sense of humor. Asked if he planned to argue the city's case in the injunction hearings before Judge Barnard, he pointed to the old adage "the man who is his own lawyer has a fool for a client" and added: "It would never do to have a fool at one end of the case and a Foley at the other."*[45]

Now, sitting around the table in Tweed's private office, they went at it again. Already that morning, news of Barnard's injunction had sparked waves of gossip that Connolly or Tweed was preparing to quit. A *Times* reporter had cornered Connolly and asked him directly if he could say anything about it. "Yes you can," Connolly had snapped. "You can say it's a ___ lie."[46] The histrionics got worse each time they met. They'd argue, then Sweeny and Hall would huddle in a corner or leave the room as Connolly sat stonily alone at the table. He was no more guilty than the rest, Connolly would insist, and would "sink or swim with his colleagues, but ... his colleagues should sink or swim with him."[47] Sweeny tried flattery, browbeating, and threats. He and the mayor made promises: If he resigned, they'd protect him and block any investigations. They'd pick a friendly replacement as comptroller whom they could all trust.

Tweed held his tongue during these arguments, refusing to speak up either for or against his embattled comptroller. The spectacle must have disgusted him, the blatant disloyalty. Tweed recognized that if Sweeny and Hall dumped Connolly, they'd likely try to dump him next. The foursome haggled for hours that day and resolved nothing, just like the day before and the day before that. Tweed certainly thanked his lucky stars when the meeting finally ended and he could go outside and get some fresh air.

That wasn't the case today, however. Instead, Tweed opened the door, saw Sweeny, Connolly, and Hall all leave to go their separate ways, and stepped out into the anteroom of his Duane Street office. Then almost immediately a newspaperman grabbed him and asked for a private interview. Tweed recognized the reporter as one of the usual crowd from the *New York Sun*, usually a friendly voice. He invited him into his private lair, sat him down, and put on a friendly face. "How are you? Glad to see you," he said.

"Well, what do you think of the matter, Mr. Tweed?" the reporter asked, starting right in, talking about Barnard's injunction.[48]

---

* As plaintiff in the case, the reformers had named John Foley, an ex-supervisor and fountain pen magnate. Foley had one of the few Irish names among the Committee of Seventy and, to press his case, he hired three high-priced Irish-named lawyers: Strahan, Barlow, and Barrett.

"Oh, I don't think it can stand," Tweed said. "It was just served on me." The reporter found Tweed in good cheer that day, happy to talk and hear his own voice. He tried to scribble down Tweed's words exactly. "I wanted to go out of town at 12 o'clock and just at that time the man came with the writ. Well, I told him, 'That's what I've been waiting for. The sooner the better.'"

"What are you going to do about it?" the reporter asked—deliberately using the language of Tweed's own mythical boast. Tweed probably squirmed at hearing the fake quote thrown in his face.

"Oh, I shall have special counsel I think… I think I shall have my own counsel. I don't know though—yes, I think I will."

"You don't seem to be very downcast."

He laughed. "Pooh! I am not afraid. What do I care? They'll find me there. I'll have pretty good counsel—pretty good counsel."

"I saw George Jones yesterday; he feels rather exulting about it."

"Yes, I suppose he does. They think it's a pretty good thing probably." A shadow crossed Tweed's face at this point—the mention of Jones, the taunting question. The reporter described the look as "contempt." The question seemed to strike a nerve, a vein of bitterness. After his weeks of careful public silence, Tweed's tongue took a life of its own. "I would have fought out this thing differently if I had been alone. (With emphasis:) Yes, Sir, I wouldn't have been so quiet, I can tell you."

"Did you read the *Nation*," the reporter asked. "You know they are going to have you lynched?"

"He's an infamous liar," Tweed snapped, Godkin's arrogant lynch threat the last straw. "The man who wrote that knows he's told a lie, and that he wouldn't dare to tell me so to my face. (After a pause:) I was born in New York, and I mean to stay here too."

"You don't seem to be afraid of a violent death. Are you?" the reporter asked.

"(Stamping his foot)—Well, if they want to come I'll be there. That's all I have to say about it. I'll be there, I'll be there, Sir. (With a smile.) The TIMES has been saying all the time I have no brains. Well, I'll show Jones that I have brains. You know if a man is with others, he must do as they do. If I had been alone, he would have had a good time of it. … I tell you, Sir. If this man Jones would have said the things he has said about me twenty-five years ago, he wouldn't be alive now. But, you see, when a man has a wife and children he can't do such a thing. (Clinching his fists.) I would have killed him...."

"I suppose you must be tired of public life, Mr. Tweed."

"Oh, yes, I am sick of it. I wish I could retire to private life and have nothing more to do with politics. I'm sick of them. Jones wouldn't have dared to say anything if I had no wife and children."

Tweed would claim later that the *Sun* reporter had misconstrued him, even if these were his exact words. He'd blame the story's "typographic display" for distorting his meaning. It's not that he'd have liked to murder George Jones but for his family duties, he explained.[49] He had "Nothing to be ashamed of."[50] Still later, he'd grumble at his own stupidity for the remark, saying: "If I go to murder a man, I want at least to escape the charge of malice prepense."[51]

These excuses hardly helped. Within a day or so, every major New York newspaper had printed the verbatim transcript of Tweed's outburst—how big bad Boss Tweed had snarled and stamped his foot and boasted of wanting to kill George Jones. In a city of brass knuckles that respected strength, he looked like a weak little boy, a frustrated bully breaking under strain.[52]

⊛ ⊛ ⊛ ⊛ ⊛

Barely had the shocks finished roiling Manhattan—first Judge Barnard's injunction freezing city finances followed by Tweed's ugly temper tantrum—when a new bombshell hit in the headlines, again shining the spotlight on "Slippery Dick" Connolly, the comptroller. Burglars had broken into Connolly's office in the new County Courthouse and stolen hundreds of vouchers from locked file cabinets, vouchers that covered the very same expense items listed by the *New-York Times* in its Secret Accounts stories.

Only a few days earlier, the citizens' investigating committee had asked Connolly to produce these very same vouchers for their examination. The theft had every sign of a cover-up, someone trying to torpedo the investigation by destroying evidence.

Connolly, already exhausted after days of harassment from his Ring "friends," heard the news on reaching his office Monday morning, September 10. Connolly's office occupied a large, high-ceiling suite on the second floor of the new Courthouse. William Murphy, a private watchman on duty Saturday night, had left his post for a three-hour break and returned to find shards of broken glass on the floor and part of the door's glass window covered by cardboard. He thought nothing of it at first, seeing nothing out of place. Stephen Lynes, the county auditor, heard the news on arriving at work Monday morning and made a quick inspection. He discovered that two locked wooden closets had been forced open, the locks ripped off. Seven pigeonholes had been emptied from one cabinet, three from another. Checking his records, he found that the empty boxes had contained vouchers—original claim forms used by contractors to support city payments—for 1869 and 1870, three thousand of them, tied in bundles labeled "armories and drill rooms," "adjusted claims," and "county liabilities." Lynes remembered seeing them in their normal places the prior Friday afternoon, he told police; someone must have stolen them over the weekend.[53]

Experts examining the door concluded that the burglars, working from the outside, had cut the glass with a diamond—and who owned a more famous diamond in New York City than Tweed? They'd made a hole just wide enough for a hand to reach inside and unlock it. Still, carrying so much paper out of the building unseen would have been difficult; the missing vouchers would have filled two bushel baskets, or three to four cubic feet. And both Murphy and Edwin Haggerty, the building's janitor who lived in an upstairs apartment with his wife, claimed they hadn't heard anyone enter the locked courthouse over the weekend.

Within hours, word of the robbery flashed all over town and newspaper reporters descended by the dozens on Connolly's office. Connolly invited several into his private room and sent for Murphy, the watchman, to tell his story. He described the robbery as "singularly unfortunate to himself" since it might have destroyed evidence that could clear him of charges.[54] Whoever had committed the crime had known exactly what to look for, which cabinets and pigeonholes to pilfer. Nothing beyond the specific cabinets had been touched; no money or other papers were missing and nothing was out of place.

Connolly's laments aside, though, the news had a startling impact. It raised the darkest suspicions: Connolly or "the Ring" must have been behind it, a desperate effort to protect themselves. It fed the worst image of Tweed's circle as desperate men willing to stop at nothing, especially after Tweed's ugly outburst against George Jones and the mayor's harassment of the *New-York Times* and *Harper's Weekly* that summer.

The news created a flurry even on the New York Stock Exchange. Shares of the Erie Railway and the Hannibal and St. Joseph, railroads in which Tweed was said to hold positions, both tumbled in value as did city bonds. Rumors swirled around the trading floor that Connolly might dump bonds on the market to punish his Wall Street enemies.[55] Anything was possible with these Tammany criminals.

But people also quickly noticed several things about the robbery that didn't make sense: For one, Connolly's office routinely kept copies of all the stolen information. They could replace it instantly. Every city expense was recorded in a ledger book, and none of the ledgers had been touched. The only items missing—the contractors' original claim forms—could be easily reconstructed from other records. If someone were trying to cover up a crime, they'd failed miserably, and anyone familiar enough with Connolly's office to know exactly which pigeonholes to rob would have known this. Besides, why should Connolly break into his own office to steal evidence? He had a key to the front door, and he could have more easily "misplaced" the documents than pretended to steal them.

But if Connolly hadn't done it, then who did? Gossips produced a long list of suspects that day: Some pointed to Oakey Hall, the mayor, perhaps trying to incriminate Connolly to drive him out of office. Others pointed to Matthew O'Rourke, the *New-York Times* writer and former comptroller employee, perhaps wanting to steal the records to prove his newspaper's charges. Others suggested the newspaper itself, fearing that the original vouchers might clear Tweed and Connolly of wrongdoing. Police investigators only added to the confusion by their own lackadaisical probe. Some officers who saw the hole in the glass door were overheard whispering: "Too thin."[56]

Whoever knew the truth wasn't talking, but guesses abounded and the accusations pointed mostly back to Connolly. The crime, after all, was committed in his office and involved his records. He'd have a hard time proving his innocence.

◉ ◉ ◉ ◉ ◉

No one reacted more sharply to news of the voucher robberies than A. Oakey Hall, His Honor the Mayor. If Hall was looking for an excuse to save himself by pushing Connolly out the door, he'd now found a dandy.

That morning, without bothering even to talk first to his comptroller, Elegant Oakey sat down in his City Hall office, took pen in hand, and laid down the law. He wrote Connolly a stern letter asking for his resignation. The 1870 Tweed charter denied him the right to fire Connolly outright, but Hall decided that now, under the circumstances, a firm demand would suffice.

"I have just been informed by the Superintendent of Police that last night the offices of the Finance Department were secretly invaded," he wrote. "Our constituents have a right to hold you responsible." No evidence had connected Connolly to the crime, but that didn't stop him from pointing his finger. Was it a way to shift suspicion away from himself? "With great personal reluctance, I officially reach the conclusion that the exigency requires your retirement from the head of the Finance Department... and ask... for your resignation."[57]

A few hours later, when Tweed welcomed Sweeny, Connolly, and the mayor for their regular daily angst session at his Duane Street office, Hall quickly pulled out the letter and used it to confront Connolly directly. He no longer asked him to resign but *insisted* on it. Sitting across the polished mahogany table from Connolly, he read the letter aloud to Connolly's face as Tweed and Sweeny watched. Connolly, a larger man physically than Oakey Hall, didn't flinch, though his eyes probably narrowed into two tiny slits behind his gold-rimmed reading glasses. "Hall, don't send me that letter," he said, according to sources. "The public demand your resignation as much as my own. We must sink or swim together."[58] He knew nothing about the voucher theft, Connolly insisted.

But Hall ignored him. He handed the letter across the table to Connolly but Connolly refused to touch it. "You may mail it to my office or to my house, but I will never take such a letter from your hands," he said.[59]

That night, Hall would send it to the newspapers. By the next morning, it would be plastered all over town, exposing the schism to the world.

Tweed barely said a word during this entire exchange. The fact that he didn't put his foot down and demand that his friends stop tearing each other apart reflected his own shrinking voice within the group. By one account, Tweed already had found himself being chastised in these private meetings: Oakey Hall had "timidly suggested" at one point that Tweed consider stepping down, to which Tweed had snapped back: "I am prepared to resign at once if the rest (Sweeny, Connolly, and Hall) will do so." Tweed, asked about the incident, denied it ever happened.[60]

Jimmy O'Brien, who still kept an office in City Hall to stay abreast of the gossip, found this story unlikely. Hall would never have dared turn against Tweed, he told people that day. "If Hall ever asks Tweed to resign, he'll never ask another man," he said. "Mr. Tweed [would] give Hall's tree such a shaking that there would be no plums left on it."[61]

In any event, after the meeting that morning, Oakey Hall seemed pleased with his own performance. He left Tweed's office on Duane Street and didn't object when a newsman from the *New York Sun* tagged along and badgered him with questions. The reporter described Hall's bubbly mood, how he stepped out onto the sidewalk wearing a reddish-gray suit looking "such as a third-rate clerk at Lord & Taylor's would disdain to wear." The mayor entertained the newsman, chatting non-stop as they walked together across Chambers Street and City Hall Park. "I've made up my mind that no earthly power will draw a word out of me. I've been dreadfully busy," he said. The reporter scribbled notes as Hall talked about the sacrifice he'd made taking public office, how he'd given only one dinner party since becoming mayor. Reaching the marble edifice of City Hall, the mayor stopped on the front steps and lifted his arm to point at a bank building across the street on Broadway with a flag on top reading "Security." "This is the flag I mean to have for the next year over the City Hall," he said.

Then, "with the air of a grand seigneur of the time of Louis XIV, the Mayor took off his hat and waved it to the *Sun* reporter as the latter bade his pleasant companion good day," the reporter wrote.[62]

Hall's good humor that morning, coming amid a storm of crises—robberies, lawsuits, and fraud charges—seemed strange and sparked its own rumors that the mayor had lost his mind. "I am so overwhelmed with business that I am in a maze," Hall told another reporter that day. "My brain is so occupied that I should hardly know what I was talking about."[63]

But behind closed doors, Oakey Hall made plans. He had every intention to force Connolly out. Legally, the city charter gave him only one recourse against Connolly if he refused to go, impeachment, but the mayor had a better idea. He invited August Belmont, the German banker and national party chairman, to visit his City Hall office that afternoon and they met privately for a full hour. Hall may have offered Belmont the comptroller's job on the spot. Belmont, a respected figure in international finance, would have restored credibility instantly to city bonds in world markets. Belmont played along. After seeing Hall, he made a point to be seen visiting the Comptroller's Office in the new Courthouse and refused to answer questions from newsmen.

That night, the mayor dined with friends at the Manhattan Club. The next day, on Saturday, he devised a newer plan: Instead of Belmont, he found another taker for the comptroller's job: George B. McClellan, "Little Mac,"

JAPANESE CUSTOMS IN NEW YORK.
Tamani Tycooni invite Connolli to Hari-Kari—No-go-he.

Frank Leslie's Illustrated, *October 7, 1871.*

the former Civil War general and 1864 Democratic presidential nominee. McClellan, sacked by Abraham Lincoln from his command of the Army of the Potomac after the Antietam bloodbath in 1862, had spent three years in Europe after the war, traveling through Switzerland and France, meeting Prussian army chief of staff Helmuth von Moltke and selling American-made munitions. He'd returned stateside in late 1868 and now enjoyed a role as elder statesman. He'd recently settled with his wife Ellen in a new home he'd built on Mt. Orange, New Jersey, just across the Hudson from Manhattan, and had accepted the post of chief engineer of New York's Docks Department and trustee of the Atlantic and Western Railroad, giving him together a healthy income of $20,000 per year.

The mayor visited McClellan, still trim at 45 years old, and "Little Mac" happily agreed to Hall's offer to become Comptroller so long as Connolly first agree to leave. The chance to be a hero again, saving the city from scandal, appealed to McClellan. The mayor left an acceptance letter for him to sign when the time came.

Things seemed to fall into place that Saturday for Mayor Hall. Through intermediaries, he heard that Connolly finally had agreed to step aside, promising to send his resignation to City Hall by 5 pm that day in exchange for Hall's promise to choose a trusted replacement as comptroller: either Belmont or McClellan.

But late that afternoon, waiting in his office for Connolly's resignation letter, the mayor grew impatient. He received a telegram from his wife Kate who was staying just across the river at their weekend retreat in Milburn, New Jersey, saying one of their daughters was ill. He should come home quickly. By then, Tweed and Sweeny both had left the city for their weekend homes, Tweed's in Greenwich and Sweeny's at Lake Mahopac. At 9 pm, hearing nothing from Connolly, Oakey Hall too decided to leave his office to join his wife and sick daughter.

He thought nothing of the silence from Connolly and didn't bother to check if anything had gone wrong. Business could wait until Monday.

• 14 •
COUP D'ETAT

"Oh, yes, I am always cheerful. You know the true philosophy of life is to take things just as they come. How was the clever definition of—let me see, I forget the name—of life? What is mind? No matter. What is matter? Never mind. That's my philosophy.... [S]ome of my newspaper enemies come out with a rumor that I was insane, mad, and all that, you know. That's the only reason why I did it, I assure you...."

—MAYOR A. OAKEY Hall, speaking with a newsman, September 18, 1871.[1]

RICHARD CONNOLLY, meanwhile, had reached the end of his rope. In his twenty years at Tammany Hall, Connolly had earned his nickname "Slippery Dick" by his cold-blooded navigation of rough-and-tumble backroom intrigues, double-crossing his friends at the drop of a hat. Now he felt his own head on the chopping block. Hall and Sweeny had turned against him and Tweed stood mute. Things had gone terribly wrong for him. Nine months earlier, Connolly had stood at the top of his game. He'd attended the Americus Club's annual January ball and been portrayed by a society writer as the happiest of men: "Comptroller Connolly, one of the old school of Irish gentlemen, who know the value of social power and the fascinations of good manners. In the boxes he was gracious, on the [dance] floor he was gallant, and at the table he was trenchant. When called upon loudly for a speech he held up his fork reprovingly, and at once proceeded to discuss his little quail."[2]

Now, Connolly found himself threatened with jail, ruin, and disgrace.[3] His wife Mary pressed him to take a stand. Known as a "headstrong woman, with a fair share of ability, and a greater amount of pluck than women generally possess,"[4] Mary held the purse strings in the Connolly household. Connolly had placed most of his fortune in her name—over $3.5 million in unregistered United States bonds alone—and she controlled it firmly. Stories circulated that Mary Connolly insisted her husband not resign, that quitting would be a confession of guilt and disgrace the family.

The week grew increasingly hellish for him. Connolly came to work Tuesday morning, spent a few hours at his office, then was pulled into the daily Board of Apportionment meeting—having to spend more hours closeted with Tweed, Sweeny, and the mayor who'd just asked him publicly to resign.[5] After that, he'd returned to his office to find it crawling with reporters. He spent the afternoon behind closed doors, refusing to see anyone except his lawyers, his Deputy Comptroller Richard Storrs, and his bond broker George K. Sistaire (a member of the Astor "whitewash" committee). Midday, he sent word to the newsmen that he was preparing an answer to the mayor's public demand for his scalp. When one reporter managed to snag him in the hallway, Connolly only shrugged and said he was 62 years old, of failing health and tired of public life, but he refused to quit until "fully vindicated."[6]

Late that afternoon, he released his answer to the mayor—a formal letter designed for printing in the newspapers. "I beg leave to differ from your Honor, in thinking the robbery of my office created any 'sudden or unexpected emergency,'" Connolly wrote, his lawyers doubtless checking his every syllable. "I am happy to assure you that it has effected no serious mischief, the archives of the department containing ample abstracts of all the stolen papers." Then he laid down his own marker. If he, Connolly, were guilty, then so too was the mayor. "My officials acts have been supervised and approved by your superior vigilance—so far as my administration is questioned, equal responsibility attaches to yourself.... I am unable to submit myself a vicarious sacrifice to satisfy the hungry appetite of adversaries for a victim."

He signed the letter as a gentleman: "Very respectfully, your obedient servant. Richard B. Connolly."[7]

That afternoon, he felt the pressure rise another notch: 250 city employees, laborers from the Croton Waterworks and uptown streets, came marching downtown to the Courthouse and pushed their way into the building to demand their salaries, frozen by Judge Barnard's injunction. The city owed each of them four to six weeks' pay for work already performed. When police blocked them from going upstairs, they began shouting "Give us our money" and "Our families must have food" and "Why don't Connolly sign the payrolls if he isn't going to resign?" Connolly was out at the time and police finally drove the crowd outside. "If we don't get our money we will dig a grave for Slippery Dick," one of them grumbled while skulking away.[8]

When Connolly came back and heard about the incident, he recognized the game afoot. His enemies were trying to destroy him politically by blaming him for the workers' plight. He immediately sat down and, ignoring Barnard's injunction, he wrote out a warrant providing money for the mens' salaries, signed it, and sent it to the mayor for approval. When nobody could find Oakey Hall, Connolly personally took the warrant and walked it across the street to the Broadway Bank and tried to draw the money on his own signature, but the bank teller refused. He was terrified of violating protocol, he said, with so many investigations afoot.[9]

Then, returning to his office, Connolly heard the latest rumor—that if he didn't resign, police were preparing to arrest him for malfeasance.

About this time, he finally snapped. Enough was enough. Richard Connolly was nobody's fool and nobody's scapegoat. He had friends. He didn't have to swallow this abuse. He'd kept up his large following in the Irish community and had contacts among the city's bankers. That night, he finally took matters into his own hands: He waited until after dark to avoid being seen. Then, traveling alone, he threaded his way across town to the home of an old acquaintance he hadn't seen in years: William Havemeyer—the retired sugar merchant, former New York mayor, and now leader of the reformers who'd chaired the mass meeting at Cooper Union and been appointed co-chair of the reformers' Committee of Seventy. Connolly as a young man had once worked as clerk in a bank Havemeyer owned and they'd stayed in touch ever since. Now he needed the older man's advice.

Havemeyer enjoyed telling the story of what happened that night: "One evening Connolly came to see me. I knew he would come," he explained. "He said they all wanted him to resign, and that the pressure was very strong. I gave him two pieces of advice. I told him; if he were innocent, not to resign, because it would be taken as evidence of guilt, and I told him, if he were guilty, not to resign, because... every little cur about the office would besmear him to curry favor with his successor."[10]

They spoke for several hours, until nearly 11 p.m. Connolly told Havemeyer all about his problems: the internal bickering within the Ring, the efforts to destroy him. He said nothing about his own crimes, the complex schemes he'd devised to skim "percentages" from city contractors, but Havemeyer didn't press him. At some point, a messenger interrupted them; Sweeny and Hall had sent word insisting they needed to see Connolly again right away—probably to renew their arm-twisting.

Connolly said he had to go. But before leaving, Havemeyer gave him one more piece of advice: He should get himself a good lawyer, in fact the best lawyer in New York City. He should go and talk to Samuel J. Tilden. Tilden would be glad to see him.

◎ ◎ ◎ ◎ ◎

Tilden had followed the Tweed drama from his perches on Wall Street and Gramercy Park, but only at a distance. He'd stayed away from the Cooper Union reform meeting on September 4 and, if he played any behind-the-scenes role in the Barnard injunction, he left no record of it. He read newspaper accounts of the new Committee of Seventy, how it met every day but accomplished nothing, but he didn't join it. "They got together and talked a great deal," complained even Havemeyer, the group's co-chairman, "everybody had a new thing to propose, and it became a regular debating club."[11] Tilden heard the gossip about the rift between Oakey Hall and Dick Connolly and enjoyed the latest joke: "When rogues fall out, honest men get their due."[12]

In early September, he began laying his plans. He sent a circular to 26,000 state party leaders about their upcoming convention in Rochester and placed the Tammany frauds atop the agenda: "Wherever the gangrene of corruption has reached the Democratic party we must take a knife and cut it out by the roots," he said.[13] But beyond this, he kept to himself. When rumors in mid-September connected him to secret talks over Connolly's plight at the Comptroller's Office, he denied them flatly: "I know nothing about it. I have had nothing to do with it," he told a reporter. "The statement, so far as it concerns me, is a pure fiction. I had no conversation whatever, directly or indirectly, with any one, or any connection with any negotiation, either for the resignation of Mr. Connolly, or for the appointment of anybody in his place."[14]

His friends Manton Marble and August Belmont cornered him at the Manhattan Club for advice on the situation, but Tilden gave them none.

Then, one afternoon, opportunity knocked. A messenger interrupted Tilden at his Wall Street office with word that someone wanted to see him, Richard B. Connolly himself. Connolly had sent a friend to ask for an appointment. Tilden answered immediately: Yes, he said, he'd be glad to see the embattled comptroller. They should meet as soon as possible, but not in his office. They needed to meet someplace private where they wouldn't be seen, such as Tilden's own home. The next morning would be fine.

It must have been an odd moment: Tilden and Richard Connolly, the stiff Swallowtail lawyer and the big, back-slapping Irish pol, sitting alone together in Tilden's Gramercy Park brownstone, perhaps sipping tea, talking face to face in quiet tones, looking out the window at elegant horse-drawn carriages on the pretty tree-lined street. Tilden and Connolly had met over the years but rarely mixed. They belonged to separate worlds. Connolly held a membership in Tilden's upper crust Manhattan Club but seldom came; he preferred the cigar-smoking, whiskey-drinking crowd at Tammany or Tweed's Americus lodge. Connolly probably needed a few minutes to make himself comfortable; once he did, he gave Tilden his proposition: He was in a fix and needed a good lawyer and Havemeyer had recommended Tilden as the best. Would he do it?

Tilden answered quickly: No, he said. "I could not be his counsel, or assume any fiduciary relations toward him," he explained later. Tilden had bigger plans and Connolly was just one piece on his chessboard. Being Connolly's lawyer might get in the way. But that hardly ended the matter. Tilden had an important message for Connolly:[15] He must *not* resign his post as comptroller. His office was vital to the reformers, and Connolly owed them a duty to hold it. His quitting would only give Tweed and Oakey Hall the chance to fill it with one of their own crooked friends. Instead, if Connolly wanted Sam Tilden's help, he'd have to make a clean breast and surrender himself to the law. That meant giving up his power, his patronage, and any leadership role in the local party.

For a lifelong politician like Connolly, these terms must have sounded steep. Still, he swallowed and agreed. When Tilden asked for a few hours' time to develop a plan, he promised to meet him again at Tilden's house that night. This time, they'd expand the group to include Havemeyer and Connolly's personal lawyers.

After Connolly left his home, Tilden headed downtown to Wall Street and his law office to study the problem. He quickly found what he wanted: There was an obscure provision in the city charter—Tweed's charter—that allowed the comptroller temporarily to transfer all his powers to a deputy while keeping his own job at the same time—a routine device to assure continuity in case the comptroller decided to take a vacation in Europe or had to leave work for a few weeks to nurse a cold. This gave Tilden an idea: Under this provision, Connolly could hold onto the comptrollership—blocking the mayor from replacing him in the office—but surrender real power to a deputy hand-picked by the reformers. This new deputy would become *de facto* the new comptroller and the mayor could not fire him. Tilden would be taking Tweed's own charter, which made Tweed's and Connolly's jobs untouchable, and using it against them.

And by capturing the Comptroller's Office—the linchpin of city finance—Tilden could effectively checkmate Tammany Hall. Tweed and his crowd wouldn't be able to spend a dime of taxpayer money without his blessing.

To play the role of new deputy comptroller, though, Tilden would need a person with special qualities: solid reform credentials, knowledge of city government, and plenty of backbone to stand up against harassment and threats. Most important, he'd need someone fiercely loyal to him. He happened to have just the right person in mind: Andrew Haswell Green. Green, the longtime Central Park commissioner recently pushed aside by Peter Sweeny, had been Tilden's close friend for thirty years. Both were life-long bachelors and, in 1845, they'd been law partners for a short time. Green had been itching to get back into government and, since his recent run-in with Sweeny, he had no sympathy for Tammany Hall.

That night, when the time came for his next meeting with Connolly, Havemeyer arrived promptly at Tilden's front door but Connolly never came. They waited impatiently for over an hour. Finally, Havemeyer stalked out into the night, grabbed his carriage, and raced across town to Connolly's house on Park Avenue. Here, he found the comptroller sick in bed in a panic. He'd been pressured again by the mayor and he didn't know what to do. "[He] said it was crucifying him," Havemeyer explained, telling the story a few weeks later. Havemeyer sat Connolly down and the two talked quietly well into the night, Mary Connolly probably poking her head in occasionally to offer an opinion. Connolly agreed to reschedule the meeting. "I put a little more backbone in him and made him promise to come to Tilden's house at 10 o'clock next morning," Havemeyer recalled.[16]

The next morning, all the conspirators met at Tilden's house on Gramercy Park for the *coup d-etat*: Tilden, Havemeyer, Connolly, and the lawyers. They'd earlier sent for Andrew Green who'd quickly joined them and agreed to accept the new post of deputy comptroller. All were prominent Democrats, a crucial point in Tilden's plan; he wanted to show the party cleaning up its own mess, stamping out corruption among its own members. Sitting with Tilden, Connolly balked again at giving up his powers, but Tilden refused to take any nonsense. He laid down the law: The Tweed Ring was going to be crushed, Tilden told him flatly. Connolly, as a criminal, would be destroyed. He had only one chance to survive: "if he threw himself upon the mercy of the public, and evinced a disposition to aid the right, the storm would pass him and beat upon the others."[17]

Before leaving Tilden's house, the lawyers drafted three letters to implement the transfer of authority: The first, from Havemeyer to Connolly, laid out the rationale for Connolly's staying in office and appointing Green as his deputy. The second, from Havemeyer to Andrew Green, urged Green to take the post, and the last, from Connolly to Green, formally offered him the job.[18] "Slippery Dick" Connolly had become a true sudden convert to reform, and now he had the papers to prove it.

They made the transfer with military precision. That afternoon, Andrew Green, along with Tilden and Connolly, rode downtown and took his oath as deputy comptroller from Judge Barbour of the state Supreme Court, the only judge they could find that day at the new Courthouse. At 5 pm, he arrived at the Comptroller's Office with a squad of uniformed police and took possession. He posted extra guards at the doors, turned on all the gaslights, and brought in a team of clerks to take stock of the records. He issued a circular saying that all papers sought by the citizen's committee would be provided and the November interest payment on city bonds would be paid promptly.

That done, he sent announcements to the newspapers. Since most papers did not publish on Sundays, most New Yorkers would not hear of the takeover until Monday morning. In all the public notices, Green mentioned only one person, William Havemeyer, as alone having engineered the complicated transfer of power. He left Tilden's name out of every document and conversation. Still, word of Tilden's role began leaking out. "Of course, Mr. Havemeyer is not the real author of this astute manoeuvre," Manton Marble would write that week in the *New York World*, "he is merely the respectable mask of a shrewder and more subtle brain. But as the cunning contriver has reasons for not avowing his work, we are willing to respect his incognito."[19]

Once Green had settled in, one of his first visitors to the office would be Samuel Tilden, ready finally to emerge from the shadows and take charge of events. He'd now seized control of the city treasury, snatched it away from Tweed in an instant, and Tweed wouldn't even know it until Monday morning.

• 15 •
NUMBERS

"Those were great days for newspaper men. There was hardly a day in which there was not a new sensation or when a reputation was not ruined by a new revelation."

—*Brooklyn Eagle* reporter WILLIAM HUDSON reminiscing years later.[1]

"The excitement in political circles in consequence of the extraordinary proceedings at the City Hall is greater than anything I have ever seen in New York."

—*New York Tribune* managing editor WHITELAW REID to Horace Greeley, September 18, 1871.[2]

MAYOR A. OAKEY HALL learned about the *coup d'etat* only the next morning, on Sunday, when a messenger delivered a copy of the *New York Herald* to his weekend home across the river in Milburn, New Jersey where he was breakfasting with his wife Kate. Elegant Oakey must have jumped from his chair. "The Municipal Muddle," read the headline, next to "Mr. Connolly's Action." Below, in tiny block print, appeared the full text of the Connolly-Havemeyer letters effectively surrendering the city Comptroller's Office to Andrew H. Green—Sam Tilden's friend—while Connolly kept the fig leaf of a title. And behind it all appeared gray-haired old sugar magnate William Havemeyer, leader of the reformers.[3]

Oakey Hall saw the game instantly. He'd been tricked. Connolly had made himself a Trojan horse, a tool for invaders, and made the mayor look ridiculous. It was treason! Hall got up from the table leaving Kate and the family behind. He'd had his own plans that weekend to settle the political impasse: throw Connolly overboard, install George McClellan in his place, and claim credit himself for cleaning up City Hall. Now Slippery Dick and Havemeyer had turned things upside down. "This movement was about the last thing that Sweeny, Tweed and Hall calculated upon," the *New-York Times* gloated that week with good reason.[4]

Stepping outside, Oakey Hall saddled his horse and rode at full gallop the six miles across New Jersey flatlands to General McClellan's house at Mount Orange. First and foremost, he had to learn if his own plan still had any life. McClellan greeted him at the door and invited him in for tea but gave him bad news. He'd gotten cold feet.

Oakey Hall had tempted fate by hitching his wagon to George B. McClellan. McClellan had a timid streak that had cost him dearly during the Civil War. As commander of the Army of the Potomac, his failure to move aggressively before the 1862 battle of Antietam—despite having a copy of Robert E. Lee's own secret orders in his hands—and his failure to chase Lee's army afterward had been the last straws prompting President Lincoln to sack him. Two years later as presidential candidate, McClellan's failure to untangle his own pro-war views from his party's Copperhead peace platform had cost him the election.

Now, in this newest crisis, "Little Mac" had wavered again. Hearing that party reformers backed Andrew Green for the comptroller's spot, he'd had second thoughts. When Hall had first raised the idea two days earlier, McClellan had expected to step into a vacant office as a conquering hero, saving the city from chaos. Now he'd be seen merely as a partisan in a fight against Tilden and the Committee of Seventy. That weekend, friends had privately warned him against tying himself to the mayor or Tweed, "whitewashing parties who are as deep in the mud as Connolly is in the mire," as his advisor William Aspinwall wrote him.[5]

Oakey Hall, sitting face to face with McClellan that Sunday morning, begged him to reconsider. McClellan tried to be polite. He promised to think it over and give him an answer by the next morning at 10 am, but gave no cause for hope.

With plans unraveling and time slipping, the mayor now left the General's house, mounted his horse and galloped off to New York City. By the time he reached the Hudson River, took the ferry across, trotted up to City Hall and climbed the stairs to his office, he had another idea. The mayor fancied himself a pretty fine lawyer. After all, he'd been district attorney before becoming mayor and argued thousands of cases before juries. Sitting at his desk, he pulled out the city statute books, opened them up, and peered through his pince nez glasses. Before long, he'd found something. Without talking first with Tweed or Sweeny, both of whom had left town for the weekend, he took pen in hand and wrote two letters. The first was to Connolly:

"I am advised that your action in [transferring to Andrew H. Green] all and every power and duty of Comptroller ... is equivalent in law to a resignation of your office," he wrote. "I hereby accept such resignation."[6] Connolly, of course, had not resigned at all, but the mayor was grasping at straws. He couldn't fire Connolly through the front door, so he'd try tricking him out the back.

Then he wrote a new letter to General McClellan. Little Mac had said he'd take the comptroller's job only if Connolly had left it vacant; now, as far as Oakey Hall was concerned, vacant it was. "I therefore tender you the office of Comptroller, and earnestly urge you to take it," he wrote.[7] He signed both letters with a flourish and sent them scurrying across town by messenger and provided copies to the newspapers on time to print in their editions the next morning. If George McClellan would only step forward and take the offer, he believed, public pressure to accept him would be unstoppable. Connolly would have to step aside.

As for Andrew Green, that interloper who now occupied the Comptroller's Office, the mayor could only sneer. Green was an invader, and Hall had determined to snub him. When a messenger delivered a copy of Green's oath of office to be filed that morning, the mayor's chief clerk, Charles Joline, flung it on the floor in front of a crowd of reporters and let it sit there while he read a newspaper. A few hours later, he returned it to Green unopened. Later, on the mayor's orders, Joline sent a letter to all city department heads: "I am directed by the Mayor to inform you that he does not recognize either Richard B. Connolly as Comptroller or Andrew H. Green as Deputy or Acting Comptroller."[8] As the hours passed from Sunday to Monday, crowds gathered around the City Hall and Courthouse buildings that sat beside each other in City Hall Park. Rumors spread that the mayor planned to install McClellan by force, sending squads of policemen storming into the Comptroller's Office and occupying it at gunpoint.

The mayor trotted up Broadway to the Manhattan Club for dinner on Sunday night, probably hobnobbing with the chef after holding court in the smoking parlor to poke fun at the political mess. The next morning, on Monday, he left his City Hall office and rode across town to the Department of Docks near the East River waterfront where McClellan worked as chief engineer. The General had made his final decision: He wanted no part of the comptroller's job, he told the mayor. He had no desire to cross swords with the reformers. In fact, before even seeing the mayor that day, McClellan had already said so to a reporter from the *New-York Times* who'd trekked out to his New Jersey home the night before: "There is not a word of truth in the report," he'd insisted. "I can assure you that I declined verbally and emphatically to Mr. Hall."[9]

Elegant Oakey knew his game was up. He left McClellan's office, rode his carriage back through the crowded cobblestone streets of lower Manhattan and stopped on Broadway for a private talk with Tweed at the Public Works Department. Tweed's reaction could not have been pleasant. Once asked if he ever planned to make Hall governor, Tweed had laughed, saying "it would take too much time to pull his wires, and he'd be sure to go off half-cocked when he ought to be as mum as a ghost."[10] He may have told the mayor so to his face now. In any event, a newspaper man saw Hall leaving Tweed's office an hour or so later "in a state of considerable excitement."[11]

The mayor walked across Broadway back to City Hall, invited a few newsmen into his office, and called their attention to his choice of clothes: "Gentlemen, some of you yesterday said that I had received a severe check," he said, referring to his setbacks with Connolly and McClellan "and, *in testimonium veritatis*, I have, as you see, put on a check suit."[12] If anyone laughed at the pun, they wouldn't say so. William Havemeyer, watching from a distance, thought the mayor had lost his sanity. "Hall is as crazy as a bed-bug," he told friends. "He shows that by the way he fights."[13]

◎ ◎ ◎ ◎ ◎

Meanwhile, across City Hall Park, wide-awake Andrew Green was living out his worst nightmare. As the city's new deputy comptroller, he faced a frigid reception. Beyond the defiance from Mayor Hall—the Tammany crowd quickly took to calling him "Handy Andy"—he faced brewing street-riots, open rejection from city department heads, and fiscal calamity. Fearing violence from the outset, Green asked twenty armed police guards to keep garrison in his office day and night and burned lamps constantly in all the windows. After the mayor had refused to accept his oath of office—a legally meaningless act—Green heard rumors that Hall planned to send police storming into his office to toss him out and put McClellan in his place. Green's own police guards braced for battle in the corridors. "McClellan will have to walk over a good many dead bodies," one was overheard saying.[14]

Isolated at every turn, Green found himself linked to an ironic partner, Slippery Dick Connolly, the only city official who'd talk to him.

Andrew H. Green.

Nothing in Andrew Green's long career had prepared him quite for this. A life-long bachelor at 52 years old, Green, slender with dark beard and mild eyes, had come to New York City as a teenager from rural Worchester, Massachusetts, studied law, dabbled in Tammany politics, and formed a lifelong bond with another bachelor, Samuel Tilden—joining Tilden's law practice for a short time in the 1840s. Since then, Green had emerged as New York's premier civic innovator. He'd headed the Board of Education in the 1840s but made his real mark leading the Central Park Commission since 1857. Here, he'd backed Frederick Law Olmstead's innovative pastoral design for the park, created the new Museum of Natural History, won authority from the Albany legislature as planner for all northern Manhattan, and earned a spotless record for honesty.

When Tweed's circle seized the Central Park Commission in 1870 under the new City Charter and put Peter Sweeny in charge, they'd kept Green as a member but Green effectively withdrew. He boycotted meetings and privately began griping to Tilden and the *New-York Times* that Sweeny's crooked management threatened to destroy his years of work on the park. For Tilden, Green was one of the handful of friends he'd sought out during August to vent his anger over the Secret Account revelations in the *New-York Times*.[15] By one account, Green had been visiting Tilden at his home on Gramercy Park when Connolly first came to see him.[16]

Now, Green had stepped into a hornets' nest. As comptroller—be it "deputy," "acting," "*de facto*," or otherwise—Andrew Green was responsible for the city's finances and, as he quickly discovered, he'd been handed a bankrupt wreck. Green's clerks counted all the cash in the city vaults over the weekend and found just \$2.5 million. Of this, every penny had to be put aside for the \$2.7 million interest payment the city would owe on its mountain of debt in November. Default would cripple credit not just for local governments but for every financial house from Wall Street to Harlem. Beyond that, he had not a cent. Annual property taxes wouldn't be due for several months and the crisis made normal borrowing from banks and credit markets impossible.

Meanwhile, bills had to be paid and Green had to find the money. Thousands of city employees—laborers, policemen, clerks, schoolteachers, and court-attendants—demanded salaries. Some had gone without pay for weeks and fumed at seeing their families starve. These workers knew how to make trouble; many had blood-stained hands from the July Orange Day riot, the May quarrymen strike, and other brawls. Mobs of hundreds gathered daily at City Hall Park clamoring for pay, mostly peaceful[17] but sometimes turning ugly and having to be chased away by club-wielding police. Green, calm and soft-spoken, often met their leaders and begged for patience but sent them away angry. He had no money.

Sitting at the receiving end, Green had little doubt who was stirring up these protests: Tweed and Sweeny, still sitting like Caliphs over the Public Works and Parks Departments, "inciting the laborers under their orders to make persistent and violent demonstrations," he wrote. "[The workers] were instructed, day after day, to hang around the finance Department and give the Acting-Comptroller all the annoyance which they possibly could."[18]

Fortunately for Green, the reformers who'd put him in office had big bankrolls and recognized the danger. Heads of the city's ten largest banks came to see Green that first week and advanced him a rare unsecured loan of $500,000 backed only by Green's handshake. This money would allow him to avoid immediate bloodshed by paying the workers a few weeks' salary. In return, Green unveiled a bold reform agenda: He issued orders immediately to forbid political monkey business on city payrolls, asked each office head to produce a list of no-show employees, and began firing them.*[19] At the same time, he threw open all the records in his office to the citizens' investigating committee, allowing clerks to come and examine them to their hearts' content.

Richard Connolly, still holding the actual title of "comptroller," chose to make the best of his awkward situation by becoming "Handy Andy"

* For instance, Green demanded that city employees be at their desks during work hours, forbade them from accepting payoffs from contractors, and barred supervisors from collecting assessments from employee salaries to support politicians—items rudimentary by modern standards but radical at the time. Such civil service reforms would not reach even the federal government until the late 1870s as small pilot programs and not be adopted on a wide scale until the Pendleton Act of 1883 in response to the 1881 assassination of President James A. Garfield.

Green's best friend. He came to the Courthouse each day and followed Green like a puppy, helping his new deputy learn the ropes and mingle with the staff. They made an odd pair side by side, Connolly tall and boisterous, slapping backs and cracking jokes, Green shorter, serious, and reserved. A newsman described Connolly that week as dressing like a sharper trying to make a good impression: black coat, white silk vest, snuff-colored English broadcloth suit. "His hair was redolent of rich perfume, and his vest glittering with a gold chain," the reporter noted. "He looked neat and trim, as if he had come out of a bandbox."[20]

During Green's first day when rumors swept the office about possible violence by police trying to evict them, Connolly had entertained the newspaper writers on his behalf. "They would not be mad enough to do that," he insisted, but, if violence came, he'd be ready to fight: "They can take me to prison, but I shall go," he recited dramatically, eyes to the ceiling.[21] To the mayor's letter declaring that he'd effectively resigned his post by appointing Green his all-powerful deputy, Connolly fired off a sharp reply: "I have not either in fact or equivalent resigned," it said. "By the appointment of Andrew H. Green Esq., as Deputy Comptroller, I have endeavored to guard the public interest committed to my care."[22] He sent a courier dashing off to the mayor to deliver it but a messenger brought the letter back a few hours later unopened.

Connolly saw threats everywhere. He refused to step outdoors that week without a bodyguard. He'd burned bridges with powerful people by crossing Boss Tweed and he still labored under a cloud of suspicion from the voucher robbery. New charges surfaced against him that week in the *Evening Post*—doubtless planted by the mayor or Peter Sweeny—that Connolly's own son J. Townsend had stolen a separate set of county vouchers earlier that year and fled the country with them. Connolly had to find three city officials willing to swear in writing that it had been James Watson, the former auditor killed in the sledding accident the prior January, not Connolly's son, who'd walked off with the twenty-four missing vouchers representing $3 million worth of city claims—possibly proof of still more frauds—and never returned them despite Connolly's repeated requests months before Watson's death.[23]

It didn't stop there. Beyond these public attacks, Connolly heard unnerving rumors that the mayor was planning to have him arrested for forgery. By early October, Connolly found the pressure unbearable. He scribbled out a resignation letter and handed it to Havemeyer—apparently the only person in Gotham he still trusted—but Havemeyer simply put it in his pocket. "I shall not part with your resignation till I secure the appointment of Andrew H. Green as your successor," he told him.[24] Connolly knew the reformers still considered him a crook even while paying him lip service. Friends speculated he'd stick to his job only so long as Oakey Hall remained mayor. "He has documents that could send Hall and the other fellows to the state prison," one said, and "wants to get satisfaction of Hall for his treachery."[25]

Capping his nerve-wracking week, Connolly had to wrestle again with his own most recent nightmare: the voucher robbery. That Wednesday night as he was sitting quietly with his wife at their Park Avenue home, a knock on the door interrupted him. It was William Murphy, his night watchman at the Comptroller's Office. Murphy had brought along a woman named Mary Conway who claimed to know who committed the crime.

Slippery Dick was all ears. He invited them in and heard them out. Mary Conway, it seemed, worked as a live-in maid for Edwin Haggerty, the Courthouse janitor who lived in an apartment in the Courthouse upstairs from the Comptroller's Office. The night of the robbery, she'd seen Haggerty, his friend Charles Balch, and an unfamiliar man in gray clothes sneaking around Connolly's office and carrying off loads of papers which they took upstairs to Haggerty's apartment and burned in the kitchen stove. The smoke had been unbearable, she'd said. She gave a description of the stolen goods—bundles of papers tied with pink ribbons—that fit the vouchers exactly. An inspection later of the ash heap in the apartment confirmed her story. Now, she said, Haggerty had threatened to kill her unless she kept her mouth shut.

Connolly, thrilled at the disclosure, immediately sent for his lawyers, who came rushing to his house that night. They wrote up Mary Conway's statement in affidavit form, had her sign it, then found a judge to issue arrest warrants for Haggerty, Balch, and Haggerty's wife. Police found the suspects on the street, took them into custody, and dragged them down to the Tombs prison well past midnight, where a police court judge ordered them held without bail. News of the arrests dominated city gossip for the next few days. Overflow crowds packed the courtroom for Haggerty and Balch's arraignment to see the two suspects, the maid, and the night watchman testify about the crime—the best entertainment in town. Even Andrew Green took a break from his Comptroller Office headaches and stopped by to enjoy the carnival.

The mystery remained, though. Despite hours of questioning, none of the witnesses shed any light on the crucial point: Who had the robbers worked for? Who had told them to commit the break-in? Haggerty and Balch kept their mouths shut and Mary Conway, the maid, gave the only direct testimony on the point: "Charley Balch done it for me, and I done it for another man," she quoted Haggerty as telling her.[26]

For now at least, though, Connolly could rest easier. Fingers were pointing at somebody other than him.*[27]

Tweed spent most of his time after the *coup d'etat* hiding from newspaper reporters in his office at the Public Works Department on Broadway. Here, he greeted the usual stream of politicos hawking gossip and favors but closed the door on newsmen. "I have nothing to say. I cannot say anything," he told a *New-York Times* writer who managed to grab him in the lobby for a minute. "You can understand my position. I don't want to complicate my friends."[28]

Behind this stoic front, though, Tweed must have bit back on a stew of emotions that would choke any weaker person: rage, fear, disappointment. That summer and fall, he'd seen a parade of former friends jump ship and betray him: Jimmy O'Brien whom he'd made sheriff, George Barnard whom he'd made judge, and now Slippery Dick Connolly. With Connolly, at least he'd had fair warning. Tweed knew Connolly's history of treachery: In 1862, when Tweed was still clawing his way up at Tammany and feuding with a rival Wigwam faction, he'd seen Connolly switch sides three times before coming back to ask favors.[29] Now, Tweed must have marveled at Connolly's

---

* Haggerty and Balch both would fight the charges; they'd be held without bail for six months, until March 1872, then released on $5,000 bond and never tried. The voucher robbery remains an unsolved mystery. Hershkowitz, in his examination of city archives in the 1970s, found "order forms" based on the same vouchers and warrants that supposedly had been stolen and destroyed a century earlier. He concluded that the more likely suspects were either (a) the contractors, Keyser, Ingersoll, Garvey and the others, because loss of the original vouchers could have freed them from charges of forgery or bill-padding, or (b) the Committee of Seventy trying to cast suspicion on the Ring.

Tweed himself later would claim fingerprints on the crime, but his story is highly suspect. In an addendum to his 1877 written confession prepared by lawyers and presented to Attorney General Fairchild while bargaining for his freedom, he'd say that Mayor Hall had come to him that weekend and told him that, if the vouchers were not examined, the prosecutions against the Ring could be blocked. Tweed said that, based on this advice, he approached W. Hennessey Cook, a Public Works official, who told him that the vouchers could be gotten and destroyed, just "leave the matter in his hands and he would attend to it." The story is doubtful because (a) it is uncorroborated and Tweed never testified orally on it, (b) he would have known that copies were kept of the key records, (c) he had not been indicted or arrested yet, and still felt confident about his case, and (d) Tweed was hardly likely to trust Oakey Hall's opinion on anything so important at this point.

Still, as a crime of incompetence prompted by panic, no suspect can be dismissed solely on logic.

gall, trying to cut a deal with prosecutors to save his own fortune while avoiding jail—leaving the Boss holding the bag.

His back to the wall, Tweed spoiled for a fight. His seat in the Albany legislature as state senator came up for re-election that year and, scandal aside, he damned well planned to keep it. The time had come to put his foot down, better late than never. Through his lawyers, he presented his own sworn statement in Judge Barnard's courtroom that week flatly denying all the charges against him—fraud, conspiracy, misconduct, neglect of duty, or anything else. It was all "untrue,"[30] a "general denial," he insisted. "I don't intend at my time of life to go fighting windmills."[31] The few reporters who did reach him that week found him unapologetic. "As to the cry about thieving—why, that's politics," he told one. "I tell you, I shall come out of this fight as clean and square as any man in the community. Only give me the chance to meet the charges openly and aboveboard. I am never so happy as when I am in a fight."*[32]

Tweed still had plenty of friends from his lifetime of favors and spoils. "All my professional and personal ability or influence is at your service at all times and upon all occasions," James C. Spencer of the State Supreme Court wrote him.[33] Leaders of the William M. Tweed Association of the Second Ward (today's lower East Side around Fulton Street) cheered him at a rally on Park Row that week and blasted his opponents as "a few political soreheads and vile ingrates."[34] Other friends formed a new Central Tweed Organization to back his re-election to the state senate.[35] Even Jimmy O'Brien, who'd brought disaster on Tweed's head by disclosing the Secret Accounts to the *New-York Times*, still spoke fondly. "Mr. Tweed is the most honorable man of the lot," he said when asked about the jousting at City Hall: "Tweed is plucky.... He knows what he is about, and they can't play any of their games on him."[36]

On September 22, just five days after the Connolly-Green-Tilden *coup d'etat* and barely twenty-four hours after the voucher robbery arrests, with anti-Tweed passions at fever pitch in New York City, Tweed's friends staged a magnificent rally for him. An estimated twenty thousand people[37] packed Tweed Plaza at Canal Street and East Broadway, an enormous crowd far larger than at the reformers' Cooper Union affair weeks earlier, "a human sea, surg-

* Tweed turned some of his hardest feeling that week against recently elected congressman Robert Roosevelt, uncle of the future president Theodore: "Why, who is Roosevelt? No one knew him till we brought him to the front and sent him to Congress: he was never at the front before—nobody knew him—we made him."

ing, interested, eager, and curious," as one reporter described it. They poured into the square from surrounding neighborhoods and filled every spot on the sidewalk, lining the rooftops, and crowding within windows of the redbrick buildings of nearby streets.[38] Flags waved from a wooden grandstand alongside a huge portrait of the Boss, all framed by gaslights. "Our Choice for Senator: William M. Tweed" or "Tweed- The Old War-Horse," read the banners in big block letters. Hundreds of Chinese lanterns strung around the square cast bright glowing halos of red, green, and purple. Skyrockets soared from bonfires as local Tweed clubs arrived marching in formation, some led by marshals on horseback.

After a few speeches, Tweed himself mounted the podium to an explosion of cheers, whistles, and applause that echoed through the alleys of lower Manhattan. He wore a dark brown coat and raised his little Scottish cap, standing for nearly five minutes without saying a word, "like a statue, while the storm of enthusiastic greeting ebbed and flowed over the great gathering," another newsman wrote.[39]

This night, standing barely half a mile from the East River near streets where he'd lived most his life, surrounded by neighbors, Irishmen from the nearby Five Points, Protestants from Cherry Street, a stone's throw from City Hall itself, Tweed threw off any shyness and shouted his defiance. "At home again, among the friends of my childhood and among their sons, I feel I can safely place myself and my record, all I have performed as a public official plainly before your gaze," he roared, his voice penetrating the cool night air.[40] "Reviled, traduced, maligned, and aspersed, as man had seldom been, I point proudly to my friends to prove my character and ask only for a full, free, impartial investigation into the official acts of my life," he yelled, "but no man can do justice to himself standing outside and fighting against those who control the public press… I expect my friends to stand by me to meet this untrue and unjust charge."

Tweed's stubbornness brought them to their feet. "Last year my majority [for the state senate] was a mere 20,000. This year I expect 30,000 and will take no less."[41] After he finished speaking, he stepped back from the podium and fireworks erupted all around the square, their glare positioned to illuminate Tweed's portrait along with the words "Our Choice for Senator."

Critics like E.L. Godkin of *The Nation* pointed to crowds like this and dismissed them as ignorant, money-bought friends, "hard-fisted bruisers, and crimps, and pimps, and grogery men."[42] Who else would ignore oceans of scandal and applaud a corrupt thief? Godkin pointed to Tweed's power, his web of city handouts—"offices, sinecures, contracts, public works, untried indictments, suspended sentences, penalties, licenses, ordinances, so on"—as his tool to bribe half the voting population of New York City.[43] But even so, Tweed evoked loyalty on these streets with his larger-than-life aura: The Boss. To many, the charges against him seemed unreal, the numbers incomprehensible, a set-up job. At a time when laborers earned $2 per day and $5,000 per year could buy affluent comfort, who could imagine anyone stealing millions? The *New-York Times* stories sounded like fantasy, hysteria, while Tweed had always been their champion in real life, providing jobs, charity, and, through his Tammany clubs, a web of friendship in a cold city.

Tweed faced his first real political test following the scandals two weeks later as the state Democratic Party held its annual convention in Rochester. He girded for battle. Reformers led by state party chairman Samuel Tilden had organized an anti-Tweed coalition led by old-liners like Horatio Seymour, lawyer Charles O'Conor, and Oswald Ottendorfer, publisher of the German language newspaper *Staats Zeitung*. They made no secret of their plan: They wanted to kick Tweed out of the party, strip Tammany of its designation as its "regular" organ in New York City, and replace it with a slate of do-gooders. By month's end, Tilden's group counted fully two-thirds of the delegates as being ready to back them in repudiating Tweed.

Tweed knew how to fight back, though. He arrived in Rochester at 10:00 pm the night before the convention leading an army of two hundred Tammany men: delegates, greeters, and strong-arm bullies. He took rooms in the Osborn House hotel where most of the delegates stayed and got to work. He threw open his suite and entertained them all night long with whiskey, oysters, and cigars. On delegate after delegate, he plied his persuasion—fixing them in the eye, touching shoulders, grabbing an arm, sharing a joke. He pledged friendship in one breath while threatening a walkout or hinting compromise in the next. "Go ahead and kick us out if you can get along without us," he told delegates from Albany, Syracuse, Utica, Buffalo, Westchester, or Yonkers.[44] All he wanted was "harmony." If the party needed to condemn Tweed or Tammany to satisfy the reformers, then go ahead. He had a thick skin; he could take the insults, but leave Tammany alone. Tammany was the party's strong workhorse crucial to winning statewide elections.

No one knows if Tweed sweetened these appeals with hard cash, promises of jobs, or other bribes. No one really doubted it.

By the time the convention opened the next morning, he'd performed a minor miracle. Despite months of scandal, outrage, and treachery, Tweed had seduced them. Instead of the majority of delegates being ready to shove him out the door, he'd sold them on compromise. He counted only forty out of over a hundred as firmly hostile.[45] Tilden would have no choice; he'd have to play along—just as he always did. Tweed had little fear of the starchy state chairman from Gramercy Park; Tilden had always backed down before. Why should things change now?

Tweed stayed away from the convention hall that day, using Brooklyn delegate William C. Dewitt as his mouthpiece on the convention floor, but soon he made his voice clear. Tilden, gaveling the convention to order, faced an embarrassing split. He knew the crowd's sympathies and, just as Tweed predicted, he straddled. He opened the session with a long speech denouncing municipal corruption but never mentioned Tweed or Tammany by name. He blamed Republican legislatures for the problem, referred to "vulgar millionaires" grasping for power, and ended by proclaiming that whoever "plunders the people, though he steal the livery of heaven to serve the devil in, is no Democrat." He pushed the convention to adopt platform planks blasting city corruption and demanding punishment, but he pointed no fingers.

Tweed had no such scruples. As soon as Tilden had finished, he delivered his counterpunch. At his direction, Brooklyn delegate Billy Dewitt jumped up on the convention floor and gained recognition. He asked to read aloud a petition signed by all sixteen Tammany delegates—all of whom had absented themselves from the convention hall that morning leaving a conspicuous block of empty seats. Recognizing the recent charges of corruption in New York City and the need for "harmony," it read, the Tammany men were voluntarily waiving their right to sit at the convention and pledged their support behind whichever candidates the delegates chose to nominate: a blank check.

A heady applause rose from hundreds of the delegates and spectators packing the stuffy auditorium. Rural hayseed or city slicker, they all got the point. Tweed had graciously spared them the embarrassment of his presence and he'd thrown himself on their mercy. How could they turn him down? Before the noise had faded, Dewitt gained recognition again. He offered a parliamentary motion: Since no delegate from New York City was in the room, he proposed that on any future roll call, "no delegation be deemed as sitting from that locality."[46] He immediately moved the previous question, cutting off debate.

Tilden was stunned. Dewitt's motion, in effect, would allow Tammany to keep its "regular" party status—since no other delegation could be recognized—without the delegates even having to vote on the issue. Tilden's own slate of reformers, cultivated over weeks of delicate diplomacy, would have the door slammed in its face. Tilden had heard talk of such a "compromise" but he'd expected the chance to confront it in open debate. Now, standing at the podium, he'd been gagged. This was too smart a move for a small-time hack like Billy Dewitt from Brooklyn. He recognized the fingerprints. Tweed had cheated him.

Dewitt insisted on his parliamentary rights and began taunting Tilden with the rulebook as Tilden stood helplessly on the podium in front of hundreds of onlookers. "The man from Kings [Dewitt] quoted the law to the veteran," a newsman wrote.[47] Mortified at the insult, Tilden still had to concede. Dewitt demanded a vote and a clerk called the roll. When they reached his name, Tilden first voted "no," then changed it to "yes," drawing snickers from the crowd. Dewitt's motion carried by a whopping majority of 94 to 4, a remarkable vindication for the scandal-plagued Boss even if half the delegates hadn't a clue what they'd just voted for. "This is the perfection of discipline," E.L. Godkin grumbled of the outcome, "simply and purely an instrument of evil."[48] Horatio Seymour, sitting on the podium and slated to take the gavel as permanent convention chairman later that day, left the hall in disgust, went back to his hotel, packed his bags, and took the next train home to Utica, claiming he had a cold.[49] Behind the scenes, state committeeman Henry Richmond was heard "cursing in [Tilden's] face the absence of all plan and all leadership," Manton Marble wrote.[50]

After the session broke up, crowds of friendly delegates swarmed to Tweed's room at the Osborn House to offer congratulations. Dozens of Tammany men marched in formation through the streets of Rochester behind a brass band, arriving at Tweed's window to present him a musical serenade. The next day, Tweed flexed his muscle again. Having heard complaints that his heavy-handed tactics had unnerved some moderate upstaters, he allowed three of Tilden's dissidents to address the convention and present their complaints, so long as the delegates agreed never to allow them a vote on their credentials. Again, the convention marveled at the Boss' generosity.

The only shadow on his victory came at the end of the second day. As the convention reached its closing hours and began choosing nominees, Tilden again mounted the podium and got the crowd's attention: "The real point involved in this controversy has not been entirely comprehended by some of the gentlemen from the rural districts," he started to explain, referring to the speeches by his New York reformers earlier that day. By keeping Tammany as the "regular" party organ in New York City, he said, they were giving Boss Tweed a license once again to steamroll the state legislature by nominating twenty-one state assemblymen and five state senators—New York City's local quota . Had they no outrage at the scandal?

Several delegates—Tweed's friends in the room—jumped to their feet at the surprise outburst. Before Tilden could finish even getting the words out of his mouth, voices interrupted him. "Point of order!" "Previous question!" Tilden looked out at the auditorium filled with hundreds of agitated faces, some cheering, others hissing. He listened quietly to a string of objections designed to shut him up, then calmly brushed each aside with a few words.

Allowed finally to reclaim the floor, Tilden drove on with his point. "I am free to avow before this convention that I shall not vote myself for any one of Mr. Tweed's members of the legislature." The room erupted again in hoots and howls, cheers and hisses. Criticizing Tweed? By name? Here? "And if that is to be considered the regular ticket, I will resign my place as Chairman of the State Committee and help my people storm this tide of corruption.... I shall cast my vote for honest men."[51]

He'd started an uproar. "The excitement threatened to become a riot," historian DeAlva Alexander wrote in describing the scene.[52] After a few minutes, Tilden moved that the convention nominate the entire state ticket—a list of names all acceptable to Tammany—then he walked away. The ticket meant nothing. The real contest would come later and Tilden had laid down a gauntlet. He could do as he pleased.

Tweed himself seemed hardly fazed at the incident; he remained focused on the job at hand. All that day, he was seen scurrying about his suite at the Osborn House, shouting orders, greeting friends, cracking jokes. Asked about Tilden's outburst and Seymour's absence, he brushed both off as "troublesome old fools." As for his own fight with reformers, he seemed to relish it: "I should like some more of the same sort. When I'm under the dog, you'll hear me howl, not before."[53]

❁ ❁ ❁ ❁ ❁

Samuel Tilden returned from Rochester angry but resolute. He'd discovered his mission. He knew he'd carried an awkward goal to the convention: to convince his party to amputate its strongest arm, Tammany Hall, that delivered thousands of patronage jobs, millions of government dollars, and dozens of winning candidates on Election Day. He'd hoped to remove a cancer without killing the patient. He'd failed, but he had walked away standing on his feet.

Ever since engineering the takeover of the city Comptroller's Office by Andrew H. Green a few weeks earlier, Tilden had gloried in his tactical triumph. He'd cut the heart out of Tweed's moneymaking operation in a single stroke and the victory changed him. Instead of hiding in his library with his books and in his uptown club, he now took every opportunity to show his face publicly—at the Comptroller's Office, at City Hall, at the Courthouse. It was Tilden who had organized the dissidents at Rochester and who constantly appeared with Andrew Green offering advice. Tilden even came to the Tombs police court alongside city prosecutors when they brought Haggerty and Balch, the two voucher robbery suspects, up for questioning.

Tilden had now conceived a two-front war on Tammany: one public, the other secret. Publicly, he planned to beat Tweed in the November elections and destroy his base in the state legislature. Privately, he aimed to build a legal case to put him behind bars. He insisted that Democrats lead every step of the reform effort. Whatever conspiracy of inner demons drove him at this key point, pushing Tilden to emerge and seize the public spotlight—outrage at scandal, personal ambition, revenge at a bully who'd mocked him over the years—he left no doubt of his commitment, pushing aside lucrative client work as the battle heated up.

Reformers, starved for a leader, delighted at the change. Ever since the Cooper Union mass meeting in early September, they'd worked as a disorganized band top-heavy with dilettantes: Wall Street magnates, uptown club members, and elite lawyers. Now, they rallied behind Tilden. "A number of active leading men at my house last night all agreed to stick by you through thick & thin," his ally Henry A. Richmond telegraphed from Buffalo that week.[54] Some even showed gratitude by showering him with money, though Tilden never asked for it: "I beg to send you herewith my check for $500- to assist in the good fight against rogues & corruption in which you are engaging & in which you have the warm support of every honest man," August Belmont wrote.[55] "*You* must not be allowed to spend any money for your election. Your noble conduct has made all honest Democrats your debtors," echoed Royal Phelps, enclosing a check for $250.[56]

Tilden alone had the stature to corral so many egos. People listened to him. When Robert Roosevelt tried unsuccessfully to pull two quarreling anti-Tweed leaders together for a meeting, he appealed to Tilden: "The only way is for you to ask them [and] then when you get us together use your authority and influence..."[57]

Tilden knew that Rochester had been a fiasco for him. He'd laid down a goal and failed miserably. No compromise, he'd said. "Action and not words can save us, but it must be complete and decisive action," he'd written an upstate friend before the convention.[58] Instead, he'd "weakly yielded" to threats and been "cajoled and swindled," as the *New York Tribune* put it. Horatio Seymour, who'd left the convention in disgust, blasted the whole affair: "The anti-Tammany men were in disgrace," he wrote Tilden from Utica.[59]

Now, all the principal anti-Tammany factions had agreed to form a new coalition based at Apollo Hall, the old theater on West 28th Street where they held meetings, including dissident Germans, Young Democrats, Swallowtails, and reformers from the Committee of Seventy. Tilden agreed to join them, even if it meant sinking his own "regular" party.

To lead the battle in November elections, the Apollo Hall group nominated an eclectic slate of candidates rich in high-profile Tweed enemies, starting with Jimmy O'Brien for state senator and Tilden himself for state assemblyman.[60] It included Republicans like former Civil War General Franz Sigel for city register, a favorite with German immigrant. To oppose Tweed for the state senate in Tweed's own heavily-Irish district, they chose Jeremiah O'Donovan Rossa, a popular, world-renowned Irish patriot recently landed in America. Rossa in Dublin had co-founded the nationalist Fenian movement and edited the newspaper *Irish People*. The British had jailed him for sedition and treason but recently granted him amnesty on condition he leave his homeland. He'd received a hero's welcome on arriving in New York City.

All October, Tilden threw himself into the campaign: He spoke to noisy rallies, torchlight parades, and street corner meetings. At every stop, he blasted Tweed and his circle. Practice made him a good rabble-rouser despite his flat voice and bland delivery. "Are you going to send selfish, unprincipled men into power—men whose object is robbery and rapine, men whose sole object is to enrich themselves and plunder the working class?" he asked ten thousand cheering supporters outside Apollo Hall one night, evoking shouts of "No, never!"[61] To an Irish crowd on 23rd Street, he appealed to self-interest: "These men had pretended to be your friend," he told them. "What is the result? Why … they have enabled your enemies … to say [it] proves beyond a doubt that you are not fit to govern yourselves at all." He drew loud applause pledging "I cannot die with a good grace until this work of redemption is accomplished."[62] To another: "They betrayed the Democratic Party. They betrayed Democratic principles. They betrayed the people of this City."[63]

When Apollo Hall's coffers drew low, Tilden dipped into his own pocket to contribute $10,000 for expenses and raised more money from friends.[64]

With the city's eyes riveted on the exciting campaign, Tilden could now turn to the secret part of his plan—building a legal case to put Tweed in jail. He'd later claim he started this work almost by accident: "happening casually in the office of the comptroller of the city of New York," as he put it, Andrew Green asked him to look at a legal paper he was preparing to send the Broadway Bank. The paper involved allegations by one of the city contractors, plumber John Keyser, that the endorsements on his paychecks from the county had been forged. Whether it was Green who asked Tilden to investigate or Tilden who pressed the idea on Green, by early October he'd thrown himself into the project.

Sam Tilden needed no search warrant or subpoena to prod the Broadway Bank into giving him any record he wanted; the imprimatur of Green and the Committee of Seventy sufficed.* The Broadway Bank, located near City Hall, was a Tammany favorite; it held accounts for virtually every key machine figure including Tweed himself. He quickly assembled a team to help him, including Henry Taintor, an accountant he'd worked with on railroad litigations, and two full-time clerks named George W. Smith and P.W. Rhoades. Together, they began wading through the oceans of data.

From this jumbled mass of numbers and accounts—the Broadway Bank records plus those of the Comptroller's Office—Tilden hoped to find a pattern, a link to connect the exorbitant city spending sensationalized in the *New-York Times'* Secret Accounts and the personal enrichment of a single person: Tweed. On its surface, the job looked daunting. Beyond the sheer mass of papers and ledgers to examine, no one item stood out. The overall

---

* In fact, many of the deposit tickets and account records Tilden took later disappeared and could not be provided for trial. Some turned up later in Tilden's personal collection. See Box 24, Tilden papers, NYPL.

pattern screamed fraud, but each individual entry appeared perfectly in order. If thieves they were, they'd covered their tracks well.

Only the Keyser warrants broke this pattern and gave Tilden his opening.

The *New-York Times* disclosures that summer had listed sixteen warrants (payments) as supposedly being issued by the county to Keyser under the 1870 Tax Levy for work on city armories and the new Courthouse. But Keyser had sworn that he'd never seen any of them and insisted his endorsements were forged. Tilden now took these warrants—essentially cancelled checks—and examined them closely. He noticed an odd pencil mark on the back of each one, the letters "E.A.W." or "E.A. Woodward," each in the same handwriting. To solve the riddle, he called in two senior clerks from the Broadway Bank, Arthur Smith and Ansel Parkhurst, both of whom handled accounts for Tweed. Tilden sat down with them and showed them the warrants, and Smith quickly recognized the pencil mark as being the initials as Edwin A. Woodward, Tweed's clerk at the county Board of Supervisors. Woodward had his own separate account at the bank, and the pencil marks suggested that Woodward had taken Keyser's warrants and deposited the money directly into his own account. Tilden quickly confirmed this fact by checking Woodward's records.

The implication was alarming. The term "money laundering" would not be invented until decades later, but the concept of moving money from account to account, hiding it under borrowed names, transforming it from cash to check to credit to cash again, all for the purpose of removing any trace of its origin or destination, struck home. To prove such a thing, Tilden would have to reconstruct the money trail for these warrants, a cumbersome process that would require his clerks to compare thousands of transactions in these accounts, scouring inputs and outputs for patterns.

It was grueling, painstaking work. Tilden and his clerks buried themselves in the Broadway Bank records, working long hours into the night, straining their eyes by gaslight and candlelight to decipher hand-written ledgers with columns of tiny numbers. They cramped their fingers making full transcripts of all the suspect accounts—Woodward's, Keyser's, Ingersoll's, Garvey's, and Tweed's. Then they laid them side by side for comparison. They tracing the warrants marked "E.A.W.," looking for withdrawals from one account and deposits into another of similar size and occurring on nearby days. In some cases, they had to "deconstruct" complex transactions into smaller pieces, examining individual deposit slips and checks. Since all the suspect Keyser warrants stemmed from the 1870 Tax Levy, they decided to reconstruct all the Tax Levy payments, comparing them with deposits and withdrawals from the accounts.[65]

In the process, they covered dozens of spreadsheets with calculations and crosschecked their entries against hundreds of bank documents. At one point, Tilden asked Smith, the Broadway Bank clerk, to produce every slip for every deposit into Tweed's account and found that many were in Woodward's handwriting, not Tweed's. Parkhurst, the teller, confirmed having seen Woodward make several of the deposits himself.[66]

Word of his secret project leaked and Tilden panicked when newspaper reporters approached him over it, not wanting to tip his hand. He flirted with them in a strange dance. Sometimes he'd hint at sensational disclosures: "Mr. Tilden is busily engaged in collecting evidence … that may be rather startling even to those who now think they have heard about all the 'revelations' that could possibly be made," one reported.[67] But when a *New-York Times* writer planned to reveal details, he pleaded for time. "Indeed, we will be successful," he coyly announced for attribution, "but a few more days will amply satisfy us, and develop more than has even yet been suspected."[68]

Having plowed through mountains of detail, Tilden now summarized his findings in an affidavit and an attached table: "Identification of the parties receiving the proceeds of the warrants drawn for allowances made by the Special Board for Audit, under section 4, of the county tax levy for 1870." Beneath this dry-sounding title lay pure dynamite. The table identified 190 payments approved by Tweed, Connolly, and the mayor under the 1870 Tax Levy and traced what became of the money in each case. Its simple visual shape pointed a clear accusing finger. It showed deposits and transfers among bank accounts laid side-by-side, column-by-column, moving sideways across the page from the county treasury to Ingersoll to Keyser to Woodward. Out of the $5,710,913.96 total approved by the county, a full $932,858.50 ended up in the final column on the page: the personal bank account of William M. Tweed.

In a separate table, Tilden showed eleven additional payments from the county to the New-York Printing Company totaling $384,395.19, and a transfer of $104,433.64 occurring on the same day to Tweed, bringing his total to just over $1 million.[69]

It was a stunning intellectual feat, one of the earliest examples of an "audit trail"—a fundamental compliance tool used today by financial regulators around the world. Tweed had pocketed the money; no one could doubt it. No longer could he hide behind Connolly, Hall, or anyone else. Tilden had tied him to the crime with a clear, direct chain of evidence. Tweed could deny it all day long but he'd only look ridiculous.

With this new evidence in hand, Tilden now played his final card. On October 17, just two weeks before Election Day, he sent a delegation from the Committee of Seventy riding north by train to Albany to meet Governor John Hoffman. Hoffman, by now utterly mortified at his Tammany friends, had spent most of September touring upstate county fairs trying to avoid the scandal. Shown Tilden's concrete evidence, he gave them what they wanted. A few days later, State Attorney General Marshall B. Champlain took the train down to New York City and visited Tilden at his Gramercy Park home. He showed Tilden a letter he had written and planned to sign the next day appointing a special agent to bring legal action against the Tweed Ring in his name. His choice for the job: 67-year-old Charles O'Conor, the wily old trial lawyer who'd recently boosted his fame by representing former confederate president Jefferson Davis in beating his post-Civil War indictment for treason. O'Conor was also one of Sam Tilden's closest legal friends.

Tilden had to be thrilled. The governor and attorney general had placed the prosecutorial apparatus of New York State virtually at his disposal. What's more, representing the attorney general, they could bypass New York City's Tammany judges and bring cases anywhere in the state—Albany, Buffalo, or wherever they could find a friendly judge.

O'Conor quickly assembled a team of prosecutors and made Tilden an unofficial member. "They will act with promptness and vigor," Tilden promised reporters when asked about the announcement.[70] A few days later, Tilden hosted them all for a meeting at his Gramercy Park home to plot strategy, making his parlor the visible center of the movement. Word began to circulate. Soon, very soon, they'd be coming after Tweed.

Supplement to The New-York Times, October 26, 1[illegible]

IDENTIFICATION OF THE PARTIES

Receiving the Proceeds of Warrants Drawn for Allowances Made by Special Board of Audit, Under Section 4 of the County Tax Levy of 1870.

FROM BOOKS IN CONTROLLER'S OFFICE.					FROM ENTRIES IN ACCOUNTS IN THE NATIONAL BROADWAY BANK.						
					INGERSOLL & CO.		A. J. GARVEY.		E. A. WOODWARD.		WM. M. TWEED.
Date.	No. of Warrant.	Payee of Warrant.	Last Indorser or Depositor of Warrant.	Amount of Warrant.	Deposits.	Checks.	Deposits.	Checks.	Deposits.	Checks.	Deposits.

16
PERSONAL KNOWLEDGE

GEORGE JONES HAD NEVER SEEN anything quite like it: a subpoena, delivered by a sheriff's deputy to his corner office on the top floor of the *New-York Times* building. It demanded he appear before a Grand Jury investigating charges of corruption against Mayor A. Oakey Hall. Jones didn't quite know what to make of it. On one hand, he appreciated that the law finally was closing its grip on a character his newspaper had labeled a "thief" and "swindler," but what could George Jones have to tell a Grand Jury? Anything he knew about the affair, he'd either already published in his newspaper or else was none of their business.

Who was the target here, he wondered: the mayor or the *New-York Times*?

One by one, reformers had started dragging Tweed Ring suspects into court through lawsuits filed by the Committee of Seventy. They'd started with the contractors—James Ingersoll, John Keyser, and Andrew Garvey. One reporter had followed Keyser to his house on Second Avenue and found him crest-fallen: "I have nothing to say except that I am sick, worried out, broken-hearted and hunted down."[1]

Elegant Oakey was the first city official on the reformers' target list. A few days earlier, Hall had been forced to appear at the Fourth District Police Court on East 57th Street to be arraigned on charges of neglect of duty, a misdemeanor crime. He'd arrived on horseback wearing kid gloves and a tartan cravat and holding a light cane in his hand. "I am here, Sir, to disappoint the malice of my partisan enemies [and] to relieve your Honor and the District Attorney of any responsibility in this matter," he'd a nnounced to the judge, shrugging off any embarrassment, then waived his legal right to examine witnesses. The judge had released him on his own recognizance.[2]

Hall's arraignment had been only the first step, though. Now a Grand Jury had been called to decide whether to bring formal charges.

George Jones, after getting his summons, walked the half-dozen blocks from the *New-York Times* building on Park Row past City Hall to the Courthouse on Chambers Street, the same building his newspaper had ridiculed all summer as neck-deep in graft. His newspaper also had lambasted the Grand Jury itself as a rigged joke. "There is a new Grand Jury, and it has been packed, depend on it," it quoted Judge Barrett, a reform lawyer, as complaining.[3] The *Times* had even charged Judge Barnard himself with picking the jury's members and selecting as foreman General William Hall, the defendant mayor's uncle, a story that turned out to be untrue.[4]

Waiting in the lobby of the ornate Courthouse, with its octagonal rotunda, its vaulting skylight, its marble floors, frescoed ceilings, and Corinthian columns, George Jones had plenty of company. He found himself rubbing elbows with all the leading players in the scandal, each having received a similar subpoena: Andrew Green, Samuel Tilden, William Havemeyer, Jimmy O'Brien, among others. Each waited his turn to sit alone before the jury and be asked the same question: Do you have any *personal* knowledge that the mayor had committed a crime by knowingly signing fraudulent warrants. Logically, the question made no sense. Other than seeing his signature on the papers themselves—which the jury could do any time it wanted—the only way anyone could have "personal knowledge" was literally to have been in the room with Hall when he signed them, seen him do it, and heard him explain why. The case against Hall rested on documents. Not surprisingly, not a single witness would be able to say "yes." Each would awkwardly have to deny having any "personal" evidence against the mayor.[5]

George Jones had every reason to expect a tough grilling. His *New-York Times* had been the loudest voice blasting Tammany. Newspaper editors had few protections while appearing in court in the 1870s; a spiteful prosecutor easily could throw him in jail for contempt if he refused to talk. Jones knew his only real power lay in the ability of his newspaper to punch back in its columns and in the bank accounts of his friends to pay bail. That October, Jones had seen harassment against his newspaper worsen. One anonymous Tammany tough, speaking through the *Star*, a Tammany mouthpiece,* had

* The *Star* had received $251,000 in city advertising from January 1869 through May 1871, despite having a circulation of only 9,000, making it one of the most highly city-subsidized journals in New York.

virtually instructed the mobs of angry unpaid workers hanging around City Hall each day to go and burn down Jones' and *Times* editor Louis Jennings' houses. It had printed their home addresses, blamed them for the workers' lost salaries, and stoked them up with angry untruths: "Jennings was paid $50,000 for his work by the Radical Club and has invested it in a house in Forty-Second Street," it told its impoverished readers.[6]

Jones and Jennings each posted extra police around their homes, though no incidents had occurred. Now, facing what looked like a Tammany grand jury run by a Tammany district attorney, Samuel Garvin, and possible jail if he refused to cooperate, George Jones treaded carefully as a guard led him into the private chamber and closed the door. He sat alone in the witness chair facing twenty-one hard-faced, impatient men—the Grand Jurors and the District Attorney—with no lawyer, no notes, and no place to hide. "Mr. Jones, what is your business," Garvin asked him promptly.[7]

"I am a publisher," Jones answered. "Of the *Daily Times* newspaper."

The jurors had scheduled over twelve witnesses that day and had little time to waste, so Garvin jumped quickly to the central issue: "Confining yourself to the complaint, will you have the goodness to state to the Grand Jury whether you have any personal knowledge as to any appropriation of the public money or misconduct of Mr. Hall in connection therewith that would throw any light on this subject to the Grand Jury."

George Jones measured his words. "I have the information that all people have who have read the statements and have opinions as to the credibility of those statements; I have no personal knowledge."

"You have no knowledge of any facts personally connected with this investigation?" Garvin repeated.

"None whatever."

For anyone else, this simple denial would have sufficed. But Jones and his newspaper had played a special role in the Tammany scandal; the *New-York Times* had been Mayor Hall's chief accuser for over a year, starting months before its publication of hard evidence with the Secret Accounts. Certainly, its publisher had to know *something* about the mayor he could share. After all, calling a man a criminal with no basis was a crime in New York State, libel, and itself could put a newspaper editor in jail.

One juror interrupted the District Attorney to demand from Jones an explanation: "I have read the editorials, probably two or three months in your paper, on this question; the paper has not ceased almost daily to brand Mr.

Hall as a thief. Can you give us of your own knowledge any information that will help us to come to a conclusion that he has proved himself to be a thief?"

Again, those words "of your own knowledge" set George Jones' on edge. "There is a difference between me as an individual and the newspaper," he explained, "the newspaper is an impersonality; I am an individual. I do not propose to answer any questions in relation to the paper. I am here as an individual."

In his twenty years at the *New-York Times*, Jones had never faced this dilemma, nor had any newspaper publisher in America in recent memory. Jones, for years the newspaper's quiet financier working in the shadow of his flamboyant partner Henry Raymond, was as poorly equipped as anyone on Park Row to navigate this minefield. For the next half hour in the closed-door session, Garvin and the grand jurors peppered him, asking over and again the same basic question using different words and angles, trying to coax a different answer, growing impatient each time Jones repeated the same dry formula. Tell us names of your informants, Garvin asked. Tell us names of the newsmen who wrote each article and each editorial so we can question them. Maybe they'd have "personal knowledge" to share.

Here, too, Jones dug in his heels. Newspapers by the 1870s had already well established the practice of basing stories on anonymous sources. Beyond protecting the source, publishers also hid the names of reporters. "By-lines" on news stories would not become common in the *New-York Times* for another forty years, well into the twentieth century. "I cannot give you the names of any one that furnishes information to a newspaper," he insisted, and "I do not propose to go into the interior working of the *New-York Times*."

Jones could only guess how badly he was irritating the jurors with his denials and evasions. After several rounds, he grew tired of the semantics and laid down his marker: "it is known to the whole of this public that moneys have been drawn from the city treasury by the signature of Mayor Hall, for which no evidence has been returned. There is a flood of evidence which is open to you and every gentleman here to see ..... I mean to say if you do not act upon what you have got, you will not act at all."[8]

He didn't convince anyone. The jurors finally let him go, perhaps just as happy to find no evidence against the mayor and be able to point to Jones, the mayor's chief accuser, as their excuse. In the end, they threw up their hands. By a "nearly unanimous" vote, they would conclude that "A. Oakey Hall has been careless and negligent in the discharge of his duties, in affixing his signature to warrants without giving the vouchers that consideration which the public interest demanded." But as to any criminal charge, they found the evidence simply too weak since no witness had come forward to testify to the mayor's criminal intent.[9]

The controversy didn't end here. A transcript of George Jones' supposedly-secret testimony that day somehow leaked from the district attorney's office. Horace Greeley, Jones' boyhood friend, got his hands on a copy and saw it as a chance to embarrass his Park Row newspaper rival. He printed the full text in his own *New York Tribune* under the headline: "Whitewashing Hall."[10] In an editorial, Greeley, who still considered the mayor a dupe and not a criminal, viciously mocked Jones for his ignorance of any "personal knowledge" of the mayor's guilt, saying it revealed just how "destitute of any moral purpose of principle" the *Times* had been in its sensational summer exposes. At the same time, he denied any need to protect the newspaper or its staff or sources in the affair. "They should have subpoenaed every reporter employed in collecting information," he argued; "their spies from the Controller's office should have been compelled to tell the little they knew."[11]

It was a strange debate between two personalities later considered pillars of American journalism, one eager to undercut the other to exploit a single-day scoop. Thomas Nast, watching the affair from his perch at *Harper's Weekly*, would draw a cartoon of Greeley applying pails of "whitewash" to the mayor.[12]

For the mayor too, this hardly ended the issue. There'd be other Grand Juries that would not be so timid at finding reasons to drag him into court.

17
MARKED

"The best philosopher that ever lived was spat upon by an antagonist who was arguing with him. He pulled out his handkerchief and wiped the saliva from his face and said: 'That is only a digression; now let's get on with the argument.'"

—A. OAKEY HALL, in his speech on being nominated for mayor, November 25, 1869.[1]

THE NEWS ELECTRIFIED New York City: Boss Tweed had been ordered arrested. Less than a week after the state attorney general had empowered them to bring charges against the Ring, Charles O'Conor and his prosecutors had marched into the chambers of State Supreme Court Judge Wilton L. Learned in Albany and charged Tweed and two city contractors, furniture-maker James Ingersoll and plasterer Andrew Garvey, with "deceit and fraud." Citing Samuel Tilden's explosive new affidavit, they demanded that Tweed return $6,312,000 in stolen loot—the total amount paid by the county under the 1870 Tax Levy vouchers, every penny of it considered suspect since none had been properly "audited" as the law required.

On Wednesday morning, October 26, they'd asked Judge Learned for an arrest warrant and he'd issued it promptly, setting bail at a sky-high one million dollars, ten times larger than the $100,000 bail set for former-Confederate-president Jefferson Davis in 1867 for treason.[2]

As word spread Thursday morning, curiosity seekers jammed Tweed's office at the Public Works Department on Broadway. A group of tough-looking men—"white-coated roughs ornamented with slouched hats," as a *New-York Times* reporter put it—lined up outside Tweed's door. "What, arrest our Boss?" one of them laughed. "You don't know him."[3] Over on Wall Street, stock exchange speculators treated it as a joke. "Tweed! Why he is the incarnation of American progress," one said. "He can steal more than anybody else. He ought to be made President (laughter) in Sing Sing."[4]

Tweed heard the news that morning and hardly flinched. He'd been absorbed that week with other problems, campaigning for his seat in the state senate. A few days earlier, he'd drawn 1,500 supporters to one rally at Centre and Pearl Streets[5] and presided at the opening of a new Tweed Club on East Broadway that drew hundreds of the Boss's friends, all described as "men above suspicion," to enjoy the brass band and sip champagne.[6]

Any normalcy for Tweed, though, was a shallow illusion. At City Hall, he kept an uneasy truce with the new regime. He still presided at the Public Works Department and met regularly with the city Board of Apportionment—Sweeny, Hall, and himself—but the board's new fourth member, "Handy Andy" Green, cast a pall on any back room chatter. They met in the mayor's office rather than Tweed's Duane Street lair and bickered constantly. Typically, when Green and the mayor locked horns one time over a question of whether to pay claims to six charities while making others wait, Tweed settled the argument by freezing Green out—in this case, by referring the decision to a special committee composed of himself, Hall, and Sweeny. Green could only watch and take notes.[7]

Stepping out on the streets, to the theater, or his favorite restaurants, he faced sneers or ridicule. Newspapers had plastered their pages with Tilden's new chart showing how Tweed had personally pocketed over a million dollars in county Tax Levy payouts, painting him a criminal; Thomas Nast's *Harper's Weekly* cartoons made him a laughable, vicious clown. Standing six feet tall and three hundred pounds, Tweed couldn't help but be conspicuous anyplace he went. His found refuge only in his office or across the sound in Greenwich.*[8]

Tweed had chaired a meeting of his Tammany General Committee a week earlier and found it demoralizing. "The Tammany 'braves' looked more like chanting the deathsong than sounding the war-whoop," one observer in the room wrote.[9] Tweed gave them a pep talk but his glum look that day sparked rumors that he'd lost $4 million in Wall Street speculation.[10]

Now, with a judge having ordered his arrest, Tweed saw final disaster written on the wall. He spent Thursday in his office working at his walnut desk.

* Around this time, Tweed also faced another blackmail threat from Jimmy O'Brien. O'Brien, through intermediaries, insisted that Tweed purchase half of O'Brien's outstanding $350,000 claim against the county in exchange for O'Brien's using his influence with Tilden and the Committee of Seventy to go easy on him. Tweed balked at first but finally agreed. He paid O'Brien $20,000 in cash and the rest in mortgages—over $150,000 altogether. In the end, for his money, Tweed in return got nothing.

He scribbled out urgent notes to friends asking them to provide bail[11] and finalizing the transfer to his son Richard of his seven most valuable real estate holdings around New York City worth some $750,000 including his Fifth Avenue home, his Fort Washington farm, and the "circle property" (Columbus Circle)—recording the deeds he'd signed in August.[12] That week, Tweed had paid $22,359 from his own pocket for salaries of Public Works Department employees, mostly pipe layers and repairmen, whose wages had not been covered yet by Andrew Green. The good will gesture only backfired, sparking more ridicule about his stolen money.[13] By then, Tweed had started burning his personal records in his office fireplace and told Ingersoll and Garvey, his codefendants, to do the same.[14]

Hours passed that day and nothing happened. At one point, Tweed sat down with one of the newspaper writers who now stalked his office constantly waiting for him to stumble. "Yes, the exhibit [Tilden's table] does look bad, very bad," he told him, "but, sir, I have not received a cent of that county money." In fact, Tweed suggested that Tilden had misconstrued a totally innocent transaction: He'd loaned money to Ingersoll and Garvey earlier and they were simply repaying the debt, he claimed. That explained the suspicious cash transfers into his account at the Broadway Bank. But Tweed never spelled out this defense, either then or later at his trial, making it sound hollow. Still, "I am not going to run away," he insisted, "you may depend upon that."[15]

Even now with his world crashing around him, Tweed enjoyed these daily verbal jousts with the newspapermen: "Although 'interviewed' and badgered at least nine times a day by 'one of our reporters, [Tweed] is always calm and great, if not perfectly grammatical—and that defect may be chargeable to the reporters," conceded even George Templeton Strong, the merchant-diarist and Sam Tilden's Gramercy Park neighbor.[16] Tweed stayed on friendly terms even with the reporter from the *New-York Times*, his chief accuser. "Good by, my son; come again any time," he told him in closing one interview that week.[17] In another, asked about a critical story, he assured him: "You have never misrepresented me."[18]

The sheriff failed to come for Tweed on Thursday and Tweed went home to Greenwich, taking the ferry across Long Island Sound to Connecticut. He could have stayed there beyond the reach of New York justice but chose instead to return the next morning, a fittingly rainy day. By the time he reached Broadway, he had to push past dozens of lawyers, newsmen, and politicos to reach his office. Reporters described him as looking tired and depressed and noted that he wasn't wearing his famous diamond pin. When word came that the arrest was imminent, he grumbled: "Well, they've been talking about this for the last six weeks. It's time they did something."[19]

At 12:30 pm, Sheriff Matthew Brennan, a stout 49-year-old with thick mustache and whiskers, appeared on the sidewalk leading half-a-dozen somber men in dark suits. Brennan pushed his way up the stairs to Tweed's office and knocked crisply at the door. "Good morning, Mr. Tweed," he said.[20]

Tweed looked up from his desk, his room jammed with people, and returned the greeting. "Good morning."

Brennan had received the arrest warrant that morning from Wheeler Peckham, one of O'Conor's lawyers who had hand-carried it down from Albany. O'Conor and Peckham wanted to make certain that Brennan personally executed the order. Brennan, a Tammany Sachem like Tweed and a member of Tweed's Americus Club, had a strong independent streak. Born in New York in 1822 of immigrant parents, he'd been one of the first American Irishmen to reach political prominence, a police captain in the 1850s and a power at Tammany, owning a saloon near the Five Points neighborhood with his brother. As comptroller through the mid-1860s, he'd been honest enough that Tweed would push him aside for Slippery Dick Connolly. Tweed had picked Brennan to run for sheriff in 1871 to replace renegade Jimmy O'Brien only as a peace gesture to reform-minded Young Democrats.

Now, O'Conor trusted Brennan for the most sensitive arrest of his career.

"Take seats, gentlemen," Tweed said as Brennan stepped forward. There'd be no whiskey or cigars this morning. Tweed's sons Richard and William Jr. sat together on a sofa; his lawyers pulled chairs up to the desk. Others stood around the Boss in a circle. One reporter described Sheriff Brennan as walking over to Tweed at this point, putting a hand on his shoulder and saying with a nervous laugh, "You're my man"—what the reporter saw as "a deliciously cool joke" since normally the sheriff would simply drag a man off by the collar.[21]

"Mr. Tweed I have an order for your arrest," Brennan announced, a half-dozen newsmen scribbling notes to record the scene.

"I expected it," Tweed said, "but not quite so soon. However, I have my bail ready and you can take it here if you will."

"I will," Brennan said. "Who are your bondsmen?"

Tweed then listed some of the richest men in New York City, all standing gloomily around the room: Erie Railway president Jay Gould who'd come to pledge $1 million, builder Terrence Farley, real estate dealer Benjamin P. Fairchild, and contractor Bernard Kelley who'd each pledge $300,000, and publisher Hugh Hastings who'd pledge another $100,000. Together, they'd secure a bond totaling $2 million, the required double amount of the $1 million bail.

Brennan then asked everyone but Tweed, the lawyers, and the bail bondsmen to leave the room. It would take three hours to complete the formalities behind closed doors as Brennan's deputy Judson Jarvis cross-examined each bondsman and drew up legal papers. After they'd finished, Tweed showed Brennan the door and the sheriff departed with his bond, a copy of which landed quickly in the newspapers. Under the arrest order, Tweed remained free but his troubles had only begun. In twenty days he'd have to answer the legal complaint, followed by a trial, perhaps indictments, perhaps jail. His bondsmen—Jay Gould especially—would face weeks of harassment.*

After Brennan had gone, Tweed spent another hour sitting privately in his office with his sons and lawyers that day, then he took the afternoon ferry home across the waters to Greenwich. Over the next week, he tried to shrug off the indignity and act as if everything were normal. He still had an election campaign to finish. The next Monday after a weekend away, he came to his Broadway office carrying toys he'd bought for his youngest sons, four-year-old George and eight-year-old Charles. Tweed had become a grandfather by now, as his son William Jr.'s wife Eliza had given birth to a baby daughter.

One of the newspaper reporters hovering about the office asked Tweed if he were going to resign. "What for, I would like to know," he snapped, having answered the same question a dozen times already. "I am here legally, and have done nothing that can remove me legally from here, and in this position I am going to remain. Is that plain enough?... I am going to fight this fight against me to the bitter end."[22]

* * * * *

As the election campaign reached its crescendo, Thomas Nast's anti-Tweed cartoons in *Harper's Weekly* catapulted him to rarified fame and he seized the opportunity with gusto. He made money hand over foot that fall from the

---

* Jay Gould at the time was facing revolt by Erie Railway stockholders and feared that prosecutors would use the bail-bond process to compromise his position, forcing him to drop off Tweed's bond in November. He would be ousted as Erie president in March 1872.

drawings that sprang so easily from his fingertips. Copies of his new 1871 "*Thomas Nast's Illustrated Almanac*" sold like hotcakes at 30 cents apiece with over a hundred original drawings and columns from humorist Mark Twain. Nast had produced two new illustrated pamphlets that year, "*Dame Europa's School*" and "*Dame Columbia's Public School, or Something that Did Not Blow Over*," both of which sold to worldwide audiences. He matched his regular cartoons in *Harper's Weekly* with drawings for the satirical weekly *Phunny Phellow* and freelance painting. All told, he'd earn $8,000 for his work in 1871 including $5,000 for his Tweed drawings alone.

Nast used his money to live well. He and his wife Sarah decided to keep the house in Morristown, New Jersey where they'd moved over the summer to avoid harassment from city bureaucrats and planned to stay there permanently. In December, Sarah would give birth to a new baby daughter, Mabel, their fourth child. Nast had become famous, popular with all except the Irish and Catholics whom he regularly insulted in his cartoons. So famous had he made the faces of his favorite targets—Tweed, Hall, Sweeny and Connolly—that a legion of copy-cats followed him with clever anti-Tammany cartoons in *Leslie's Illustrated*, *Harper's Weekly*, *Phunny Phellow* and other magazines. One of them, R. Hoyt, enjoyed drawing Tweed and Hall in exotic costumes, either as Sioux Indians marching off to the "Happy Hunting Ground" or as Japanese Samurai warriors: "Japanese Custom in New York: Tamani Tycooni invite Connolli to Hari-Kari—No-go-he," read the caption on his parody of the Connolly resignation farce.[23]

Nast kept his own focus on Tweed, though, and as the scandal deepened, his images grew darker. He drew a cover for *Harper's Weekly* in October that showed Tweed, Hall, Sweeny and Connolly facing ultimate justice, standing in the shadow of four nooses, Tweed himself bowing to the gallows, "The Only Thing That They Respect or Fear."[24] Nast had become the lynch mob. He filled every *Harper's Weekly* issue that autumn with multiple cartoons on the scandal. When workmen blamed reformers for their lost paychecks, Nast gave them the answer: a cartoon showing a huge vault marked "City Treasury" that was "Empty" to starving workers but "Full" for Tweed and his friends seen toasting themselves with champagne over a sumptuous feast. Tilden's Apollo Hall reformers printed thousands of copies to use as leaflets in the election campaign.[25]

For the Election Day issue, Nast outdid himself. He brushed off an old sketch he'd made during his 1860 travels with Garibaldi of Rome's ancient coliseum and updated it to show Tweed as Emperor presiding over a gruesome scene on the coliseum floor: the Tammany Tiger, terrifying and fierce with blood dripping from its teeth, having just killed Lady Columbia, symbol of law and liberty, and ready to kill again. "The Tammany Tiger Loose: 'What are you going to do about it?'" read the caption. Even a child couldn't miss the point—Tweed the evil dictator, flaunting his power, persecuting the weak. New Yorkers bought over 300,000 copies of the edition; they posted the drawings on newsstands, in saloons and clubs, handed them from neighbor to neighbor, laughed at them over dinner tables, cringing at the villains, appalled at the crimes.

"The only thing they respect or fear."
Harper's Weekly, *October 21, 1871.*

Nast had perfected the art of outrage. In the process, he'd turned Tweed into a vulgar image, a scoundrel, an object of disgust, fat, evil, far removed from a human being. That was how most of New York and the country now knew him.

Somehow, he survived. Despite Nast's cartoons, Tilden's proofs, the arrest, the disclosures, and the heroic Irish opponent, Tweed won his seat in the New York State Senate that year, defeating Jeremiah O'Donovan Rossa by 12,300 votes. Four regiments of state militia soldiers had joined police in guarding the ballot boxes against cheating but that didn't stop the *New-York Times* from charging fraud and rowdyism[26] in the victory. Rossa himself claimed that he'd out-polled Tweed by 350 votes and been "counted out," but his appeal went nowhere.

Everything else that Election Day for Tweed spelled disaster. Apollo Hall reformers won every important contest: all fifteen state assemblymen, four out of five state senators, and all fifteen aldermen. Jimmy O'Brien hooked

"The Tammany Tiger Lose: What are you going to do about it?"
Harper's Weekly, *November 11, 1871.*

his seat in the Albany state senate and Tilden was elected to the assembly.

Meanwhile, the birds started to fly. Andrew Garvey and E.A. Woodward both ran to Canada to avoid prosecutors. Keyser fled south to Florida, a short boat ride from Cuba. Ingersoll had disappeared the morning after Tweed's arrest, telling friends he'd gone to Portland, Maine on a business trip. "He will be back here," Tweed told them, "he won't run."[27] In fact, Ingersoll ran to Canada, then France, having already sold four of his lots in Manhattan for $45,000 to finance the trip.[28] Henry Hilton resigned from the Parks Department a few days later.[29]

Peter Sweeny disappeared as well. He resigned as Parks Commissioner just before Election Day and followed his brother James to St. Catherine's, Canada, and then Paris, far from American justice.[30] Two weeks later, Oakey Hall recognized realities and appointed Andrew Haswell Green the city's permanent comptroller, making the *coup d'etat* official.[31] Connolly had resigned two weeks earlier contingent on Hall's pledge to appoint Green.[32]

Connolly too finally met his end. Just before the Thanksgiving holiday, while hanging around his old Comptroller's Office with his new friends Tilden and Green, he looked up to see Matthew Brennan coming his way. He got up to shake the sheriff's hand but Brennan brushed it aside. "Mr. Connolly, I've got an unpleasant duty to perform," he told him. "You are my prisoner."[33]

"There must be some mistake," he had said, turning to Tilden. "Mr. Tilden, the Sheriff has arrested me."

Connolly had considered himself safe under protection of the reformers. After all, he'd helped them win the game by handing over his office at the height of the crisis. Now he learned how wrong he'd been. Tilden came over, looked at the arrest order, and simply nodded. "What is the bail, Mr. Brennan," he asked. It was $1 million, the same as Tweed's and signed by the same judge in Albany. "I am surprised at this. But it is so, Richard." Tilden actually had little reason for surprise; the arrest was based on Tilden's own affidavit signed just a few hours earlier.

Of all the arrests, Connolly's became the oddest farce. Rather than take him to jail, the sheriff agreed to let him first visit a few allies to try and raise bail. They lunched together at Delmonico's restaurant on Beaver street—Connolly, Tilden, Brennan, and William Havemeyer. Unable to find bondsmen, Connolly spent the next four nights at the New York Hotel in custody of police guards as his lawyers negotiated for his freedom. At one point, they actually reached a deal. The prosecutors, recognizing Connolly's help in surrendering the Comptroller's Office, agreed to free him and let him settle his entire case with the government—which on its face demanded repayment of the same $6.3 million as Tweed's—by paying just $1 million in restitution and promising to testify against other Ring defendants.

They went to Connolly's house on Park Avenue to settle the bargain, but here things went awry. It was Mrs. Connolly, the ex-comptroller's wife, who controlled their household money, and she now took over the talks. As the hour grew late and time came to ante up, she left the lawyers in the parlor, went upstairs, then returned a few minutes later with $1 million worth of United States treasury bonds—the agreed price. As she laid them on the table, though, Charles O'Conor, the lead prosecutor, hesitated. If she could produce this much money so easily, he though, there must be plenty more. He now demanded an additional $500,000.

Mary Connolly balked. She refused to pay another dime. Her husband pulled her aside and begged her frantically to relent: "I must pay $1,500,000 or go to jail," he insisted.[34]

"Richard, go to jail!" she told him.

So he did. Connolly spent all that December at the Ludlow Street Jail; friends who accompanied him there heard him cry as guards locked his cell door behind him. He stayed there until New Year's Day when Sheriff Brennan finally agreed to lower the bond and let him go. On leaving the jail, Connolly promptly went home, packed his bags, and left New York for Connecticut. From there, he reached Canada, then sailed to Europe where he'd already sent much of his fortune. Connolly would spend the next ten years in Egypt, Switzerland, and France growing sick with Bright's disease, poor, and depressed, never to see American shores again.

Horace Greeley, finding the whole situation amusing, scribbled an epigram on Slippery Dick's flight: "Dick cut and ran; so proved himself, for once, a *non est* man."[35]

Of all the famous "Tweed Ring," only Tweed and Elegant Oakey Hall remained in New York City. All the others had gone. For Tweed, too, the noose tightened. The same week as Dick Connolly fled, Tweed finally resigned his post as New York's Commissioner of Public Works and gave up his seat as a director of the Erie Railway Company.[36] By now, he'd transferred title on another fifteen of his city real estate holdings to his son Richard, including his Duane Street office and his Broadway property on 21st Street, totaling some $2 million in value and allowing Richard to qualify as a bail bondsman.[37] Tweed had almost nothing left. His yacht, the *William M. Tweed*, was seen in Bridgeport, Connecticut, bobbing behind a tugboat apparently being towed away to escape creditors.

In mid-December, a Grand Jury met in New York City and indicted Tweed on charges similar to those in the earlier O'Conor complaint and Sheriff Brennan came to arrest him again. As before, his sons and lawyers rushed to his side. But this time, instead of greeting Brennan with a friendly "Good Morning," Tweed asked wearily: "Must I go to prison tonight?"[38] Brennan took Tweed into custody at the Metropolitan Hotel and rode with him in a carriage down to the Tombs on Centre Street. Here, a judge ordered him held without bail; Tweed only escaped a night in the penitentiary by the good graces of Judge George Barnard who intervened on his behalf. Barnard issued a writ of *habeas corpus*, set bail at $5,000, and allowed the Boss to go home to the Metropolitan Hotel, a tired, sad man.[39]

Just before New Year's Eve, Tammany Hall itself, Tweed's club for twenty years, threw him overboard as well. Weeks earlier, the Tammany Sachems had asked Tweed to resign and save them the trouble, but Tweed had dragged his feet. Now, they met privately, without Tweed even in the room, and voted

THE TAMMANY CHIEFS ON THEIR MARCH TO THE SETTING SUN.

A cartoon by R. Hoyt, one of many artists following Nast's example in satirizing the Tweed Ring.

to replace him as Grand Sachem with banker Augustus Schell. The day before, Tammany's General Committee had met and removed Tweed as its chairman.[40]

It was a remarkable fall. Six months earlier, William Magear Tweed, the Boss of Tammany, had stood at his height, the Monarch of Manhattan, lavished with diamonds, praise, and statues. Now, he'd been reduced to a criminal and a laughing stock, shunned by friends, un-pitied, and losing his fortune. Even poor workmen on the street without a dime turned their backs on him. "What the divil's the use o' stickin' to 'm, whin there's nothin' to stick to," one Irish street laborer was heard saying.[41]

In the cruel, arbitrary world of 1870s America, Tweed had become a marked man, literally a cartoon character—villain and chief swindler, presumed guilty, beyond fairness. There was no place left for him in respectable society.

• PART IV •

Fall

"STONE WALLS DO NOT A PRISON MAKE." —*Old Song*.

"NO PRISON IS BIG ENOUGH TO HOLD THE BOSS."

IN ON ONE SIDE, AND OUT AT THE OTHER.

Harper's Weekly, *December 18, 1875*.

• 18 •
LAW

"It is a great, a splendid and a noble victory, Sir.... Tweed and his gang are doomed. This is only the commencement, and before many days pass it will be made so hot for the arch robber that New-York will not hold him.... We will now see what can be done to have refunded the enormous amounts stolen from the City and County Treasury."

—SAMUEL J. TILDEN, on the election victory of the Apollo Hall reformers over Tammany, November 7, 1871.[1]

"I have got twenty more years of life to live yet. I'm only fifty years of age. Time works wonders, they say, and it will work a change in this. I guess I shall live it all down."

—TWEED, after his first criminal trial, January 31, 1873.[2]

GENTLEMEN, HAVE YOU AGREED to your verdict," Judge Noah Davis asked the twelve men sitting in the jury box of the crowded court of Oyer and Terminer—the criminal trial branch of New York's Supreme Court —on Friday morning, January 31, 1873.[3]

The foreman rose to his feet. "No, sir."

The trial had lasted seventeen days, heard dozens of witnesses, and consumed hours in legal arguments. The jury had been deliberating since the prior afternoon, locked up over night, and taken over forty fruitless ballots. Tweed had come early each day to the Courthouse on Chambers Street though the coldest part of winter; snow clogged the sidewalks and the thermometer at Hudnut's Pharmacy in the *New York Herald* building had dropped to a bone-chilling three degrees the night before. Wearing a dark suit and white tie, he sat surrounded by family, his sons Richard and William Jr. and older brother Richard, and lawyers enough to fill a small jail.

Now, the judge and jurors glared at each other. "Gentlemen, is it likely that, with any little longer time for consideration, you can agree?" Judge Davis looked more sad than angry in his crisp black tie and black robes.

"I think not," the foreman said. After a few minutes, he sheepishly sat down.

"Is there any other juror who wished to state anything on the subject?" Juror five stood up and explained that they'd all agreed at 7 am that morning to give up. "I suppose you have exerted the efforts to agree, and I do not see that any benefit can result from keeping you out longer," Davis sighed. "Then you are discharged, gentleman."

A hung jury. Tweed was free, at least for now. He showed little emotion in the courtroom. It had taken a full year since his fall from power for prosecutors to bring him to trial. Grand juries had filed eight separate indictments against Tweed in New York's Court of General Sessions on charges from forgery to corruption to abuse of power to neglect of duty—felonies, misdemeanors, big and small. The whole Tammany gang—Tweed, Sweeny, Connolly, Hall, Garvey, Woodward, Ingersoll, Sweeny's brother James—all stood charged in the scandal, including five indictments against the mayor alone. Tweed's total bail topped $1.5 million.

But he'd beaten the rap.

For Tweed's trial, State Attorney General Francis Barlow had stacked the deck by bringing in two high-priced outside lawyers to argue the prosecution case: Wheeler H. Peckham, forty years old, thin, mustached, son of a sitting New York appeals court judge in Albany and brother of future Supreme Court Justice Rufus W. Peckham, had practiced law in New York City since 1864 and been counsel to the Committee of Seventy. Backing him up was Lyman Tremain, a former district attorney, state attorney general, and speaker of the state assembly. To win a quick conviction, they'd chosen to prosecute Tweed on the easiest charges to prove: the so-called "big" or "omnibus" indictment, a package of 220 counts—"More counts than in a German principality," the judge himself had quipped.[4] The charges stemmed primarily from the 1870 Tax Levy, by now the most heavily audited transaction in history, and centered on two basic violations: that Tweed had neglected his legal duty to "audit" claims for payment from the county (three statutory counts) and that Tweed had been corrupt by abusing his public position (one count). These four counts were then applied to each of fifty-four specific incidents: individual payouts under the Tax Levy package.

Since each violation was only a misdemeanor crime, it demanded a lower standard of proof to a win conviction. But it also carried a smaller penalty: a $250 fine and a jail term up to one year, generally limited to one sentence per indictment. Peckham had had to justify to a skeptical jury why all the fuss over such a small punishment: "We are not here to try any petty question; petty with regard to the consequences," he'd explained in his opening trial statement, but rather "the safety, ... the existence of the institutions under which the community is now organized, and under which we now live."[5] They wanted Tweed convicted and behind bars, and this was the quickest way to get him there.

Then they had the judge, hand-picked for the job. Noah Davis, a thin-lipped, clean-shaven, 54-year-old Republican from upstate Albion, New York, near Buffalo. Davis had long, deep roots in anti-Tammany "reform" politics. He'd sat for ten years as a state judge in Albion before winning election to the United States Congress in 1867. In 1870, he'd come to New York City to join a lucrative law practice and President Ulysses Grant had made him the local United States Attorney. Both as congressman and as federal prosecutor, Davis used every chance to score points with the "reform" crowd. After the 1868 Tammany voting frauds, he'd sponsored legislation in Washington to strip local New York courts of their authority to naturalize new citizens and make immigrants wait six months after taking their oaths before being allowed to vote.[6] He'd joined the New York City Bar Association's executive committee and served alongside Samuel Tilden, Wheeler Peckham, and other anti-Tammany activists.

When the Committee of Seventy decided to offer its own slate of "reform" candidates in November 1872 to capture the city government, it trusted Noah Davis for the empty seat on the state supreme court, making him available to preside over the Tammany trials.[7] They waited until he took office before scheduling the case. Tweed's was Davis' first major trial after the election.

Now, though, Davis and the prosecutors had been blocked. Tweed had hired his own team of top-shelf lawyers to defend against this onslaught. They were led by David Dudley Field, brother of trans-Atlantic Cable leader Cyrus Field. Tall and articulate, Field had made his name in the 1850s by modernizing the state's civil and penal codes, then turned to defending Wall Street moguls like Jay Gould's Erie Railway. Now he lived opposite Samuel Tilden on exclusive Gramercy Park and catered to one of America's richest clienteles. Joining Field at the defense table was John Graham, an experienced trial

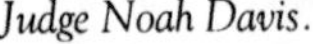
Judge Noah Davis.

Lawyer Wheeler Peckham.

tactician, and six others lawyers including 28-year-old Elihu Root, a future Secretary of War, Secretary of State, and recipient of the Nobel Peace Prize.*

From its start, Tweed's trial had been an eye-catcher. Boss Tweed was an American living legend in 1873. Thomas Nast's *Harper's Weekly* cartoons had made him a national icon, the fat, thieving politician with the diamond pin. Sensational stories had pumped estimates of his Tweed Ring's supposed thefts to $60 million or more, an amount that dwarfed every other scandal in the country's history, be it the Whiskey Ring, Credit Mobilier, or Civil War profiteers. Newspapers touted Tweed's personal fortune at $20 to $25 million[8]—ten times higher than Tweed's own sworn valuation of his property at $2.5 to $3 million at its height. Frontier outlaws like Jesse James and John Wesley Hardin might terrorize the west by robbing trains and murdering townsfolk, but they didn't live like kings in Fifth Avenue mansions. No dime novels appeared to glamorize Boss Tweed. Instead, Nast in his cartoons now portrayed the ex-Boss as a beaten, humiliated oaf sitting amid ruins.

Once the trial began, prosecutors had produced two star witnesses: First came Samuel Tilden, now a rising political celebrity as state legislator and

* Root would be appointed Secretary of War by President William McKinley in 1899 and Secretary of State by President Theodore Roosevelt in 1905. He'd win a seat in the United States Senate after that. His 1912 Nobel Peace Prize recognized contributions to several international treaties plus Root's work as a member of the Permanent Court of Arbitration at the Hague and as President of the Carnegie Institute for International Peace.

likely next governor of New York State. Tilden had seized the chance to appear before the galleries to testify on his now-famous chart tracing over $1 million in county Tax Levy payments directly to Tweed's personal account at the Broadway Bank. Tilden drew unintended laughs when asked in cross-examination if he'd had any "antagonisms" against Tweed. "We haven't sympathized very much," he said. "But I never had any malice toward him." He mentioned his opposition to Tweed's 1870 charter but insisted, "I acted on my own hook—an independent personal hook."[9]

The other surprise witness had been John Garvey, the "prince of plasterers" whose $2.8 million in inflated claims had been a mainstay of the *New-York Times* Secret Account stories. Garvey had fled the country to Switzerland after the disclosures but now, a year later, he'd come back to testify against Tweed and Oakey Hall. Prosecutors had promised him immunity and hadn't asked him to return a penny of his ill-gotten gains. Tweed grew so angry at Garvey at the trial that, during one recess, he'd followed Garvey into a courthouse lobby and loudly chewed him out. Asked about it by reporters, Garvey refused to repeat Tweed's exact words except to say "His language was blasphemous."[10]

Tweed's defense lawyers had called only a handful of witnesses. Instead, they'd relied on logic. No evidence had shown that Tweed had intentionally stolen anything, they argued. His acts were ministerial. Tweed was no auditor and had no ability to look behind the claims presented to him. If anyone was guilty, they explained, it was contractors like Garvey who'd submitted the inflated bills or James Watson, the dead county auditor, who'd prepared the fraudulent paperwork.

The strategy worked. Tweed sat in court each day with his sons looking serene and bored. Asked how he was holding up, he'd whisper "Oh, I feel all right, thank you" or "I'll feel better when it comes my turn to put witnesses on the stand."[11] After Judge Davis had sent the case to the jury, Tweed waited in the Courthouse lobby hobnobbing with reporters and politicos until after 11 p.m. that night, talking with anyone who'd approach him, smiling and shaking hands.

Then, the next morning, the jury had announced its stalemate: no conviction, no acquittal. Within minutes, Peckham, the lead prosecutor, had stood up in the courtroom and voiced his indignation. "We… move the immediate trial of the case again, at the present moment, and ask the court to direct a panel of jurors to be summoned and proceed with the trial." But

Tweed's lawyer David Dudley Field recognized the bravado as pure bluster. He too stood up and addressed the court. "We think, You Honor, this request is novel and remarkable," he said calmly. "We are all exhausted."

The judge agreed reluctantly. Davis had other trials to preside over that winter, including murder cases carrying death penalties. And the prosecutors needed time to assess the damage and lick their wounds.

After court adjourned, Tweed led an entourage of well-wishers out onto the icy sidewalk and up Broadway to his office on Duane Street where he spent the afternoon entertaining them, doubtless opening the old liquor cabinets for a round of drinks and cigars. "I expected an acquittal," he said. "What it was all done for is to harass and persecute me."[12] Most of the talk that day centered on the jury and its stalemate. Prosecutors speculated openly that Tweed must have paid a handful of them to produce the deadlock, though several jurors denied any outside influence. Tweed saw it differently: "I only know what they tell me. What they say is that they stood eleven for acquittal and two for conviction." Reminded that there were only twelve jurors, not thirteen, his blue eyes twinkled. You're forgetting the judge, he said. "I think Judge Davis is a very clever lawyer; but I think he was judge, counsel, witness, jury, and all in this case."

Besides, he said, "It was only a political trial.... I know they will never get a jury to convict me."

◎ ◎ ◎ ◎ ◎

Tweed had spent a painful year waiting for his day in Judge Davis' courtroom. During the months after his fall from power in late 1871, he'd nearly fallen apart. Booted out of Tammany and City Hall, betrayed by friends, humiliated and vilified, his mind and health had collapsed. "I myself was almost exhausted," he later admitted. "The huge personal expense added to the other things kept me under such constant pressure that, as I have said, my brain was threatened."[13]

His career in ruins, Tweed had still come to his Duane Street office most days in early 1872 but rarely showed himself. Glum and sickly, he hid behind lawyers and refused to answer questions. His Americus Club had cancelled its annual January ball that year though it re-elected Tweed the club's president. The *Leader*, the Tammany-sponsored newspaper that had delighted Tweed by backing him until the end, closed its doors in December 1871 when the new Sachems cut off its funding.

Early that January, Tweed had suffered an emotional jolt when his friend Jim Fisk, the chubby playboy prince of the Erie Railway, was shot dead in the Grand Central Hotel by society upstart Ned Stokes after a tawdry, public argument over Fisk's former mistress Josie Mansfield. The assassination had shaken the city, a cold-blooded murder, and certainly made Tweed contemplate the prospect of some deranged gunman taking a shot at him as well. Hearing the news, he'd dropped everything that night and rushed to the hotel room where Fisk lay dying with a bullet in his stomach surrounded by doctors. "Well, William, you have had a great many false friends in your troubles, but I have always stood by you," Fisk had murmured on seeing the Boss. When Tweed asked how he felt, Fisk told him a story: "When you were a boy did you ever run away from school and fill yourself with green apples? I feel just as I used to feel when I filled myself with green apples. I've got a belly-ache."[14] He died the next morning of the bullet wound.

Two months later, Tammany Hall had slapped Tweed again by electing a full slate of new Sachems replete with born-again reformers: Sam Tilden, Charles O'Conor, and Horatio Seymour, all men who'd happily dance on his grave. "Tammany don't amount to anything now," Tweed could only grumble about his old club.[15] "I am not now in politics," he pronounced.[16] He never bothered going to Albany to claim his hard-won seat in the state senate, fearing the legislature would only hit him with charges and investigations.

Humiliation had taken a toll on Tweed's family as well. As he waited in New York for lawsuits and indictments, his wife Mary Jane ran out of patience. She'd left him to cross the ocean for an extended tour that summer in Europe, far from the local hysteria and her disgraced husband. She brought along their son William Jr. and his family. Tweed claimed later that the trip cost him a small fortune, $30,000, coming on top of legal bills and shrinking investments. He'd already transferred virtually all his real estate to his son Richard who now owned his Fifth Avenue home, his Duane Street office, his carriage, his upstate farm and his yachts. Tweed kept only a few land parcels in Queens and Putnam counties.[17] To raise cash, he'd even put the top story of his Duane Street office up for rent.

With money tight and friends scarce, he had to ask his son Richard to help keep him out of jail by becoming his bondsman for $1.2 million worth of bail; Jay Gould had withdrawn from Tweed's bond in November after prosecutors had threatened to interrogate him under oath about his Erie Railway financial schemes.[18]

Nast's "Finger of Scorn" following A. Oakey Hall.
Harper's Weekly, *January 4, 1873.*

All that year, Tweed could only watch helplessly as reformers tore apart his political machine. Oakey Hall had managed to finish his term as the city's mayor, but only after surviving an impeachment attempt* and two criminal trials. Prosecutors had presented no evidence in either of the mayor's trials tracing city funds to him as Tilden had done with Tweed or showing that Hall knew that the warrants he'd signed were frauds, the same problem of crimi-

* The complicated impeachment affair on New Year's Day 1872 pitted the outgoing board of alderman—defeated in November voting—against the new incoming "reform" board. The old board voted to impeach Hall that day in order to appoint a new mayor who would, in turn, reappoint them and thus block the new "reform" alderman from taking their seats. Hall, however, frustrated their plan by backing the reformers who promptly rescinded his impeachment. His first criminal trial, in March 1872, had ended in a mistrial when a juror died; his second, in November 1872, had produced a hung jury—five for acquittal, seven for conviction.

nal intent that had frustrated Hall's original grand jury. Still, prosecutors were busily planning a third attempt to put him in front of a jury.

After Elegant Oakey had stepped down from the mayoralty on New Year's Day, 1873, Thomas Nast had produced a *Harper's Weekly* cartoon showing him leaving City Hall followed by a giant hand floating in midair and pointing a finger down from above: "The Finger of Scorn shall follow them, if law (sometimes called justice) can not."[19] Nast would make his "finger of scorn" a regular feature in his cartoons following Hall, Tweed, and the rest. Hall didn't seem to let it bother him, though. In late January that year, he slipped on an icy New York sidewalk and suffered a painful broken leg that crippled him for weeks. Still, he made a joke of it: "I am inundated with ball tickets from around the country, two or three being appropriately in aid of hospitals," he wrote in a letter. "In every way I realize I am like poor France —- disordered— and especially in the Boneypartes."[20]

At the same time, Tweed saw Samuel Tilden use his new perch in the Albany legislature to destroy Tweed's judges, long a pillar of his New York power. In quick order, Tilden had led the state assembly in bringing charges against George Barnard, John McCunn, and Albert Cardozo, demanding impeachment of each. Cardozo resigned after a long hearing.* McCunn died of heart failure a few days after being unanimously ejected from the bench in July, with only Tweed and Jimmy O'Brien absent from the vote. The state senate convicted Barnard after a five week trial in August on charges of favoritism, conspiracy with Jay Gould and Jim Fisk, and conduct unbecoming a judge. His 1871 betrayal of Tweed by granting the reformers their original anti-Ring injunction won him no sympathy now.[21]

Meanwhile, Tweed saw the public treating his enemies as heroes, saviors of civic morality for having toppled his Ring. Thomas Nast ranked first among equals in this pantheon. His *Harper's Weekly* cartoons had made him a national celebrity. Nast had visited Washington, D.C. in February 1872 and received a royal welcome. President Ulysses Grant himself had led the applause by inviting him to an intimate family dinner in the White House. Nast savored the limelight. "I had a very pleasant chat with [the president] about everything in general, and I was very much pleased with the open way in which he spoke to me," he wrote home to his wife Sarah that week. "Every-

* Cardozo's son Benjamin, two years old at the time, would overcome the family scandal; President Herbert Hoover would appoint him in 1932 to the United States Supreme Court for the seat vacated by Oliver Wendell Holmes.

body knows me, everybody is glad to see me, everybody thanks me for the work I did during the Tammany war."[22] Nast visited Capitol Hill where leaders invited him to step out onto the House and Senate floors. He dined with House Speaker James G. Blaine and Vice President Henry Wilson and heard flattery from dozens of senators and cabinet members eager to see their faces in his cartoons.

In New York City, voters had elected William Havemeyer, the seventy-year-old former sugar merchant who'd co-chaired the reform Committee of Seventy and pressed Slippery Dick Connolly to surrender his Comptroller's Office to reformers, their new mayor to replace Oakey Hall.* And Jimmy O'Brien too would soon enjoy his reward for leaking the Tammany Secret Accounts to the *New-York Times*: a seat in the United States Congress.

Tweed's topplers literally fought over the franchise. When Samuel Tilden at one point appeared to claim too much credit, the *New-York Times* scolded him for blowing his own horn. "[Tilden] denounced [Tweed only] when it was no longer dangerous to denounce," it proclaimed in late 1872, reminding readers of Tilden's silence through much of the fight. "Just at present it is a comparatively comfortable thing for… Mr. Tilden… to throw mud on the grave of the Tammany Ring." Instead, the *Times* took credit for having challenged the Boss at his height. "Mr. Tilden was throughout this period as quiet as a mouse," it claimed. "He cut loose [from Tammany] in the very nick of time to save his own reputation."[23]

Tilden, cultivating his own rising prospects, jumped at the chance to respond by scribbling out a fifty-two page dramatic narrative detailing his own heroics in the fight, called "*The New York City 'Ring:' Its Origin, Maturity and Fall*." He blanketed the state and country with copies.[24]

Tweed, the arch-villain, couldn't escape being made an issue even in the oddball 1872 presidential campaign that pitted President Grant running for reelection against Horace Greeley, the eccentric *New York Tribune* publisher running as a "Liberal Republican" (Republicans who considered Grant too corrupt) and Democrat.** Republicans turned reality on its head by claim-

* Havemeyer would die of heart failure after less than eleven months in office, catching a bad chill after walking two and a half miles on a cold day after his train had stalled during a visit to Long Island.

** Rounding out this peculiar field were Tilden's friend Charles O'Conor, who put aside his role in the Tammany prosecutions to run for president as a "Straight-Out Democrat" (Democrats who refused to accept Greeley) and Victoria Woodhull, candidate of the People's Party, the first women to seek the White House.

ing a connection between Greeley and Tweed and smearing him over it, ignoring Greeley's years' of fighting Tammany voting abuses long before Nast or George Jones ever got involved. Not only had Greeley accepted Tammany support in the 1872 campaign, but Republicans dug up evidence that he'd once invested in a business venture, "The Tobacco Manufacturers Association," that included Tweed as a partner. They used it mercilessly to whip the Sage of Chappaqua.[25]

Nast turned loose his talented *Harper's Weekly* pencil to crucify Greeley in cartoons that portrayed him and Tweed as bosom buddies: In "The Cat's Paw," he showed Tweed the cat holding Greeley the kitten in full embrace. In "Save me from my tobacco Partner," he placed Tweed peering over Greeley's shoulder as a grinning cigar-store Indian in front of the "Tweed, Greeley, Sands, & Co. Tobacco and Snuff Factory" while a policeman carries "Warrants for Arrest of all the Tammany Ring Thieves," as if Greeley were one of them."[26]

"I have been so bitterly assailed that I hardly know whether I have been running for the Presidency or from the Penitentiary," Greeley wrote in a letter shortly after losing the vote.[27] He died a few weeks later.

As the world turned around him, Tweed could only sit and wait for his day in court: "the biggest club in New York could not drive him away," his lawyer John Graham assured reporters after one of the endless rumors of Tweed's imminent flight.[28] He waited for a full year, until January 1873 when finally it came. Now, having survived the seventeen-day trial in Judge Noah Davis' courtroom and having escaped conviction, he saw a ray of light. The state's $6.3 million civil suit against him had come up in Albany and Tweed's lawyers had managed to stop it in its tracks as well, tangling it up in legal appeals over jurisdiction.[29] Tweed could win this fight after all. He seemed to find a new lease on life, even though the verdict, a hung jury, meant that prosecutors could try him all over again.

Feeling free and vindicated, Tweed decided to travel. He left New York City in April 1873, two months after the trial, and headed east to Boston with his wife Mary Jane and two of their children. Then he went to Chicago. In the summer, he visited California. One published report that spring placed him as far away as Ontario, Canada, supposedly preparing to sail to Europe. Instead, each time, Tweed surprised critics by coming home back to New York City.[30]

He spent languid days that summer at the Americus Club on Connecticut's Indian Harbor enjoying its panoramic vistas of the Long Island Sound and afternoons at his Greenwich estate tending his garden: vines, figs, and flowers. For privacy, he'd built a fence around the Greenwich property complete with iron gate and two iron dogs. The thoroughbred horse "Boss Tweed" still won two-mile races at Jerome Park in the Bronx but Tweed himself never showed his face there. In July, his 81-year-old mother, Eliza, died; she'd been living in an old home on East Broadway where Tweed visited her every week but kept her ignorant of the scandal.

In the fall, he took time even to comment on politics, spouting opinions as if he still held power at Tammany. Republicans had lost badly at the polls that year after the October collapse of Philadelphia's Jay Cooke & Company, the country's richest private banker, sparking a massive financial crisis. The "Panic of 1873" had forced the New York Stock Exchange to halt trading for ten days, hundreds of firms to declare bankruptcy, and thousands to lose jobs. "[B]read and butter is one of the most potent questions in politics," Tweed lectured like a professor when asked, "and when I had any influence that question always received my earnest consideration."[31]

If Tweed relished his freedom, perhaps he recognized its transience. Prosecutors and reformers recoiled at the spectacle of the criminal Tweed as a free man, prancing about the country, flouting his wealth, speaking his views. Lawyers and politicians who'd built their "reform" careers on denouncing him found it an embarrassment; Tweed's freedom only exposed their own failure to convict him. Their defeat in Judge Davis' courtroom the prior January only whetted their appetites for a second or even a third attempt to put him behind bars. Wheeler Peckham openly complained that he'd lost the first trial only because the jury had been "corrupt."[32]

In February, a new grand jury brought four more indictments against Tweed, Connolly, Woodward, and Ingersoll, forcing Tweed to appear before Judge Noah Davis yet again to plead his innocence. By November, the prosecutors were ready for a second bite at the apple.

* * * * *

Tweed's second criminal trial began almost ten months to the day after he'd escaped the first on a hung jury. Judge Noah Davis presided again, having just completed the trial of Ned Stokes for the murder of Tweed's friend Jim Fisk. The jury had convicted Stokes of manslaughter and Davis had sentenced him to four years in the state prison at Sing Sing. For Tweed's case, the courtroom again buzzed with excitement, jammed with newspaper men from across the country, teams of expensive lawyers, and hordes of curiosity seekers.

This time, though, things turned sour from the outset. On the first day in court before the trial had even begun, Tweed's lawyers launched a radical strike. They handed Judge Davis a petition charging him with bias and requesting he disqualify himself from the case. Davis had formed an "unqualified and decided opinion unfavorable to the defendant," they argued, and could not preside over a fair trial.[33]

The strategy backfired. The petition's last-minute timing made it look like a cheap delay tactic and a personal smear of the judge. Davis glowered with anger. "[S]ome of its statements are entirely inconsistent with the truth," he snapped in open court, glancing at the document for the first time. "One statement is entirely untrue." Apparently flustered, he recessed the court for an hour to confer with other judges, then came back and took a hard line: "I shall proceed with the case," he insisted, because "self-respect" demanded it, but he reserved the right "to vindicate the dignity of the court and the profession itself from what I deem a most extraordinary and unjustifiable proceeding."[34] But he refused even to discuss the bias issue until *after* the trial.

This left Tweed's lawyers in a painful box; the judge's anger at the perceived insult now threatened to shade their every step during the trial. Lawyer John Graham begged Davis for a chance to explain the petition. "I ask that you give me an opportunity to show that our facts are true," he argued. "You leave us through the whole trial under an imputation which we feel to be utterly unjust."

"No, Sir," Davis ruled.

Failing that, Graham asked the judge at least to allow Tweed to select a new team of lawyers who hadn't offended him. "We fear that it will injure our client," added lawyer Willard Bartlett.

This too Davis denied. "The trial must proceed." There would be no explanations, no substitutes, no delays. Tweed would have to live with the result. "I will give no time to counsel to mutiny against their client."[35]

It then took seven days to choose a jury, twelve men in New York City who could credibly claim impartiality on the subject of Tweed. Dozens had to be rejected, including fourteen on the first day alone, most for admitting to be biased in the case. Charges of jury tampering erupted almost immediately: Peckham had hired four Pinkerton detectives to shadow the jurors, prospective jurors, and even Tweed's brother Richard around the courthouse to prevent foul play, and he'd assigned lawyers to investigate each potential juror for hints of prejudice.[36] Tweed's lawyers, in turn, hired their own detectives to shadow the Pinkertons—sleuths trailing sleuths. On the sixth day of jury selection, one of the Pinkertons reported something suspicious: He had followed the jurors on a lunch break and seen juror eight, a man named Ellis H. Lubry, speak briefly with Police Captain Walsh after he'd seen Walsh talk privately with Tweed, then seen Walsh talk privately to Tweed again. Walsh took the witness stand and insisted the detectives had made a mistake, that he was personal friends with Lubry and Tweed both and hadn't discussed the case at all, but Davis quickly dropped Lubry from the panel.[37]

At the same time, for the final jury seat, Davis approved a man named John Calvin Lloyd who openly admitted bias. Asked if he thought Tweed and his gang guilty, he'd said "Some of them were undoubtedly guilty," and he acknowledged a prejudice against Tweed "on account of his moral character."[38]

The actual trial took just four days to complete as prosecutors repeated mostly the same testimony from the first trial, only more briefly. At issue was the same "omnibus" indictment with 220 misdemeanor counts. Witnesses included clerks from the Comptroller's Office and the Broadway Bank. Sam Tilden made a return appearance to explain his famous chart. J. McBride Davidson, a safe maker, described submitting false bills to the county through auditor James Watson and contractor John Keyser, also home with immunity, explained his Tax Levy warrants. Prosecutors chose not to re-call plasterer Andrew Garvey, fearing Tweed's lawyers would embarrass him on cross-examination, but instead they produced Garvey's brother John who recounted a conversation two years earlier where Tweed told him it would be better for him if John's brother Andrew stayed away in Europe.*

Tweed's lawyers called just three defense witnesses, including Bill Copeland, the clerk who'd copied the original Secret Account disclosures that ended up in the *New-York Times*. Copeland acknowledged that he'd never seen Tweed sign any of the warrants.

Judge Davis gave the case to the jury late Wednesday night, November

---

* Andrew Garvey earlier had claimed that C. Hennessey Cook, a Tweed aide at the Public Works Department, had threatened to kill him if he testified against the Boss, and claimed this was the main reason he had fled the country during the scandal, rather than fear of his own prosecution for fraud. "The job has been put up and I am to do it," he had Cook saying. "There won't be any pistol or noose, but you will be got out of the way so that nobody won't know." The story has no corroboration. Cook had left the country by this point and could not deny it. Given Garvey's own indictment for forgery, it should be taken with a large grain of salt.[39]

19. He read aloud his final instructions by the light of candles placed in empty beer bottles on his desk to supplement the gas chandeliers on the ceiling. Tweed waited in the courtroom until after midnight as the jurors deliberated. Reporters described him as jittery and restless, jumping up and down, holding brief whispered talks. When the judge adjourned the court at 3 am, Tweed went home for a few hours' sleep but appeared again early the next morning with his son William Jr. When Judge Davis called the jurors in at 10 am to check on their progress—they'd been locked up overnight to work—they reported they still hadn't reached a verdict and asked Davis to explain one of the legal counts in the indictment. Then they retired for more talks.

Forty-five minutes later the jurors came back. "How say you, is William M. Tweed guilty or not guilty?" Davis' clerk, a Mr. Sparks, asked them. This time, they had an answer. The foreman stood at his chair. "Guilty," he said, "guilty on all four of the counts." He handed the clerk a list:

"Guilty–1,2,3,4 counts.
"Davidson accounts–Counts 213 to 216, inclusive.
"Garvey Accounts–Counts 37 to 60, 69 to 100, 122 to 200.
"Keyser Accounts–Counts 1 to 36, 61 to 68, 100 to 112, 113–116, 117–123."

Judge Davis quickly deciphered this complex formula to mean that the jury had convicted Tweed on fifty-one of the fifty-four items in the indictment, each with four subparts: 204 counts altogether. He polled them to confirm their unanimity, then he let them go: "Gentlemen of the Jury: You have had a very arduous work… The Court feels bound in discharging you to tender you thanks for the attention you have paid and for the anxious manner apparent to do your whole duty in this case. You are discharged."[40]

After the jurors had left their box, Davis then asked the sheriff, Matthew Brennan, who had arrested Tweed originally two years earlier, now to take Tweed into custody again and hold him until Saturday—three days later—when lawyers would return to argue procedural motions and Davis would pronounce his sentence. Then he gaveled the court adjourned.

Tweed looked pale as Brennan led him out through a side door and down a corner stairway to Chambers Street to avoid crowds in the corridors and on the sidewalks. A reporter described Tweed, his son and his son-in-law Arthur Maginnis as in tears. A carriage whisked them away to Tweed's office on Duane Street. After some time alone with his family, Tweed left the building and rode up Broadway to see his lawyer John Graham, then he spent the night at his son's home on Fifth Avenue, formerly his own mansion. As a convict under Sheriff Brennan's custody, two deputies dogged his every step. They even stayed in Tweed's bedroom at night as he slept, refusing to leave him unguarded.

Thursday morning, Tweed left his son's home at 10 am, rode to Duane Street and stayed in his office until 7 p.m. before going home; messengers brought him breakfast from Delmonico's restaurant. An "intimate friend" described the Boss as being in "excellent spirits" as he worked through the day arranging for possible time in jail, transferring more properties to his son Richard and, through Richard, to his daughter-in-law Eliza, William Jr.'s wife. Friday he spent at his lawyer's office again preparing for the case.

On Saturday, Tweed returned to Judge Davis' courtroom along with the two deputies and his sons. As he reached the doorway to the crowded chamber, Sheriff Matthew Brennan pulled him aside privately, looked him in the eye, and took his hand: "I hope you will bear up, Bill," he said.[41]

"Ah, I have tried to bear up, Matt. I never thought it would come to this."

As Tweed entered the courtroom, a reporter noted how Tweed had changed just in the past few days since the conviction: "Physical and mental prostration marked his step, his carriage and his look; there was no bravado and no cringe."[42] Tweed took his seat quietly, no greetings, no handshakes. As lawyers jousted over opening arguments, Tweed shifted his hands, crossing them, dropping them, swinging them at the wrist, reaching into his pockets, gripping the wooden chair arms.

Prosecutor Lyman Tremain, a tall, plump man, then rose to his feet and addressed the judge. It was time for Davis to impose sentence. Tremain's proposal jolted the room. Rather than asking for a single penalty of $250 in fines and a year in jail—the maximum for a misdemeanor—he asked instead that Judge Davis impose separate sentences for each of 102 separate offences based on the 204 counts on which the jury had found Tweed guilty. That would produce a total punishment of more than a hundred years behind bars and a fine of over $25,000.

Tweed had expected it—Tremain had hinted at the unusual request on Wednesday—but hearing the words spoken out loud hit a nerve. His face turned pale; he held his head in his hand. "Your motion is perfectly startling," his lawyer John Graham argued, jumping to his feet. This abrupt, surprise change in the ground rules put the entire trial under false pretenses, he argued: "That we should have been [sitting] upon a volcano like this from the beginning [and] that the jury should have been kept in utter ignorance of the fearful consequences that were to follow from its action."[43] He quoted Wheeler Peckham's own opening statement from the first trial where Peckham explained the basis of the small single penalty and Judge Davis' own holding then that "there can be but one single judgment" in the case.

When prosecutors stuck to their point, Graham became emotional. "Your Honor, we are taught, from the time we enter this world, to ask for mercy; and those prayers which we put up in our own behalf must teach us to render deeds of mercy to….."[44] He stopped in mid-sentence.

Noah Davis would have none of it, though. He'd been waiting over a year for his chance to send Tweed to prison and wasn't about to lose it now. Sitting stiffly at the bench in his black tie and black roles, his cheeks turned red, he heard the arguments and brushed Graham's points aside. The lawyer's quotes from him and Peckham had come from the first trial, not the second, and he had researched the point again in the meantime. Any misunderstanding by jurors on the issue "could have no legitimate effect even if expressed."[45]

"Mr. Tweed, stand up," the judge's clerk finally insisted. Tweed rose at his chair. "William M. Tweed, have you anything to say why sentence of the Court should not be passed upon you?" Tweed, perhaps confused—he hadn't spoken a word out loud during the trial—held his tongue as lawyer Graham interrupted: "Nothing… he has spoken through his counsel."

As Tweed continued standing, Judge Davis now began speaking, his eyes focused on the defendant, referring to pages of notes. "William M. Tweed, you stand convicted by the verdict of an intelligent and honest jury of the large number of crimes charged against you in this indictment," he began, building momentum as words tumbled off his tongue. "Holding a high public office, honored, and respected, by a large class of the community in which you lived, and, I have no doubt, beloved by your associates, you… saw fit to pervert the powers with which you were clothed, in a manner more infamous, more outrageous than any instance of a like character which the history of the civilized world contains."

As Davis continued this lashing, he tone noticeably shifted: "he grew red and excited, uttered his words with strong emphasis, and struck his clenched fist on the desk," one reporter wrote.[46] Tweed stood at his place the whole time. The judge's oration lasted thirty-one minutes; in it, he accused Tweed of "defiance" merely for acting calm during the trial. Reporters noted how Tweed straightened himself to stare back in Davis' face, at times gripping both his hands to the back of a chair. "Few honest men could have looked as honest," one wrote of him at that moment.[47]

"It is the duty of this court to pronounce upon you a sentence that may be in some degree adequate to your crime," Davis finally concluded.[48] He now explained his own complicated math for setting a sentence. He specified fifty-one of the 102 counts on which Tweed had been convicted and fined him the maximum $250 on each—$12,750 altogether—plus three other counts on which he fined him six cents each. At the same time, he specified twelve groups of guilty counts on which to base a jail term of twelve years, triple the term he'd recently given Ned Stokes for murdering Jim Fisk. Because the crimes were misdemeanors, he ordered that Tweed serve his time in the city penitentiary on Blackwell's Island, a place no less notorious than the state prison at Sing Sing.

Then, before adjourning the court, he announced plans to settle one other score. He ordered Tweed's lawyers to return to his chambers the following Monday to address their earlier charge that Davis was biased. Davis hadn't forgotten it. He'd give them all a tongue-lashing, charge them with contempt, and fine three of them $250 apiece.[49]

Sheriff Matthew Brennan led Tweed from the courtroom out a side door to a private nearby lobby where Tweed stood shaken with his sons and brother. One reporter described him as "utterly broken," despondent and tired;[50] another wrote how Tweed hid his face in his hands and wept.[51] They left him alone some time, then guards brought him downstairs to Sheriff Brennan's private office to wait while his lawyers scoured the city, still hoping to find a judge willing to intervene and stop the proceeding. At one point, they arranged for dinner to be sent over from Delmonico's restaurant. As Tweed picked at his food, his mind wandered and he thought of Slippery Dick Connolly, his former comptroller who'd deserted him to the reformers and fled to France. "Dick is living in clover on $3,000 a year, and he is the cause of all this trouble and ought to be where I am," he muttered.[52]

After a while, Tweed recovered his composure enough to grumble at the judge who'd just sentenced him to over a decade behind bars. When a reporter slipped into the room and asked him about it, Tweed blasted it as "pretty severe" and Davis' attitude as unprofessional. "I can't help my looks, but I know I didn't cry; but I never felt defiant," he said. "He had no business to keep me standing all that time to be lectured; his duty was to pass sentence and no more."[53]

Tweed napped on the couch as the clock ticked past midnight. Finally, at 1 am, the sheriff told him it was time to go to jail. A crowd still jammed the sidewalks outside on Chambers Street at that hour, still hoping for a glimpse of the ex-Boss. Deputies twice had sent empty carriages with shades drawn rushing off into the night trying to trick them into leaving. Now, they led Tweed to a corner of the building where lights had been darkened and two carriages had pulled up to the entrance. Tweed stepped out into the night and scampered across the sidewalk and entered the front carriage, which he shared with his brother, the sheriff, and one of his lawyers. After a short ride through the bumpy cobblestone streets, they reached the Tombs, the city jail. They led Tweed inside through the iron front gate. Here, Tweed happened to spot a familiar face, a watchman he knew from the neighborhood. He stopped to shake the man's hand. "John, how are you? I never expected to meet you here like this."[54]

"Yes, Mr. Tweed, I am sorry," the man answered, shaking his head.

The night warden was caught unaware by the arrival of his new celebrity inmate. He'd assumed that Tweed would be taken to the jail on Ludlow Street to hold him until his transfer to Blackwell's Island. He had them wait in a hallway while a cell was prepared. Finally, Tweed shook hands with his son and then followed the warden past sleeping convicts through the jail's lower tier. They stopped at cell six, a dark, narrow cave with cement floor and iron bed that smelled from thirty-five years of urine, sewage, and despair. Here, the warden locked Tweed inside. Exhausted, he slept soundly on his first night in jail.

• 19 •
PRISON

"The reporters did this."

—TWEED, on reading newspaper coverage in his cell in the Tombs, the morning after his sentencing by Judge Davis. November 24, 1873.[1]

THE TOMBS, BUILT IN 1838 on landfill over a swamp, got its name from its odd architectural design, based on a photograph of an ancient Egyptian crypt. Its stone basements had long ago sunk in the mud causing walls to crack. Foul sewage smells permeated the lower floors; disease, lice, rats, and filth thrived in the dampness. Obsolete and overcrowded, the prison contained two hundred narrow cells that often held two or three prisoners apiece, including fifty reserved for women. Most inmates lived on starvation diets: dinners of bread and tea, breakfasts of bread and coffee, and a bowl of soup for lunch. Cigars, tobacco, or fruit could be purchased only through a black market at twice their normal value.

For Tweed, Sunday in this depressing dungeon seemed a virtual reprieve. He spent the day in his cell reading newspapers and writing a long letter to his wife. When Sheriff Brennan came to visit and asked how he felt, he said: "as well as I can be under the circumstances. I am cold."[2]

By Sunday night, the warden had moved Tweed into a larger room in the front of the building, heated and furnished with a bed, chairs, and a green carpet; he even had a broken window fixed for his new guest. Tweed, able to spend his own money on comforts, arranged to have meals delivered from Matron Foster's Restaurant, a popular nearby haunt, rather than touch the prison's food. His wife Mary Jane and daughter Josephine both came to visit along with his son William Jr., brother Richard, and former private secretary Foster Dewey. Tweed asked the warden to keep newspaper reporters away from his distraught family, and the warden agreed.

Rather than a quick stop *en route* to Blackwell's Island, though, Tweed ended up spending a full week in the Tombs. Sheriff Brennan decided to wait before moving him, both to give Tweed's lawyers a chance to find a friendly judge to intervene and to give "the old man" time to prepare. Matthew Brennan had never been close with Tweed during their Tammany hay-day, but now he showed concern. Brennan even joined Tweed in jail on Thanksgiving Day to share roast turkey with Mary Jane, the older Tweed children, and lawyer John Townsend. Tweed's plight became a popular theme for Sunday church sermons all over the city and country, an object lesson in sin: "The sight or thought of William M. Tweed in a convict's dress will do more to enlighten the men who most need the enlightenment," the *New York World* opined.[3]

Religion aside, though, city fathers had little charity for the former Boss. Reports of his sentimental Thanksgiving family dinner set tempers flaring. The next day, District Attorney Francis C. Barlow sent Brennan a blistering note scolding him for his leniency, accusing him of "violation of duty." When the sheriff demurred, Barlow issued firm orders: "that William M. Tweed be at once removed to the place of imprisonment designated by the court."*[4]

Brennan made the transfer the next day. Tweed's family came to the Tombs to see him off; Mary Jane and three of his daughters waited with him in a parlor on the Leonard Street side, barely holding back tears. At 2:40 pm, when the order came to move, Tweed held his wife once more and let his son help him put on his coat. They walked together over the "Bridge of Sighs"—the prisoners' name for the corridor connecting their prison cells to the in-house police court—then stepped out onto Centre Street. A few policemen nodded their heads in respect as Tweed walked past. "Here's Tweed!" shouted bystanders waiting on the street to see him. Tweed still drew a crowd, part well-wishers, part vagabonds and street urchins. Deputies had to push them away for Tweed to reach the carriage that carried him through narrow allies to the pier at 26th Street on the East River. Here, they boarded the steam ferry *Bellevue*. "Perhaps I ought to be grateful to [my enemies] for affording me the pleasure of a carriage ride and a sail," Tweed cracked, standing with his son and a few lawyers on board as the boat drifted away from shore and out

---

* No good deed goes unpunished, and Brennan would later suffer for his kindness to prisoners. About a month after sending Tweed off to Blackwell's Island, Brennan would take custody of another Tammany-ite, former state senator Henry Genet convicted of stealing government property. When Brennan's deputy allowed Genet a few last liberties, Genet returned the favor by slipping away and escaping to Canada. An angry trial judge punished Brennan and his deputy both by imposing fines of $250 and 30-day sentences in the Ludlow Street Jail.

onto the currents and they watched the squat brick buildings and church steeples of Manhattan recede into the distance.[5]

Blackwell's Island, just 800 feet wide and less then two miles long, sat halfway between Brooklyn and New York, a cold, windswept place. No bridges or telegraph lines connected it to either city; treacherous East River currents swept along both its banks making even the routine boat passage bumpy and dangerous. The city had purchased the island in 1828 as a place to banish undesirables, the sick, the poor, and the insane. It now held a prison, an almshouse, and hospitals for contagious diseases like smallpox. Its stone quarry, worked by convicts from the penitentiary, had produced materials to build one of the hospitals and the new lighthouse on its northern tip. The Charity Hospital alone held 763 patients including some 150 quarantined with fevers and twelve diagnosed with smallpox; the Lunatic Asylum held another 1,400 inmates.[6]

Reaching the Island, Tweed looked down at the dirt while crossing the gangway. He embraced his son William Jr. one last time before a sheriff's deputy led him to the penitentiary and delivered him to Warden Joseph Liscomb. Liscomb had promised newspaper reporters that he'd treat Tweed just like any of the four hundred other inmates under his change, including nine he punished by having iron balls chained to their legs. A guard sat Tweed down and asked him to state his name and age. Tweed gave his age as 50 years old, his profession as "statesman," his religion as "none" though he explained that his relatives were Protestants. They measured his weight at 268 pounds then took him to the barber to shave off his beard and crop his hair, then gave him a bath. They took away Tweed's clothes and gave him a convict's uniform to wear: striped pants, shirt, cap, and a "larceny jacket," though none properly fit over Tweed's large body. A prison doctor examined him and pronounced Tweed fit enough to live in one of the prison's cells, each being seven feet long and 3-and-a-half feet wide with stone floor, iron bedstead, and a small grated iron door.

Tweed's own personal physician had sent a note suggesting he be placed instead in the prison hospital, noting his recent shocks, delicate condition and history of apoplexia-anguinea, but the doctor disagreed. Instead, they moved him into cell 34 on the second tier, then left him alone.

Tweed slept badly the first night. His body didn't fit in the tiny cot, a bare iron frame with stretched canvas and no mattress. He suffered chronic diarrhea, shivers, and prostration. He breakfasted on the standard coarse bread and coffee and spent the day inside his cell with William Jr., his only visitor. Occasionally he stood at the cell's door, head bowed. "You have brought me here to die," he told one official who examined him.[7]

The second day, Tweed's personal physician, Dr. Schirmer, came to see him and again argued to move him to the prison hospital. That night, the prison doctor reexamined him and agreed. Warden Liscomb ordered Tweed moved. There were rumors that Tweed had only hours to live. Myer Stern, a member of the Charities and Corrections Commission that oversaw the prison, visited the Island that day and gasped at Tweed's condition. "Tweed would have been killed in forty-eight hours" without a change, he later claimed.[8]

Rules demanded that all prisoners on Blackwell's Island do forced labor; most convicts worked in the stone quarry, the carpentry shop, the shoe shop, or the bakery. Some served as nurses in the Lunatic Asylum. For Tweed, they now assigned work as an orderly at the prison's hospital, which would allow him to eat and sleep with the sick prisoners, a sharp improvement from his cramped cell. The hospital occupied a large room on the prison building's fourth floor; it held seventeen patients on two rows of cots, with two desks, cases of medicine, a window facing the city and a hot stove.

The change suited Tweed. Here, he would work under direction of the doctor and a senior orderly; his duties included changing patients' bandages, giving them medicines, keeping their records and keeping them company. His spirits lifted over the next few days and his health returned. He fell into a pattern: He woke each morning at 6:30 am and enjoyed the freedom of the orderly room. Making the best of prison life, he soon managed to win some privileges. Warden Liscomb began to trust him; perhaps he enjoyed hearing Tweed tell stories of backroom politics from the city. He sympathized with Tweed's age, his bad health and soft living, things that made him different from the other inmates. After a few weeks, he allowed Tweed to move into a private room in the prison's center building where officials stayed. The room was sparse but it had a bed, desk, chairs, and a window.

Commissioner Stern, for his part, began giving passes to Tweed's sons William Jr. and Richard and his private secretary Foster Dewey so they could visit him regularly, despite prison rules that generally limited visits to once a month. Tweed's wife Mary Jane came too, every ten days or so. Tweed had hardly been the best husband to her during their twenty-eight year marriage. It's not unlikely he was unfaithful to her, given his long trips to Albany and his high-living style. Still, he'd kept any affairs highly discreet; rumors of mistresses remained rare and unproven despite hostile newspapers hungry for slander against him. She stayed loyal to him now, even if her own health had begun to break under the stress. A degenerative eye disease was starting to steal her vision. In a few years, she'd be functionally blind.

All Tweed's visitors brought him newspapers so he could follow events in the world from his solitary island. That December, as Tweed adjusted to the penitentiary, he read that Oakey Hall, the only one of his old Ring cohorts who'd stayed in Manhattan and faced his accusers, had won an outright acquittal in his third criminal trial. A jury had found him "not guilty," issuing its verdict on Christmas Eve and sparking celebrations in the courtroom, cheers shouted and hats thrown in the air. Well-wishers had mobbed Hall as he crossed the snowy sidewalk to his carriage; congratulations poured in from respectables like Peter Cooper and Henry Ward Beecher who weeks earlier had treated him like a leper.

With Elegant Oakey now exonerated and free, Tweed found himself the only Ring member being punished. His name had been blackened far beyond the others. Even behind bars, he caused controversy. When another Charities and Corrections Commissioner, Lambeer, came to Blackwell's Island in mid-April for an inspection, he learned of Tweed's living arrangements and acted shocked. He'd seen Tweed with his door open, unguarded, a dozen steps from the exit on the verge of escape, he claimed. "A woman comes [to Tweed's room] in the morning, cleans his room and lights his fire. He boards at the Warden's house. He goes to his breakfast from eight to nine, to his dinner between nine and two, and to his supper between five and six," Lambeer told newspaper reporters, and repeated rumors that the prison carpentry shop had produced "costly furniture, tables, aquariums, flower stands, &c.," all for Tweed. "People at the Union League Club told me, 'Why, Tweed lives on the fat of the land,' and I denied it."[9]

"Luxurious treatment!" screamed the newspapers, demanding investigations.

Myer Stern, the commissioner who'd ordered Tweed's original transfer to the prison hospital, had to defend himself from charges of favoritism and whispers of bribery. "The sentence which consigned Tweed to prison did not enjoin us to torture him or to undermine his health," he insisted.[10] He described Tweed's private room as merely a "large cell" justified by the ex-Boss's age, size, and poor health. "William M. Tweed might, in the eyes of his bitterest antagonists deserve no greater consideration than the meanest culprit, the burglar, the highwayman, or the shoplifter, but he certainly is entitled to no less consideration."[11]

After a loud public meeting, the commissioners agreed that Tweed must return to the hospital. But a few days later, when word of the transfer reached the prison, several inmates who'd befriended "the old man" faked having cases of smallpox, causing a panic on the Island and giving Tweed a few more days of comfort.[12]

Two months later, on June 19, Tweed enjoyed his first chance to leave the penitentiary since becoming a prisoner. Foster Dewey, his former private secretary, had filed a lawsuit claiming he'd been cheated on a $1,000 payment he'd made to the Seventh Ward Tweed Association and the lawyers had asked that Tweed come to testify as a witness. Warden Liscomb accompanied Tweed for the passage by rowboat across the East River that morning; a coach carried them to the Courthouse on Chambers Street—the same building where Judge Noah Davis had sentenced him to prison and where Andrew Garvey's frescoes still decorated the ceilings. Crowds gathered on the sidewalk to see the former Boss on his first reprieve in six months. "There he goes." "There's the old man," people said as he walked by. He wore a white straw hat with black band, eyeglasses dangling from a black cord around his neck, his white necktie neatly knotted. Tweed's beard had grown back but now had a ghostly white color. Still, friends noted a healthy, ruddy pink in his cheeks. His smile revealed that he'd lost an upper front tooth. He basked in the attention, shaking hands, waving, winking as he made his way up the courthouse stairs. Inside the judge's chambers, he laughed several times listening to the lawyers' arguments, a novelty after his months of isolation.[13]

Tweed had written a letter to his sister-in-law Margaret, Richard's wife, around this time saying that he got plenty of exercise in prison, ate well, and walked a quarter mile each day. He slept soundly.[14]

When Tweed's turn came to testify, all eyes in the courtroom turned his way. He kissed the bible after taking his oath and spoke quickly. His largely backed Dewey in his testimony,[15] then he lingered in the courtroom after the trial had ended. When the warden led him back outside to the street and a cheer greeted him on the sidewalk, he broke into a grin; an "expression of almost tearful pleasure suffused the face of the fallen chieftain," a reporter noted.[16]

Warden Liscomb took Tweed directly back to Blackwell's Island that day and Tweed returned to his daily hospital work. He'd have to wait six more months for another chance to cross the East River again. By then, he'd served more than a full year behind bars—the legal maximum penalty for a misdemeanor crime—and his lawyers had applied for a *habeas corpus writ* to free him. Judge Noah Davis himself had broken the law, they argued, by imposing a sentence larger than the statutes allowed. Now, they said, Tweed was being held illegally.

The warden again accompanied Tweed across the river for his court appearance, this time taking the steam ferry rather than a rowboat because of cold December winds. Tweed wore a low-crowned felt hat that covered his white hair; friends again commented on his healthy look, how the "enforced regularity of the life and the salubrity of the air on the Island" had agreed with him; gone was the "defiant confidence" that had once defined him.[17]

Tweed's court appearance that day proved inconclusive; the judge, Comstock, deferred action until the next week. The warden took Tweed back to prison but they returned to New York again and Tweed this time entered the court surrounded by ten lawyers including his son, William Jr. Newsmen described him as talking vivaciously with a circle of relatives, politicos, policemen, and clerks while waiting for the judge to start. He read a newspaper as lawyers argued other cases. When his own came up, he snapped to attention, but the hearing again ended inconclusively. Judge Comstock refused to release Tweed but he set the stage for a hearing before the state Court of Appeals in Albany.

Tweed returned to Blackwell's Island that night and he soon spent his second Christmas in prison, enjoying a dinner of corned beef, vegetables, soup and bread served in the prison hospital. A few of the inmates deprived themselves of their meals to save extra portions for "the old man" so he could eat seconds.

⊚ ⊚ ⊚ ⊚ ⊚

The world went on without Tweed. Voters in New York State elected Samuel Tilden their new governor in 1874. Noah Davis, the judge who'd sentenced Tweed to prison, won promotion to chief justice of the state supreme court. Lyman Tremain, the prosecutor who'd recommended Tweed's long sentence, won election to the United States Congress. Each had built his career on the same high-profile credential, his role in punishing the villain now locked away on Blackwell's Island.

Oddly, one of Tilden's first acts as governor was to issue a pardon for James H. Ingersoll, the city contractor whose inflated bills for repairing county armories had dominated the *New-York Times'* original 1871 disclosures. A jury had convicted Ingersoll of felony fraud shortly after Tweed and sentenced him to five years in prison, making him the only other Ring member to see the inside of a penitentiary. Now Tilden had freed him solely on condition that he testify against other defendants. Which ones? With Sweeny and Connolly in Europe and Oakey Hall acquitted, Tweed didn't take long to figure out that he was the only one left.

Tweed's own lawyers stayed busy too. Following his appearance before Judge Comstock in December, they took their case to the Court of Appeals in Albany that would take another six months, until June 15, finally to rule on the merits. Finally, good news for the former Boss: They ruled for Tweed unanimously. Judge Davis had been wrong, they decided. He'd overstepped. Tweed had been tried under a single misdemeanor indictment and could only be sentenced to a single misdemeanor penalty—a $250 fine and one year's imprisonment—despite the fact that the jury had convicted him on 204 individual counts. That meant Tweed should have been released from prison the prior November 22, seven months earlier. They ordered him now released immediately.

The ruling brought a rush of excitement. Foster Dewey, who'd gone to Albany to help Tweed's lawyers on the appeal, was thrilled and ran back to tell the Boss. He took an overnight train from Albany and reached Blackwell's Island by 11 am the next morning. "We have got it!" he shouted, finding Tweed.

Tweed reacted coolly. He'd been disappointed before and, after nineteen months on Blackwell's Island, he'd grown comfortable with the routine—waking early, working in the hospital now as its recording clerk, keeping the books and noting each patient's coming and going, his medications, diagnosis, and progress. "Well, I expected it, but not so soon," he told Dewey,[18] showing little interest in leaving right away.

In fact, Tweed apparently smelled a rat. Samuel Tilden now reigned as governor in Albany with an eye toward a presidential nomination the next year and he had no intention of setting him free. Tilden had made Tweed the centerpiece of his "reform" resume, the reason voters had sent him to Albany in the first place. Tilden had anticipated the Appeals Court ruling and taken precautions. He'd quietly pushed through the Albany legislature a new law, the Public Remedy Act, authorizing the state to sue for funds stolen from local governments. Using it, he'd sent his prosecutors Charles O'Conor and Wheeler Peckham to file a new civil lawsuit against Tweed demanding repayment of $6.3 million—similar to the earlier suits stalled on appeal. They'd brought the case to Judge Noah Davis in New York City. Davis, sporting for a chance to re-engage, had promptly issued new orders for Tweed's arrest, to be executed whenever Tweed was freed from Blackwell's Island, if ever.

Noah Davis had reason to embrace this new line of attack. Having himself been the judge who had issued Tweed's twelve-year prison term, he'd taken the appeals court's reversal personally. Charles O'Conor had wasted no time taunting him over it. In a letter to Davis that month, he described how the decision gave Tweed the "grim satisfaction [of a] public humiliation of the judge who pronounced the illegal sentence."[19] Davis now obliged by setting things straight; he fixed bail on the new lawsuit at $3 million, the largest bail ever yet imposed on any person by any judge in the United States and triple the amount of county funds ever actually traced to Tweed by Tilden's famous chart. And, O'Conor boasted, if they needed to raise it to $5 million to keep Tweed from walking free, they'd happily do so.*

At the same time, as extra insurance, prosecutor Wheeler Peckham convinced the local New York District Attorney, Benjamin Phelps, to apply for a fresh warrant for Tweed's arrest based on an old 1873 indictment charging Tweed with fraudulently obtaining the mayor's signature on one of the original Tax Levy warrants. Around the sheriff's office, old timers spoke nostalgically of Tweed—"He was the best of the lot." or "He stood his imprisonment like a man."—even as they prepared to lock him up again.[20]

Tweed, meanwhile, looked frantically for an exit from the maze. He waited on Blackwell's Island as his lawyer, David Dudley Field, made the rounds in Manhattan trying to find any wealthy soul willing to stand as bondsman for all or part of the $3 million bail. He got cold shoulders wherever he went. Anyone standing with Tweed could expect blistering public criticism plus prosecutors' probing into their personal finances and business affairs—all likely to land in the newspapers. With Tilden as governor, who would want to link themselves to Tweed?

* Bail in American courts today is limited today almost exclusively to criminal cases, not civil lawsuits, and while failure to pay a civil judgment today can result in bankruptcy, it is not a cause for imprisonment. Debtors' prisons in America generally were phased out a century ago. Under modern practice, the state's entire plan to keep Tweed locked away by setting unreachable bail on civil cases would be invalid.

The prosecutors, taking no chances, now sent a deputy sheriff to Blackwell's Island to take Tweed into custody immediately on his release. Finally, on June 23, a full week after the Appeals Court's ruling, the odd game of musical chairs began. The warden ordered Tweed to be freed. He sent word to the prison hospital late that night after other inmates had gone to sleep. Tweed got up from his cot in the dark room, took his packed bag, and followed a guard to the warden's office. Here, they weighed him, measured him, and returned his civilian clothes. Then the deputy, McGonigal, stepped forward and took him into custody. "You are my prisoner, Sir," he told Tweed, to which Tweed replied "Oh, I know that. I'm ready to go with you."[21]

Tweed wore a dark suit as a rowboat carried him and the deputy across the East River through the midnight darkness. In Manhattan, a carriage took them to the home of Tweed's nephew Alfred Sands on East 26th Street to spend the night. The next morning, Tweed and the deputy rode together to the District Attorney's office on Chambers Street in the new Courthouse, Tweed wearing a black coat, blue trousers, white vest and tie. His pocket watch dangled from a black cord across his shirt. He sat on a sofa and drank several glasses of ice water as the lawyers haggled over last-minute details. Friends who hadn't seen Tweed since he'd entered prison nineteen months earlier gasped at the changes in him. He looked weak and fragile now. "His hair has become white," a reporter noted, "his figure, once erect, is now bent. He is still robust, but his corpulency [sic.] appears to be unhealthy."[22] Still, they noted, he "walked briskly and with an upright bearing, now and then nodding smilingly in response to the salutation of some friend."[23]

Tweed took his place in the Court of Oyer and Terminer and stood as District Attorney Phelps asked that he enter pleas on the two latest indictments. His lawyer David Dudley Field objected: Tweed had already pleaded "not guilty" on twenty-two other indictments and he'd had no opportunity to study the newest charges. After some argument, they all returned to the District Attorney's office to iron out details for posting bail: $4,000 for the two new charges and $1,000 each on fourteen older indictments.

Afterward, Tweed led the entourage—his sons, the lawyers, and the deputy sheriff—out into the sunshine on Chambers Street where a crowd of curiosity seekers instantly surrounded them. While waiting for a carriage, Tweed leaned against an iron stair railing and stared blankly into space. They rode the short distance to Tweed's office on Duane Street—a place he hadn't seen in over six months—where deputy sheriff McGonigal now arrested him again on the $6.3 million civil suit and demanded $3 million in bail. This time, Tweed had none to offer.

With his prisoner in custody, they all piled back into carriages again—Tweed, the sheriff, his sons—and rode up Broadway to Delmonico's restaurant where they enjoyed lunch in a private parlor off the main dining room. Then McGonigal and Tweed left the others and stepped outside for the final leg of their journey, the brief ride to Ludlow Street where the jail stood. Here, the warden, William Dunham, had prepared a first floor apartment for the former Boss with a bedroom and sitting room facing the street. He slept well that night; it seemed he only slept well now in jail.

Ludlow Street Jail looked more like a library than a prison with its red brick front, walled-in exercise yard and eighty-seven cells, each with bed, wash-basin, and wide, barred window, placed smack in the commercial district of lower Manhattan next to the Essex Street Market.* Originally designed as a debtors' prison, it now housed both "boarders"—prisoners who paid for their keeping—and non-paying inmates. For fifteen dollars a week, one could eat decent meals at a dining table and sleep in a sparse but comfortable room. Those who couldn't afford it lived upstairs in a ten-foot-by-ten-foot cell, emptied their own slop-pails, and ate by themselves.

Tweed had reason for hope on returning to Ludlow Street, just half a mile from his old boyhood neighborhood and three blocks from what they used to call "Tweed Plaza." His lawyers had filed two new sets of motions to win his freedom: one to reduce his bail from $3 million down to a manageable size and the other to quash the backlog of over thirty indictments hanging over his head. Meanwhile, Tweed asked to be left alone. He refused to see reporters or politicians, limiting his company to his family, his doctor, and his lawyers. He studied the daily newspapers and bristled at one story saying he kept a stock of fine wines to drink behind bars; Tweed claimed he'd stopped drinking altogether on the advice of his doctor.

In late July, though, the picture darkened. Judge Barrett, the latest to hear his legal motions, rejected them all. He refused either to lower Tweed's impossible $3 million bail or to vacate any of the old pending indictments filed since December 1872. Tweed knew that no appeals judge would help him

* Today, it is the site of the Seward Park High School.

now; he'd become too hot to touch. Looking forward, he saw an endless web of prosecutions. Eleven criminal indictments still hung over him in addition to the state's $6.3 million civil suit. If he beat one, they'd only arrest him to face another, with bail set deliberately out of reach. So long as Sam Tilden sat in the governor's mansion with an eye toward the White House, he could expect no mercy. Meanwhile, his lawyers' bills had grown astronomically, nearing $400,000. His losses on real estate topped another $1 million and family expenses were draining him $50,000 per year. At this rate, he'd soon be a pauper. He hadn't been allowed to see his two youngest sons, six-year-old George and ten-year-old Charles, in almost two years.

Oakey Hall, now basking in celebrity as the vindicated ex-mayor, had written a play called *The Crucible* that was set to open in mid-December at the Park Theatre on 22nd Street with Hall himself appearing on stage as an actor playing the lead role: an innocent man named Wilmot Kierton, wrongly convicted of theft. Elegant Oakey played the role well, even off stage. The *New-York Times* now cooed him as a victim: "We do not now believe—much as appearances at first were against him—that he ever shared in the profits of the old Ring Government," it announced in a note on the new play, "and we ... have now no worse wishes for him than that he may win both fortune and fame in his new enterprise."[24]

Only Tweed, it seemed, still deserved the scorn of mankind. Prosecutors seemingly had thrown up their hands on pursuing any of the other Ring members. Tilden as governor had pardoned Ingersoll and made no effort to extradite Sweeny or Connolly from Europe. In October, prosecutors settled with the widow of James Watson, the dead county auditor, for just under $600,000, closing that case as well.

Tweed, in effect, faced spending the rest of his life in prison, dragged from court to court, jail to jail, despite his having been convicted of nothing but a misdemeanor for which he'd already served the sentence. In October, yet another arrest order was issued against him on a newly-filed civil suit demanding $1 million in restitution and prompting an additional $1 million in bail. In November, the state Court of Appeals rejected his lawyers' challenges to the pending $6.3 million civil suit for its lack of a bill of particulars. Even the *New-York Times* began to question why Tweed alone was being punished: "because he is the only leading member of the Ring who has faced the ordeal of the courts," it asked, "[ought he] to be made to bear the punishment due his associates?"[25]

Tweed made the best of things at Ludlow Street Jail. He took a liking to a black prison servant named Louis "Luke" Grant and began paying him to act as a personal aide. Through his window, he could hear the women shopping each day at the Essex Street Market and grew attuned to the neighborhood. During meals, he became friendly with Charles Lawrence, a silk smuggler serving time with him in a nearby room on the jail's first floor. Lawrence had been arrested in England and sent home to stand trial. He fascinated Tweed with his stories of the legal fine points, the fact that some European countries had no extradition treaties with the United States to handle such cases. Tweed decorated his own room with photographs of family members and of his Greenwich estate. He clipped and saved a newspaper drawing of himself entering prison and hung above his bed a silk-sewn tapestry with the motto "In God we Trust." He stocked his desk with papers and filled a shelf with books to read.

Every few weeks, he even convinced the warden to let him leave the jail building and go outdoors, always accompanied by guards. Sometimes they'd take a carriage and ride out into the country around Central Park to walk under trees and stop on the way back to have dinner with his family. The warden had allowed Tweed this privilege at least four times during the summer and fall that year and perhaps as many as seven or more.[26] Sometimes, he son William Jr. would pick him up in his personal carriage and they'd enjoy the outside walk together. Most recently, they'd allowed Tweed to spend Thanksgiving Day at his son's dinner table.

Early in December, Tweed again asked the warden for the chance to go out and the warden agreed, sympathizing with Tweed over his "delicate" health. A neighbor on Ludlow Street remembered seeing them leave the jail at about 1 pm that day, Saturday, December 4, in a new carriage with a folding leather top, William Jr.'s carriage. Along with Warden Dunham and Keeper Edward Hagen, they rode north through the city past Central Park and crossed the Harlem Bridge into the Bronx to enjoy the rural countryside. On the way back they stopped in the park and sat on a hill to talk and stretch their legs. Afterward, they rode back to 60th Street and parked the carriage on the corner with Madison Avenue. From here, they walked down the sidewalk to Tweed's son Richard's house, a four-story brownstone on Madison near 59th Street. They came inside and met Mary Jane, Richard, and Tweed's daughter Josephine and son-in-law Frederick Douglas for a family visit.

Tweed sat in the front parlor by a bay window for over an hour talking to his sons. Then at one point he excused himself to go upstairs for a word with his wife who was sick in bed. By now the hour had turned late, nearly 6:30 pm. The sun had gone down and the streets outside had turned dark. After a few minutes, Warden Dunham asked William Jr. to go upstairs and fetch his father for the trip back to Ludlow Street and jail.

William Jr. disappeared up the stairway and came back a few minutes later. He had a startled look on his face. Father was gone.*

* Joseph Johnson, a former "Big Six" fireman under Tweed, would tell reporters it was "well known" that Tweed's imprisonment on Ludlow Street was "merely nominal" and several of his excursions were "to the residence of a lady in Fifth Avenue, near Thirty-ninth street." The address vaguely matches that of a Mrs. MacMullin, mentioned in similarly unsubstantiated Tweed rumors eighteen months later. But there is no evidence that Tweed enjoyed more than the seven or eight "excursions," or that he visited her on any of them.[27]

• 20 •
ESCAPE

"Now, is it likely I'm going to run away? Ain't my wife, my children, my children's children, and everything and every interest I have in the world here? What would I gain by running away? ..."

—TWEED, after resigning as Commissioner of Public Works, December 29, 1871.[1]

"I shall follow him wherever he may have gone or go; anywhere this side of the infernal regions, for I do not care to follow him there. He must be found, however, and found he will be, either sooner or later, go where he may. Every effort will be made to secure his return to the Court, and, if necessary, the effort will be a lasting one."

—WHEELER H. PECKHAM, prosecutor, on hearing of Tweed's escape, December 4, 1875.[2]

TWEED HAD KEPT HIS PLAN utterly secret. He'd told no one—not his family, not his lawyers, not his friends. He simply disappeared. That evening, as he'd entered his son's house on Madison Avenue escorted by the two Ludlow Street Jail guards, he'd noticed a mark on the stoop at the front door. This was his signal. All through dinner he hid his nervousness by overeating and telling stories. Then, afterward, he slipped away, took a hat and coat from the rack, and stepped out the front door. He hid in a shadow by the street until a covered wagon drove up at precisely 8 o'clock, the agreed time. On its signal, Tweed hesitated, then climbed inside.[3]

The wagon pulled away from the curb onto Madison Avenue but, before going far, the driver pulled it to a stop. A crowd of people had blocked the road; a streetcar had gone off its tracks and workmen had gathered to try and right it. Police on horseback stopped to help. Tweed, cowering behind the canvas, felt his heart race in his chest. What if they decided to search the wagon? What if they found him? He'd never felt anything like it. He was a fugitive.

Moving again, the wagon creaked its way across uptown cobblestone streets until it reached a deserted spot along the Hudson River. Here, it stopped and Tweed got out. Following orders, he climbed into a small wood rowboat that waited for them in the darkness by the shore; a man at the oars took the boat out onto the river. Silently, they made their way across, dodging occasional sloops and ferries that plied the waters this time of night. Reaching New Jersey, they landed on a rocky shore beneath the Palisades, the rugged cliffs that dominate the river from the New Jersey side. They were not far from the spot where, 70 years earlier, another Tammany Boss, Aaron Burr, had shot dead his rival Alexander Hamilton in a duel.

Tweed stepped off the boat in New Jersey as a wagon rode up to meet them. It carried him away from the water and up into the rocky New Jersey hillside, an area with few roads, miles of thick woods, and occasional broken-down farmhouses. Few visitors came this way. After several miles, the wagon stopped at an isolated shack and Tweed got out. A stranger greeted him at the door. His host—a man whose name remains unknown—invited him inside and gave him food to eat and a bed in which to sleep.

The next morning, Tweed woke early and stepped outside to find himself in a secluded woods near Weehawken,* a short walk from the edge of a cliff looking back across the Hudson giving him a panoramic view of Manhattan. From his perch, he could see steeples of Trinity and St. Paul's churches, the outlines of Central Park and Croton Reservoir, and the rising brick towers of the Brooklyn Bridge beyond.

Here, he waited. All he needed had been provided in his New Jersey hideout; his two keepers cared for him, cooked his meals, got him newspapers, and kept away strangers. He spent his time indoors, going out only in the early morning for walks. He developed a disguise: He shaved his beard, cut his hair short and began wearing a reddish-yellow wig and gold spectacles. He took the name "John Secor," an invalid wanting rest and fresh air. Mostly, he passed the hours reading newspapers and following the most intriguing story in the country that week: his own.

Tweed's escape had thrown New York City into turmoil. It dominated newspaper headlines, political talk, and saloon arguments for days. "GONE AT LAST," announced the *New York Herald*.[4] Police searched frantically for

---

* Weehawken is today the site of the New Jersey end of the Lincoln Tunnel, connecting traffic to mid-town Manhattan.

him; witnesses came forward claiming to have seen Tweed on the run in Canada, Long Island, Savannah, Cuba, Texas, and other exotic places.[5] Others speculated he might still be hiding in New York right under their noses. Tweed followed the search closely through the newspapers, keeping his own bags packed and ready to move if anyone came near.

Sheriff William Connor, who stood personally responsible for the escape, offered a $10,000 reward for Tweed's capture. Suspicions pointed everywhere: Warden Dunham and Keeper Hagen of the Ludlow Street Jail faced withering criticism for allowing Tweed to enjoy jaunts in Central Park and family dinners at his son's house, making a joke of his incarceration, not to mention negligence or complicity for the escape itself. Two of Tweed's jail mates also drew questions: Charles Lawrence the silk smuggler and a Vermont bank robber calling himself "Bliss" who conceded he'd once offered to help Tweed break out, but that Tweed had laughed off the idea. "What could I do with myself?" Tweed had told him, pointing to his own conspicuous body. "Where could I hope to hide myself?"[6]

Tweed must have winced at reading how the escape had again embarrassed his own family. His son William Jr., who'd seen his own career wrecked by the scandal but who'd stood by his father throughout his court trials and prison terms, was described as having run downstairs after discovering Tweed missing crying "I am ruined" and pulling his hair. Tweed's son-in-law Frederick Douglas also was described as acting "like an insane man." Tweed saw his wife Mary Jane, already sick from the strain, portrayed as being utterly confused that night, huddled upstairs with her daughters while denying to skeptical police she had any idea where her husband had gone.[7]

For now, all he could do was wait. Utterly secluded, Tweed made himself comfortable, passing his days playing cards, talking walks, making small talk with his keepers, or jotting occasional notes in a diary. After a few weeks, he got to enjoy the strange sensation of following his own trial in *absentia*. He still faced the $6.3 million civil lawsuit brought by Tilden's prosecutors and State Supreme Court Judge T.R. Westbrook insisted that the case go forward. Tweed had left his lawyers no instructions and his escape had made their job daunting: "Flight is always interpreted as a confession of guilt," Wheeler Peckham pronounced, and Tweed's own top lawyer David Dudley Field agreed, calling it "a great mistake."[8]

Still, following the twists and turns in the daily press from his New Jersey hideout, Tweed saw his lawyers mount a spirited defense. David Dudley

Field delighted at putting the prosecutors themselves on trial for bias and incompetence. As the trial dragged on through February and March, Field attacked them daily for "letting all the alleged wrongdoers go free, and attempting to fix the responsibility for this [entire] $6,000,000 upon Tweed." Where were the cases against Connolly, Keyser, Ingersoll, and Sweeny, he asked? He ridiculed them in open court as cowards who "once bowed before [Tweed], and there wasn't one of them, so hasty now to prosecute, that did not almost cringe at his feet."[9]

Tweed grew hopeful reading the accounts and began to think his legal magician actually might win the case, despite the negative hoopla over his own disappearance. Perhaps he might then be allowed to come home, pay a fine for the escape but be considered vindicated on the larger charges.

Fortunes changed in mid-March, though, when Charles O'Conor, the 71-year-old lead prosecutor who'd been sick in bed for most of the trial, finally returned to court. Seeing the case foundering in his absence, O'Conor had dragged himself out of bed, rode a coach through snowdrifts over the long distance from his home at Fort Washington—the northern tip of Manhattan Island far above Central Park—and arrived at the courthouse unannounced. He first day back at the prosecutors' table, he raised a series of objections and convinced Judge Westbrook to disallow much of Field's defense. It wasn't the prosecutors who were on trial, he argued, it was Tweed. The tenor changed. Ultimately, the jury would take just one hour to rule against the former Boss for the full $6.3 million.

Any hope of vindication had gone out the window.

In early May, Tweed and his two keepers packed their belongings and left the hideout atop the New Jersey Palisades, his home for over three months. They traveled south to nearby Staten Island around Fort Wadsworth facing the harbor Narrows.* They found an abandoned hut that local shad fisherman used for shelter and made it home. They hid here by day but sometimes ventured out onto the choppy waters at night in a small rowboat. One time, they ventured all the way across the harbor to Brooklyn to enjoy a few hours in a lively saloon, Tweed introducing himself as "Secor" and hoping no one would recognize him in his red wig, clean-shaven face, and glasses.

Finally, after about two weeks, Tweed and his keepers left the hut one

* Within a few blocks of the Staten Island end of today's Verrazano Bridge, the start of the New York City Marathon.

night, got into their small boat and rowed far out to a spot outside the harbor where a small schooner, the *Frank Atwood*, waited to meet them. All his life, Tweed had feared the water. He'd rarely sailed his own yachts on Long Island Sound; he was prone to seasickness. Now he'd have to spend weeks learning to live with it.

The *Frank Atwood* headed south along the Atlantic coast past the New Jersey, Virginia, and Carolina beaches. Days grew longer and waters tropical as they reached northern Florida. Here, the schooner left Tweed along a strip of sandy beach near a lighthouse—his next hideout. His two keepers from New Jersey stayed behind.

Things had been arranged. Tweed walked over to the lighthouse and found the master and his family ready to board him as a guest. Again, he introduced himself only as "John Secor" and soon was joined there by another traveler, a man identified only as "William Hunt," a guide who would lead him on the rest of his journey. Hunt, much younger than Tweed, would introduce himself to strangers as Secor's nephew. Theories abound over Hunt's actual identity. One report pegged him as Arthur Maginnis, Tweed's son-in-law from New Orleans, another as a cousin, still another as a coachman whom Tweed had employed in New York City to drive his carriages while he was still Boss of Tammany.[10]

Whoever he was, they left the lighthouse and "Hunt" led Tweed on an excursion through the Florida interior, camping in the everglades and nearby pine forests. As the summer grew hot, they settled near St. Augustine along the ocean. Tweed used this free and private time to think, about prospects for his future and mistakes of his past. In June, he and Hunt left St. Augustine for the Florida Keys, then found passage on a fishing boat to Cuba, which was then part of Spain, a country with no extradition treaty with the United States.[11] From Cuba he could embark to the Spanish mainland and perhaps find refuge. "I should have lived in Spain my whole life," he'd confide years later, "I had designed to go into some quiet part, like Catalonia or somewhere where living was inexpensive, and I have always been prudent in my appetites and personal living. I could have lived there for the rest of my life."[12]

Reaching Cuban waters on about June 12, the fishing boat carrying Tweed and Hunt refused to come into port; it had no papers and feared being stopped by authorities. Instead, it left Tweed and Hunt on a deserted beach about ten miles outside the port of Santiago de Cuba near the Island's eastern tip. Tweed and Hunt camped the first night under a moonlit sky. The next morning, a local fisherman found them and offered to lead them to town. Tweed, overweight, short of breath, and suffering from diabetes, found the hike exhausting. An observer described him reaching Santiago as "terribly sunburnt, his face being as brown as a berry and very much blistered."[13] A custom official approached and asked to see their passports. Seeing that "Secor" and "Hunt" had no visas, he ordered them both arrested—apparently not knowing who they were.

Cuba in 1876 was a country at war. Thousands of Spanish troops faced independence rebels aided often by American "filibusterers" or "adventurers." Just three years earlier, Spanish troops had captured twelve Americans on a ship called the *Virginius* and, ignoring diplomatic protests, had executed them all as "enemies of the state." Spain had recently sent a new hard-line Captain-General to Havana, Joaquin Jovellar, who'd issued orders to detain suspicious Americans on sight—a new diplomatic sore point. Tweed and Hunt, arrested and held on the Spanish man-of-war *Churrucca*, feared nothing more than being mistaken for "filibusterers" and getting tangled in the bloody fray. Fortunately, his Spanish captors recognized "Secor"-Tweed as too old or sick to be a rebel fighter. They treated him courteously and help soon arrived in the form of the American consul in Santiago, a young diplomat named Alfred Young of Cincinnati, who came aboard and won their release on bond.

Given the freedom of the town, Tweed and Hunt moved into a local rooming house, the *Hotel de Shy*, while waiting for Spanish authorities to resolve their status. The town of Santiago de Cuba offered many charms: walks by the harbor, carnivals in the square, and receptions at the hotels. As "Secor," Tweed enjoyed socializing with others prisoners, mostly American, French, and English merchants whose ships likewise had run afoul of customs officers. He celebrated the Fourth of July with fireworks from the balcony of the *Hotel Lascelles* and even hired a local customs clerk to teach him Spanish. "As soon as I got free I pitched in to study the Spanish language, and kept at it with as much intentness as I ever did to make a political point," he'd say later.[14]

He kept his distance from strangers, though, always fearful of being recognized. "I felt indisposed to talk, to meet acquaintances," he explained.[15]

During those weeks, Tweed also took time to read and hear about curious goings on back in his own country. His own escape seemed forgotten, eclipsed by newer, more exciting events. America was celebrating its Centennial birthday in 1876; a great exhibit in Philadelphia was drawing 200,000 visi-

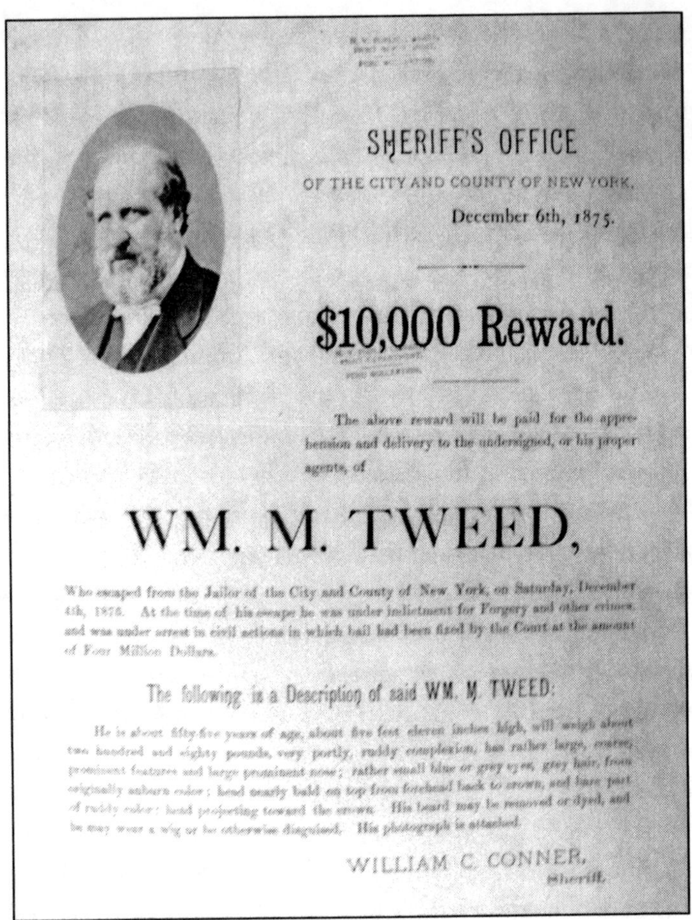

SHERIFF'S OFFICE

OF THE CITY AND COUNTY OF NEW YORK.

December 6th, 1875.

$10,000 Reward.

The above reward will be paid for the apprehension and delivery to the undersigned, or his proper agents, of

WM. M. TWEED,

Who escaped from the Jailor of the City and County of New York, on Saturday, December 4th, 1875. At the time of his escape he was under indictment for Forgery and other crimes, and was under arrest in civil actions in which bail had been fixed by the Court at the amount of Four Million Dollars.

The following is a Description of said WM. M. TWEED:

He is about fifty-five years of age, about five feet eleven inches high, will weigh about two hundred and eighty pounds, very portly, ruddy complexion, has rather large, coarse, prominent features and large prominent nose; rather small blue or grey eyes, grey hair, from originally auburn color; head nearly bald on top from forehead back to crown, and bare part of ruddy color; head projecting toward the crown. His beard may be removed or dyed, and he may wear a wig or be otherwise disguised. His photograph is attached.

WILLIAM C. CONNER,
Sheriff.

tors and thousands came each day to Washington, D.C. to celebrate at the White House and on Capitol Hill. News from the western frontier had shocked the country that month: General George Armstrong Custer, commander of the Seventh Cavalry, had been massacred along with two-hundred-and-fifty of his soldiers by Sioux Indians in the Dakota territory near the Little Bighorn River.

Even more striking to Tweed was the news on American politics: Democrats meeting in St. Louis, Missouri, that summer had nominated as their candidate for President of the United States a curious choice, Tweed's old nemesis Samuel Tilden.

He also learned something else: He'd been spotted.

❂ ❂ ❂ ❂ ❂

Samuel J. Tilden looked older now in 1876 after two years in the state legislature, two as governor, and months plotting for the presidency. Age had turned his hair gray, set against his formal black suits and stiff while collars. As governor, he worked long hours, straining his eyes and suffering chronic indigestion. He demanded as much from his staff. When a young lawyer hired to help on the Tweed case complained to him once about conflicts with other work, Governor Tilden lost his temper. "Sir!" he'd screamed, "a man who is not a monomaniac is not worth a damn!"[16]

As governor, Tilden had set up residence at the state capitol in Albany, renting a large home on Eagle Street and asking his sister Mary Pelton to come and manage his household. Rumors circulated in late 1875 that he'd suffered a stroke or "softening of the brain." Even close friends believed it for a time because of Tilden's chronic poor health. But he still kept a regimen of daily horse-riding, purchasing a sealskin coat to brave even the coldest Albany winter days, earning him the nickname "Sealskin Sammy."

Tilden had won the New York governorship by 50,000 votes in 1874, as big a margin as Tweed had produced for John Hoffman in 1868 with all his shenanigans. Tilden used the perch to strengthen his crime-fighting credentials by tackling the upstate "Canal Ring," a cabal of contractors and legislators who embezzled millions of dollars on fraudulent bills for repairs to the Erie Canal and other waterworks, not unlike Tweed's bill-padding in New York City. He'd built his presidential campaign with his usual painstaking care. He'd placed in charge two close confidantes: Abram Hewitt and Edward Cooper, both Gramercy Park neighbors and long-time allies from railroad and coal investments. He organized a "Literary Bureau" to pump out friendly news stories and pamphlets and had a special telegraph wire laid from St. Louis, where Democrats planned to hold their nominating convention, to his governor's mansion in Albany.

He campaigned on a single theme: reform! Tilden had found his moment.

Scandals had shaken America in the 1870s, making earlier swindles—Civil War-era profiteering, local graft, or anything else—look like child's play. Critics called it the "Era of Good Stealings,"[17] a time of unprecedented graft at every level of government, especially in Washington, D.C. Scandal had tarnished President Ulysses Grant's administration to the point that "Grantism" became an insult. Grant appeared personally honest but surrounded by looters. The Whiskey Ring frauds reached Grant's own personal secretary Orville Babcock and Indian land scandals forced the impeachment of his Secretary of War William Beklnap. The Credit Mobilier implicated dozens in Congress, not to mention Congress' own "salary grab," the James G. Blaine "Mulligan Letters" scandal, and graft by reconstruction governments in the South.* Who better to clean up the mess than Sam Tilden, the honest man who'd beaten the blackest corrupt conspiracy of them all: Boss Tweed's Tammany Hall.

Tilden's 1876 Democratic platform called for "reform" of almost everything: the civil service, the currency, homesteading, taxes, and crooked politicians. Republicans too saw the light and nominated their own self-styled "reformer," Ohio governor Rutherford B. Hayes who promised to drain Washington's political patronage swamp. The holier-than-thou "reform" versus "reform" contest made practical politicians on both sides hold their noses.**

Among Democrats, Tilden only serious opposition came from a small circle of people who knew him best, old New York friends like August Belmont, Augustus Schell, and Tammany Hall's John Kelly, an early ally who'd grown tired of Tilden's arrogant style. Tilden's agents managed to gag them all in St. Louis at the convention; they held New York's seventy delegate votes in line with a strict Unit Rule and, when Kelly tried formally to attack him in a speech to the convention, they had him ruled out of order. Tilden won the nomination easily on the second ballot, defeating Indiana Governor Thomas Hendricks whom he chose as his vice presidential running mate, but Kelly never forgot the insult.

Now, with the nomination in hand, Tilden found himself dogged by old news: Tweed. With bitter irony, Republicans were trying to smear him by tying him to the same Tweed Ring he'd helped destroy.

Tilden had gladly testified at Tweed's *abstentia* trial in New York City the prior February hoping to remind voters of his role in toppling the Ring. On cross-examination, though, Tweed's lawyer David Dudley Field had embarrassed him by producing evidence painting he and Tweed as best of friends:

---

* The Whiskey Ring frauds involved corruption in implementing federal liquor excise taxes; the Credit Mobilier involved graft and bribes in building the transcontinental railroad; the 1875 "salary grab" was an attempt by Congress to double its annual pay, including two years of retroactive salary at the higher level, repealed in response to the public outcry; and the "Mulligan letters" detailed Blaine's suspicious dealings with the Little Rock and Fort Smith Railroad, a scandal that followed him for life.

** It would be New York's Senator Roscoe Conkling, a Republican, who'd blast Hayes civil service reforms the next year by saying: "When Dr. Johnson defined patriotism as the last refuge of a scoundrel, he was unconscious of the then undeveloped capabilities and used of the word 'reform.'"[18]

an 1866 letter from Tilden inviting Tweed to join him at a Philadelphia political rally, a letter form Tilden requesting for a job for a mutual ally, and a $5,000 check Tweed had given Tilden as an 1868 campaign contribution. "You and Tweed went to Philadelphia and stood shoulder to shoulder to fight for the constitutional liberty of this great republic?" Field asked mockingly at one point, prompting waves of laughter in the courtroom as Tilden bit his lip and forced a smile but didn't answer.[19]

Tweed's escape from Ludlow Street Jail had caught Tilden unaware. His first reaction was to insist that the getaway was not his fault, which would have been a severe embarrassment. "The sheriff alone is responsible," he told reporters, "the whole responsibility is on the sheriff."[20] He must have scowled at seeing the latest cartoon from Thomas Nast in the July 1, 1876 *Harper's Weekly*. Called "Tweed-le-dee and Tilden-Dum," it showed he and Tweed in cahoots once again. In it, "reformed" Boss Tweed (dressed in a striped prison suit with diamond on his chest and a belt saying "Tammany police") is seen arresting two young boys from the street. "If all the people want is to have somebody arrested, I'll have you plunderers arrested," the "Reform Tweed" says, "You will be allowed to escape; nobody will be hurt, and then Tilden will be in the White House, and I to Albany as Governor."[21]

Still, with Tweed on the run and in hiding, at least Tilden could count on Tweed's mouth being shut for the rest of the campaign. He could rest easy on that score. Or at least so he thought.

President Ulysses Grant had mostly stayed out of the contest. Looking forward to retirement with just eight months left as president, Grant was spending a quiet summer at his vacation home by the seashore at Long Branch, New Jersey, far from the White House. Grant did not especially like Rutherford Hayes whose "reform" talk often sounded like personal backbiting, but he didn't like Tilden either. That summer, Grant became intrigued over a possible role he could play in the contest. His State Department had picked up the trail of Sam Tilden's nemesis on the run. Grant, like other Republicans, savored the prospect of Boss Tweed, captured and in their custody, being used as a weapon against Tilden. And for Grant himself to get credit for catching the fugitive would be a welcome feather in his hat.

Grayer and stouter now than during his days as Civil War commander, Grant had learned of the discovery in July. Henry Hall, the American Consul in Havana, had contacted his State Department superiors on June 23 to report the landing of the two Americans "John Secor" and "William Hunt" aboard a schooner from St. Augustine, Florida. Secor, being over fifty years old and in poor health, made an unlikely "filibusterer" but Hall suspected he might be a fugitive. Secor and Hunt both carried passports issued in Washington, D.C., on April 3, 1876 but with no visas. The passports had been mailed to "Jon Brown, New Court House, New York City."[22]

A few days later, Hall had alerted his colleague Alfred Young, the consul in Santiago de Cuba, that "Secor" might be the infamous Boss Tweed of New York City. He enclosed a photograph and the description of Tweed from the New York sheriff's wanted poster[23] and asked Young to investigate. A few days later, Young confirmed: "Vessel Arrived Safely"—code for Tweed—though he noted separately that Tweed appeared much thinner now, suffered from heat and disease, and might die if detained by police.[24]

Hearing the news, Grant's Secretary of State Hamilton Fish ordered that a trap be set. "If Secor is Tweed and is still in Cuba ask [the new Spanish] Captain General Jovallar would he deliver Tweed to United States officials if a ship was sent to Santiago," Fish directed.[25] Jovallar apparently agreed—despite the absence of an extradition treaty—but said he needed time to confer with his superiors in Madrid. Meanwhile, Hall made arrangements to identify the fugitive, take him into custody, and inform the press at the proper time.

Everything seemed ready for the takedown except for one: Tweed himself had other plans.

◎ ◎ ◎ ◎ ◎

It's not clear how Tweed learned about the trap. "No sooner had I got to Havana than old Jovellar learned in some way that I was a nice fat goose that he could pluck to feather his nest," he'd claim later.[26] If Tweed did pay the General a hefty bribe, then he got good value for his money. But he got even more from a use of simple charm to win another ally: Alfred Young, the helpful American Consul in Santiago de Cuba.

Young would later admit knowing Tweed's real identity almost from the start. Hunt had told him, he said, and Tweed had spilled the beans to his wife. In fact Mrs. Young, the consul's wife, became quite taken with the elderly fugitive she enjoyed socializing with that summer around the bar of the *Hotel de Shy* and at diplomatic receptions. "[H]is wife had great influence over him," the State Department would later conclude of Alfred Young, "[and] she was very much interested in Tweed's condition."[27]

Tweed, recognizing the closing net, decided he needed to leave Cuba immediately and booked passage on a Spanish ship bound for Barcelona and Vigo, the *Carmen*, paying $548 for himself and Hunt. He had a problem, though. The ship was scheduled to leave port on July 22 and Spanish authorities still hadn't approved his passport. He remained a prisoner in Santiago. Tweed approached the *Carmen*'s captain and convinced him to wait a few days, agreeing to pay the demurrage, or harbor fees, while the ship sat idle. But that wasn't enough; he needed to push the Spanish authorities to release his passport.

Here, Alfred Young, the American consul, proved very helpful. At Tweed's behest, he personally applied to Spanish officials for "Secor" and "Hunt's" passports and found he was getting help from unexpected places: The Captain of the Port, who reported directly to General Jovellar, "had rec'd orders to let Secor [Tweed] go wherever he pleased," Young explained later, and the local British vice consul too had heard appeals from New York City business friends to help Secor.[28] Someone was pulling strings from high places.

Within a few days, Young had broken the logjam and presented Tweed and Hunt their passports. Finally free to leave, Tweed signaled the *Carmen*'s captain to set sail. But Young hadn't finished yet. He did Tweed two more crucial favors: He helped Tweed financially by changing $620 in American greenbacks into Spanish gold and converting a $2,200 bank draft into local currency, sending some of the cash back to Tweed's son William Jr. in New York City. Then he misled his superiors. He waited until the eve of the ship's departure before telegraphing Henry Hall in Havana that Tweed was about to leave. Hall, receiving the telegram at 6:30 pm, commandeered a carriage and galloped the eight miles to General Jovellar's home outside Havana to request he immediately detain "Secor." Telegraphs flashed orders to Santiago de Cuba and a warship was sent in pursuit, but the *Carmen* had reached the open ocean.

Why did Alfred Young go so far beyond the call of duty on behalf of the friendly fugitive? Young denied ever receiving a penny from Tweed or even knowing much about the Tammany scandals. "I thought Tweed was a persecuted man," he explained, "and I wished to help him,"*[29]

---

* Henry Hall blew the whistle on Young in a letter to Washington, and Young submitted his resignation to Secretary of State Hamilton Fish shortly thereafter. His career in the diplomatic service ended abruptly.

"I am at this moment in receipt of a telegram from Havana saying 'do not send vessel. Treachery somewhere,'" Secretary of State Hamilton Fish reported as news reached Washington of Tweed's latest escape. "So it is, 'the best laid plans of mice and men.'"[30] Fish ordered that telegrams be fired off now to Spain itself. It was essential that Tweed be tracked.

◎ ◎ ◎ ◎ ◎

Tweed had little time to celebrate his narrow escape. He'd avoided arrest in Cuba, but had become a prisoner at sea. It would take the *Carmen* forty-two days to cross the Atlantic Ocean. Along the way, rolling on the ocean swells, Tweed suffered miserably. Wracked by seasickness, his large body magnifying the nausea, he couldn't look at food. "I try to eat what is provided, but I can not do it; my stomach instantly turned when I get a taste of garlic, and as that is the only flavoring they use in cooking, I am sure to get it in the first mouthful. I have not eaten more than two plates of soup and a few soda biscuits in two days, and I begin to feel the necessity for food," he wrote in a journal. His body weight fell precipitously; clothes no longer fit him. "I still keep on the cloth [summer] pants, a pair made for me in June 1873," he complained. "They are about ten inches too large around the waist, so I think I must have decreased some in size since that time."[31] When he did eat, he limited himself to soup for breakfast, soup and biscuits for other meals, and an occasional glass of sherry from the ship's doctor.

Reaching Spain, the *Carmen* headed directly to the port of Vigo on the Atlantic coast. It cast anchor in the town's harbor near a small island called San Simon that held the port's quarantine station. Here too, Tweed had little chance to enjoy the respite. Barely had they arrived when Tweed was startled to see the local governor come aboard leading a squad of soldiers. He came directly up to Tweed: "the old fellow [Tweed] had no coat on nor any shoes or stockings, and his trousers and his sleeves were rolled up and he was scrubbing the deck," a local seaman said later, describing the scene to reporters.[32]

"Mr. Tweed, put on your coat and shoes," the governor said, "we want you to go with us, we are going ashore."[33] He was under arrest.

◎ ◎ ◎ ◎ ◎

Behind the scenes, Hamilton Fish had once again set a trap. President Grant had taken a personal interest in the chase. "I think it will be advisable to ascertain if the Spanish authorities propose to give 'Secor' up in Spain," he'd wired Fish from his vacation home by the New Jersey seashore, "and if so if there is a Naval vessel handy to take charge of him."[34] Following Grant's lead, Fish had sent a cipher telegram to Caleb Cushing, the American Minister in Madrid, shortly after Tweed had flown the coup in Santiago: "Ascertain secretly and cautiously if he can be returned to Cuba."[35]

Cushing, a 75-year-old veteran diplomat, former congressman and former attorney general, was preparing to leave Madrid for a summer holiday to the United States via Paris and London, but left the matter in the hands of his young charge d'affairs, 33- year-old Alvey Adee. Adee, an upstart in the foreign service who'd hiked the Alps before learning civil engineering from an uncle, had come to Spain in 1869 as a personal aide to family friend Daniel Sickles, the flamboyant one-legged former Civil War general who'd famously shot his wife's lover in 1850s Washington, D.C. and won acquittal from a jury. President Grant had appointed Sickles the new American ambassador. Soon, Adee had won the staff's respect and become secretary of the Legation.

"I am directed by the Secretary to instruct you to ask for the return to Cuba of both Secor and Hunt," Adee read as diplomatic cables flashed between Washington and Madrid that summer.[36] Taking the initiative, Adee met with Spanish officials and quickly had things arranged. The main problem would be identification, both of the vessel and Tweed himself. Spain had on its lists over thirty ships named *Carmen*; finding the right one would require covering every port of entry. As for Tweed, Adee had no photograph to provide Spanish officials who'd be making the arrest. Like most Americans, though, he'd seen the Tweed drawings by *Harper's Weekly* artist Thomas Nast. He asked a friend named Don Benigno S. Suarez who had a *Harper's Weekly* subscription if he could borrow a recent copy; he picked out Nast's "Tweed-le-dee and Tilden-dum"—the drawing of Tweed arresting the two children—and passed it along to the Spanish.[37]

Spain posted alerts all along its Atlantic coast as the *Carmen* approached. The fact that Spain had no extradition treaty with the United States never became a problem. Spain had decided to play along, eager not only to return Tweed to Cuba but to surrender him directly to the U.S. Navy—thereby avoiding any legal process on either side of the ocean. Tweed's arrest in Spain would be totally outside Spanish law, American law, or international law—no judge, no lawyer, no hearing, no magistrate, no delay. In fact, Spain didn't even ask for identification of Tweed or Hunt beyond the Nast cartoon.

Spain understood the *quid pro quo*: "The generous conduct of the Span-

Harper's Weekly, *July 1, 1876.*

ish Government, which has not hesitated to deliver up these criminals [Tweed and Hunt], notwithstanding that no treaty of extradition exists, ought to be well appreciated by the North American Republic, which, in its turn, will take pleasure in doing us the same service if it be necessary," it announced.[38] By turning over Tweed, Spain had earned a diplomatic favor: Topping its wish list: the right to do as it pleased in Cuba, to demand that America return Cuban rebels seeking refuge, and to continue arresting American "adverturers" who got in the way.

To make the transfer, Adee arranged for the U.S. *Franklin*, a 47-gun frigate on a scheduled stop at Gibraltar, to change course for Vigo. "I hope you will find among your officers someone familiar with Tweed's personal appearance," he alerted the captain, "or that other means of identification (such for instance as a recent file off Harper's Weekly with Nast's caricatures)."[39] On September 7, Adee could report home: "Tweed, traveling as Secor, is arrested, together with one William Hunt, said to be his nephew, the baggage of both being sealed."[40]

Washington wired back: "Luggage should be guarded and no papers allowed to be taken."[41] Tweed himself was to be kept quiet. The *New York Herald* sent a reporter to interview him, but Adee denied him access to the fugitive.[42]

At the last minute, though, the State Department reversed itself on one key point: They wanted Tweed only. "Say also [to the Spanish] that we learn nothing about Hunt and do not desire his detention, but will also receive him if so desired," Fish wired Adee, who relayed the message.[43] Why would the U.S. government release Hunt, an obvious accomplice in Tweed's escape, before even questioning him? It created a mystery: Could the State Department have learned a deeper secret: that Tweed's entire escape had been aided or engineered by people whom President Grant's administration had reason to protect? People whom "Hunt" could identify? The list of possible conspirators was long: Republican politicians whom Tweed had threatened to expose, New York prosecutors tired of risking their reputations in court, or police officials who'd taken bribes?

Or was "Hunt" just an innocent nobody? By letting him go, Fish left the question forever unanswered.[44]

* * * * *

Word of Tweed's arrest caused a sensation back in New York City when news arrived by telegraph. "Where is Vigo?" people asked. The rich irony that Spanish officials had used a cartoon by Thomas Nast to identify him became instant grist for legend. Accounts told how, seeing the drawing, Spanish officials had assumed at first that "Twid" was a kidnapper or child abuser, not the Boss of Tammany Hall.[45]

The timing of the arrest raised suspicions, though, coming just as the presidential contest had reached fever pitch.

The Tilden-Hayes campaign had grown strikingly dirty for two candidates bent on "reform." Republicans attacked Tilden with every possible smear. They dredged up his Civil War-era Copperhead ties, proclaiming "not every Democrat was a rebel, but every rebel was a Democrat." They accused him of defending slavery, evading income taxes, and defending corrupt railroads while calling him a thief, a liar, and a drunk, "Slippery Sammy" or "Soapy Sam."[46] "Reform," the original buzzword, got lost in the shuffle: "The word 'reform' is not popular with the workingmen," Horatio Seymour warned Tilden as the contest heated up. "To them it means less money spent and less work."[47] Tilden's high-minded appeal became replaced by a simple "Turn the rascals out."[48] His campaign would spend over half a million dollars that year on expenses, including $100,000 from Tilden's own bankroll.

And now, Tweed was back. All that year, Tilden had seen his early ties to the ex-boss thrown back at him. Copies of Tilden's testimony from the Tweed *abstentia* trial in February had appeared under the headline "Tilden and Tweed; The Twin Leaders of the New York Democracy."[49] "Samuel J. Tilden was personally responsible for the rise of the Tweed Ring," the *New-York Times* itself declared, "and he did nothing whatever to break their power until their ruin had been accomplished."[50]

With Tweed now captured, rumors exploded that Republican politicos had engineered the arrest to make trouble. A quick ship could return the ex-Boss to New York City by late October, weeks before Election Day with plenty of time for mischief. Some newspapers openly charged that a deal had been struck: That Tweed had agreed to come home, pay a million-dollar fine, and be immediately released; in return, he'd testify against Tilden on a laundry list of scandals. Tweed would win his freedom and get his revenge in one fell swoop. "The capture of Tweed is no accident," announced the *New York Sun*, "it is a put up job."[51]

President Grant, from his vacation home on the New Jersey seashore, didn't deny it. Instead, he personally instructed Secretary of State Fish to prepare quick transit: "a Naval vessel should be on the spot to return [Tweed] to Mr. Tilden who must be anxious to see him," he telegraphed on September 7, hours after the arrest.[52] In another telegram a few days later, he reminded Fish of the key issue: "The [New York] Herald is very anxious to learn whether it is true that Tweed is to be used as a witness against Tilden...."[53]

❁ ❁ ❁ ❁ ❁

Tweed knew none of this. Arrested on reaching port in Spain after forty-two days at sea, his luggage, papers, and diaries all seized, he found himself held incommunicado in the *Lazaretto* , the quarantine house at Vigo harbor. Then, after a full week, a squad of *Carabineros*, local soldiers, came and marched he and Hunt up a steep rocky hill to the Vigo fortress that overlooked the town. Here, they threw him into a dungeon with stone walls, stone floors, and stone ceilings. Nobody spoke English to him and Tweed's broken Spanish barely allowed him to communicate. He could only guess what was happening.

The local American consul at Vigo, a Mr. Molins, took the initiative to see "Secor" and reported him as a "respectable" man with "social standing." Adee, reading the dispatch, smelled a rat: "These details, from a stranger, lead me to the inference that some of Tweed's friends are, or have been, working for him at Vigo," he reported.[54] He quickly put a stop to any such friendly visits.

Tweed, from his dungeon cell, paid money to an old Spanish women to bring bedding, food, and beer for he and Hunt from a local tavern. After several days, another squad of *Carabineros*— some thirty soldiers in bright red and yellow uniforms—came and marched them back down the hill to the harbor to board yet another ship, a handsome Navy frigate called the *Franklin*. Here among the greeters he spotted his son Richard, the first member of his immediate family he'd seen in nine months. The two happily embraced; Richard shared a few warm words with his father and gave him a few gold coins before having to leave the ship.

On board the *Franklin*, the soldiers delivered Tweed and Hunt to the ship's captain, Samuel R. Franklin, who finally told Tweed the full story—that he'd been given orders to carry him back to New York City and prison. Franklin assured Tweed he'd be given every courtesy during the passage, including use of the private stateroom usually reserved for visiting Navy brass and privileges of the officers' mess. But Tweed would be guarded day and night, sentries inside and outside his cabin, and his porthole kept shut.

To Hunt, the captain gave a choice: either passage home on the *Franklin* or immediate release in Spain. Hunt didn't need to think it over; he quickly took his leave and returned to shore, never to be heard from again.

The voyage home offered no relief. Stormy seas followed them across the ocean. Instead of the planned thirty-day crossing, headwinds, fogs, and gales slowed the *Franklin* to a crawl and made Tweed constantly seasick. Most days he awoke at 7 am and stayed in his room where he took meals and read books, including a Bible and a copy of McDuff's "Words and Mind of Jesus," gifts from his wife Mary Jane. He buried himself in military histories of the Civil War and talked of stocking a library when he got home to New York City. Other times, he played cards, solitaire when alone and cribbage with ship's officers who came for conversation. "His behavior was that of a perfect gentleman. He was always glad to see any of us when we called on him," one of them said. "Though everything on the ship was at his disposal, he made no extra demands. He did not smoke, nor did he drink, either wine or spirits, unless when unwell."[55] Only once during the long voyage did Tweed emerge from his cabin to walk on deck; he found the experience of being escorted by guards more humiliating than the relief of fresh air.

He grew morbid alone in his cabin. "He evidently regards himself as a sort of martyr, pursued by malignant fiends," a shipmate wrote.[56] Tweed apparently considered suicide, but rejected the idea as "wicked."[57] More than once, the ship's doctor ordered him to drink sherry to relieve chest pains.

After thirty-eight days at sea, the *Franklin* had covered barely half its route, reaching St. Thomas in the Virgin Islands where it stopped for coal and fresh food. The final leg of the journey would be worst of all. A heavy storm described as a "hurricane" hit the Atlantic seaboard as the *Franklin* steamed north off the New Jersey coast, pushing it far from shore.[58] Tweed had gorged on tropical fruit loaded at St. Thomas—oranges, bananas, and alligator pears—which magnified his seasickness. At one point, feeling desperately nauseous, he managed to entertain the crew with what one described as "very amusing remarks signifying his willingness to try the experience of Jonah and to attempt to get ashore in a whale's belly, or on the back of a porpoise."[59]

They finally reached New York on November 23 and newspapers covered every step of Tweed's return like a royal pageant. As soon as word hit the city of his approach, crowds jammed the Battery. A Navy tug, the *Catalpa*, left port carrying Sheriff Conner, District Attorney Benjamin Phelps, and other dignitaries to intercept the *Franklin* off Sandy Hook and collect the prisoner; an armada of boats from the major newspapers followed them.

Reaching the *Franklin*, Sheriff Connor climbed aboard, presented his papers to Captain Franklin, and followed him to Tweed's cabin. Coming out, he joked: "It's the old man. I found him at his usual occupation, playing cards."[60] Tweed said little as he followed the sheriff from his cabin onto the deck wearing a black hat, gray coat, and eye-glasses hung over his vest. A newspaper writer watching from a nearby boat described him as looking exhausted:

"[w]alking slowly... stooping and with some appearance of feebleness, leaning upon a cane [with] pale and somewhat haggard features and a full gray board."[61] Every member of the *Franklin's* crew came on deck and formed a line so Tweed could shake their hands before leaving.

He walked unsteadily down the gangway to the *Catalpa*, then sat with the sheriff in the tug's wheelhouse as it steamed up New York harbor toward the city. He occasionally asked the sheriff questions, mostly about local politics: "Is Reilly elected Sheriff? ... And Gumsleton was elected County Clerk?" When Connor remarked that, yes, they were, Tweed said "I thought so." Nearing the Battery, seeing Castle Garden and the South Street piers approaching from the distance, Tweed marveled at the progress made on the Brooklyn Bridge's towers during his absence. "I see they've got the wires across at last," he said. Still, he couldn't hide his gloom. A crewman who'd known him in his hay-day described Tweed simply as "careworn and very much thinner."[62]

Thousands of curiosity seekers mobbed the Hudson and East River banks with opera glasses and telescopes as the *Catalpa* approached, hoping for a glimpse of the ex-Boss. Now they cheered as his boat reached Pier No. 47 on the Hudson. Legs wobbly, Tweed tripped and almost fell while walking down the gangway; an Irish workman caught him by the arm and yelled "Hooray for the 'ould Boss."[63]

He threaded his way across the wharf, stopping to shake hands or share a smile with an occasional friend. At the curb, he boarded a waiting carriage and sat in the back as a policeman closed the door behind him. As it rode off, crowds followed, carriages with reporters and people chasing on foot. One newsman described how Tweed sat quietly in his carriage seat peering out a window, seeing the streets of home for the first time in eleven months, and stroking his white beard. At Ludlow Street, spectators jammed the sidewalks all around the jailhouse as the carriage entered through a gate directly into the jail's courtyard. After a few minutes, Warden Watson stepped outside and announced: "Yes, gentlemen; Tweed is locked up in his room."[64]

On seeing the warden for the first time since causing so much trouble by his escape, Tweed told him simply, "Well, I thought I'd come back to you."[65]

He ate dinner privately that night with his son William Jr., his former secretary Foster Dewey, and his brother Richard. They stayed and talked well into the night. "He is crushed and broken. He has lost his old buoyancy and defiant spirit," Dewey told reporters afterward. "He seems desolate and desirous of companionship more than anything else. He is a mere wreck of his former self."[66]

Of his time away, Tweed had spent almost four months at sea, mostly nauseous and seasick, traveling from New Jersey to Florida to Cuba to Spain and back again to New York City, and weeks more behind bars on Cuba and in Vigo. "His curious, ill-conceived escape netted him ten months of running from the frying pan to the fire," historian Leo Hershkowitz would write.[67]

Tweed would later admit to paying $60,000 in bribes to arrange the breakout, a remarkably large transaction arranged from his jail cell in total secrecy. Just as remarkably, no accomplices ever would be identified or charged in the escape, even "Hunt," whom Spanish authorities had delivered into American hands. Tweed would never reveal any of them, except to say that no New York City official or policeman had been involved. Nor would anyone betray Tweed for the $10,000 in reward money. Pressed about it later, Tweed would argue he hadn't really broken out of anything. "I did not escape from the jail," he'd say, "but left my own house."[68] Only one thing was clear. This was the last time. Asked if he would ever permit Tweed to visit his family, the sheriff said "No, sir.... Tweed shall not escape from me again."[69]

• 21 •
LAWYERS

"For Tweed there was some sympathy as a man who had been broken down by the prosecution and who had some manly qualities, but for a greedy thief like Connolly and a wily trickster like Mr. Peter B. Sweeny—'brother, there is none."

—EDITORIAL COLUMN in the *New York Tribune*, June 8, 1877.[1]

"The abuse you get only shows the outrageous injustice which public officers who do their duty get."

—FRANCIS BARLOW, in a letter to Attorney General Charles Fairchild, June 25, 1877.[2]

"These men are dead socially and politically. Let us force them to put the money they have stolen back into the City Treasury and leave their punishment to a higher power."

—An unnamed "PROMINENT LOCAL POLITICIAN" commenting on Sweeny, Connolly, and Tweed, June 7, 1877.[3]

FRIENDS JOKED that Tweed himself had overseen the building of the Ludlow Street Jail near his old neighborhood on the lower East Side back in the early 1860s: "If Mr. Tweed had known he was going to patronage it," one said, "he would have made the rooms ... more commodious."[4]

He adjusted quickly back to life behind bars, but eleven months on the run had taken a toll. Dr. William Schirmer, his personal physician, examined Tweed on his first day back and found him a physical wreck. Tweed had lost a full hundred pounds of body weight since leaving the city—mostly from nausea and seasickness during the ocean crossings. His blue eyes had "lost their brightness," the doctor reported, and his voice had turned feeble; he spoke now in an undertone, walked with a cane, his hair and beard ghostly white. What's more, Tweed's diabetes had worsened and weakened his lungs, leaving him often breathless. Still, he retained "remarkable possession of all his faculties."[5]

For days after returning to dry land, Tweed could barely look at food: "I can't get the motion of the ship out of my head," he complained.[6]

Slowly, he began to heal. The warden gave Tweed the same two-room suite on the jail's first floor he'd occupied before the escape, though he now charged Tweed $75 a month for the privilege. Here, he could look out his own window at shoppers from the Essex Street market or carriages on Grand Street. He decorated the room with flowers, a piano, and photographs, and he convinced Luke Grant, the prison servant, to again act as his personal aide for a small fee. After a few days, Dr. Schirmer found Tweed walking circles in the jail's brick-enclosed courtyard side-by-side with his son, William Jr., who came most days to visit. He enjoyed entertaining old friends like veteran Republican wire-puller Thurlow Weed who'd come to "try to cheer him up," he said.[7] He avoided politics like the plague. Sent a reporter's written question as to whether he planned to make damning exposures against Samuel Tilden as the newspapers had speculated, Tweed returned it with the word "No" written in large letters and underlined heavily in blue pencil.

Why cross swords with Tilden now? Tweed had his own problems. Even putting aside bad health, his future looked utterly bleak. He faced jail for the rest of his life. Having lost his trial in *abstentia*, he owed the state $6.3 million and, even if he could free himself under debtor laws,* he still faced trial on twenty-eight criminal indictments. The state already had confiscated all his property they could find. Poverty, unimaginable a few years earlier, now haunted his future. Tweed's real estate holdings worth over $2 million in 1871 had lost fully two-thirds their value since he'd transferred them to his children, who'd sold them to raise cash. His savings had trickled away: legal bills of $445,000, family expenses of $40,000 each year, $450,000 in losses on the Metropolitan Hotel, $30,000 to send the family to Europe in 1872, $100,000 in bank settlements, among many others. "I have recklessly parted with a great deal of money," he conceded.[9] Scandal had destroyed his credit. "Sir; Physically and financially I am in trouble," he wrote to James Ingersoll around this time, asking if he'd have "the goodness" to drop several lawsuits against his family.[10] One nephew, Frank Tweed, son of his brother Richard, couldn't find work at all in New York City; "the name of T—d rendered it difficult," his sister-in-law complained, as if the name itself had become a curse.[11]

---

* He would attempt to win release that summer under the so-called 60-Days Act that allowed debtors, on petition of a creditor, to assign their property away and, this done, be released. The effort failed because the State of New York, his largest creditor, refused to cooperate.[8]

He faced a grim reality—he might not have long to live. More than anything, he wanted to go home and spend his last years in Greenwich with his wife and children and find some dignity.

That winter, hope came to him in the form of an idea. E.A. Woodward, who had been Tweed's clerk at the county Board of Supervisors back during his glory days and had once helped Tweed arrange payoffs and "percentages" for his circle, had fled New York City after the disclosures but was arrested that summer in Chicago and brought back to stand trial. Woodward had found a way out, though. Held like Tweed in the Ludlow Street Jail, he'd hired a lawyer who'd quickly negotiated a "compromise" with prosecutors for his release. He agreed to pay $150,000 in restitution, make a full confession, and testify against any other Ring members brought to trial. Woodward had stayed loyal to Tweed during the scandals and Tweed was glad when he came by for a talk one day during his first week back in New York City.

Woodward had a suggestion: Tweed should speak to his new lawyer, John D. Townsend, and get some new advice.

John Townsend, short, with receding hair, small eyes, and a crisp mustache, had been a child prodigy when he'd started Columbia University at just thirteen years of age in the late 1840s, but he'd left soon to see the world. He sailed as a junior officer on the clipper ship *Flying Cloud* on its record-breaking 89-day trip to San Francisco and tried his luck at the California gold mines. Failing there, he came back to Harvard Law School and launched his legal career. Now, 41 years old, Townsend barely knew the famous Boss Tweed when he came to his room at Ludlow Street Jail. Townsend had no illusions that Tweed was anything but what the newspapers said he was: guilty as charged. Still, he sympathized. "Personally, Tweed was the pluckiest man I ever met," he said of their first meeting. "Not a man in a thousand could have survived the terrible strain he has lived under for more than a past year."[12]

Townsend saw only one way for Tweed to save himself: to stop his denials, admit his guilt, and pay his penalty. After two years in prison, ten months as a fugitive, and facing a hopeless future, Tweed had little desire to fight and was ready to listen. Also, he now had something to get off his chest—the truth. His truth, something he'd thought about during his months as a fugitive. Only Tweed wanted to tell it in the right forum and under the right conditions. His truth had value; it should set him free. Free, that is, from jail.

"At first it was not an easy matter to induce Mr. Tweed to beg for mercy," Townsend recalled.[13] Ever since the first *New-York Times* disclosures had appeared in July 1871, Tweed had adamantly denied doing anything wrong. He'd prided himself in keeping secrets and protecting friends—even long after they'd betrayed him. Beyond sheer stubbornness, Tweed knew his enemy. He'd seen how the prosecutors had strong-armed his case, vilified him, and tried to destroy his family. Worst of all would be going hat-in-hand to Samuel Tilden, a man from whom he expected nothing but scorn. He and Tilden had been enemies for years and, besides, Tilden as a "reform" candidate for President of the United States had no reason to waste his mercy on Tweed.

Sitting with the Boss in jail that day, Townsend had an answer: Why not go *around* Tilden? Tilden was governor, but the state had delegated responsibility for prosecuting the Ring cases to Charles O'Conor. Townsend knew O'Conor from his work on the Woodward "compromise" and everyone respected O'Conor's reputation: a hardliner but honest, above politics, and fiercely independent.

With Tweed's blessing, Townsend made the long trip by carriage up to Fort Washington at the northern tip of Manhattan Island past Central Park and the rural areas beyond, where O'Conor lived stoically in semi-retirement on Washington Heights overlooking the Hudson River. O'Conor, gruff, moody, gray-haired with start features, had served for five years without pay as the state's lead prosecutor of the Tweed Ring by the time Townsend came to visit him in mid-December 1876. He was tired. At 71 years old, his career since the 1840s had been legend: district attorney, brilliant litigator, bar association leader. An unapologetic states rights ideologue and Civil War Copperhead, O'Coner had built a national profile and received 21,559 votes for President of the United States in 1872 running on the "Straight-Out Democrat" (states' rights) ticket. Harshly opinionated, he'd made waves just that month by slamming President Grant as "The drunken Democrat [from] the Galena gutter, besmeared with the blood of his countrymen slain in domestic broil."[14]

O'Conor had viewed the Ring prosecutions through a stark moral prism. His goal had been civic vengeance, to punish thieves and make them suffer visibly for their crimes. Now, he recognized the effort had largely failed. Most of the Tammany crowd had escaped his noose by fleeing the country or turning state's evidence. No civil lawsuit had been brought against Oakey Hall and no effort had been made to extradite Sweeny or Connolly from Europe.[15]

Only a pittance of stolen money had been returned to the city and none but Tweed had spent much time behind bars. No wonder the public increasingly considered him a scapegoat.

O'Conor invited John Townsend into his house that morning and, sitting in the parlor by a warm fireplace, he listened to Townsend's proposition: a Tweed "compromise" similar to Woodward's, complete with a full confession. He was intrigued. The proposal offered him a new chance. "[T]he spectacle of Tweed upon his knees asking for mercy and consenting to be a witness against his associates in crime would have more effect as a preventive against future associations of like nature, then would the recovery of all the money that had been stolen," Townsend recalled his saying.[16]

John Townsend hurried back downtown to Ludlow Street. Telling Tweed the news about O'Coner's reaction, the former Boss agreed to try the approach. Tweed sat down at the small wooden desk in his jail cell, put pen to paper, and poured his heart out onto the page: "All further resistance being hopeless, I have now to make and only seek ... unqualified surrender," he wrote. Tweed, in the letter, proposed to O'Conor that he would hand all his property to the state, answer every question, confess his crimes, and help the prosecutors however he could. "I am an old man, greatly broken in health, and cut down in spirit and can no longer bear my burden [facing] hopeless imprisonment, which must speedily terminate my life."[17]

When he finished, Tweed sealed the letter in an envelope and handed it to Foster Dewey, his loyal former clerk, who went riding up to Fort Washington to hand it directly to O'Conor. O'Conor looked it over; before answering, he felt obliged to discuss it with the governor.

◎ ◎ ◎ ◎ ◎

Samuel Tilden had reason to be distracted when Charles O'Conor came to his door at Gramercy Park that day in mid-December. Just four weeks earlier, on November 7, he'd won a remarkable victory. He'd soundly defeated Rutherford Hayes in the popular vote for President of the United States, and he held a lead in electoral votes: 184 to 165, one short of victory. A cloud hung over the outcome, though. Three Southern states remained undecided, Florida, Louisiana, and South Carolina, as did a single electoral vote from Oregon, amid charges of violence, bribery, and ballot box fraud. Each campaign had sent squads of "visiting statesmen" to monitor the final vote counting by local boards in the contested states. Some Democrats threatened violence should

Hayes' Republicans cheat them out of their victory. President Grant, taking the talk seriously, had brought troops marching into Washington, D.C. in case things got out of hand. Just days earlier, on December 6, the four contested states each had sent competing slates of electors to the U.S. Congress, charged under the constitution to untangle the mess. But Congress itself was stalemated, split between a Democrat-controlled House and a Republican-controlled Senate.

Now, amid the chaos, here was his old friend Charles O'Conor coming to talk to him about Tweed. Tilden had known O'Conor for almost forty years; he'd been one of his earliest friends and mentors since coming to New York City in the 1840s. O'Conor had helped Tilden start his legal practice and had even drafted the papers incorporating Tilden & Company, the family business run by Tilden's two brothers in upstate New Lebanon. O'Conor had joined Tilden as a founding member of the Manhattan Club in the 1860s, had commiserated with him during the Civil War, and been one of the first people Tilden confided in on the Tweed Ring.

Even so, Tweed was a topic for which Tilden had little patience at this point.

Tweed had arrived back in New York City too late to affect actual voting, but with the presidential contest still unsettled, Tilden had to see him as a dangerous loose cannon. The ex-Boss had been quoted making threats during his voyage home from Spain: "I've got secrets enough of his to damn him as bad as I am damned."*[18] Tilden had faced criticism all through the campaign over the inept Tammany prosecutions. Critics charged him with pardoning "about nine out of ten men who were confessedly guilty," as one biographer put it.[19] Right up until Election Day, he'd worried that Tweed's arrest in Spain had been a trick. He'd had Abram Hewitt, his campaign chairman, issue a public letter trying to minimize the impact: "I… caution the public against a pretended confession of William M. Tweed seeking to implicate Gov. Tilden in the New-York Ring frauds, which, I am informed, is already in type in advance of the arrival of the United States steamer Franklin," it said, declaring it a fraud in advance.[20]

Now, with the voting over, talk that prosecutors were considering a "compromise" with Tweed created new headaches. How could Tilden think of free-

* This quote is almost certainly a fabrication from a reporter who was not abroad ship during the voyage, but Tilden would have no way of knowing this for certain.

ing the criminal around whom he'd built his "reform" reputation? Still, the talk gained currency, fueled by news that another Tammany fugitive, Peter B. Sweeny, the supposed "Brains" of the Tweed Ring, had accepted an extraordinary offer to leave his cushy exile in Paris and come home to face trial in New York on the $6.3 million civil case. Prosecutors had promised Sweeny full immunity, assuring him he would remain "unmolested"—not arrested on any of the his three pending indictments or any other civil or criminal actions—not only during his trial but for thirty days afterwards. This way, even if Sweeny were found guilty or if settlement talks failed, he'd still have time to escape and leave the country again.[21] Critics sneered at the one-sided deal, but Tilden hadn't objected.[22]

Tilden still had three weeks left as Governor of New York State and an epic political crisis to navigate. For him, a "compromise" with Tweed made sense only if it gave him control over Tweed's mouth—not a likely prospect—but he would always listen to any idea from his old friend Charles O'Conor.

Sitting together now in Tilden's parlor lighted by windows facing pretty tree-lined Gramercy Park ringed by brick townhouses of the city's elite, O'Conor showed Tilden the remarkable "surrender" letter he'd received that week from Tweed at Ludlow Street Jail. Tilden listened as O'Conor walked him through the proposal. It had its attractions: a Tweed confession would vindicate Tilden and the prosecutors by proving they'd been right all along; his testimony could save the city millions of dollars by protecting it from lawsuits while also providing evidence against yet-unpunished Ring members like Sweeny, Connolly, and Oakey Hall; and its moral weight—the sight of the once-powerful Boss begging for mercy—would deter corruption.

But Tilden, his strained eyes focused on the letter O'Conor held in his hands as he spoke, had no sympathy for the argument. Embroiled in a cliffhanger presidential contest, Tilden saw little to like in any compromise with Tweed, only a maze of traps. He needed answers to questions: What new information could Tweed possibly provide that they didn't already know? Could anything he said be trusted? Would he have documents to back up his story? And the spectacle of Tweed's being set free—what moral effect would *that* have? How could he justify it? Before agreeing to any arrangement, O'Conor should first insist on hearing Tweed's full story and seeing all his evidence, Tilden told his old friend. Then he could make a more considered judgment.

O'Conor agreed; Tilden's circumspection made sense. But it also raised an ethical point: Tweed had approached him in confidence. Until they decided whether to pursue his offer or not, O'Conor would feel duty-bound to treat his evidence as secret and private. He wouldn't be able to share it with anyone, not even the governor. Any leak would be a break of faith, he explained.

Once again, Tilden didn't see it that way. He wanted to see Tweed's story himself; in fact, he insisted on it. Any statement from Tweed had to be submitted to him personally. Until he, Tilden, was satisfied, he refused to allow O'Conor to give Tweed any assurance of a deal. As governor, he had that right.

Charles O'Conor recognized the impasse and saw no reason to press the issue. He saw that Tilden had other urgencies; the house buzzed with newspapermen and politicos fishing for any scrap of news on the presidential stalemate. He also knew politics: Tilden the politician wanted to use Tweed's confession for his own purposes, kill any parts embarrassing to him, and highlight any charges against his rivals. Why else would he dare to intrude on O'Conor's independence as the Attorney General's designated prosecutor? O'Conor knew that a Tweed confession could embarrass prominent citizens of both parties, perhaps even Tilden himself. But that was the reason he as prosecutor had to reject the interference.

O'Conor excused himself, took his hat and coat and left. The old lawyer knew he could not accept the governor's demand and he recognized that Tilden would not back down. Within a few days, he sent a letter resigning from the Tweed prosecution team giving no reason other than his age and health.[23] Shortly after that, he returned the Tweed "surrender" letter to its sender.

On January 1, 1877, Tilden ended his term as New York's governor with the presidency still undecided. He presided in Albany at the inauguration of his successor, the new governor, a handpicked protégé named Lucius Robinson. Afterward, he took a carriage to the train station to return to New York City. Only a handful of well-wishers came to see him off. "He attracts few people," his biographer John Bigelow wrote of him, even after Tilden had won the popular vote for President of the United States, "and no one in Albany cares for him."[24]

◎ ◎ ◎ ◎ ◎

Tweed had to be disappointed learning that O'Conor and Tilden had rejected his "surrender." He knew he couldn't avoid another fight now but had only dwindling resources to wage it. He decided to hire John Townsend formally as his new lawyer but insisted on pinching his pennies. As his fee, he agreed to pay Townsend ten promissory notes worth $1,000 apiece. Only half would be paid up front; the rest, the second $5,000, was made contingent. Townsend would receive it only after winning Tweed's release from prison or successfully defending him against another criminal conviction.[25] A few weeks later, when David Dudley Field asked Tweed if he would provide $1,000 to appeal the judgment in the $6.3 million civil case, Tweed refused.[26]

With Charles O'Conor now out of the picture, Townsend tried his next plan; he sent Tweed's original "surrender" letter back up to Albany to the office of Charles Fairchild, the state attorney general. He had no illusions; even with a new governor in Albany, Fairchild, a smart, ambitious man, took his cues from the person who had put him on his pedestal, Sam Tilden.

Fairchild's star had risen quickly in the New York legal constellation. Just 34 years old, a Harvard-educated son of a prominent upstate lawyer, Fairchild had had the good sense to marry Helen Lincklaen, a favorite niece of former governor and presidential candidate Horatio Seymour, still New York's most popular Democrat. Stern-faced, clean-shaven, sharply dressed, Fairchild had used his political ties to help him become the state's deputy attorney general in Albany just seven years after joining the Bar. With Tilden's blessing, he'd won the top job for himself in 1874. Tilden as governor had made Fairchild a central cog in his political operation: treasurer of the state party committee during his presidential campaign and a top lieutenant at Tilden's nominating convention in St. Louis. "Of course Tweed was aware that when he applied to Mr. Fairchild... he was submitting himself as much to the tender mercies of Mr. Tilden as if he applied to him personally," Townsend explained.[27]

Still, things looked promising. Shortly after receiving Tweed's "surrender" letter, Fairchild had jumped at the prospect. He took the train down to New York City and rode over to Ludlow Street Jail to meet Tweed privately for a long face to face conversation. "I... talked with him awhile," Fairchild said later, describing the meeting, "no statement was made or anything of the kind; I told [Tweed] if he was of use to the public we would consider how much use and whether it would justify doing anything for him."[28] In fact, as the two sat together in Tweed's room that day, the old Boss laid out a long list of people he could provide testimony against, starting with four state senators and seven assemblymen. According to notes from the meeting, he mentioned Jimmy O'Brien who was then suing the city for his $350,000 claim in supposed sheriff's expenses that Tweed and Connolly had rejected years earlier. Tweed also included as targets his closest Ring associates, the old "lunch club" gang: Oakey Hall, Peter Sweeny, and Slippery Dick Connolly, each of whom Tweed claimed he'd had "frequent conversations" with "in reference to their interests in the spoils."[29]

Fairchild seemed satisfied with what he'd heard. The next days saw a flurry of activity: Wheeler Peckham, now given hands-on control of the case, approached Townsend to arrange follow-up meetings with Tweed and a go-between named Carolyn O'Brien Bryant began representing the Attorney General. Bryant had gained Tweed's trust earlier by writing a sympathetic article on his jailbreak for *Harper's Weekly*.[30]

All through March, the work went on. Apparently, an obstacle had disappeared. In late February, Samuel Tilden had lost the presidency.

⊛ ⊛ ⊛ ⊛ ⊛

On March 5, Rutherford Hayes took the oath of office in Washington to become the nineteenth President of the United States. Most Democrats cried foul, that Tilden had been robbed. Congress had created a special 15-member commission to decide the disputed ballots; it had consisted of five Senators and five Congressmen—split equally between Republicans and Democrats—and five Supreme Court justices, slanted three to two in favor of Republican appointees. By party-line vote, they'd assigned each and every one of the contested electors to Hayes, giving him a one-vote electoral victory.

A few weeks after entering the White House, Hays would order the withdrawal of federal troops from the last two Southern states where they remained, ending post-Civil War "Reconstruction" and dooming black voting rights for the next eighty years. It was part of a murky arrangement reached in a hotel room to convince Southern congressmen not to block Hayes' inauguration by filibustering the vote count. The stigma of fraud—"His Fraudulency," "RutherFraud" Hayes—would shadow the rest of his term.

Tilden too suffered criticism for his handling of the contest. Rather than coming to Washington or politicking behind the scenes to marshal his forces, Tilden had spent days in his law library as the outcome teetered writing detailed legal briefs on the constitutional issues—hoping to win the contest by words on paper rather than flesh and blood human contact, the stuff of politics. He'd opposed creation of the Electoral Commission but never communicated the fact clearly to supporters in Congress who could have blocked it. "[H]e refused to lead... he had no counsel to give... he was speechless and without resource," even the friendly *New York Star* said.[31] "Unwilling to bargain for the presidency, and unable to muster the moral and physical energy needed to take charge of the struggle and lead his disorganized supporters in Congress, Tilden reacted the way most people react under stress: he reverted to type," noted historian Roy Morris, Jr.[32]

For Tilden, reverting to type meant withdrawing. In March, after Hayes' swearing in, he refused to make speeches and buried himself in biographies of Oliver Cromwell and Scottish historian Thomas Carlyle. The strain had affected him physically; arthritis made his left hand almost useless, a "numb palsy" that would worsen during the rest of his life. He walked in a shuffling gait, his face pale, his voice a raw whisper. "Physically he was an old, broken man," said biographer Alexander Flick, "but his mind was still keen, and all his faculties at instant command."[33]

Still, even during this period, barely a week after losing the presidency, Sam Tilden found time to climb out of his shell and meet with the Tweed prosecutors. "[Fairchild] accepted Tilden's invitation for himself and his wife, and will be at Gramercy Park over Sunday next," O'Brian Bryant, Fairchild's go-between, reported to Tweed's lawyer John Townsend that week. "He expects to go to Fort Washington [O'Conor's home] on Sunday with Tilden and arrange the enlargement of *our* client [Tweed] immediately. The future conduct of the affair will be confined strictly to O'Conor and the Attorney-General."[34] The next week O'Brien Bryant telegraphed an update: "The understanding is absolute, as I said, and all is right for a close next week."[35]

It is doubtful that Sam Tilden gave a green light to a deal with Tweed in these post-election private talks. What was more likely, based on later events, was that Fairchild asked Tilden's advice on how to string out the convict, get from Tweed all the value he could, then cast the old man away.

❁ ❁ ❁ ❁ ❁

"The talk of a compromise with Tweed is now becoming so general that perhaps it may impose some responsibility on me," New York City corporation counsel Charles Whitney wrote to Fairchild in mid-March.[36] Progress, in fact, appeared substantial. Fairchild returned to New York in late March for another talk with Tweed at Ludlow Street Jail. He happened to pick a day when John Townsend, Tweed lawyer, was out of town but Tweed met alone with him anyway. The next day, Fairchild came back and this time left Ludlow Street taking with him loads of documents, Tweed's old checks and ledgers. "I saw [Tweed] again at the jail, and I saw him a second time, next day for a few moments," Fairchild explained. "I then told him I did not propose to ask him questions about various individuals and people, but if he had any statement to make of facts that were within his knowledge, to prepare such a statement and submit it to me, and I would see whether it was of any value to the public."[37]

Townsend, hearing what had happened, rushed over to the exclusive Buckingham Hotel uptown on 50th Street where Fairchild stayed and asked how things had gone. What Fairchild told him, his exact choice of words, remains a mystery, but Townsend came away with a definite impression: that Fairchild had all but decided to set Tweed free. "Mr. Fairchild did not fix any date for his discharge, but he clearly intimate to [me] that he would order the discharge within a few days," he recalled.[38] He rushed back to Ludlow Street and told Tweed, who asked him quickly to visit Greenwich and tell his wife Mary Jane to expect him home soon. That week, Townsend received a follow-up telegram from O'Brien Bryant: "*Buckingham* [code for Fairchild] all right. Took my paper down this morning."[39]

The flurry of messages back and forth heated up; telegrams to Ludlow Street Jail came in disguise, addressed to "Luke Grant," Tweed's aide. Now was the time for Tweed to put his cards on the table.

Following up on Fairchild's idea, he and Townsend sat down over the next few weeks and prepared a detailed written "confession." The remarkable document, a narrative, covered the history of Tweed Ring, its rise to power, its division of spoils, its skimming of city contractors, and Tweed's bribery of the state legislature, all things that Tweed had denied for years. The confession took special aim at Tweed's three closest Ring cohorts, still running free: Oakey Hall, Connolly, and Sweeny, spotlighting their central role in all the Ring scandals. To back up his claims, Tweed included lists of canceled checks, names of witnesses who could back his story, and a full inventory of his real estate holdings.[40] The document also specified Tweed's offer to prosecutors: that he'd surrender his property, testify for the city against lawsuits, provide checks, papers, and other documents, and appear in court whenever they asked.

Before finalizing the "confession," John Townsend took a copy of the draft and rode up to Fort Washington to show it to Charles O'Conor and ask his opinion. O'Conor declined to read it but gave his view regardless: "He says he has no doubt you will be discharged, and that after receiving the statement they could do nothing else," Townsend told Tweed.[41] O'Brien Bryant, who happened to be visiting O'Conor when Townsend dropped by that day, put it slightly differently. The evidence—the checks, the statements, the interview notes—he said, were now "in Tilden's hands."[42]

Townsend rode the train up to Albany and handed the "confession" to Fairchild in unsigned form in mid-April. Almost immediately, a lengthy, detailed description of it appeared in the *New York World*. It caused a stir in the state capitol. Tweed talking? Who knew how many lives and careers the old Boss could scuttle with his secrets? "Since his troubles most of those whom he had looked upon as his friends in the palmy days had held themselves aloof from him," Townsend warned in a comment to the newspaper, "he does not propose to recognize any further claim upon him for silence."*[43]

More leaks followed and the behind-the-scenes maneuvering became a public circus. "It is pretty well understood here that any of the Tilden-O'Conor-Kelly gang who want to hit the head of an enemy have only to send the name to the 'Boss,' and they will be furnished [charges]—provided always that Tweed is promised a full pardon for his crimes and release from imprisonment," the *New-York Times* sneered at the process.[45] In fact, Tweed already had been asked if he had any special dirt to throw against Republican state senator William Woodin or Republican publisher Thurlow Weed—both enemies of Tilden—or against the New York Central Railroad, then represented by Fairchild's father, who was acting as an advisor in the case.[46]

Still, by early May, despite all this hoopla and constant meetings, nothing had changed. Tweed sat in jail growing increasingly restless. Why hadn't Fairchild freed him yet? Or even answered his offer? "My mind is not easy at the long delay of the Attorney-General in deciding, and I fear he will delay until the suspense will be more of a torture than at present," he wrote.[47]

The emotional turmoil was taking a physical toll on him. Tweed's body could no longer absorb stress. "He is suffering intensely from diabetes, and

* How or why the "confession" leaked is another mystery. Townsend felt concerned enough to send Fairchild a prompt denial: "I notice that the 'World' has several columns today giving what they say is the Confession of Tweed [and] assure you that I have furnished no part of it," Townsend wrote. The fact that he was ready with a newspaper comment, though, still points in his direction.[44]

since he had been under the excitement attending his anticipation of release his troubles have been greatly aggravated. *He absolutely needs rest of mind and opportunity to obtain exercise and sunshine*," his physician William Schirmer wrote after examining him in early May.[48] Admittedly, Tweed came to enjoy mingling with some of the prosecutors, a chance to reminisce about his days in power. "If possible, have the Counsel to the Corporation, Mr. Whitney, call today," he asked Townsend that week. "I would much like to see him. My mind and thoughts are now fresh on the matter and I can explain fully all he desires."[49]

By now, Tweed had firmly convinced several of the prosecution lawyers of his value. Whitney, who was responsible for defending the $1 million "water meter" cases,* was eager to use him as a witness in court. "Tweed's testimony will so key up and strengthen the case that I should be of the opinion that it would save the city in the end from the payment of this claim," he wrote Fairchild. "Personally, I feel much averse to seeing Tweed at liberty.... But in my position... the money side of the questions looks big."[50]Wheeler Peckham, responsible for the Peter B. Sweeny trial, agreed. "Pursuant to your suggestion I saw Tweed and examined him," he wrote. "His testimony would be important & ... He seemed quite ready to talk."[51] "Whitney & I saw [Tweed] today & got all out of him we could on the points you suggested," Peckham reported a few days later. "He would be of decided use in the Sweeny case."[52]

⚙ ⚙ ⚙ ⚙ ⚙

The time had come for Charles Fairchild to make a choice: what to do about Tweed? Sitting in Albany at the state capitol, he heard a gaggle of advice, Sam Tilden talking in one ear, Tammany Boss John Kelly in another, his own staff of lawyers flooding him with letters and appeals. He tested the political winds: "I consulted with several people as to their view of the general policy of trying to make any use of Tweed, what the public sentiment was on the subject," he conceded.[53] Certainly, he saw his own political future affected by the outcome. Releasing Tweed would outrage the reformers; keeping his in jail could spark a backlash of sympathy for a sick old man. And his own credibility

* These cases involved claims by a Joseph Navarro who'd contracted to sell the city 10,000 defective water meters for $70 each, and which the city refused to accept. Navarro demanded payment. Tweed, who'd signed the original contracts in 1870 as Public Works Commissioner, was prepared to testify that the contracts had been riddled with fraud and need not be honored.

too had been questioned: Even if Fairchild hadn't explicitly promised Tweed his freedom, he'd planted enough seductive hints to create that impression.

Another factor arose at this point tipping the balance, the chance to seal a deal with Peter Sweeny—the biggest fish from the Tammany scandal after Tweed himself—and collect some money for the city treasury. Ever since Sweeny had returned to New York City that winter, attorney Wheeler Peckham had been meeting secretly with Sweeny's agents in his New York office.[54] They'd traded proposals for an all-money settlement; Sweeny had already raised his original proffer of $100,000 to $250,000 and perhaps they could get more. These were small sums compared to the $6.3 million claimed under the lawsuit or the $4 million in bail demanded of Tweed but hard cash nonetheless. Peckham justified a deal to Fairchild by painting a gloomy picture of the evidence: Sweeny, he argued, not been a member of the 1870 interim Board of Audit and had not signed any of the suspect Tax Levy warrants that year, thus other proof would be needed to show that he'd taken his split of the money. True, Peckham had bank records to show that ten percent of the Tax Levy proceeds went to James Sweeny, his brother, who'd transferred large sums to Peter, but James had died in Paris the prior March and could not testify in court.[55]

After that, he argued, the case became tissue-soft. Only one thing could save it: Tweed. "In my view the trial of the case without Tweed gives us less than an even chance for success unless we can prove the case on the def't himself," he argued, "Now having given you the facts I leave it to your decision...."[56]

Sweetening the pot was that fact that Slippery Dick Connolly too had made recent overtures from Europe about a "compromise," perhaps with a partial payment as well. An agreement with Sweeny could pave the way for both: two large feathers in Fairchild's hat.

He decided. He'd settle with Sweeny and take the money. Tweed could wait.

* * * * *

Peter B. Sweeny came to the courtroom on Chambers Street in a jaunty mood to start his scheduled trial on June 7, "laughing and talking... looking very little disturbed," according to a reporter.[57] Life in Paris had worn well on him; he'd aged little, with barely a touch of gray in his heavy black hair as he sat at the defense table flanked by lawyers. As the judge gaveled the room to order, he announced that a settlement had been reached in the case. Jaws dropped around the room, though, as the details became clear. The city would collect $400,000 in restitution, but Sweeny himself wouldn't pay a dime of it. All the money all would come from the estate of his recently-deceased brother James. Even more striking was Judge Westbrook's statement from the bench: "It may be proper for me to say in passing that the terms of the arrangement, so far as they have been communicated to me, involve no concession or reflection upon the defendant."[58]

He'd been "fully exonerated," Sweeny gloated after the announcement. "[A]ny settlement [was on] condition that my responsibility or culpability is expressly defined." And since not a penny had been asked from Sweeny himself, his culpability had been defined as zero.[59]

Almost immediately, even the prosecutors themselves disowned their own handiwork, shocked at the one-sided whitewash. "I was no party… to any agreement that Mr. Sweeny should be in any way exonerated or declared exonerated. I say that very emphatically," William Whitney insisted when asked by a reporter.[60] Pechkam too denied having approved the judge's exonerating statement, even though he'd been standing at the prosecution table at the moment the judge made it and hadn't objected.[61]

Reactions from the public at large were even harsher. New York mayor Smith Ely, Jr., hearing the news, couldn't believe his ears. Sweeny had originally offered to pay the city $600,000 to settle the charges before he'd left for Europe back in 1873, Ely told reporters, and he blasted Fairchild now for agreeing to accept $200,000 less.[62] Tammany Boss John Kelly accused prosecutors of having given Sweeny a special back channel to Tweed "compromise" talks so he could scuttle any agreement that might hurt him.[63]

For Tweed, the Sweeny deal meant something worse: he'd been cheated. His testimony had become worthless though his draft "confession" had doubtless been used as a bargaining chip. John Townsend, hopping mad, wrote a quick note to Fairchild insisting he keep his bargain: "I am just informed that you have effected a settlement in the case against Peter B. Sweeny & there is reason to believe that the amount obtained was secured, in a great degree, by the use you have made of the statement I furnished to you… by direction of my client, Mr. Tweed. Under the promise that he should be discharged if any use was made of that statement, I now request the fulfillment of your agreement."[64]

Fairchild, stung at the criticism, made Townsend wait six days for an answer. He denied everything: "After careful examination I have come to the conclusion that the testimony which said Tweed could give as shown by said statement would not justify his release," he wrote in a terse letter, returning the package, failing to mention any of the hints or understandings he'd made with Tweed or his lawyer.[65] In fact, Fairchild hadn't even bothered waiting for Townsend to receive the answer before he leaked the letter to a gaggle of reporters after a late-night dinner at the Manhattan Club.[66] Townsend read it in the *New York Tribune* before he'd even seen it.

Recriminations came quickly.* Excuses aside, though, Fairchild had crippled his political prospects in New York State; neither Sam Tilden nor Horatio Seymour, his two mentors, could help him. Fairchild's own allies gasped at his bungling of the case. "You have refused to let Tweed out to tell the story of these frauds, and so we must look elsewhere," William Whitney complained. Tweed, in his statement, had suggested a Public Works deputy, William King, as someone who could corroborate his claims. "Now why is King kept away, and why should not he be allowed to come back," he asked.[70] "That Fairchild attempted to suppress the full truth about the Tweed Ring seems clear," Whitney's biographer, Mark Hirsch concluded.[71]

Even Noah Davis, the judge who'd originally sentenced Tweed to twelve years' imprisonment on Blackwell's Island, blasted the attorney general's decision on the Sweeny case. "The worst feature of [the Tweed ring crimes] is,

---

* Townsend responded with an angry public letter detailing the entire course of back-channel talks with Fairchild, accused Fairchild of "incompetence" and ""dishonesty," and charged him with sharing Tweed's private "confession" with political friends. According to a *New York Tribune* reporter who saw the document, "The copy submitted to Mr. Fairchild, when returned yesterday, bore marks of having passed through many hands; for there were annotations in different chirography after almost every name on the list of those whose checks Tweed holds," each person apparently having been checked with. Fairchild later would claim he'd shown the "confession" to only six people: Tilden, Peckham, Whitney, Bigelow, Nash, and his father S.T. Fairchild.[67]

Fairchild, in his own defense, published a report a few weeks later pointing to "fatal variances" between Tweed's written and his oral statements, claiming that "in one of my interviews with Tweed, he volunteered a statement to me which I knew must be false." He also argued that Tweed's property had no value to the state and that the statute of limitations had passed on most of the people against whom Tweed might have testified.[68]

The most vicious finger-pointing came from Carolyn O'Brien Bryant, Fairchild's go-between, who published a scathing series of letters claiming, among other things, (a) that Tweed had lavished money on two secret paramours, a Miss Garrett and a Mrs. MacMullin, "whose influence had been as potent for evil, as that of his estimable wife had been for good on his career," (b) that Tweed had had a chest in his room at Albany's Delavan House filled with $1,000 bills to pay off legislators, and doled out $150,000 in the 1868 Erie fight alone, and (c) that Tweed openly planned to lie in his confession, saying "if swearing was all that was necessary, he would give them all they wanted!" Tweed denied all of Bryant's charges, they had no corroboration, and were not pursued by the aldermen's investigating committee.[69]

that notwithstanding that all these crimes have been so clearly proven …, nevertheless the whole body of those conspirators against the city and its treasury go substantially unwhipped of justice," he announced from the bench that December. "To my mind, this presents a spectacle so abhorrent to my notion of justice,… a parody of public justice."[72] With one exception: Tweed.

That year, the state Democratic party snubbed Fairchild at its annual convention by denying him re-nomination to his post as Attorney General, courtesy primarily of Tammany leader John Kelly, offended at Fairchild's duplicity in the affair.

In December, meanwhile, Peter Sweeny left New York City and sailed for Havre on the steamship *France*, where he would spent the next twelve years living in Paris and raising his one son, telling anyone who'd ask that he'd been fully exonerated in the Tweed Ring scandals and had a judge's statement to prove it.

• 22 •
CLEAN BREAST

"I can't; I am in the same condition as a man who is a good swimmer—you tie his hands and throw him in the water, and say: 'Swim, you are a good swimmer,' but he will drown… Give me [books and records] to refresh my memory, and I will tell you all I know in that connection."

—TWEED, asked to testify about bills in the Albany legislature he'd influenced seven years earlier, September 21, 1877.[1]

"Nathaniel Sands was taken care of as Tax Commissioner, at fifteen thousand dollars a year'; Mr. Henry was made Dock Commissioner; Joseph F. Daly was made a judge, at fifteen thousands dollars a year, for fourteen years."

—TWEED, asked how he'd "taken care of" the New York Citizen's Association to stop it from criticizing his regime. September 28, 1877.[2]

MONTHS PASSED and still he sat in jail. Summer came and the hot sun made the neighborhood around Ludlow Street stink from wretched smells of garbage abandoned in the filthy streets and nearby market. Tweed kept a photograph of his estate in Greenwich with its wide green lawns and soft, cool breezes off the Long Island Sound—a place he hadn't seen in four years. He hung it on the wall and thought of it often while locked inside the stuffy, crowded jail.

Tweed had given up trying to defend himself against the barrage of lawsuits that prosecutors still threw at him; he had no more money to lose. He figured his financial worth now at barely $5,000, compared with $3 million at its height, and he knew he'd never walk free except by an act of kindness from the state. Following Townsend's advice, he formally instructed him to confess judgment in every case. "My defenses … have been disclosed to the Attorney General personally in several interviews on his personal assurance to me that if I made such statement I should be released from confinement," he wrote, Fairchild's double-cross still sticking in his throat. Ultimately, he'd confess to three more lawsuits raising his total outstanding debt to some $25 million.[3]

Tweed still wanted to talk, now more than ever, and plenty in New York City still wanted to hear him, even if not the Attorney General. He wasn't without friends, even now, people prepared to help him for their own reasons.

For instance, there was John Kelly. Kelly, square-faced and full-bearded, had never fit with Tweed's crowd when they held the whip hand at Tammany Hall. Kelly had grown up poor on New York's Hester Street but was good with his fists and smart with numbers, a quiet, serious man. He'd risen fast in the rough-and-tumble Tammany of the 1850s, an early Irish face in the party's upper hierarchy. He became a Sachem while winning elections as alderman, congressman, and ultimately sheriff, a job where he'd admitted collecting a fortune of $150,000 in fees for arresting criminals, collecting fines, and running local jails. Here he'd won his nickname "Honest John."* Tilden's reform crowd had hand-picked Kelly to challenge Oakey Hall for mayor in 1868 against Tweed's machine, but Kelly had fallen sick that year, chronic bronchitis worsened by public speaking and a parade of personal tragedies: Kelly's wife and his 21-year-old son both had died of consumption and a daughter had shown worsening symptoms.

Kelly needed rest. He left the city that year and spent the next two years abroad traveling with his daughters in Europe, North Africa, and the Holy Land. He returned in late 1871 just as Tweed's regime was collapsing in scandal, bringing home from Italy four large religious oil paintings that he donated to the new St. Patrick's Cathedral. Back in New York, reformers turned again to Kelly, this time as a fresh face to rebuild a demoralized Tammany Hall. Kelly seized the chance and took firm control. He had himself appointed Comptroller, the same post earlier held by Slippery Dick Connolly and reformer Andrew H. Green, so he could watch the city's money and keep things clean. He made a sensation by ousting two corrupt city police board members, backing Governor Sam Tilden's war against the upstate Canal Ring, and keeping Tammany free of scandal. Soon, he controlled virtually every appointment in Gotham.

---

* "Honest John" would later be accused by Mayor William Havemeyer of charging the county more than $30,000 in excess costs for his sheriff's department work, but it would never be proven. "Fraud permeates every part of your bills to such an extent that one honest spot would be a sort of relief," Havemeyer would say in a letter. Kelly sued Havemeyer for defamation over the attack but Havemeyer died before the suit came to trial. See Werner, p. 278-279; *New-York Times* and other newspapers, December 1 and 2, 1874.[4]

Critics called him a "dictator," but Kelly denied it. "I never dictate the nomination of any man," he once told a reporter with a wink. "My advise is often asked, and I always give it freely and frankly."[5] He held court each day in a small brownstone on Lexington Avenue behind closed shutters and dim chandeliers—the gloomy darkness suited him— wearing a plain suit and a small gold watch chain. But people who knew him never trifled with the figure behind the mild blue eyes and gentle nature. "John Kelly is a man who never forgets an injury," Oakey Hall said of him. "Beneath [his] mastiff face and neck slumber the passions of hatred and revenge."[6]

John Kelly felt particular hatred these days toward Charles Fairchild for his high-handed treatment of Tweed. Kelly had volunteered to act as a go-between during the "compromise" talks and heard Fairchild give the same misleading come-ons as Tweed had. He felt he'd been used when Fairchild torpedoed the deal. Kelly recognized value in the old Boss. Tweed was a disgraced man, but many of the city's immigrant poor still admired him. He'd stolen money, but paid his penalty in prison and now wanted to make amends. To "Honest John," Tweed's case presented an opportunity: Let him talk. The old man on the witness stand publicly confessing his crimes, fingering all the crooked thieves of his era, would prove how serious the new "reformed" Tammany was in cleaning its own house.

Kelly pulled strings and things happened. He gave his blessing and, on July 17 that year, the city's Board of Aldermen voted to launch its own investigation of the Tweed scandals and the state's bungled prosecutions. They appointed a three-member committee with Democrat Samuel Lewis as chairman. Its charge would be broad: to take public testimony on "all the facts and circumstances connected with the organization known as the 'Tweed Ring.'" Its star witness, speaking out for the first time, would be the former Boss himself.[7]

Tweed arrived by carriage for his first day before the aldermen wearing a blue flannel suit, the color contrasting starkly with his white hair and white necktie. From his jailhouse carriage, he got out and hobbled up the marble steps of City Hall, escorted by Deputy Sheriff McGonigal, the same officer who'd arrested him at Blackwell's Island two years earlier and now helped the old man along. The walk made Tweed breathless by the time he reached the Common Council room, a large chamber with high ceiling, cut crystal chandeliers, a polished wood dais, tall windows facing the park, and public galleries behind a brass rail.

Tweed had shaved off his beard and now wore a thick gray mustache; those close enough to see remarked how well he looked sitting at the witness table. When he stood up, though, they saw the cost of his years behind bars. Tweed could barely take two steps without a cane, his legs too weak to carry his large body. "He stoops more than usual in walking, and the scanty hair on his head has been bleached somewhat whiter," a *New York Herald* writer noted.[8]

The session lasted just a few minutes that day. John Townsend, Tweed's lawyer, had taken sick and couldn't attend and Tweed refused to testify without him. The aldermen agreed to a delay. Three days later, though, he came back and this time he didn't disappoint either the panel or the small, curious crowd dotting the chamber—a mix of reporters, politicos, and old cronies. Sitting at the witness table with his now-healthy lawyer at this side, Tweed took his oath and cleared his throat. Hugh Cole, the committee's lawyer, began the questioning. "I believe you are a native of the State of New York, Mr. Tweed?"

"I am, sir."[9]

"When did you first enter into public life?"

"In 1852, I think, sir," he answered. "I was Alderman in 1852 and 1853. I have been Supervisor, Commissioner of the Board of Education, Representative in Congress, and State Senator."

It didn't take long for Tweed to find his voice and startle the crowd. As the counsel led him through a description of his early days with the county supervisors in the 1850s, Tweed quickly launched into a detailed account of bribes given and taken, skimming of county contracts, and plots to fix elections, naming names of county officials who played along, dead and alive. A week later, at the aldermen's next session, he identified long lists of city contractors who'd cooperated in the bill-padding schemes, including even Jimmy O'Brien, the famous ex-sheriff now basking in celebrity as source of the *New-York Times*' famous "Secret Account" disclosures. Tweed detailed how O'Brien had attempted to extort $150,000 from him during the 1871 disclosures and how he'd sold his unpaid claim of "sheriff's expenses" many times over. Then at the next session, he told the origins of the 1870 "Tweed Charter" and explained the bribes, favors, and backroom deals he'd made to win its approval in the state legislature, again naming senators and assemblymen who'd played the game.

Tweed gained confidence as he spoke. "Mr. Tweed manifested no nervousness, but answered the questions... promptly, fully, and with the old-time rapidity of speech," a reporter wrote.[10] His disclosures—particularly his finger pointing—startled former friends all over town, people who'd long ago disowned him, assuming he'd never squeal. Tweed had always kept his tongue; "the most timid never dreaded being betrayed by Tweed," the *New York Tribune* noted, "no one doubts that he is telling a great many awful truths."[11]

Each time he'd testify, people he'd mentioned by name would virtually stand in line to call him a liar. "There is not a word of truth in it," Isaac Oliver insisted of the Supervisor disclosures.[12] Jimmy O'Brien angrily rounded up reporters after Tweed's revelation of his extortion attempts. "There is no truth in the story. I never sold Tweed my claim against the city," he insisted.[13] At the next session, Tweed slammed him back by producing a copy of the actual sales document from O'Brien and presenting it publicly. "That settles Jimmy O'Brien," he told the panel.[14]

Similarly, after Tweed had detailed some of his pay-offs to newspapers, the *Albany Argus* flatly denied his claims: "it is simply and wholly false; false in detail and false in total, without one shadow of foundation from the commencement to the end."[15] Tweed opened his next day before the aldermen by presenting a package of letters and cancelled checks proving $778,000 paid to that newspaper. "Men whom I have benefited in every way think that I am not able to defend myself, but I want them distinctly to know that I am—and that I am going to do it."[16]

By the fourth session, Tweed's regular dissertations to the aldermen at City Hall had become a hot ticket. Crowds crammed the galleries and nearby hallways long before the opening gavel, wondering whom the old man would finger next. By his fifth day, the flood had become a torrent. "Several hundred persons were turned away yesterday from the Aldermanic chamber," the *New York Herald* reported. "Every seat in the gallery was filled," echoed the *Sun*; "the seats and every foot of standing room within the rail which divided the commoners from the sacred persons of the Aldermen were occupied by politicians."[17]

The committee settled into a pattern of meeting once or twice a week all through September and October and Tweed came to relish the carriage rides from Ludlow Street Jail to City Hall, about a mile away, the fresh air, the exercise, and the attention. The more he spoke, the more fluently the words rolled off his tongue as he sat at the witness table, particularly as he explained the inner workings of the Ring, the 1870 Tax Levy central to so many probes, his splitting of spoils with Sweeny, Connolly, and Oakey Hall. "He seemed bursting with facts and figures, and a pertinent question would open a floodgate of volubility," a *New York Tribune* reporter put it.[18] Sometimes he took on a "jaunty air," wrote another reporter, "the promptness with which his answers were given almost baffled the skill of the short-hand reporters."[19]

Tweed recognized that the public had its eye him and that his future freedom could depend whether people believed we was leveling with them. When his lawyer John Townsend told him not to answer one particular question on election frauds because it was overly broad, Tweed bickered with him in public. "Well, you must recollect that if I don't answer the [question] they will say that I don't want to answer them," he argued. When Townsend suggested he should let his lawyer take the blame, Tweed snapped back: "Yes; but they won't blame you for it. They will only blame me."[20]

He spent hours preparing for these bi-weekly performances. Tweed asked the aldermen to send him city records, minutes from old aldermen and supervisor meetings, so he could study before answering their detailed questions. It frustrated him that some old friends who could help freshen his memory refused for fear of being blackballed in the press; "men who could inform me and come in to see me are afraid. When they come in they tremble all over until they get out," he complained.[21]

At times, the sessions grew heated. When one alderman confronted Tweed with questions raised in a newspaper interview by John Morrissey, the former prize-fighter and recent Tammany power, Tweed answered with a blistering attack on Morrissey's own record: assaults, burglaries, fighting, gambling, and various terms in an Albany penitentiary. When the aldermen ruled him out of order, Tweed exploded: "Must I sit here and be abused by every thief that stands on the corner, and who chooses to wag his tongue at me, and then be told that I have no opportunity of defending myself? I am tied hand and foot; I am in jail; I have no means of communication with any one outside; I cannot send out a messenger," he argued. "I shall fight back at everybody that fights at me. I can't be crushed out because I am unfortunate."[22]

Other sessions turned starkly political. Rufus Cowing, the sole Republican on the panel, handed Tweed a full Tammany membership list at one point and asked him to identify each one he'd been associated with during his reign—a way to smear almost half the local Democratic party. Lewis, the committee chairman, objected, calling it a partisan trick and demanded Tweed read a similar list of prominent Republicans. When pressed, though, it was Tweed who found the diplomatic fix. He absolved them all: "I have read it [the list] over carefully, and there is not a name there connected with the

Ring frauds," he said simply.[23] Pressed another time to explain why his testimony now differed from stonewalling answers he'd given at an earlier probe of Albany corruption, Tweed simply shrugged: "What I swore then was false; what I swear now is true." Asked why he'd lied in the earlier case, he explained, "men's families and themselves should be protected all through… done to save men and their families."[24]

In mid-October, the proceedings were jolted when the *New York Herald* managed to get its hands on a full copy of Tweed's original written "confession" from the prior spring and printed the full text, including long lists of people who'd received checks from Tweed over the years, hundreds of names. Most were utterly innocent: grocers, doctors, politicians, or charities. Tweed had to spend hours that day before the aldermen explaining each check to avoid tarnishing reputations. He went out of his way to exonerate leading figures he'd been close to: "I cannot say anything against Mr. [John] Hoffman or Mr. [Thurlow] Weed," he insisted when asked,[25] and was especially gracious to John Kelly, his current Tammany patron who'd given him the chance to speak: Asked if Kelly had had any role in the scandals, Tweed said: "on the contrary, he was always quarreling with the Ring, and was well known to be opposed to us"[26]

By the time he stepped down in late October, Tweed had testified for eleven days before the aldermen and answered hundreds of their questions. His testimony filled 375 pages of transcript. More than the fingering of other culprits, most remarkable was what he'd said about himself. He'd taken responsibility for every crime assigned to him. He neither denied, nor boasted, nor glorified his actions, but laid them out in the clinical, unflinching way of a person who'd come to terms. He'd made a clean breast, disclosed his personal finances as well as his political record, with verbatim transcripts printed in the major newspapers. Did he skew his testimony and admit far more crimes than he'd ever actually committed in an attempt to curry favor and improve his odds of being released? Maybe. Tweed certainly had nothing to lose and felt pressure to tell a good story, he had no corroboration for many incidents, and his words had enough gaps to raise doubts. "His testimony is open to a good deal of conjecture if not suspicion," historian Leo Hershkowitz noted. "How much was true? How much was false? Probably no one will ever know."[27]

The aldermen did not stop with Tweed. After he'd finished, they called twenty additional witnesses, including major city contractors, Tweed's clerk E.A. Woodward, and even prosecutor Wheeler Peckham. Notably missing were the three other core members of the Ring: Oakey Hall and Connolly both in Europe and Peter B. Sweeny, still in New York but hiding behind his generous grant of immunity.[28] The testimony, 750 pages altogether, built damning cases against them all. The aldermen's findings read like a catalogue of greed: Tweed's "Ring" had "fraudulently diverted" between $25.5 and $45 million from the city and county treasuries just during the three-and-a-half years from January 1868 to July 1, 1871, they concluded. This enormous sum, almost $1 billion in modern dollars, accounted for more than half the increase in the city's debt load during the period and was divided among dozens of players—Tweed, Connolly, Sweeny, the mayor, the contractors, the bookkeepers, and smaller lieutenants.*[29]

But as for Tweed's being the master villain, calling the shots, guiltier than the rest, they said nothing.

Just as damning were their conclusions about the prosecutors. Of all the missing money, their six years of legal wrangling had recovered only $1,119,000, a tiny percent of the total. The bulk came from two dead men: $558,000 paid by James Watson's estate and $406,000 from Peter Sweeny's dead brother James. At the same time, Peckham and his lawyers had charged over $240,000 in fees, wiping out a large fraction of the recovery. "At present all the thieves, with one single exception [Tweed], are at large, several of them are living in or near New York, in elegant ease, if not in ostentatious luxury, and all of them claim entire immunity," the aldermen found.[30] The Sweeny settlement particularly rankled them; they found it "incomprehensible," allowing the "Brains" of the Ring "to save some shred of his own reputation at the expense of that of his dead brother."[31]

◎ ◎ ◎ ◎ ◎

More months passed and still Tweed sat in jail. Seasons changed again, summer to fall to winter. His cell, unbearably hot in July, gave him chills in December. Depression haunted the old Boss, even after his public testimony.

---

* This conclusion cited an analysis by Henry Taintor, an accountant with the prosecution team, who had examined some $30 million is city payments under the Tax Levy, the Courthouse, and other accounts, and estimated than only about 15 percent —$2.5 million—had gone for legitimate purposes, the rest being graft. Applying these proportions to all accounts would raise the fraud estimate to $45 million. Total city and county debt rose from $36.3 million in January 1869 to $97.3 million on September 14, 1871.

Later estimates would peg the total plunder by Tweed's regime much higher, up to $200 million according to Matthew O'Rourke writing years after the fact. These stratospheric numbers, which have become staples of the Tweed legend, have to be assumed to contain a good share of fluff and drama.

In October, he gave a rare interview to a *New York Herald* reporter he'd met during the aldermen hearing and painted a bleak picture. Sitting at the table in his room at the Ludlow Street Jail, nibbling a piece of oyster pie, Tweed's face grew animated telling stories: He poked fun at the two Presidents he'd met personally: Franklin Pierce, "almost a nonentity," and Millard Fillmore, "a poor stick." Stephen Douglas, the Illinois Senator and 1860 party White House nominee, impressed him more. "I was pretty well acquainted with him. He seemed to be a high-minded man with plenty of temperament," Tweed recalled. "I was a Douglas democrat up to the beginning of the [Civil] war and a war democrat after that." Closer to home, he made fun of his own big stomach when the reporter asked about his health. "I have gained nearly one hundred pounds since I came back from Spain. My old clothes begin to fit me again."[32]

Turning to his old Tammany cronies, though, made him sour. Of Oakey Hall, Tweed could only shake his head: "I think, [he] has been crazy, or going crazy, for years. He was a dreadfully tiresome fellow, with his weak little puns." He described Peter Sweeny as "a hard, overbearing, revengeful man. He wants his way and treasures up wrath.... We were so opposite and unlike that we got along very well." He saved the worst for himself, though: "I was always ambitious to be influential and in control," he said, explaining his own rise to power. But now looking back, he couldn't think of a single accomplishment to take pride in: "Nothing. My vanity sees nothing to delight in. I recall nothing eminent."[33]

Even now, he looked forward only to one thing, possible freedom. "I should go to New Orleans or to the West. Idleness is my aversion," he told the reporter, thinking out loud how he'd spend his life if given a new chance. "My son-in-law is in business in New Orleans and I could make myself useful to him as traveling agent or in some other way—enough to give me employment and a living. If I did not go there I would start life far out West."[34] Of politics, he'd had his fill. "I never bother my head about politics. I don't expect ever to vote again."[35]

Outside his jail cell, a movement had started. Tweed's sheer persistence had captured an audience, especially his days bearing his soul in front of the city aldermen. Now they demanded fairness for the old man. After issuing their report, the aldermen themselves voted 13 to 6 for a resolution calling on the attorney general to free Tweed, recognizing the severity of his punishment, the value of his testimony, and the unfairness of imprisoning him while allowing others to go unpunished. The vote was bipartisan; two Republicans joined Democrats in supporting it while chairman Lewis had joined the Republicans against it.[36] At the same time, publisher Hugh Hastings of the *Commercial Advertiser* newspaper began circulating a petition for his release and collected pages of signatures.

A new attorney general replaced Charles Fairchild in Albany in January 1878: Augustus Schoonmaker, a state senator from upstate Kingston, who'd won the post with support from John Kelly and Tammany. The change of faces quickly sparked a new round of efforts to release the former Boss. Schoonmaker had sat on one of the legislative committees investigating Tammany abuse and knew the case well. He recognized he'd been handed a hot potato—from Tilden to O'Conor to Fairchild to Kelly to the Aldermen and now to him.

Still, his political pedigree raised hopes on Ludlow Street. "[Schoonmaker] will, it is believed, be guided by John Kelly in the matter," even the *New-York Times* reported.[37]

In February, Tweed's lawyer John Townsend started the process by submitting a new formal petition on his client's behalf. Publicly, Schoonmaker kept his distance from the issue: "Tweed's case must stand, like every other case, on its own merits, legal and equitable," he told reporters; he was reluctant to act without some "expression of public opinion as would amount to an approval of his course by those who have been injured by his robberies."[38] He was terrified of the possible backlash; still, he kept an open mind.

Townsend's appeal was followed by one from a higher authority, "Honest John" Kelly himself speaking his mind from New York City. Kelly wrote a public letter to Schoonmaker in mid-March pleading for Tweed's release on humanitarian grounds, but he couldn't resist venting his spleen one more time at the broken promises by Schoonmaker's predecessor. "I feel it to be my duty both as an individual and as a public officer, to urge upon you the discharge of William M. Tweed, who is now confined in the debtor's prison of this city," he wrote. "Mr. Fairchild did state to me that he would discharge Mr. Tweed if he made a full confession and surrendered his property," he argued. "As a citizen I feel that the State is being dishonored by this breach of faith."[39]

What happened next behind the scenes is unclear. Schoonmaker apparently reached an informal understanding with Kelly and Townsend and assured them privately in late March that he would let Tweed go once the legislature had gone out of session, easing any political backlash.[40] Kelly passed the word to Tweed. "It is doubtless true that Mr. Kelly promised to release him [Tweed.] If Mr. Schoonmaker does not straightway consent to Tweed's release he will be made to feel the power of Mr. Kelly's wrath," a *Utica Observer* reporter wrote around this time.[41] Townsend claims that the promise was explicit: "That gentleman [Schoonmaker] gave assurance to Mr. John Kelly, to [me] and others that he would discharge him after the legislature adjourned. This assurance was made in the latter part of March, 1878."[42]

Tweed himself, sitting in jail, had survived a minor heart attack that winter and recognized his own time as limited. If he weren't freed soon, it might not matter at all. Hearing new promises from the politicians in Albany, he had to resist getting excited; the stress exhausted his weak system. As the time for his promised freedom neared, though, he couldn't help but get his hopes up. Day by day, he waited, feeling the disappointment with each day the news didn't arrive.

Charles Fairchild had left Albany abruptly after finishing his term as state attorney general and set up a legal practice in New York City. Still young, he had plenty of time for his career to recover from his bloody nose over the Tweed affair. He'd been visiting friends in upstate New York's Madison County, though, when he saw the letter from John Kelly printed in the newspapers. It made such a direct attack on his personal honesty that he felt compelled to answer. Fairchild put pen to paper and scribbled out his own letter to Attorney General Schoonmaker designed for publication in the newspapers, intended both to clear his own name and to drive one last nail into the coffin of the movement to release the old Boss. John Kelly's claim that he'd broken promises was "false," in fact "absurdly false," he wrote. He'd rejected Tweed's confession not because of politics but because it was worthless. "Of what use to the Attorney General could be a full confession from Tweed! The Attorney General and the public already knew well enough about Tweed's crimes," he argued. "Tweed did not offer evidence the use of which would at all justify the consent of the Attorney General to his discharge."[43]

There is no evidence that Fairchild spoke with Samuel Tilden that week before writing or sending the letter, but he didn't have to. He knew Tilden's mind on the issue. They'd talked it over many times before. When Fairchild finished, he mailed the letter and, as expected, it caused a public stir. No answer from Schoonmaker ever appeared... just a clear, eloquent silence.

⊛ ⊛ ⊛ ⊛ ⊛

Tweed read Fairchild's letter printed in the newspapers on the morning of April 2. He pointed it out to his bondsman Charles Devlin visiting him in his room on Ludlow Street and Devlin recalled the reaction: "I saw at once that it was this thing that finally broke him down."[44] All was now in the hands of the Attorney General, but Fairchild's letter had doomed the case. Freeing Tweed was political suicide.

Foster Dewey, who now saw Tweed almost every day in jail, conceded that the old Boss had told him "as many as five hundred times since his return from Spain that he wanted to die."[45]

Tweed read the Bible each day in prison now and made his room a comfortable cocoon, its walls covered with pictures of his wife, his children, and his Greenwich estate, a Brussels carpet decorated with red roses underfoot, a high wooden clock, and chairs upholstered in blue. He enjoyed nights of playing poker with Foster Dewey and old-time cronies from the Seventh Ward who came to visit. He'd stopped eating much; Dewey remembered how sometimes Tweed would sit at the window looking at the busy street and call out names of people he recognized, sometimes one out of every four who passed by. He'd remember the names and addresses of their parents, the businesses they'd owned, the favors he'd done for them, and the interesting events in their lives.[46]

John Townsend found the scene depressing and started keeping his distance. "I felt I could be to him of no further use [and] I saw he was giving way to despondency."[47] Tweed's wife Mary Jane had gone to Europe that spring, her own health broken from the years of strain. She'd lost all the sight in one eye and most of the sight in the other; she was practically blind. And traveled under the name "Weed" to avoid any connection with her jailed husband. Their two eldest sons, William Jr. and Richard and their families, went with her, leaving Tweed without their company in his final days. His eldest daughter Josephine and her husband Frederick Douglas—his only children left in the New York area—Foster Dewey, Tweed's brother Richard, his bondsman Charles Devlin, and the doctors became his daily circle, his last set of companions.

Tweed celebrated his 55th birthday in jail on April 3; by then, his heart condition had worsened. Around this time, he caught a cold, perhaps on his birthday from the prison dampness or perhaps from his final trip to testify at the County Courthouse. The cold worsened into bronchial pneumonia. A few days later, he died.

• 23 •
LEGACY

"The politicians who make a lastin' success in politics are the men who are always loyal to their friends, even up to the gate of State prison, if necessary; men who keep their promises and never lie.... Some papers complain that the bosses get rich while devotin' their lives to the interests of the city. What of it?"

—Tammany leader GEORGE WASHINGTON PLUNKETT, 1905.[1]

"Tammany Hall, for years, has unfairly and unjustly been stigmatized as something sinister and evil."

—CARMINE DE SAPIO, the last Tammany "Boss," February 1961, ninety years after the fall of Tweed.[2]

"There is no boss over me. The only boss I have is the people of the City of New York."

—ROBERT WAGNER, mayor of New York City (1954-1965) denying charges he followed orders from "Boss" De Sapio, January 13, 1960.[3]

"[I]f Tammany could lay its hands on the State Treasury for four years, it would put the state in debt for generations [as it had] New York City by a succession of municipal administrations sponsored by the gangster-infiltrated Tammany Hall political machine."

—Future U.S. SENATOR JACOB K. JAVITS, running for state Attorney General in 1954.[4]

THE FIGHT FOR HIS LEGACY began almost immediately after Tweed sighed his last breath. "[H]is life, as a whole, was a wretched failure, in every possible way and from whatever point of view it may be regarded," pronounced the *New York Tribune* the day he died,[5] even as hundreds of well-wishers and curious gathered around City Hall and the Courthouse on hearing the news. Reformers could not ignore the reservoir of good will for the dead Boss. "The bulk of the poorer voters of this city to-day revere his memory, and look on him as the victim of rich men's malice," E.L. Godkin warned in *The Nation* that week. "The odium heaped on him in the pulpits last Sunday does not exist in the lower stratum of New York society."[6]

A *New York Herald* reporter visiting Tweed's old neighborhood by the East River heard recriminations not against Tweed but against his prosecutors: "It was broadly stated that he had been made a scapegoat."[7] Many agreed with Tweed lawyer John Townsend's depiction of the state attorneys general as shady cowards. "Schoonmaker had been just as bad as Fairchild was [except] Fairchild failed to [release Tweed] through dishonest motives; Schoonmaker failed to do it because he was afraid."[8]

Responsible voices condemned Tweed for his crimes, but the Boss had struck a chord with many by the way he'd carried himself during the last years of his life—despite his acknowledged epic-scale corruption. It created an awkward ambivalence: "Undoubtedly [Tweed] was not a malignant scoundrel," noted even the hostile *Harper's Weekly*, whose star illustrator Thomas Nast had been at the forefront of his downfall and continued to draw cartoons of him as a pathetic jail bird, "he was a hearty boon companion, a lover of his friends, and generous to 'the boys.' Should he, therefore, not have paid the lawful and not extravagant penalty of offenses that thin and morose men would have paid if they had committed?"[9]

Tweed's story of pride, fall, and redemption, its stunning highs and tragic lows, defied snap judgments. Sunday church sermons across the country chewed at the moral lessons. "To prove that this life is an awful peril, I point to the wreck of Friday at Ludlow Street Jail," Brooklyn's widely-read Reverend T. De Witt Talmadge told his church flock that week. "Let him that standeth take heed, lest he fall."[10] Others pointed to basic compassion for a lost soul. "It is a mercy to him that he has been taken away," offered the *New York World*.[11]

Tweed's own family kept his funeral low key. The scandal had already shattered their lives, bringing shame on the household and poverty to the door. Tweed's body was packed in ice and was taken from Ludlow Street Jail to the home of his daughter Josephine on 77th Street. Telegrams went out to family members scattered around the world: Word came quickly from Tweed's two married daughters in New Orleans, Lizzie and Mary Amelia. Lizzie and her husband John Maginnis started immediately for New York to attend the funeral, but the older sister Mary Amelia claimed to be too ill to travel. Tweed's wife Mary Jane and his oldest sons William Jr. and Richard wired back from Paris to proceed without them. His two youngest sons, 10-year-old

George and 14-year-old Charles, kept away from him in New England boarding schools for the last five years, were not told about their father's death.

On the day of the funeral, crowds formed early on the street outside the black-draped house where Tweed's body lay. Stoops around Madison Avenue and 77th Street swarmed with people, men and women both, perhaps a thousand altogether. Most were rough looking, many Irish, "almost exclusively of the poorer classes," a reporter noted, "drawn from all parts of the City by feelings of gratitude."[12] They stood quietly in the cold, a brief vigil, waiting for a chance to see the old Boss' coffin go by and say a last hurrah.

Inside the house, the service itself drew just a scattering of old-timers; "the only mourners at Tweed's funeral were his kinsfolk, a few old friends, and a few poor people whom his bounty had warmed and fed," a reporter noted.[13] Rufus Cowing, the single Republican on the aldermen's investigating committee, Warden Liscomb of Blackwell's Island prison, Tweed's lawyers John Townsend and William Edelstein, his aide Luke Grant from the Ludlow Street Jail, and a handful of retired aldermen, city clerks, and firemen mingled with family members and friends like bondsman William Devlin and Foster Dewey. Everyone else stayed away. Not a single leading politician of the day showed his face, nor any of the reformers, nor any members of the former Ring.

Reverend Dr. Joseph Price, the same cleric who'd married both the Boss himself and all the Tweed children, now an old man with a long white beard and broken voice, led a brief service. Afterward, the family opened the front door and invited the people standing outside on 77th Street to come in and walk single file through the parlor to see Tweed's body in its open rosewood casket, dressed in black suit and white tie, its head resting on flowers—lilies, roses, violets—with a pillow nearby embroidered to say "Our Father." Hundreds took advantage of the gesture.

Only eight carriages followed Tweed's coffin down Madison and Fifth Avenues to the Hamilton Ferry at the foot of Broadway and across to Brooklyn's Greenwood Cemetery. "If he had died in 1870, Broadway would have been festooned with black and every military and civic organization in the city would have followed him," Coroner Woltman remarked.[14] One lot owner at Greenwood Cemetery complained about Tweed's being buried there at all, citing a cemetery rule that forbid "any person … to be interred therein who shall have died in any prison or shall have been executed for a crime." He backed down only after being assured there would be no "striking monument" erected for Tweed.[15] The family buried him next to his parents under a simple marker inscribed "To Our Father," with room left for his wife later on.

The Boss would leave no Tweed dynasty behind him, no Tweed fortune, no Tweed homestead. Instead, for the next century, the family would guard its privacy and disappear into the woodwork. He left no will; he'd long ago transferred any property of value to his children who'd lost most of it in forced sales. They sold the Greenwich estate, held in his wife's name, in May 1879 to a businessman named Joseph Millbank for a reported $75,000, well below its actual worth.[16] Tweed's daughter Josephine lost more money on an insurance scam. She'd purchased a $10,000 life endowment policy on her father back in 1868 at his height. It had cost her $1,000 per year in premiums and was supposed to pay her back the full face value in ten years or at the time of his death if earlier. After she'd paid in $9,000, though, the Knickerbocker Life Insurance Company, which issued the policy, decided to cancel payment, citing a clause that required Tweed to get its permission before he could travel abroad—a provision he broke by fleeing to Spain during his ill-fated jail break. Josephine sued, but the court ruled against her and she lost the entire amount.[17]

The Tweed children chose to surrender only one piece of the remaining property to satisfy their father's outstanding court judgments, the land in upstate Putnam County he'd purchased in 1870 to secure the city's water supply. They sent the deed to John Kelly as comptroller of New York City, in gratitude for Kelly's help in pressing for their father's release from jail before his death. "[Y]ou were the only officer who had publicly asked that good faith be kept with him," they wrote him through a lawyer.[18]

After that, the family scattered itself to the winds. The Maginnis daughters stayed in New Orleans; the younger Tweed sons settled in Connecticut, as did William Jr. Many of his immediate family remained abroad: Mary Jane would die in Paris in 1880, barely two years after her husband, as would his son Richard in 1884. The only Tweed descendant apparently to make a public mark in Connecticut was a grandson, John H. Tweed, a World War I Navy flier who became a well-known aviator in the 1920s and helped develop a local field which today bears his name: the Tweed New Haven Regional Airport. Otherwise, they are largely lost to history.

Of Tweed's inner circle atop the Ring—A. Oakey Hall, Peter B. Sweeny, and Richard Connolly—none spent a day in prison (other than Connolly's brief arrest in late 1871) but each would carry scars, sheepishly denying his role in the scandals but never escaping the "finger of scorn" that Nast had drawn to follow them through the years.

Oakey Hall ended his run as an actor at the Park Theater in his play "The Crucible" in early 1876 after just twenty-two performances. He gave up acting and would rotate between London and New York during the rest of the 1870s and 1880s. He tried his hand at journalism in brief stints at the *New York World* and a small newspaper called the *New York Truth*, but mostly he supported himself practicing law. His most famous client in later years would be a 25-year-old Russian-émigré rabble-rouser named Emma Goldman, later to emerge as America's foremost "anarchist." Charged in 1893 for inciting a crowd of unemployed workers in Union Square to seize bread off the tables of wealthy homes on Fifth Avenue, young Emma gave a gushing description of the elderly lawyer who took her case. "A. Oakey Hall was a great jurist, besides being a man of liberal ideas. He had once been mayor of New York, but had proved to be too human and democratic for the politicians," she wrote in her memoirs, glossing over the corruption scandal. "[D]istinguished-looking, vivacious, [he] gave one the impression of a much younger man than his white hair indicated."[19]

Elegant Oakey could not save Emma Goldman from a year in Blackwell's Island prison in that case, despite what she described as his "brilliant" defense. He dropped her as a client after she ignored his advice not to address the court on sentencing. Hall remained a social butterfly throughout his old age, taking up with an actress named Ella Morgan Davies at one point and, shortly after his wife Kate died in March 1897, marrying for a second time, to a woman named Mrs. John Clifton-Clifton.

All the while, he obsessed over the stain on his reputation from the Tweed scandals. To hear him, you'd think he'd never known Tweed at all, owed him nothing, and had become mayor all on his own. On a trip to London in the 1880s, Hall sued a well-known British writer named James Bryce for publishing a history of the United States, the *American Commonwealth*, that included a description of the Tweed Ring with Hall as a charter member. The suit languished for years before being dropped without trial.[20] Later, back in New York City, he was thrilled in 1898 when Noah Davis, the judge who'd presided over the now-famous Tweed trials twenty-five years earlier, came to his defense. Davis startled a group of retired jurists one night by commenting during an after-dinner speech that "Mr. Hall was innocent of the charge under which he had rested for years. He [Davis] knew … of his personal knowledge of the utter baselessness of the charge."[21]

Hall may have badgered the old judge into making the remark. He lived a few more months, until October 1898, and converted to Catholicism shortly before his death. The immense scrapbooks of newspaper clippings he'd saved about himself during his glamour days as district attorney and as Tweed's mayor of New York City in the 1860s and 1870s today fill many volumes of archives in the New York Public Library, a window on a happier time of his life.[22] Dominating its pages, though, is the scandal he claimed to have nothing to do with.

Peter B. Sweeny would return to New York in 1886 after twelve years' exile in Paris and rent an office on East 41st Street trying to worm his way back into city society, but it never took. A reporter visiting him for an interview in 1889 found Sweeny dressed in carpet slippers and a gray suit and described him as a fit-looking 65-year-old man: "solidly built, [his] head liberally covered with thick hair, showing a sprinkling of the gray dust of time, a bright, clear eye, a sallow complexion, bronzed to a healthy ruddiness by the sun, a short, heavy mustache, and an expressive mouth capable of forming itself into a peculiarly pleasant smile or into one of cynical bitterness."[23]

Asked about the famous scandal—as he constantly was—Sweeny had a quick response. He had nothing to do with it; "after seven years of the closest investigation I was publicly exonerated in open court of any imputation in connection with the 'ring frauds,'" he'd say, pointing to his 1877 settlement with prosecutors.[24]

In finding a "respectable" skirt to hide behind, Sweeny managed to one-up even Oakey Hall. When George Jones, the *New-York Times* publisher who'd led the paper's anti-Tammany campaign in the 1870s, died in New York in August 1891, Sweeny sent a letter to the *New York World* the next day claiming that Jones had given him full absolution just before passing away. Sweeny, according to his own story, had visited Jones at his home on West 37th Street and they'd had a long talk about old times in which Jones had commiserated with Sweeny's supposed suffering and scribbled out a private note to his managing editor saying: "There is nothing against Mr. Sweeny. I wish you would treat him most generously."[25]

The story is probably nonsense. George Jones by all accounts never wavered from his conviction in the Ring's guilt. No note from him ever surfaced, nor had he apparently mentioned the incident to anyone before his death, nor had Sweeny either. Almost nothing about the story rings true except for one thing: Sweeny's unquenched thirst for a clean name. He'd live another twenty years in the New York area, until 1911. His son Arthur, raised in Paris, would become a respected assistant city corporation counsel. But Sweeny himself would never escape the cloud; he'd be identified even at death as "One of the 'Big Four' of the Tweed Ring," the "Brains" of the operation.[26]

Slippery Dick Connolly fared worst of all. Already 61 years old when he fled New York after the disclosures, Connolly got little credit for his role in helping the reformers by turning over the Comptroller's Office at the height of the 1871 crisis. Craving obscurity, he traveled first to Egypt but even here he couldn't find peace; Nast's cartoons had made his face instantly recognizable. An American visitor who spotted him sitting on the piazza at a hotel popular with tourists described him in pathetic terms, "shunned by everybody, with trembling hands and vacant eyes."[27] Connolly had brought most of his fortune with him into exile, but he reportedly lost the lion's share speculating in Egyptian bonds. After that, he moved north and spent what money he had left settling into two homes, one in Switzerland and the other in Marseilles along the French Mediterranean. He wasn't able to enjoy life there either; he soon began suffering from Bright's disease, a form of kidney failure requiring painful treatments but never healing.

In December 1877, Connolly instructed his lawyers to confess judgment in New York City in the same $6.3 million lawsuit the state had brought against Tweed. He accepted liability for $8 million that included six years worth of interest, an amount he knew he'd never pay. "He was a very old man, worn out by an incurable disease, which was only relieved by frequent surgical operations," his lawyer told the court at the time.[28] He'd die in Marseilles about two years later.

On the other hand, those who claimed a hand in toppling Tweed's regime were treated as heroes and amply rewarded. Voters sent Jimmy O'Brien to a term in the United States Congress, though they refused to elect him mayor of New York City. Judge Noah Davis won promotion to chief judge of New York's state supreme court. Prosecutor Wheeler Peckham went on to enjoy a thirty-year career in private legal practice and editor Louis Jennings of the *New-York Times* returned to England to be elected a Tory Member of Parliament. Andrew H. Green, after stabilizing the city's finances as comptroller, became New York City's premier urban visionary, with a hand in creating the New York Public Library (as an executor of Samuel Tilden's estate), Riverside,

Morningside, and Fort Washington Parks, and the Bronx Zoo, and driving the 1898 consolidation that added Brooklyn, Queens, and Staten Island into modern New York City. At 83 years old, he was shot to death by a jealous lover mistaking him for the elderly man who'd stolen his girlfriend.[29]

Even Charles Fairchild, the state attorney general who rejected Tweed's "surrender" and "confession" and lost his job as a result, rose to prominence again in 1885 when President Grover Cleveland asked him to join his administration in Washington, D.C., ultimately as Secretary of the Treasury.

Of all the reformers, though, three names shared top honors in bringing down the Tweed Ring: Samuel Tilden, Thomas Nast, and the *New-York Times*. None of them held positions in government at the time; Tilden was still a private lawyer, through a state party official. The other two had no official power at all. Nast simply scribbled cartoons and the *New-York Times* was just a newspaper. Each would enjoy lavish accolades for a time.

Tilden built a national political career on his fame from the case, bolstered by his defeating the upstate Canal Ring as governor, making him the preeminent crime-fighter of his era. He rode the momentum all the way to the gates of the White House in 1876. Supporters would raise his name for Democratic presidential nominations again in 1880 and 1884 but Tilden had no taste left for it and would send word disowning the efforts.* Realistically, his chances for the presidency had suffered a blow in October 1878 at the hands of another newspaper digging ambitiously for a hot story, this time the *New York Tribune*. The *Tribune* that fall managed to unearth and decode secret "cipher" telegrams sent by Tilden's agents at the height of the 1876 electoral dispute, apparently offering bribes to vote-counters in the contested states: $50,000 for Florida, $80,000 for South Carolina, and $5,000 for the single vote from Oregon.[30]

Tilden denied knowing anything about it and was cleared of any personal wrongdoing, but the scandal damaged him. No longer could he pose as the pure, untarnished "reformer" above the normal grubby plane of politics, his principal calling card in 1876.

Instead, after losing the presidency in 1876, Tilden went on a long European vacation and then came home to focus on his law practice. In later years, his health failing, he turned to art and philanthropy. He renovated his

---

* Typically indecisive, though, Tilden in 1880 would leave his friends hanging until the last possible moment, waiting until actual convention balloting had started to pick a presidential nominee, before sending his letter of withdrawal.

Gramercy Park home into a showpiece with interior stained glass ceilings and dome, a Victorian sandstone front, and Italianate word-carved fireplaces and moldings. It survives today as home to the National Arts Club, designated as both a New York and a National Historic landmark. On his death in 1886, Tilden willed most of his $5 million fortune and enormous book collection to form what would become the New York Public Library, one of the world's foremost research centers today. Fittingly, its famous building on New York's Fifth Avenue and 42nd Street with its stone lions guarding the front gate stands just across the street from where Tweed's own Fifth Avenue mansion had been a century before.

Critics have given Tilden mixed grades for his role in the Tweed affair. He came late to the crusade; he didn't throw down his gauntlet until weeks after the *New-York Times* had made the case in July 1871 through its Secret Accounts expose. Up until then, he'd virtually cowered before Tweed's person and bowed to his machine, giving credence to later charges of complicity with the Ring. But by two surgical strokes—the capture of the Comptroller's Office and the tracing of the Broadway Bank accounts—he put a fatal dagger in the operation.

His later role as governor, overseeing the prosecutions, stretching the law to keep Tweed behind bars as other Tammany suspects went free, raised eyebrows even during his lifetime. By letting politics and personal malice appear to shade his judgment, he ironically accomplished what Tweed could never do himself. He turned the Boss into a martyr. There had never been a case before like Tweed's and Tilden had no script to follow but his own instincts.

Nast and the *New-York Times* generally get top honors for bringing down the Boss. Working together, they demonstrated a power of media persuasion never before seen in America, galvanizing public outrage into a potent political force. It set a sobering precedent. Media-made hysteria itself was a mixed blessing: in the right hands it could be a power for reform, but prone to endless manipulation. In 1898, "yellow press" hoopla over the sinking of the U.S. battleship *Maine* in Havana Harbor would take the country to war before anyone knew who'd actually exploded the ship. Even Tweed's case raised concerns: Nast and *New-York Times* publisher George Jones both had launched their assaults on the Boss long before concrete evidence against him emerged with the Secret Account disclosures. Both wrapped themselves in virtue, but the question remained: Had Tweed been innocent, could anyone have stopped their juggernaut, and would it have been any less effective?

The power of newspapers, magnified by new technologies of visual image and mass steam printing, placed heavy new responsibility on editors and publishers. Nast's visual images did not depend on facts and numbers to support them, as seen in his ability to place incriminating words in Tweed's mouth—whether he said them or not—and make them stick by repetition. The *New-York Times* too in chasing the story often mixed fact-finding and analysis with name-calling, slander, and moral grandstanding.

In Tweed's case, the evidence did finally emerge to vindicate the attacks, and George Jones likely knew from the start it was there, even if he couldn't print it. His and Nast's courage in the face of official harassment became the stuff of legend, and it paid dividends: it boosted circulation by gist of a good story and it won the confidence of a generation of readers in a responsible free press. Nast and the *Times* had pioneered a new role for newspapers as independent public watchdogs, far different from the political party lapdogs or attack dogs most had been until that time. Muckraking reporters of the Progressive Era would perfect the model, which remains a standard for investigative journalists to the present day.

The *New-York Times* would barely survive a near-bankruptcy in the coming years to enjoy its new fame. George Jones, now in full control, would show his independent streak again in 1884 by bolting the Republican Party, his traditional patron, to support "reform" Democratic governor Grover Cleveland for the presidency that year. Republican readers and advertisers, furious at the defection, would desert him; circulation would shrink and profits would fall by two-thirds, from $188,000 in 1883 to $56,000 a year later. By 1890, after a brief rebound, costs of constructing a new building sent profits tumbling again.

George Jones' death in 1891 left the newspaper marooned. After forty years as its financial chief, he alone understood its archaic bookkeeping. He left control in the hands of two heirs, his son Gilbert Jones and his son-in-law Henry Dyer, but neither took to the job. They raised the paper's price from 2 to 3 cents and lost thousands of readers to the "yellow press" journalism of Joseph Pulitzer and William Randolph Hearst. A group of *Times* editors tried to revive the paper's glory days by purchasing control for $1,000,000 in 1893, but Jones' heirs kept ownership of the *Times*' Park Row building and its accounts receivable; imminent bankruptcy placed it under judicial receivership by the mid-1890s.

Rebirth for *New-York Times* came with the arrival of a next-generation founding giant, 38-year-old Adolph S. Ochs, a successful Tennessee publisher who took control with a $75,000 investment in 1896, brought the paper out of receivership, cut costs, gave it a new mission, and soon turned it profitable again. That October, he placed his new motto on the front page: "All the News That's Fit to Print." The modern *New-York Times* dates its lineage from this point. Today, a century later, a direct family descendant of Adolph Ochs, his great-grandson Arthur Ochs Sulzberger, Jr., sits as publisher and chairman of the New-York Times Company.

Thomas Nast emerged from the Tweed affair as the most celebrated graphic artist of his time. His influence already had been profound, establishing the political cartoon as a powerful voice and building a language of symbols still ubiquitous: Uncle Sam, the Democratic donkey, the Republican elephant, and our modern Santa Claus. For twenty years after Tweed, he wielded his pencil as a scimitar over American politics. Presidents and senators dreaded his lampoons; and his friendship could tilt national contests. Success made him rich. By the early 1880s, Nast had accumulated a small fortune of $125,000, enormous for a newsman. *Harper's Weekly* paid him an annual retainer of $5,000 plus hundreds more per drawing. He earned a total of $25,000 in 1879 alone, more than triple the $7,500 salary then paid to United States Senators and more than double the $10,000 paid to the vice president and cabinet members.

But Nast, perhaps because he'd enjoyed so much success so early, failed to change with his times. Competitors cropped up like Joseph Keppler's satirical weekly *Puck*, *The Judge* magazine, and the *Daily Graphic* that began to win away his audience. He adapted poorly to new technology: *Harper's Weekly* in 1880 changed its method for turning artwork into typeset, switching from the hand-engraving of wooden blocks to photochemical reproduction. For Nast, this meant abandoning the soft pencils he'd used for years and turning to ink pens that gave him a thinner, weaker line. At the same time, *Harper's Weekly* began playing down its pure political content to reach a broader family audience. Unthinkably, in the early 1880s, it began rejecting many of Nast's drawings.

Nast had quit the magazine briefly in 1877 in an argument over editorial policy; he left for good in 1886. Without steady income, his saving eroded. He lost $30,000 in a single shot by investing in a new Wall Street firm called Grant and Ward, headed by his longtime hero General Ulysses S. Grant; the firm collapsed in 1884 when the junior partner, Ferdinand Ward, turned out

The lasting image of Tweed as money-grabbing pol, created by Thomas Nast. Harper's Weekly, *October 21, 1871.*

to be an embezzler. After that, Nast mortgaged his home in 1893 to start his own new illustrated journal, *Nast's Weekly*, which failed in the marketplace, losing him thousands more.

Theodore Roosevelt, a lifelong fan, jumped at the chance to help the struggling artist when Roosevelt became president in 1901. He offered Nast a political appointment—American consul to Equador, the only overseas spot then readily open. Nast, loathe to travel but strapped for cash, accepted. Asked by friends what he planned to do in his far-off post at Guayaquel, he quipped, "I am going there to find out how to pronounce the name of it."[31] Four months after arriving in mid-1902, he died there of yellow fever at 62 years old.

And what of Tweed, the old man who'd once ruled the city as Tammany Grand Sachem only to die behind bars at Ludlow Street Jail? More than a century later, Tweed remains part of the American political vernacular, but usually just as a cartoon character, the image framed by Nast and the *New-York Times*: the fat, corrupt, arrogant political Boss who stole a fortune from the public and defied them by saying "What are you going to do about it?"

Tweed didn't invent civic corruption or ballot box stuffing, but he and his Tammany crowd elevated the techniques to stunning proportions. They committed frauds gigantic on any scale, even if Tweed was personally guilty for only a small fraction of the while. In later years, estimates of "Tweed Ring" total plunder jumped from the relatively-modest $25 million to $45 million range of the 1877 Aldermen's Committee to fully $200 million (at least $4 billion in modern dollars), a figure clearly inflated for dramatic impact but never scrutinized. It became part of the legend.[32] Tweed lived in a corrupt time, the Gilded Age, but he defined that era and pressed its boundaries. Even by his own day's standards, to call something "A Worse Fraud than Tweed's" spoke volumes.[33] Tweed inherited a culture of graft endemic to New York City for generations and pushed it to its logical extreme, forcing the reformers to crack down. After his excesses, no city in America could tolerate his style of wide-open graft or ballot box abuse. Urban corruption didn't disappear but it evolved and became more subtle. "A villain of more brains would have had a modest dwelling and would have guzzled in secret," E.L. Godkin wrote in the aftermath.[34] George W. Plunkett, a Tammany leader of the next generation, well understood the point. "The politician who steals is worse than a thief," he'd say in 1905. "He is a fool."[35]

It's hard not to admire the skill behind Tweed's system, though. The Tweed Ring at its height was an engineering marvel, strong and solid, strategically deployed to control key power points: the courts, the legislature, the treasury, and the ballot box. Its frauds had a grandeur of scale and an elegance of structure: money laundering, profit sharing, and organization. It took the brilliance of a Samuel Tilden just to unravel the basic cash flow.

So sturdy was the frame that even after the *New-York Times* had printed its disclosures and citizens had mobilized, Tweed remained entrenched. The Ring had only one fatal flaw: its humanity. Human beings composed it, governed by greed, vanity, and fear. Greed ultimately took control; they stole too much and lost their nerve. Treachery broke the Ring more than any outside force: Had Jimmy O'Brien not leaked the Secret Accounts, had Judge George Barnard not handed the reformers their pivotal injunction, had Slippery Dick Connolly not handed the Comptroller's Office over to Tilden and Andrew Green, had Tweed himself shown better leadership and insisted his gang stick together in the crisis, it's easy to envision their weathering the storm and walking away.[36]

At its foundation, Tweed's system had an irresistible political equation: Everyone benefited, rich and poor alike, and nobody seemed to get hurt. Money for graft as well as good came mostly from outsiders. Taxes stayed low; Connolly financed city operations mostly with debt, selling bonds and stock to investors in Europe and on Wall Street, pushing off payment until another day.

For the wealthy, Tweed produced dynamism and growth. His regime spent $10.4 million on Central Park up through 1869 and millions afterward. Wasteful and riddled with graft? Certainly. But during this time the value of real estate in the three surrounding wards more than tripled, from $26.4 million to over $80 million between 1856 and 1866 generating millions in tax revenue, and the total value of property in the city rose 82.5 percent in the decade form 1860 to 1870—a product of many forces totally beyond Tweed or Tammany, but Tweed's fingerprints cannot be ignored.[37]

Along with growth came a dose of city pride, grand projects like the Brooklyn Bridge, paved uptown streets, and the new Courthouse. Even Andrew Garvey, the plasterer, in describing how he squeezed millions in graft from city projects, reminded investigators: "Mr. Tweed has frequently told me to try to have the work done well."[38]

By contrast, in the mid-1870s with Tweed disgraced and the local economy crippled by the panic of 1873, this frenzied building came to a halt. William Havemeyer, the new mayor, refinanced the city's debt and restored credit, but he saw only waste and graft in Tweed's public works. Hundreds of men who dug quarries, leveled streets, and hauled boulders lost their jobs. Havemeyer threatened to halt funding even for the Brooklyn Bridge, turning frugality into a moral stance against "large and centralized schemes of local government."[39] Andrew Green as comptroller cut every spending request that reached his desk during this period. After a decade of Tweed excess, citizens no longer trusted their money in the hands of activist government.

For the down and out, Tweed offered even more. The marriage of Tammany to the immigrant Irish poor had a pragmatic root. Tweed viewed the immigrants not as charity cases to pity, judge, or befriend. Instead, he respected them as voters to bargain with, to woo and court. He won their loyalty by providing tangible service when government "safety net" programs barely existed. His aid took many forms: state money for schools and hospitals, lumps of coal at Christmas, and city patronage jobs to put bread on family dinner tables. If winning their votes meant getting public aid for Catholic Church schools, Tweed was happy to lead the charge in the legislature, enjoy the credit, and take the political heat.

To Tweed, helping out poor greenhorns had less to do with kindness than politics, a more durable force. By welcoming the newcomers under its wigwam, Tammany gave them a share of power and a sense of community. To be a "Tweed repeater"—a foot soldier in Tammany's army to steal elections—was a bragging right to many, a badge of belonging and often the ticket to a job. Tweed was no Robin Hood. He stole, but not just from the rich, and he kept a large cut for himself. Still, compared with anyone else, the poor saw it as a pretty good deal.

Critics sneered at this appeal to the city's "lower stratum." Many elite politicians of the Victorian age cringed at the concept of popular sovereignty: allowing the unwashed, ignorant masses to outvote respectable taxpayers. They threw up their hands at "ruling vast bodies of human beings, containing a large percentage of the vicious, the ignorant, the criminal, and the unfortunate," as journalist Charles Wingate put it.[40] Tweed rejected this. He'd proved the city could be governed even after the maelstrom of the Civil War draft riots, though he'd clearly lost his touch by the time of his own scandals.

The problem was, Tweed's system was based on lies. Stealing was wrong, even then, and Tweed and the others knew it perfectly well. No regime based on it could last, or deserved to last. Eventually, the bills came due, the creditors got nervous, and the house of cards collapsed. Meanwhile, democracy itself almost drowned in the process: self-government meant little when elections were won by the side that cheated best. Tweed's style of running a political party—rigorous organization, ethnic inclusion, and tough discipline—became staples of big city machines for a century, fitting the lofty theories of democratic government to the rough realities of life. But with it came a dark-edged tradition: corruption on one side and overbearing celebrity prosecutors on the other.

The man behind the image can only be appreciated as a mass of contradictions. "Tweed was a bold, bad, able man, who had far higher ambition, far higher skill, [and] played with great recklessness the very game which carries other men … to the senatorships, chief-justiceships and governorships, and gives them the petites entrees at the White House," E.L. Godkin wrote of him at the time.[41] As a politician, Tweed had a human touch others could only envy. Stories abounded of his good nature. Firemen spoke of how he carried ladders through snowstorms to save a burning building or how he enjoyed a good fistfight with a rival squad: "Why, bless you, I've seen him wade [into a brawl] alone with a trumpet and clean out a whole hook and ladder company who tried to keep ahead of us in the car track," one told reporters.[42]

Locked away in jail, Tweed found a good word ever for the reporters who'd put him there: "If I could have bought newspapermen as easily as I did members of the Legislature, I wouldn't be in the fix I am now," he told the *Brooklyn Eagle* 's William Hudson. "The most of those—'cusses would refuse money when they didn't have enough to get 'em a decent meal."[43]

He did everything on a grand scale and left a trail of clashing images: The outgoing, backslapping leader uniting the city and helping the poor; the conniving schemer lining his pocket and monopolizing power; the victim of politically-driven prosecutors; the guilty architect of the largest municipal fraud in history. Tweed proudly insisted he had always kept his word, even while fixing a vote or skimming a contract. In the end, even after his epic crimes became public knowledge, people respected his integrity, especially in facing his accusers, serving time in jail, and, in the end, in confessing his guilt. It made him an oddly moral man for the most outrageous thief of his generation.

A century later, the fog has barely lifted. Professor Leo Hershkowitz, after studying Tweed's court records and municipal archives as closely as anyone, could conclude that Tweed was hardly a criminal at all and had been framed by slanted newspapers and prosecutors: "Tweed's testimony, his confession, his lack of facts and figures, his altogether pitiful figure suggest he was indeed a paper tiger, a bench warmer, watching the pros at work," he wrote.[44] On the other side sit the two closest things to smoking guns painting him the master swindler: Samuel Tilden's chart tracing $1 million in county Tax Levy payouts directly to Tweed's account at the Broadway Bank, and Tweed's own confession to the city aldermen.

"Tweedism" didn't die with Tweed. Tammany Hall would bounce back and remain a power in New York City politics for another ninety years, well into the 1960s. A parade of strong leaders starting with "Honest John" Kelly would clean house and restore discipline.[45] In the twentieth century, Tammany would spawn progressive leaders like Alfred E. Smith who would transform its traditional immigrant roots into an agenda of social legislation at the foundation of Franklin Delano Roosevelt's New Deal. But for every Al Smith,

Tammany would create a score of crafty fixers like wisecracking Mayor "Jimmy" Walker (1926-1932), popular for defending the nickel subway fare and pushing to legalize Sunday baseball but who resigned under fire over corruption charges and bad publicity from his high-profile extramarital affair with actress Betty Compton.

In 1927, Tammany would leave the old wigwam Tweed had built for it on 14th Street, its home for sixty years, and move to a new home on 17th Street across Union Square.* The 1930s would see a decline. Fiorello La Guardia (1935-1945), elected mayor in 1934 on a Fusion-Republican ticket, would cut off Tammany from its traditional City Hall patronage. By 1943, Tammany would have to sell its Union Square building and move into rented space at 331 Madison Avenue. That year, the New York County Democratic Committee would cut its formal tie to the club, though the label "Tammany Hall" would stick for another two decades.

The 1950s would see a renaissance with Tammany's last true "Boss," a media-savvy powerbroker named Camine De Sapio who'd rise to prominence behind respected leaders like Mayor Robert F. Wagner and Governor W. Averill Harriman. De Sapio would court publicity; his picture would make the cover of *Time Magazine* in 1955 with the Tammany Tiger peering over his shoulder.[46] Still, charges of "Bossism" would follow him and prompt a revolt. He too would be undone by a new generation of "reformers" led by Wagner, Eleanor Roosevelt, and U.S. Senator Herbert Lehman. His final defeat would come in 1963 in a race for leader of a Greenwich Village district at the hands of a young firebrand named Edward Koch, later to become Mayor of New York City.

Ironically, of his generation, only Tweed today has an official city building with his name on it: the "Tweed Courthouse" on Chambers Street by City Hall, scene of so many pivotal events in his life: the notorious graft, the "voucher robbery," and his conviction for fraud and sentencing to twelve years on Blackwell's Island. Originally budgeted in 1858 at $250,000, costs on this architectural wonder ultimately topped $4 million and perhaps $12 million or more, rich in gravy for all involved.[47] The building had become dilapidated, stigmatized for scandal, until the city began a major renovation in the mid-1990s. It spent $85 million to remove eighteen layers of paint, re-

---

* The structure survives today and houses the New York Film Academy, the Union Square Theater, and a liquor store.

place the ceiling and external marble cornices, reconstruct the marble and glass-tile floors, and repaint the elegant interior. Today it houses the city Department of Education.

Nobody intended for the gesture to be taken as a tribute or a vindication of the old Boss; the building's formal name remains simply "New York County Courthouse." Calling it for Tweed simply reflects what everyone knows: that Tweed built that building, just as he retains a hold on the imagination of the city. His swagger is as much a part of modern New York City as the steel, the concrete, the noise, and the traffic. That's good enough of a monument for him.

SOURCES

Archive Collections:

Library of Congress ("LC"):

- Henry Dawes papers.
- Hamilton Fish papers
- Horace Greeley papers.
- Andrew Johnson papers
- Abraham Lincoln papers
- Manton Marble papers
- George B. McClellan papers
- Edwin Stanton papers.
- William Seward papers
- Stanton papers
- Andrew Johnson papers

National Archives ("NARA"):

- State Department, Ministry to Spain.
- United States Marshals, Treasury Department.

New-York Historical Society ("NYHS"):

- Richard Connolly papers.
- Charles Fairchild papers.
- Andrew H. Green papers.
- A. Oakey Hall papers.
- Thomas Nast papers.
- Henry Fox Taintor papers.
- Samuel J. Tilden papers.
- William M. Tweed papers.

New York Municipal Archives ("NYMA"):

- John Hoffman mayoral files
- A. Oakey Hall mayoral files
- New York County Board of Supervisor files

New York Public Library ("NYPL"):

- George Jones papers
- A. Oakey Hall scrapbooks

- John T. Hoffman papers
- Thomas Nast scrapbooks
- Samuel J. Tilden papers
- Tammany Hall scrapbooks
- William M. Tweed papers

New York State Library ("NYSL"):
John Hoffman papers.
Legislative reports (cited below)
Tammany Scrapbooks

New-York Times archives ("NYTA"):
- Fletcher Harper Sr./Jr. papers
- George Jones papers.
- Henry Raymond papers.

Newspapers and Journals

- *Brooklyn Eagle*
- *Congressional Globe and Congressional Record*
- *The Daily Register*
- *The Evening Free Press*
- *The Evening Post*
- *Frank Leslie's Weekly Illustrated*
- *Gotham Gazette*.
- *Harper's Weekly*
- *The Leader*
- *The Nation*.
- *The Star*
- *New York Journal of Commerce*
- *New York Evening Telegram*
- *New York Herald*
- *New York Sun*
- *New-York Times*
- *New York Tribune*
- *New York World*
- *Pomeroy's Democrat*
- *Washington Post*

Government Reports

- "*Charges Against Justice Albert Cardozo.*" Judiciary Committee, New York State Assembly. ("Cardozo Impeachment") Report No. 1111. 1872.
- "*Evidence before the Grand Jury in the Case of A. Oakey Hall.*" ("Hall Grand Jury") New York. 1871.
- "*Gold Panic Investigation.*" United States House of Representatives, Report No. 31. 41st Congress, 2d Session. March 1, 1870.
- "*Charges Against George G. Barnard, and testimony thereunder, before the Judiciary Committee of Assembly.*" ("Barnard Impeachment") New York State Assembly. 1872.
- "*New York Election Frauds.*" ("Frauds") United States House of Representatives, Report No. 31. 40th Congress, 3d Session. February 23, 1869.
- "*Tweed Ring: Report of the Special Committee of the Board of Aldermen appointed to investigate the 'Ring' Frauds, together with the Testimony elicited during the Investigation.*" ("Aldermen") New York City Board of Aldermen, Document No. 8. January 4, 1878.

Books, Articles, Pamphlets:

- Ackerman, Kenneth D. *The Gold Ring: Jim Fisk, Jay Gould & Black Friday, 1869*. New York, Dodd Mead & Company. 1988.
- Adams, Charles F. Jr. and Adams, Henry. *Chapters of Erie and other Essays*. Boston: James R. Osgood and Company. 1871.
- Alexander, DeAlva Stanwood. *A Political History of the State of New York*. New York: Henry Holt and Company. 1909.
- Anbinder, Tyler. *Five Points: The 19th-Century New York City Neighborhood that Invented Tap Dance, Stole Elections, and Became the World's Most Notorious Slum*. New York: Plume. 2002.
- Anbinder, Tyler. "Tweed, William Magear." *American National Biography*. Volume 22. New York: Oxford University Press. 1999.
- Berger, Meyer. *The Story of The New-York Times, 1851-1951*. New York: Arno Press. 1970.
- Bernstein, Iver. *The New York City Draft Riots: Their Significance for American Society and Politics in the Age of the Civil War*. New York: Oxford University Press. 1990.

- Bigelow, John, editor. *Letters and Literary Memorials of Samuel J. Tilden.* ("Tilden letters") Port Washington, N.Y.: Kennikat Press. 1908.
- Bigelow, John. *The Life of Samuel J. Tilden.* New York: Harper & Brothers Publishers. 1895.
- Bigelow, John, editor. *Writings and Speeches of Samuel J. Tilden.* ("Tilden writings") New York: Harper and Brothers. 1885.
- Boller, Paul F. Jr. *Presidential Campaigns.* New York: Oxford University Press. 1984, 1996.
- Bowen, Croswell. *The Elegant Oakey.* New York: Oxford University Press. 1956.
- Breen, Matthew P. *Thirty Years of New York Politics, Up-to-Date.* New York. 1899.
- Bridges, Peter. "An Appreciation of Alvey Adee." *American Diplomacy.* December, 2001.
- Brummer, Sidley Davis. *Political History of New York State during the Period of the Civil War.* New York: AMS Press, Inc. 1967.
- Bunker, Gary. "*Thomas Nast's Rare Lincoln Political Caricatures.*" C.A.R.I.C.A.T.U.R.E.S. August 25, 2003. (*http//www.lib.niu.edu/ipo/iht820129.html*)
- Burrows, Edwin G. and Wallace, Mike. *Gotham: A History of New York City to 1898.* New York: Oxford University Press. 1999.
- Calhoun, Charles W., editor. *The Gilded Age: Essays on the Origins of Modern America.* Wilmington, Delaware. SR Books. 1996.
- Callow, Alexander B. *The Tweed Ring.* London: New York: Oxford University Press. 1965.
- Clews, Henry, LL. D. *Fifty Years in Wall Street.* New York: Irving Publishing. 1908.
- Coleman, Charles H. *The Election of 1868: The Democratic Effort to Regain Control.* New York: Columbia University Press. 1933.
- Cook, Adrian. *The Armies of the Street: The New York City Draft Riots of 1863.* University Press of Kentucky.
- Cook, Theodore P. *The Biography of Samuel J. Tilden.* New York: H.S. Goodspeed & Co. 1884.
- Cornwallis, Kinehan. *The Gold Room and the New York Stock Exchange and Clearing House.* New York: A.S. Barnes. 1879.

- Daniels, Jonathan. "Mr. Jones and the Tiger." *Neiman Reports*. Vol. XX, No. 4. December 1966.
- Daniels, Jonathan. *They Will be Heard: America's Crusading Newspaper Editors*. New York: McGraw-Hill Book Company. 1965.
- Davenport, John I. *The Election and Naturalization Frauds in New York City, 1860-1870*. New York. 1894.
- Davis, Elmer. *History of the New-York Times, 1851-1921*. New York: The New-York Times. 1921.
- Fairfield, Francis Gerry. *The Clubs of New York*. New York: Arno Press. 1975.
- Flick, Alexander C. *Samuel Jones Tilden: A Study in Political Sagacity*. New York: Dodd, Mead & Company. 1939.
- Foord, John. *The Life and Public Services of Andrew Haskell Green*. New York: Doubleday, Page & Company. 1913.
- Gellman, David N. and Quigley, David. *Jim Crow New York: A Documentary History of Race and Citizenship, 1777-1877*. New York: New York University Press. 2003.
- Goldman, Emma. *Living My Life*. New York: Alfred A. Knopf, Inc. 1931. [Internet version: Anarchist Archives.]
- Hale, William Harlan. *Horace Greeley: Voice of the People*. New York: Harper & Brothers.
- Harper, J. Henry. *The House of Harper: A Century of Publishing in Franklin Square*. New York: Harper & Brothers, Publishers. 1912.
- Hershkowitz, Leo. *Tweed's New York: Another Look*. New York: Anchor Books/ Doubleday. 1977.
- Hershkowitz, Leo. *Boss Tweed in Court*. Bethesda, MD: University Publications of America. 1990.
- Hirsch, Mark D. "More Light on Boss Tweed." *Political Science Quarterly*. Vol. 60, Issue 2. June 1945.
- Hirsch, Mark D. "Samuel J. Tilden: The Story of a Lost Opportunity." *The American Historical Review*. Vol. LVI, No. 4. July 1951.
- Hirsch, Mark D. *William C. Whitney: Modern Warwick*. New York: Dodd, Mead & Company. 1948.
- Hood, Clifton. *722 Miles: The Building of the Subways and How They Transformed New York*. Baltimore: The Johns Hopkins University Press. 1993.

- "*How New York is Governed.*" (Pamphlet) New York: The New York Daily Times. 1871.
- Hudson, Frederick. *Journalism in the United States from 1690 to 1872.* New York: Haskell House Publishers Ltd. 1873, 1968.
- Hudson, William C. *Random Recollections of an Old Political Reporter.* New York: Cupples & Leon Company. 1911.
- Jackson, Kenneth T., editor. *The Encyclopedia of New York City.* New Haven: Yale University Press. 1995.
- Katz, Irving. *August Belmont: A Political Biography*. New York: Columbia University Press. 1968.
- Keneally, Thomas. *American Scoundrel: The Life of the Notorious Civil War General Dan Sickles*. New York: Anchor Books. 2002.
- Kessner, Thomas. *Capital City: New York City and the Men Behind America's Rise to Economic Dominance, 1860-1900.* Simon & Schuster. 2003.
- Klein, Maury. *The Life and Legend of Jay Gould.* Baltimore: The Johns Hopkins University Press. 1986.
- Kluger, Richard. *The Paper: The Life and Death of the New York Herald Tribune*. New York: Vintage Books. 1986.
- Leonard, Thomas C. *The Power of the Press: The Birth of American Political Reporting*. New York: Oxford University Press. 1986.
- Lynch, Denis Tilden. *"Boss" Tweed: The Story of a Grim Generation.* New York: Boni and Liveright. 1927.
- Mandelbaum, Seymour J. *Boss Tweed's New York.* New York: John Wiley & Sons. 1965.
- McCullough, David. *The Great Bridge.* New York: Simon and Schuster. 1972.
- McFeely, William S. *Grant: A Biography*. New York: W.W. Norton & Company. 1981.
- McJimsey, George T. *Genteel Partisan: Manton Marble, 1834-1917.* Ames, Iowa: The Iowa State University Press. 1971.
- McLoughlin, J. Fairfax. *The Life and Times of John Kelly, Tribune of the People*. New York: The American News Company. 1885.
- Mitchell, Stewart. *Horatio Seymour of New York*. Cambridge, Massachusetts: Harvard University Press. 1938.

- Morphet, David. *Louis Jennings, MP: Editor of the New-York Times and Tory Democrat*. London: Notion Books. 2001.
- Morris, Lloyd. *Incredible New York: High Life and Low Life of the Last Hundred Years*. New York: Random House. 1951.
- Morris, Roy Jr. *Fraud of the Century: Rutherford B. Hayes, Samuel Tilden and the Stolen Election of 1876*. New York, Simon & Schuster. 2003.
- Mushkat, Jerome. *The Reconstruction of the New York Democracy, 1861-1874*. New Jersey: Fairleigh Dickinson University Press. 1981.
- Mushkat, Jerome. *Tammany: The Evolution of a Political Machine*, 1789-1865. Syracuse University Press, 1971.
- Nevins, Allan. *Hamilton Fish: The Inner History of the Grant Administration*. New York: Dodd, Mead & Company. 1936.
- *The New-York Times Jubilee Supplement, 1951-1901*. New York: The New-York Times. September 18, 1901.
- "*Official Document on Extravagance of the Tammany Ring*." (Pamphlet.) New York City Council of Political Reform. New York. 1871.
- "*Official Proceedings of the Democratic National Convention of 1868*." [internet site]
- Paine, Albert Bigelow. *Th. Nast: His Period and His Pictures*. New York: The Macmillan Company. 1904.
- Pratt, John W. "Boss Tweed's Public Welfare Program." *New York Historical Society Quarterly*. Volume XLV. October 1961.
- Reeves, Thomas C. *Gentleman Boss: The Life and Times of Chester Alan Arthur*. Newtown, Ct: American Political Biography Press. 1975.
- Riordon, William L. Plunkett of Tammany Hall: A Series of Very Plain Talks on Very Practical Politics. New York: New American Library. 1995,
- Ritchie, Donald A. *American Journalists: Getting the Story*. New York: Oxford University Press.1997.
- Salwen, Peter. *Upper West Side Story: A History and Guide*. New York: Abbeville Press Publishers. 1989.
- Sears, Stephen W. *George B. McClellan: The Young Napoleon*. New York: Ticknor & Fields. 1988.
- Sirois, A.L. *Boss Tweed's Dinosaurs*. Amherst Jct., Wisconsin: Hard Shell Word Factory. 2002.
- Spann, Edward K. *Gotham at War: New York City, 1860-1865*. Wilmington, Delaware: SR Books. 2002.

- Strong, George Templeton. *The Diary of George Templeton Strong: Post-War Years, 1865-1875*. Allan Nevins and MiltonThomas, editors. New York: The MacMillan Company. 1952.
- Summers, Mark Wahlgren. *The Era of Good Stealings.* New York: Oxford University Press. 1993.
- Swanberg, W.A. *Jim Fisk: The Career of an Improbable Rascal.* New York: Charles Scribner's Sons. 1959.
- Sweeny, Peter B. "*On the 'Ring Frauds' and other public questions. Taken from his Interviews and other papers.*" (Pamphlet.) New York: John Y. Savage. 1894.
- Sweeny, Peter B. "*The Political Situation, resulting from the Last State Election.*" (Pamphlet.) New York: The Jackson Association. 1869.
- Tilden, Samuel J. *The New York City "Ring:" It's Origin, Maturity, and Fall Discussed.* (Pamphlet.) New York. 1873.
- Townsend, John D. New York in Bondage. New York. 1901.
- Vinson, J. Chal. *Thomas Nast: Political Cartoonist.* Athens: University of Georgia Press.1967.
- Walling, George W. *Recollections of a New York Chief of Police.* Montclair, New Jersey: Patterson Smith. 1972.
- Watterson, Henry. *History of the Manhattan Club: A Narrative of the Activities of Half a Century.* New York. 1915.
- Werner, M.R. Tammany Hall. New York: Doubleday, Doran & Company, Inc. 1928.
- Wingate, Charles F. "An Episode in Municipal Government." *North American Review.* ("The Ring," in volume 119, October 1874; "The Ring Charter," in volume 121, July 1875; "The Shattering of the Ring," in volume 123, October 1876. Cited as Wingate I, II, and III, respectively.)

REFERENCE NOTES

1. Alone *(pages 1–8)*

1. "Well, Tilden and Fairchild…": *New York Sun*, April 13, 1878.
2. "I hope they are satisfied now.": ibid.
3. "honest graft": Riordan, p. 3-6.
4. "I am an old man, greatly broken…": Letter from Tweed to O'Conor, December 5, 1876, published in *Harper's Weekly*, April 14, 1877.
5. Eleven days of riveting public testimony…: See testimony in "Aldermen."
6. Suspicions he'd exaggerated his own guilt..: See particularly Hershkowitz, *Tweed's New York, Another Look*.
7. "Under promises made to me …": *New-York Times*, March 27, 1878.
8. Fairchild issued a public letter denying …: Letter from Fairchild to Schoonmaker, April 1, 1878. Fairchild papers, NYHS. See *New York World* and other newspapers, April 2, 1878.
9. "Behind all these phases of disease…": *New York Tribune*, April 13, 1878.
10. "My wife!…": *New York Herald*, October 26, 1877.
11. "Nine men out of ten either know me …": Tweed testimony, Frauds, page 266.
12. "Poor old man, poor man, ": *New York Tribune*, April 13, 1878.
13. "Other people will regret his death…": *New York Herald*, April 13, 1878.
14. "Such talents as [Tweed] had…": *New-York Times*, April 13, 1878
15. "[I]f it be right that men should be punished…": *Harpers Weekly*, May 4, 1878. For Nast cartoons, see *Harpers Weekly*, January 26, 1878.
16. "Without his boldness and skill…": *New York Herald*, April 13, 1878.
17. "As long as I count the ballots, …": *Harper's Weekly*, July 10, 1871. See, e.g., Wingate, p. 150; Wingate, III, p. 386; and Lynch, p. 370.
18. "The career of Tweed…": *Washington Post*, April 13, 1878.

2. Riots *(pages 11–36)*

1. "*As the representative of the Seventh Ward* …": Lynch, p. 83-84; New-York Times, December 30, 1852. I've used portions of the quote from both sources.
2. Governor Horatio Seymour was spending : This incident is from Mitchell, p.321-322; Cook, fn. 57 on p.287.
3. Seymour, a … Peace Democrat: Seymour claimed to oppose slavery but saw it as no reason for war. As his biographer described his position: "to destroy the United States because of slavery would be as mad as to drag all Europe into a war in order to abolish serfdom in Russia or polygamy in Turkey." Mitchell, 206.
4. "the bloody, treasonable, revolutionary doctrine…": *New York Herald*, July 6, 1863; Mitchell, p. 303-306.
5. Opdyke … "In his person he symbolized…": Lynch, p. 258.
6. "My friends.": *New York Tribune* and *New-York Times*, July 15, 1863. See Mitchell, p. 324, and Appendix (p. 581-584) which includes side-by-side texts from the *New York Express*, *Evening Post*, *World*, *Times*, *Herald*, and *Tribune*.

7. "If the conscription law will not bear…": *New York World*, July 15, 1863.
8. "[L]eave your interests in my hands…": *New-York Times* and *Herald*, July 15, 1863.
9. "Send away those bayonets.": *New York Tribune*, July 15, 1863.
10. "Gov. Seymour has just made a speech …": Letter from Goodell to Lincoln, July 14, 1863. Lincoln papers. LC.
11. "Bring out the Mayor" … "We still have law": *New York Herald*, July 13, 1861. Spann, p. 100.
12. "a tall overgrown man…": Wingate, I. p. 363-364.
13. Tweed … story about the first time he came out to vote: Lynch, p. 42-43.
14. Kansas-Nebraska Act … supported: See, for instance, Tweed to Jim Murphy, March 1, 1854. Tweed papers. NYHS. ("Do for God's sake keep Strong [an opponent of Tweed's stance] out of this anti-Nebraska business… I don't care a curse whether he opposes it or not, prudence (as he is known to be one of my warmest & best friends) requires that he should not by hasty action compromise (that's the word) us…. Talk to him on the subject."
15. "what for? I can't talk, and I know it….": *New York Sun*, April 13, 1878; Werner, p. 109. On the postmastership, see Tweed letters to Jim Murphy, January 9 and March 1, 1854. Tweed papers. NYHS.
16. Tweed … Order of United Americans: Anbinder (*American National Biography*), p. 60.
17. "If I don't [move]…": Letter from Tweed to Henry Davis, March 13, 1847, in Hershkowitz, p. 6.
18. Tweed and Seymour had sparred politically: Mitchell, p. 284-287.
19. Tammany Hotel … Nassau and Frankfort Streets: Prior to 1812, Tammany had earlier "Wigwams" on Broad Street and Spruce Street. The Hotel took its name from the organization, not *vice versa*.
20. "Supervisor Tweed, Judge [John] McCunn, and…": *New York Herald*, July 16, 1863.
21. Loyal Republicans … demanded a crackdown: See, for instance, *New York Tribune*, July 24, 1863; letter from lawyer David Dudley Field to President Lincoln, July 15, 1863 ("We must have more military force and a military head for New York,"), and letter from Opdyke et al to Lincoln, July 21, 1863. Lincoln papers. LC.
22. He barraged President Lincoln with letters: See, e.g., Seymour to Lincoln, July 19, 1863. Lincoln papers. LC.
23. statistics to prove his point: Seymour argued that the draft quotas assigned to New York were politically biased, with democratic districts given disproportionate targets. In response, Lincoln reduced the state's quota by thousands. See letters from Seymour to Lincoln, August 3, 1971, and Lincoln to Seymour, August 11, 1863. Lincoln papers. LC. Political enemies branded Seymour a coward over the issue; Horace Greeley's *Tribune* ridiculed him for trembling at "Irish servant-girls" who he feared "will, in case the draft is enforced, turn incendiaries in a body, and burn down their masters houses." *New York Tribune*, July 24, 1863; Mitchell, p. 329, paraphrasing *New York Tribune*, July 24, 1863.

24. "We are contending …": Letter from Lincoln to Seymour, August 7, 1863. Lincoln papers, LC.
25. "Looking to *time*, …": Letter from Lincoln to Seymour, August 16, 1963. Lincoln papers. LC.
26. Lincoln … ordered… authority to proclaim martial law: See letters from Lincoln to Sanford and Stanton to Dix, both August 15, 1963. Lincoln papers, LC. As the date approached, Lincoln also ordered Major General Charles W. Sanford, commander of New York's state militia, to report to Dix.
27. Lincoln was prepared…: Sharpening Lincoln's stance were reports of Seymour's disloyalty. See Dix to Stanton, July 25, 1863. Stanton papers, LC. ("[Seymour] is surrounded by many bad men, who are bitter and vindictive & whose influence on an individual like him of weak resolution is of the worst nature."); Dix to Stanton, August 16, 1863 Stanton papers, LC. ("I have twice asked Gov. Seymour if I could rely on him to use the military force of the State to enforce the draft in case of resistance to it, and have received no answer."); and anonymous letter to Stanton, August 11, 1863 ("Seymour wants time in order to array his copperheads against the government. Do not allow the time; push matters at once.").
28. City Court Judge John McCunn issued *habeas corpus* writs…: *New-York Times*, July 15 and 26, 1863. Oakey Hall, as District Attorney, would later win a state Supreme Court ruling depriving McCunn, as City Judge, of jurisdiction to issue writs at all. See "*In the matter of the habeas corpus on relation of Louise Nash*," in *New-York Times*, August 3, 1863. See also *New-York Times*, July 26, 1863, and McCunn's response on July 28, 1863.
29. Democrats had paid $2,500 to one Republican simply for staying home when the board chose voting inspectors: Tweed testimony, Aldermen hearing, pages 16-19. See also Townsend, p. 18.
30. "[T]here was hardly a time when our three votes …": Tweed testimony, Alderman, page 19-20. On supervisor graft generally, see Alderman report, p. 15-16, and testimony by Woodward and Ingersoll.

    Mayor Opdyke … had tried to stop this abuse: See Supervisor minutes, July 28 and August 5, 1863, NYMA; and Spann, p. 49, Municipal Archives.
31. Orison Blunt … "pepper-box gun": New-York Times, April 22, 1879.
32. August 28,… special public meeting: Supervisor minutes, August 28, 1863, NYMA.
33. "The committee [Blunt and Tweed] were received…": *New York Herald*, November 11, 1863; Hershkowitz, p. 93.
34. "Tammany Hall, representing more than half…": Letter from Dix to Stanton, July 25, 1863. Stanton papers, LC. Dix, before the war, had been a New York canal commissioner, state assemblyman, United States Senator, and postmaster, all as a Democrat.
35. Stanton "highly commended [the plan]…": *New York Herald*, November 11, 1963.
36. Tweed … not meet with Lincoln personally: Lincoln's official papers never mention Tweed by name and Tweed acknowledged that he had never met "privately" with Lincoln—though certainly the two had met in larger groups. Ori-

son Blunt did meet with Lincoln several times, including once over the draft, though not on this trip. See *New-York Times*, April 22, 1879.

37. wheel … selected … Tweed … loud, good-natured cheer: New York Herald, August 27, 1863.
38. "[I]f the duties of the Board are arduous…": *New York Herald*, September 26, 1863.
39. "performing their duties with eminent satisfaction…": *New-York Times*, September 11, 1863.
40. By September 29, out of 1,034 draftees : *New-York Times*, September 29, 1963. By then also, investors purchased over $829,000 worth of the new "Soldiers' Substitute Bounty Redemption Bonds" by September 4 alone. The Broadway Bank, where Tweed kept personal accounts, took the largest share: $500,000. *New-York Times*, September 2, 1863
41. "No money, no trust was ever more honestly administered…": *New-York Times*, September 11, 1863.
42. FN: Tweed, of course, was no innocent at war profiteering.: Lynch, p. 241, in Callow p. 23, Kessner, p.147.
43. epidemic of war profiteering: Details on the corruption are from Spann, p. 178-183.

    116,382 recruits: Spann, p. 178. Many of these recruits came from places other than New York, but were drawn to the city by the bounty money.
44. "He is a live man, …": Mushkat, p. 344 and 349.
45. Harper & Brothers: The company was founded in 1817 as J.& J. Harper, later renamed Harper and Brothers, by the four sons of Joseph Harper.
46. "Go finish your picture,": Vinson, 1.
47. prizefight between …Heenan and … Sayers: The fight lasted 42 rounds before police broke it up and the *Illustrated News* devoted an entire issue to Nast's drawings. Nast had earlier covered the 1858 fight between Heenan and New York's John Morrissey at Long Point, Canada.
48. "It is full of life and character": Bunker, 7. When Harper had launched its new *Harper's Weekly* in 1857, Nast had wanted to join immediately and had sold a freelance piece called "Police Scandal" as early as 1859.
49. "Compromise with the South": *Harper's Weekly*, September 3, 1864.
50. new scandal …tricking soldiers into signing blank ballots: Generally n the soldier fraud scandal, see *New- York Times* and other newspapers, October 28, 1864, et seq.
51. Nast preferred to work from his home.: Many readers were surprised to learn that Nast had not seen the Civil War battlefront when he drew his famous early wartime images. He got his first look in mid-1863, traveling to Fort Moultrie in South Carolina and then joining General Phil Sheridan's troops in Virginia.
52. "I think you are a lucky fellow…": Paine, p. 84.
53. "earnest and definite way …": Harper, p. 120.
54. "How Copperheads Obtain their Votes": *Harper's Weekly*, November 12, 1864.
55. Lincoln would carry New York State: Lincoln's War Department sent 10,000

troops to New York under Union General Benjamin Butler to guard against Election Day disruption, citing reports that Confederate agents had infiltrated from Canada.

56. "Thomas Nast has been our best recruiting sergeant": Harper, p. 188. Some of Nast's earlier Lincoln drawings were less flattering. After the 1863 Union debacle at Fredericksburg, he drew a cartoon in *Phunny Phellow* with the caption: "Lincoln is sleeping on the job. That's What's the Matter, or Who's to Blame—A Tragedy."

3. Ballots *(pages 37–59)*

1. *"The fact is New York politics…*: Tweed interview, *New York Herald*, October 26, 1877.
2. Manhattan Club … Tweed: In fact, it's not clear if they ever allowed Tweed to join at all. One Club history lists him as a member (Fairfield), another leaves him out (Watterson), and a Tilden biographer insists Tweed was never invited. (Flick, p. 152)
3. William E. Dodge … private receptions: See Invitation to Dawes from W.E. Dodge, December 26, 1868. Dawes papers. LC.
4. "a jolly, good-hearted, free-and-easy …": Cornwallis, p. 34.
5. Robert Murray … best cigars and brandy: See e.g. letters from Murray to William Seward, July 21, 1865,June 4, 1864, May 2, 1864, Dec. 8, 1863, Oct. 19, 1864. Seward papers, LC.
6. "I take for granted that the stuffing of ballot-boxes…": Murray testimony, Frauds, P. 52-53.
7. Tweed … foreign-born constituted half to three-fifths: Tweed testimony, Frauds, p. 270.
8. Rosenberg … operating from a lager-beer saloon : See *New-York Times*, October 22, 1868; Butts testimony, Frauds, p. 18. Democrats had several such offices in Irish and German neighborhoods. Saloons were convenient gathering places, with men always around to act as witnesses in exchange for a glass of beer or a few dimes.
9. "a system was established whereby four oaths…": *New-York Times*, October 23, 1868. The apparent frauds reached upstate as well. Stories floated down from towns along the Hudson River—Newburg, Fishkill, and Poughkeepsie—of local Democrats wiring New York City for bushels of fake naturalization papers.
10. Hendrick … "gang of repeaters": Hendrick testimony, Frauds, p. 237-252
11. "State to the Committee…": Tilden testimony is from Frauds, p. 257.
12. "his clothes never seemed to fit …": Flick, p. 109.
13. "Please at once communicate…": Text of the Tilden letter, dated October 27, 1868, is in Frauds, p. 109.
14. Tilden had disowned the letter: "[N]o such paper was ever written, signed, issued or authorized by me, or with any participation or knowledge on my part," he'd insisted in a card to *The Evening Post*, November 5, 1868.
15. "I did not," Tilden repeated.: Tilden testimony, Frauds, p. 258.
16. because it was the usage…": Hall testimony, Frauds , p. 275.

17. clients … half the railroads: These included the Cumberland Coal & Iron Company, Erie Railway, Pittsburgh, Fort Wayne, & Chicago railroad, Pennsylvania Coal Company, Michigan Southern & Northern Indiana Railroad.
18. Tilden … independent streak: He'd also bolted his party in 1848 to support the Free Soilers and their presidential candidate, family friend Martin Van Buren.
19. He … campaigned against Lincoln: Tilden described Lincoln as "a man whose whole knowledge and experience of statesmanship was derived from one term in Congress, a long service in the county conventions at Sangamon, …and some acquaintance with the lobby at Springfield," who now confronted "the greatest questions and most complicated forces of modern history." Lynch, p. 243.
20. "As a rule people did not like Tilden…": Flick, p. 110.
21. "found a fairly satisfactory substitute …sexual foolishness.": Flick, p. 108.
22. friends had urged him to seek the New York governorship: See, for instance, Dix to Tilden, May 15, 1868. Bigelow (Tilden letters), p. 227. See also Flick, p. 167.
23. Seymour … he enjoyed his life as retired elder statesman: See letter from Seymour to Tilden, Nov. 29, 1867. Bigelow (Tilden letters), p. 211-212 Seymour tried to organize state leaders that year on the presidential campaign: "I think eight or ten men should meet at Albany…—say, Sweeny, Tweed, Brennan, Hoffman, etc., etc."he suggested to Tilden. This small group did apparently convene in Albany in March in Tweed's room at the Delavan Housel, but agreed only to endorse no candidate for president. See Seymour to Tilden, Dec. 13, 1867, Bigelow (Tilden letters) p. 214-215; *New York Herald*, March 12-13, 1868; and Flick, p. 173.
24. "My God Tilden, what shall I do?": *New York World*, July 10, 1868, in Flick, p. 177.
25. "Now that you and others …": Letter from Seymour to Tilden, November 10, 1862. Bigelow (Tilden letters), p. 168. Tilden's personal aloofness rankled the outgoing Seymour; they "respected but did not quite trust each other and it was always Seymour who sought a better understanding." Flick, p. 114.
26. "many demands for attention…": Letter from Tilden to Hogeboom, July 28, 1863. Tilden papers, NYPL, and in Bigelow (Tilden ltters), 180-181. See also letter from SLM Barlow to Tilden, July 15, 1863. Tilden papers, NYPL.
27. Seymour's agent to … Lincoln : Seymour described Tilden to Lincoln as "thoroughly acquainted with my opinions and purposes." Letter from Seymour to Lincoln, July 19, 1863. Lincoln papers. LC.
28. "Call your committee …" "Patriotism clearly commands…": Telegrams from Randall to Tilden and S.M.J. to Tilden, October 15, 1868. Tilden papers. NYPL. See also letter from Wallace to Tilden, October 17, 1868.
29. "No authority or possibility …": Tilden, Belmont, and Schell to Hoover, October 15, 1868, printed in *The Evening Post*, October 16, 1868. See also Tilden to Marble, October 20, 1868. Marble papers, LC. ("Your danger now is of making a merely defensive campaign on what you reference as our weakened point. That won't do. Attack. Accuse the republicans … turn the charge upon them…. Carry the war into Africa.")

30. After Election Day… bickering over money: See Tweed to Tilden, October 29, 1868. Marble papers. LC ("I would be much obliged if you would send the statement of your disbursements and if you have any funds on hand give me a check therefore.), and, from Tilden papers, NYPL, see Sweeny to Tilden, November 23, 1868, ("A week ago I wrote you a respectful note in regard to advances made by me which you guaranteed and payments made at your respect. You have not made any reply or taken any notice whatever of my communication. May I ask the reason of the apparent discourtesy."), Tweed to Tilden, December 1, 1868, and Sweeny to Tilden, December 16, 1868. Notably, these letters are omitted from Tilden's correspondence published in 1908, edited by John Bigelow.
31. "I did not know very much of the details …": Tilden testimony, Frauds, p. 259.
32. "Mr. Tilden, you cannot escape …": Letter from Greeley to Tilden, in *New York Tribune*, October 29, 1869.
33. "I was never drunk…": *New York Herald*, October 26, 1877.
34. "State your official position" … "I am deputy street commissioner": Tweed testimony, Frauds hearing, p. 266-7.

    Tweed had increased the committee's size: Mushkat, 355-356.
35. the "lunch club": Tweed "Confession," *New York Herald*, October 10, 1877.
36. Sweeny as Tammany's real power: The *New York Herald* called Sweeny "chief minister and master spirit of the party" and "commander-in-chief of the democratic forces." Hershkowitz, 135. His middle initial, B, usually appeared as "Brains" or "Bismarck."
37. "[S]anguine, active, and exuberant…": *New York Herald*, September 1867, in Hershkowitz, 125.
38. preparing to move uptown: Tweed and his family lived at 41 west 36th street until moving to the Fifth Avenue property in early 1870.
39. Tweed … his private clubs: He also belonged to the Blossom, American Jockey, and possibly the Manhattan.
40. contractors …agreed to pay … 35 percent: See Aldermen report, p. 14-18; Ingersoll testimony, Aldermen, p. 567; and Ingersoll affidavit, *New York Times*, June 3, 1875.

    In 1866 and 1868, the New York Citizens Association: See Hershkowitz, 113, 116. See Alderman report, p. 15.
41. "They [Tweed and company] are well paid: Bernstein, p. 207.
42. New-York Printing Company: Frauds report, p. 12-13; Wilbour testimony, Frauds, p. 448.
43. Tweed … new Assembly Speaker: Tweed's choice was Walter Hitchman, a Tammany committeeman.
44. "I found it was impossible: Tweed testimony, Aldermen, p. 29.

    Black Horse Cavalry: See Tweed testimony, Aldermen, 212-213.
45. "legalizing counterfeit money": Werner, p. 177.
46. Gould-Vanderbilt face-off… orgy of bribes: See Adams, p. 52-55 ("“The full and true history of the legislative campaign will never be known," but at its height, "fabulous stories were told of the amounts which the contending par-

ties were willing to expend.... The wealth of Vanderbilt seemed pitted against the Erie treasury, and the vultures flocked to Albany from every part of the state." When Vanderbilt finally conceded and cut off further bribes, "the lobby was smitten with despair, and the cheeks of the legislators were blanched." The full and true history of the legislative campaign...")

47. Tweed's keeping a mistress: Lynch, 279. See also Werner 106-7, citing Wingate, I, p. 364.
48. Tammany ... protect its own base: See, for instance, letter fromNelson Waterbury to Seymour, July 16, 1868. Seymour papers, NYSA, in Mitchell, 437.
49. "Temporary Headquarters ...": See letterhead on letter fro Tweed to Tilden, October 29,1868. Manton Marble papers, LC.
50. Superior Court... Common Pleas: These courts were both city tribunals whose judges were chosen in citywide elections. The Supreme Court, which heard appeals from the city courts, was a state tribunal whose judges sat in local districts; voters in each district elected their own judges. These three courts—Superior, Common Pleas, and Supreme—were merged in 1895.
51. Republicans ... challenge all immigrant votes: They'd caused similar problems in Pennsylvania that October. See *New York Herald* and *New York World*, October 20, 1868.
52. "Challenge! Sharp challenging...": *Evening Post*, November 2, 1868.
53. Tammany ... in ... wards and neighborhoods: *New York Herald*, November 1, 1868; *New-York Times*, November 28, 1868.
54. "More in the nature of a request ...": Tweed testimony, Aldermen, p. 135.
55. "[t]heir next step will be ...": *New York Herald* and *New York World*, October 20, 1868.
56. "I feared there would be some trouble ...": O'Brien testimony, Frauds, p. 379.
57. "I ordered them to arrest ...": O'Brien testimony, Frauds, p. 381
58. "Unscrupulous, designing, and dangerous men, ...": Hoffman Proclamation, October 31, 1868, from Hoffman testimony, Frauds, p. 99, and newspapers.
59. "[N]ext to the Roman army ...": Sweeny interview. *New York Herald*, November 26, 1869.
60. arresting Republican vote-watchers... deputy pulled a revolver": *Evening Post*, November 4, 1868, and other newspapers.
61. "ruffians" ... "turned off the gas ...": *Evening Post*, *N.Y. Sun*, November 4, 1868.
62. "I want very much to show ...": Letter from Godkin to Marble, November 3, 1868. Marble papers. LC.
63. "He was not approachable ...: Tweed interview, *New York Herald*, October 26, 1877. Tweed went on: "If he had not been so cold, John T. Hoffman was about the best" of the New York politicians.
64. "O, I hear rumors...": Tweed testimony, Frauds hearing, p. 266 et seq
65. "Perhaps I contributed ... about $10,000...": Congressmen at the time made annual government salaries of $5,000.
66. "I don't suppose that I have been ...": Tweed testimony, Frauds, p. 268.
67. "no one really in need ...": Tammany minutes, March 5, 1867. NYSL; Hershkowitz, p. 137.

68. "The ballots didn't make …": Tweed testimony, Alderman, p. 133-134.
69. "The frauds were the result …": Frauds report, p. 4.
70. Of the 156,054 votes … 50,000 had been fake … 8 percent: Frauds report, p. 5.
71. presidential electors: Congress would grapple with this issue only after the disputed 1976 presidential election between Tilden and Republican Rutherford Hayes where allegations of voting fraud in three Southern states would be resolved by a special, extra-constitutional bipartisan commission.
72. "a hifalutin and long-winded …": *New York Herald*, February 24, 1869.
73. "A Stock of Stale Slanders": *New York World*, February 24, 1869.
74. Judge Barnard … grand jury: *New York Tribune*, November 16 and December 1 and 2, 1868.
75. "manifestly unfounded … comparatively trivial.": Grand July minutes, in *New York World*, February 24, 1869.

4. Spoils *(pages 60–87)*

1. "*Tweed was not an honest politician* …": Lynch, p.417; Callow, p. 12.
2. "I've been called the king …": Callow, *The Tweed Ring*, page 34.
3. "Whilst Council fires …": Tammany scrapbooks. NYHS.
4. "Somehow or other the press …": Werner, p. 119.
5. "Few persons have as many *tried* friends …": Bowen, p. 51.
6. "the strongest man …": Sweeny ("On the Ring Frauds"), p. 56.
7. John Kelly… withdrew late in the race : Tilden's circle never found another candidate. On Kelly's role generally, see *New York Herald*, November 20, 1868; McLaughlin, p. 258-60. Republicans that year nominated merchant Frederick Conkling, brother of U.S. Senator Roscoe Conkling, "honest, frank, earnest, … not plausible, not voluble, nor all things to all men, and is of course doomed to be beaten." *New York Tribune*, November 28, 1868.
8. "It will be refreshing ….": *New York Herald*, in Bowen, p. 55.
9. "He calls a spade a spade …": Bowen, p. 106.
10. "Hall's all right …": *New York Sun*, April 13, 1878; Bowen, 61.
11. "a Metropolis without … boulevards …": Hall letter to the *New-York Times*, April 29, 1869.
12. "not to give approval to schemes …": Undated newspaper clip, Hall Scrapbooks. NYPL.
13. "Mayor Hall does not intend…": *New York Telegram*, in Bowen, p. 69.
14. "glittering regalia and bearing a silver war hatchet…": *New York Herald*, July 6, 1870.
15. Americus Club … dress code : Fairfield, p. 204.
16. "the American eagle sits supinely…": *New York Herald*, August 3, 1869.
17. "I never saw so many persons…": *New-York Times*, September 1, 1869.
18. "a palatial mansion, with a brownstone front …": *New York Sun*, March 15, 1870, in Werner, p. 188.
19. "That's Tweed. Drinks wine at 1 o'clock …": Hudson, p. 37.

20. Senator Tweed … sponsored bills: Hershkowitz, 130, 132.
21. widening Broadway … Critics charged graft: Hershkowitz, p. 138-9. Hershkowitz points to a January 1871 submission by New York's Commissioners of Estimate and Assessment listing property owners to be compensated for related damages, which fails to include Tweed or any of his close associates.
22. cut-glass decanters, steel-engraved wall hangings, rose-decorated porcelain cuspidors: Description of Tweed's suite at the Delavan House is from Lynch, p. 288.
23. subsidies for Catholic parochial schools: Tweed's plan, adopted as part of the 1869 annual Tax Levy, authorized the city to spend 20 percent of its excise tax proceeds from 1868 to support free schools other than public or charity schools. Before 1825, a handful of Catholic and Protestant schools had received city funding through special grants, and religious-sponsored charities continued to receive aid through the annual charities appropriations. See Pratt, p.404.
24. "no Catholic parent will be permitted…": *New-York Times*, March 26, 1869; Pratt p. 404-406.
25. Annual charity appropriation bill: See generally Pratt.
26. "Do not forget to put through …": Letter from Roosevelt to Tweed, April 12 and May 10, 1870, in Hirsch, p. 275.
27. "He appears to take to…": *New-York Times*, March 20, 1868.
28. "we expected to get the employment …": Tweed testimony, Aldermen, p. 130.
29. Barnard and Cardozo… injunctions: . See Ackerman, p. 28-31,237-243; Hershkowitz, p. 143-144.
30. "playboy side of Fisk …": Lynch, 299. . See also, for instance, Fisk to Tweed, May 27, 1870. NYHS.
31. "He was a powerful man…" " We could not get along …": Tweed interview, *New York Herald*, October 26, 1877.
32. "why, because you won't make money …": *New York Tribune*, June 9, 1880.
33. "The bills of the *Democrat* …": Tweed to Connolly, July 16, 1870.
34. "Dear Dick: For God's sake pay …": *New York Sun*, April 13, 1878; Werner, p. 194.
35. One list of vouchers … $3.3 million …: Taintor testimony, Alderman, 393-398, 435 et seq.
36. "Mr. Hall knew nothing …": *New York World*, December 8, 1869.
37. "mysterious glamour …": Wingate, P. 368.
38. "I am not, and never claimed to be…": Sweeny interview, *New York Herald*, November 26, 1869. Instead, he said: "If there is anyone entitled to that designation among the Democracy of our city, it is Senator Tweed…. He has remarkable executive ability, and is a recognized leader."
39. "As a taxpayer… I am not …": Sweeny, ("On the 'Ring Frauds'"), p. 12. There's a story that when Sweeny…: Lynch, p. 151-152.
40. Sweeny … paid $60,000 : Tweed testimony, Aldermen, p. 105.
41. "an almost perfect document …": Hudson, p. 31.
42. "All this was agreed to," …": *New York Sun*, March 30, 1870.

43. "Why the greediness of the Young Democrat…": *New York Sun*, March 30, 1870.
44. "They were young, …": Wingate p. 127.
45. Tweed admitted … entered the bribery contest..: Tweed testimony, Aldermen, p. 29.
46. "to walk up and down the hill …": Tweed testimony, Aldermen, p. 74.
47. Tweed … $40,000 apiece among five Republicans: Tweed testimony, Aldermen, p. 73.
48. Checks for $67,250 … "My greatest wish …": Checks and Norton's note to Tweed dated January 16, 1869, in Hirsch, p. 270.
49. newspaperman barged into Tweed's …demanded a $40,000 cut… : Hudson, p. 24.
50. Tweed … resigning his post …: See telegram from John Morrissey to Marble, March 22, 1870. Marble papers. LC.
51. " He sat in his [Duane Street] …": *Evening Post*, March 29, 1870.
52. "They've killed me dead, they think …": Hershkowitz, p. 152.
53. "It has become a personal fight …": Tweed testimony, Aldermen, p. 86.
54. "calmly reposing …" "It astonished me ": *New York Sun*, March 29, 1870.
55. election reform bill: The Election bill tightened rules for registering and challenging voters that, "if carried out, give us as near an approach to honest elections as we can hope for," said the *New York Tribune*, April 9, 1870.
56. petition supporting Tweed's charter : See Petition to the Honorable Senate of the State of New York, April 2, 1870, in Townsend, p. 33.
57. "They were convinced…": Tilden, writings, I, 566.
58. "The Committee is met to hear the advocates …": Partial transcripts of the hearing appeared the next morning in the *New York Tribune*, *Herald*, and *Times*, April 5, 1870.
59. "We shall be happy to hear …": *New-York Times*, April 5, 1970.
60. "not as fidgety…" "the general tone …": *New York Herald*, April 5, 1870.
61. "I don't care if any archangel …": *New York Sun*, April 5, 1870.
62. The *Evening Post*, … would blast Greeley …: *New York Herald*, April 6, 1870; *New York Tribune*, April 6, 1870.]
63. "forcibly but briefly": *New York Herald*, April 5, 1870.
64. "highly laudatory": *New-York Times*, April 5, 1970.
65. last witness … Samuel J. Tilden: Coming up to Albany from New York City that morning Tilden had shared a railroad car with Greeley. By one account, he spent the first four hours bending Greeley's ear on city policy resulting in "Mr. Greeley's profound sleep," complete with loud snoring. *New York Sun*, April 5, 1870.
66. He'd … deny backing O'Brien: See Tilden's non-denial denial in Bigelow (Tilden writings),p. 567. ("I entered into no alliance with the 'Young Democracy' for future political power, and for weeks was ignorant even of their meetings."); on Marble's role, see McJimsey, p. 140-142.
67. "inconceivable that Tilden …": Lynch, p. 323.

68. "more than ungentlemanly ...": Letters from Belmont to Manton Marble, March 30, 1869, March 1, 1870, in Katz, p. 187. That same month, Tweed may have attempted to depose Tilden from the state party chairmanship, but, if so, he failed in the state committee. Lynch, p. 315; McJimsey, p. 138.
69. "restore both the judiciary and *the bar*...": Bigelow (Tilden writings) p. 565.
70. Tilden wrote Cardozo... Russell Sage : Flick, p. 202.
71. "I paid you a retainer for Erie ...": Letter from Gould to Tilden, February 11, 1870. Tilden papers, NYPL.. See also Bigelow,(Tilden letters, p. 258. Erie railroad records indicate Tilden received a total of $20,000 from the company between 1869 and 1871. See also Gould letters to Tilden, February 24, March 9, August 2, and October 20, 1869. Tilden papers. NYPL.
72. "without any agency of mine...": Letter from Tilden to Gould, February 14, 1870. Tilden papers. NYPL. Bigelow (Tilden letters), p. 258.
73. "He don't stand in the way...": *New York Herald*, November 26, 1869.
74. "I am sick of...": *New-York Times*, April 5, 1870. The *New York Sun* had a slight variation: "I am *out* of the discussion of his question." *New York Sun*, April 5, 1870.
75. Tweed ... face ... every sign of contempt : Flick, p. 207.
76. Tilden ... failed to make an impression: See e.g. *New York Herald*, April 5, 1870.
77. "ashy white"... "repressed rage": Flick, p. 207.
78. "typical of the timorous, ...": Lynch, 327.
79. "I felt more scorn...": Bigelow (Tilden writings), p. 568-9.
80. "would close his career in jail...": Alexander, p. 265; Flick, p. 207.
81. "As to myself don't mention my name ...": Letter from Tilden to Marble, April 5, 1870. Marble papers, LC.
82. "No one was more thoroughly cowed ...": McJimsey, p. 142.
83. The next morning : After the hearing the prior afternoon, Tweed had rushed to the Senate chamber and moved that the charter come up the next day as the first order of business. Senator Henry Genet, of the recently defeated Young Democrats, interrupted: "Is not the Police bill the special order for to-night? I think..." Tweed stopped him with a simple glare: "I thought you said you were not going to oppose the motion," he said, speaking "*softo voce*" as one reporter put it. "I am not opposing it; but I don't like this thing." Genet said. The senators approved Tweed's motion 23 to 1, Genet casting a solitary "no."
84. "Tweed's good natured face ...": *New York Herald*, April 6, 1870.
85. "surrenders the City ...": *New York Tribune*, April 6, 1870.
86. "it takes a general ...": *New York Herald*, April 6, 1870.
87. Chester Alan Arthur ... "Tweed Republicans": Reeves, p.49-50.
88. Tweed as Commissioner of Public Works ... Peter B. Sweeny to head the Public Parks Board: Hall proclamation, April 9, 1870. Hall papers. NYMA.
89. "I beg you to take [it] ...": Letter from Hall toTweed, April 5, 1850. Hall papers. NYHS.
90. "Senator Tweed is to take charge ...": *Albany Argus*, April 12, 1870, in Hall scrapbooks, NYPL.

91. "It would give me great pleasure ...": Letter from Cooper to Tweed, May 28, 1870, in Hirsch, 275.
92. "to reimburse ... those...": Tweed testimony, Aldermen, p. 92.
93. Garvey... Ingersoll, ...$50,000 ... Keyser and Oakey Hall $25,000: Werner, p.184 and Aldermen testimony.
94. "Republican Legislature had to be bought,...": Woodward testimony, Aldermen, p. 699.
95. Tweed's ... direct account of the meeting : Tweed testimony, Aldermen, p. 78.
96. "a very confidential man" ... "had my confidence ": Tweed testimony, Aldermen, p. 75.
97. *"That the County Auditor [Watson] collect ..."*: Text of resolution from Tweed testimony, Aldermen, p. 142. Tweed would claim that the Board never met at all, that the record was forged later by Oakey Hall after the public scandal had begun. See Tweed testimony, Aldermen, p. 141
98. Courthouse ... budgeted at $250,000 ... graft ... none ever proven.: See e.g. Hershkowitz, p. 112-114.
99. "Woodward brought me over a batch...": Tweed testimony, Aldermen, p. 76.
100. "see [Oakey] Hall and tell him ...": Tweed testimony, Aldermen, p. 77.
101. Woodward... $932,858.50 ... account of William M. Tweed: See spreadsheet titled "Identification of the parties receiving the proceeds of warrants drawn for allowances made by Special Board of Audit, under Sec. 4, of the County Tax Levy of 1870." box 23, Tilden papers. NYPL.
102. $384,395.19 to the New-York Printing Company: See spreadsheet titled "Deposits to credit of New-York Printing Company." box 23, Tilden papers. NYPL. Company president Charles Wilbour later would claim that Tweed had sold his stock in the company on April 4, 1870, about two months before these transactions, though Tweed's lawyers would never raise this point in his criminal trials to dispute the implication that these transactions amounted to a pass-through of government funds. See affidavit of Charles E. Wilbour in the New-York Times and other newspapers, September 4, 1871.
103. "[Watson] told me that he had to pay ...": Woodward testimony, Aldermen, p. 691-692.
104. months James paid his brother a total of $228,120 ...: See spreadsheet slabeled "Payments by James M. Sweeny for account of Peter B. Sweeny, by checks on Tenth National Bank" and "Deposits by James M. Sweeny in the Nassau Bank from May 6th to August 23rd, 1870," in box 23, Tilden papers. NYPL. See also checks attached to Tweed confession, *New York Herald*, October 10, 1877.
105. Oakey Hall ... Suspension Bridge and Erie Junction RRG : See spreadsheet labeled "Suspension Bridge & Erie Junction R.R.G." in box 22, Tilden papers. NYPL.
106. Garvey ... Connolly's private home: Garvey testimony, Aldermen, p. 551-2; Garvey testimony in Hall trial, October 25, 1872, in *New-York Times*, October 26, 1872.
107. $96,300 to Smith, Gould, Martin and Company: The cancelled check is in the Tweed papers. NYHS.

108. tax bills … uncollected: $907,158.86 : Townsend, p. 39.
Total 1870 taxes … *pre capita* in New York…: Hoffmann papers, p. 321-322, NYSL.
109. New York …l debt… $36.3 million to … $73 million : See "Statement of the Debt of the City and County of New York taken from the Reports and Statements of the Comptroller." Hall papers. NYMA.
110. Seligman … House of Rothschild … Discounts Gesellschaft: Mandelbaum, p. 77, and cites therein. See also list titled "7% Revenue Bonds, County Payable December 1, 1871," in box 23, Tilden papers. NYPL.

5. Park Row *(pages 91–104)*

1. "My doctor says peremptorily…": Letter from Jones to Raymond, April 6, 1869. Jones papers. NYTA.
2. Jones … "suggestions" : See e.g. letter from Jones to Raymond, July 1, 1863. Jones papers. NYTA.
3. Raymond … actress named Rose Eytinge : Berger, p. 30-31.
4. "I shall never sell the Times …": *Harper's Weekly*, February 22, 1890. See also Davis, p. 83.
5. "it takes a steamer three days …" Juggernaut saturnalia festival: Morphet, p. 35, 41, 42.
6. "I have seen a good deal of Jennings …": Letter from Raymond to Jones, July 17, 1868. Jones papers. NYPL.
7. "He was the most lovable man …": Letter from Jennings to Jones, June 22, 1869. Jones papers, NYPL.
8. "the most abusive pen …": *New-York Times, Jubilee Supplement*,..
9. "jolly, genial, and off-handed …": *New York Sun*, March 26, 1870.
10. "Senator Tweed is in a fair way …": *New-York Times*, April 8, 1870.
11. "far above the average …": *New-York Times*, April 13, 1870.
12. D. George Wallis … three sinecure positions at City Hall: *Evening Free Press*, August 31, 1870.
13. *Albany Argus*, for one, received…: Tweed testimony, Aldermen, p. 239.
14. $2.7 million … to the press : Booth committee report, in Townsend,, p. 38. The *New York Herald*'s James Gordon Bennett, far too wealthy for bribes, Mayor Hall had appointed Bennett's friend Gunning Bedford assistant district attorney and had assigned a policeman to guard Bennett's mansion on Washington Heights. Wingate, p. 389.
15. *New-York Times* …"necessary legal advertisements…": See certificate dated August 9, 1867. NYTA.
16. paychecks from City Hall jump to over $21,000 and $29,000 : *New York Sun*, July 22, 1871.
17. *Leading New York newspapers* : Table is from *New York Herald*, September 8, 1871; F. Hudson, p. 687.
18. I would not exercise…" "I shall not enter …": Letter from Connolly to Jones, July 14, 1868. Jones papers, NYPL.
19. "serious evil that hordes of Irish …": Morphet, p. 72.

20. "Senator Tweed in a New Role": *Harper's Weekly*, April 16, 1870.
21. Nast... cartoons ... Tweed... in the background: See, for instance, "The Ecumenical Counsel, at Albany, New York" (Paine, p. 139) showing Governor Hoffman holding court dressed like the Pope: "I am infallible Pius Hoffman. You are infallible Cardinal Sweeny, We are infallible Tammany Ring," a sign behind him says, as he and all the Tammany leaders meditate over a box labeled "Tax Payers and tenants Handy Cash." Tweed, almost lost in the crowd with a grin on his face and a hand on his big stomach, wears a Cardinal's hat labeled "Big Six" with a pussycat's face drawn on it, a tamed version of the tiger emblem of his fireman days.
22. "We should like to have a treatise...": *New-York Times*, September 20, 1870.
23. "Perfect Harmony ...": *New York World*, September 21, 1870.
24. "the whole convention rose ...": *New York World*, September 22, 1870.
25. Tilden's name on a slate of malcontents ...reject ... 242 to 23: *New-York Times*, April 19, 1870.
26. Tweed had threatened to Lieutenant Governor Allen Beach...: Bigelow (Tilden writings), p.. 569. Tilden claimed he responded by saying "You had better try it," though it is not clear when he said it.
27. O'Brien-ites declined—"unless they could be...": *New-York Times*, September 22, 1870; Wingate, II, p.130-131.
28. Tilden's ... 500 tickets ... stolen: Wingate, II, p. 130-131.
29. "assured [the convention] that the City ...": *New York World*, September 22, 1870.
30. "The audience was put to sleep ...": *New-York Times*, September 22, 1870.
31. "Tammany is supreme. ... ": *New-York Times*, September 22, 1870.
32. "Mr. Tilden as the Slave of the 'Ring'": *New-York Times*, September 23, 1870.
33. "Will the [*Times*] tell us what ...": *New York World*, September 24, 1870.
34. "We hope [Mr. Tilden] has a realizing sense ...": Flick, 205.
35. Clubs in his honor popped ...": For instance, the Fifteenth Ward William M. Tweed Association that week opened a new clubhouse on East 9th, a "fine brown-stone building... elegantly furnished throughout at the expense of several thousand dollars" with public reading room, billiard tables and library for its 250 members, most calling themselves "personal friends of William M. Tweed." *New-York Times*, September 24, 1870.

6. Whitewash *(pages 105–122)*

1. "Mildly startled": Berger, p.36.
2. "King Tweed ..."" "The firman [edict] of an Eastern potentate ...": *New-York Times*, September 28, 1870.
3. "Mr. Tweed passes his Sundays..." "Mr. Tweed was worth less ...": *New-York Times*, November 2, 1870.
4. "Tweed and Fisk are bold ...": *New-York Times*, November 29, 1870.
5. "No man can answer newspaper attacks ...": Hershkowitz, p. 160.
6. Tweed ... New York Mutual Insurance Company, the New York Gas Light

Company, the Guardian Savings Bank, the Bowling Green Railway Company, the National Broadway Bank, and the Third Avenue Railway Company: Hershkowitz, p. 156.

7. FN: "None less than Brooks Brothers": Spann, pp. 46-50.
8. "Why Attack Mr. Tweed?": *New-York Times*, September 29, 1870.
9. "I am always in the habit …": *New York Sun*, March 26, 1870.
10. 1,300 names to its payroll… "ruffians" : *New-York Times*, September 26, 1870.
11. "Where is Connolly's Report?" "The Comptroller, Mr. Richard Connolly…": *New- York Times*, October 21, 22, 1870.
12. "[W]e charge them …": *New-York Times*, October 22, 1870.
13 "We of New York …": *New York World*, October 28, 1870.
14. Belmont … "canaille," :McJimsey, p. 139.
15. "Every Democratic vote… ": *New York World*, October 28, 1870.
16. "I … have never in my life spoken …": *New-York Times*, November 6, 1870; Lynch, p. 346.
    One exception was the Sixth Ward: Anbinder, p. 327.
17. the mayor's "cool judgment, perfect self-possession …": *New York World*, November 8, 1870.
18. : "we … certify the account books of the department …": See newspapers and Lynch, p. 347.
19. "These names [Astor and the others] represent …": Davis, p.98.
20. "full and fearless vindication," … "No one ever questioned…": *New York World*, November 8, 1870.
21. "used as a cover and a shield …": Wingate, II, p. 139.
22. "Jimmy, I think as much of you …": *New York Sun*, March 30, 1870.
23. "We shall cut off their supplies": *New York Sun*, March 29, 1870.
24. O'Brien … claims for sheriff's office expenses … $350,000 … "supplies to county jail..": See Tweed testimony, Aldermen, p. 50-51; Tweed confession, *New York Herald*, October 10, 1877.
25. "Our boss was at the time …": O'Brien testimony, Frauds, p. 432.
26. "I can hardly get a street sweeper …": *New York Herald*, January 8, 1871.
27. "You've been a kind friend…""Tears as big as black walnuts…" : *New York Sun*, January 3, 1871.
28. Twenty years later sitting on a veranda …: *New York World*, August 16, 1891. See also Harper, p, 289, Paine, 167.
29. "[A] smooth, smiling fellow …": O'Brien interview, *New York World*, August 16, 1891.
30. Connolly… at O'Brien's …Jackson Club: See, for instance, *New York Sun*, March 26, 1870.
31. "a seemingly inoffensive fellow…": Wingate, II, p. 141.
32. "I told Mr. O'Brien about them …": Copeland testimony in Hall trial, in *New-York Times*, October 26, 1872.
33. "I could not hear anything …": Copeland testimony, Hall trial, in *New-York Times*, October 26, 1872.

34. "every person in the office ...": Copeland testimony in Tweed trial, in *New-York Times*, January 17, 1873.
35. "it was utterly impossible...": Copeland affidavit, in *New-York Times*, October 3, 1871.
36. Garvey ... to meet privately with Watson: Garvey testimony, in *New-York Times*, October 29, 1871.
37. "very angry if he found out ...": Copeland testimony, Hall Grand Jury, p. 18-19; Wingate, p. II, 141.
38. O'Brien ... arrangement ...county supervisor: Tweed confession, *New York Herald*, October 10, 1877.
39. "The applause was deafening ...": *New York Sun*, January 3, 1871.
40. "more closely approximate ...": *Evening Democrat*, in *New-York Times*, December 29, 1870.
41. "like a planet in his shirt ...": Werner, p. 188.
42. "blue uniforms, liberally upholstered ...": *The Star*, clipping from January 1871, Hall scrapbooks, NYPL.
43. "The Monarch of Manhattan ...": *The Evening Telegram*, January 6, 1871. Hall scrapbooks, NYPL.
44. clog dancing...: *The Star*, January 19, 1871.
45. Tweed's city was booming: see Kessner, p. 49,78.
46. "The Mayor was dressed ...": Unidentified newspaper clip, 1870. Hall scrapbooks, NYPL.
47. "Here [in New York City] you enjoy ...": Bowen, p, 69.
48. "[Hall's] first message as Mayor ...": Bernstein, p. 199.
49. "Mr. Peter B. Sweeny is said ...": *Evening Free Press*, October 15, 1870.
50. Sweeny, ...Victor Hugo ... Baron Haussmann ... Jean Corot: Leonard, p. 109.
51. city park expenses ... to over $550,000 in 1870: Wingate, II, p. 122.
52. "The greatest fault which Mr. Sweeny can find ...": *New-York Times*, June 17, 1871.
53. "alleged to be of the pre-Adamite..." "a science which,...":Wingate, II, p. 123.
54. Green, ...refused to attend meetings: See letters from Sweeny to Manton Marble, June 6 and December 8, 1870. Marble papers. LC.
55. Green's ethic of frugal penny-pinching and long-term planning: Kessner, p. 139. On Green generally, see Kessner, (chapter 2, "New York's Napoleon,") and Foord.
56. $15,000 to the Fenians: *New York Herald*, January 31, 1871.
57. Croton Aqueduct ... Tweed had paid $25,000: Hershkowitz, p. 156; *New-York Times*, February 3 and 16, 1871.
58. "Oh, Boss, put another naught ...": Werner, p. 194.
59. "Some Stolen Money Returned."... "When a man can plunder...": *New-York Times*, December 29, 1870, January 2, 1871.
60. "That donation, as you call it,... ": *New York Herald*, January 8, 1871
61. "A man's family is dear ...": New York Herald, January 8, 1871.
62. "That's the last straw" : Harper, p. 287; Paine, p. 158.

7. Fate *(pages 123–128)*

1. O'Brien… whether he paid Copeland money: Two years later, after the Ring had been toppled, the New York State Senate would pay Copeland a $2,500 reward for the service. The *New-York Times* itself would deny that Copeland received any compensation from the press, but was silent as to O'Brien. See *New-York Times*, April 13, 1872; O'Brien interview, *New York Sun*, September 13, 1871.
2. Tweed, Sweeny, and Connolly met: On this meeting, see Wingate p. 142, *New York Tribune*, August 4, 1871, and O'Brien interview, *New York World*, August 16, 1871.
3. "is said not to have been…": *New York Tribune*, August 4, 1871.
4. fired… for "political reasons,": Copeland testimony, Hall Grand Jury, p. 18.
5. "I wanted to stop O'Brien's tongue …": Tweed testimony, Aldermen, p. 50-51.
6. "Sweeny not unwisely insisted …": Wingate, II, p. 142.
7. "Mr. O'Brien wasn't against …": Tweed testimony, Aldermen, p. 51.
8. "Tweed had done me a favor …": O'Brien interview, *New York World*, August 16, 1891.
9. "He asked me to luncheon …": *New York World*, August 16, 1891; Wingate, II, 142-3.
10. Watson's private stable ..: Description, and information on the horses, is from *New-York Times*, March 16, 1871.
11. Watson … worth almost $600,000: His estate ultimately would pay $590,435.94 to settle Ring suits. See Martin testimony, Aldermen, p.826.
12. Ludlow Street Jail …jailhouse record-keeper: See Werner, p. 161.
13. "I did a big day's work …": Ingersoll affidavit, *New York Times*, June 3, 1875; Wingate II, p.143 (though Wingate mistakenly attributes quote to Andrew Garvey.)
14. Watson had been *en route* to see Jimmy O'Brien : See Wingate, II, p. 143, and *New York World*, August 16, 1891
15. "[Tammany] is the real power": *New York Herald*, January 8, 1871.

8. I Pledge Myself to Persevere… *(pages 129–141)*

1. "Is it a hopeless fight?": *New-York Times*, January 24, 1871.
2. Jones… two published reports of Tweed's muscling him out of the *Times*: Articles from *Rochester Chronicle* and the *Philadelphia Ledger*, and Jones' denial, are in the *New-York Times*, November 23 and December 5, 1870.
3. Jerome… real estate holdings with Tweed: See *New-York Times*, February 22, 1871, under "Ring Jobbery," sub-head "Purchases at Spuyten Duyvil Creek."
4. "went like sheep to Mr. Connolly…": *New-York Times*, November 7 and 12, 1870.
5. Jones probably knew much more … having seen figures … November 1870 : See *New-York Times* supplement, July 29, 1871 (""we were allowed to see the figures already printed, and some others held in reserve, fully nine months ago") ; Wingate, II, p.153, and *New York Times*, November 7, 1870 (which

asked: "Is it, or is it not the fact that Messrs. Andrew J. Garvey, (plasterer) Ingersoll, Watson & Co, (furniture dealers) Keyser & Co., (plumbers) and George S. Miller (carperter) … have received nearly *seven millions of dollars* from the Controller?"

6. without hard evidence … legal penalties—libel actions: Leonard, p.120, suggests Jones and Jennings withheld evidence during these months for tactical reasons; it "gave Tammany nothing to refute and no single issue that could clear its name," a mistake they'd made prior to the Astor committee's report.
7. "the rowdies and vagabonds…" "Tweed's Lambs.": *New-York Times*, September 26, 1870. The newspaper carried no by-lines, but Foord is identified as the reporter in Daniels, p. 23.
8. Broadway Hotel … to widen the street: *New-York Times*, February 13, March 5, 1871.
9. "Fraud" … "stupendous frauds." … "It is now known …": *New-York Times*, February 15 and 16, 1871.
10. "Another Street Job" : *New-York Times*, March 4, 1871.
11. "Whenever large quantities of property …": *New-York Times*, February 22, 1871.
12. "No Proof That The Ring Pay Taxes ": *New-York Times*, December 9, 1870.
13. "although every Democrat is not …": *New-York Times*, October 3, 1870.
14. "coarse and illiterate man.": *New-York Times*, November 23 1870, quoting the *Trenton Gazette*.
15. "Tweed Republicans" … "With Mr. Tweed's chains…": *New-York Times*, October 13 and 16, 1870.
16. "Has Tweed gone mad …": *Evening Post*, March 11, 1871.
17. "Statues are not erected to living men …": Letter from Tweed to Shandley, March 13, 1871.
18. Marble came to terms with Peter Sweeny… revenue exploded : McJimsey, p. 142.
19. "The decline of the New-York Times…": *New York Sun, February 3, 1871*.
20. "dishonest and disingenuous …": *Evening Post*, March 10, 1871.
21. "We are informed that negotiations …": F. Hudson, p. 642.
22. putting the paper in receivership : See "The Next Move of the 'Ring,'" *New-York Times*, March 28, 1871.
23. "They will kill off your work": Paine, p. 142.
24. Two things elected me …": Paine, p. 129.
25. Nast … single drawing for $350: *New-York Times*, May 6, 1871.
26. wealth … $75,000: Letter to Nast from Shepherd, May 31, 1869. Nast scrapbooks, NYPL.
27. "Please see my picture …": Telegram from Nast to Young, April 20, 1869. Nast papers, NYHS.
28. "The Democratic Scapegoat": *Harper's Weekly*, September 11, 1869.
29. "Greek Slave ": *Harper's Weekly*, April 16, 1870.
30. "The Power Behind the Throne," … "Our Modern Falstaff," Paine, p. 155,156.

31. "Emperor Tweed": *Harper's Weekly*, April 22, 1871.
32. "universal conviction" … "familiar to every citizen": *Harpers Weekly*, March 13 and 18, November 11, 1871, in Leonard, p. 111. Around this time, Nast worked increasingly in tandem with the *New-York Times*. When the *Times* attacked Tweed's alleged Broadway widening scheme, Nast drew a *Harper's Weekly* cartoon on the issue showing Tweed and Sweeny studying a map with a crooked street: "To make this look straight is the hardest job I ever had," Tweed says. "What made Watson go sleigh-riding?" *Harper's Weekly*, March 4, 1871
33. Harper … *Maria Monk*: See: Robert P. Lockwood, "The Lie of Maria Monk Lives On," Catholic League for Religious and Civcil Rights; Burrows & Wallace, p.545-546.
34. "I have not seen your 'handwriting …": Bowen, p. 74.
35. Tweed … in Central Park; Nast smiled: Harper, p. 294.
36. "Gentlemen, you know where I live": Daniels, p. 25; Paine, p.159. The Board of Education's ban against Harper & Brothers textbooks would last until the day after Election Day in November 1871. Wingate, III. 390.
37. "The New Board of Education" : *Harper's Weekly*, May 13, 1871.
38. "Under The Thumb": *Harper's Weekly*, June 10, 1871.
39. Tweed's agents … Raymond's widow: Wingate, II, p. 152-3; *New-York Times*, July 19, 1871; Davis, p. 104-105.
40. "It is my duty to say…": *New-York Times*, March 28, 1871.

9. The Wedding *(pages 142–149)*

1. "aglow with rich silks …" "confusion of white arms…" Werner, p. 190.
2. "white corded silk, décolleté, …": *New York Sun*, in Werner, p. 191.
3. sailing sloop, the "*General Tweed*"… racehorse, the "*Richard M. Tweed*" …" receiver of the Commonwealth Fire Insurance: See *New-York Times*, April 2, June 9 and 27, 1871.
4. William Jr. ... Excelsior Guards: *New York Sun*, July 5, 1871.
5. Tweed … $800,000 in city improvements … *New-York Times* cried foul: *New-York Times*, April 27, 1871.
6. "from Boulevards and cross-streets …": Kessner, p. 139; Burrows and Wallace, p. 931;
7. $20 million …"improve the water-front…": *Pomeroy's Democrat*, June 18, 1871.
8. "It is quite generally understood …": *Pomeroy's Democrat*, July 1, 1871.
9. Apportionment Board… applications for charitable donations, : *New-York Times*, May 10, 1871.
10. *Zeitschrift fur Kapital und Reute* had sent shudders: quoted inn Mandelbaum, p.78.
11. "[O]rdinarily very determined …": *New-York Times*, November 29, 1870.
12. "all from my own place…""A magnificent supper…": *New York Sun* and *New York Herald*, June 1, 1871.
13. "a cross of eleven diamonds,": *New-York Times*, June 1, 1871
14. "Seven hundred thousand dollars!": *New York Herald*, in Werner, p. 193.

15. "on such a hot night ...": Bowen, p. 84.
16. These figures were my protection ...": O'Brien interview, *New York World*, August 16, 1871
17. Michael Norton and Henry Genet... received checks: See Tweed confession, *New York Herald*, October 10, 1877. Tweed characterized them as "loans," but with no evident obligation to be paid back.
18. "There wasn't one of them ...": O'Brien interview, *New York Worlds*, August 16, 1891.
19. "O'Brien hated Sweeny ...": Wingate, II, p. 144.
20. FN: Hall family descendants...: Bowen, p. 83.
21. O'Brien... checks of $6,000 each ...promissory note for $12,000: Tweed confession, *New York Herald*, October 10, 1877; promissory note and refusal to repay are from Hirsch, ("More Light on Tweed"), p. 272.
22. "You can have anything ....": *New York World*, August 16, 1891.
23. "I didn't want..." "[I]mmediately after I had..." "I couldn't get ..." "At all events, I think..." "I didn't let him...": O'Brien interview, *New York World*, August 16, 1891.
24. "cut [Jennings'] heart out": Morphet, p. 112.
25. "There is not another municipal government ...": *New York World*, June 13, 1871, in Paine 146.
26. O'Rourke ...resigning the job on May 19: It's not clear, when O'Rourke resigned to county auditor Stephen Lynes, how much he revealed of his record-copying: See letters from O'Rourke to Lynes, July 31, and response on August 5, 1871, in the *New York Herald*.
27. he'd visited professor Dexter Hawkins: See *New-York Times*, June 30, 1871.
28. "More Ring Villainy" ... "Reliable and incontrovertible evidence ...": *New-York Times*, September 8, 1871.

10. July *(pages 153–166)*

1. "*[W]e find [the wealthy uptown landowners* ...": *New-York Times*, December 30, 1852.
2. quarrymen ...around Yorkville—strike: Generally on the May strike, see *New York Sun*, May 2, 3,4, 18, 1871, *New-York Times*, May 2, 3,18, 1871, and Bernstein, p. 229-230.
3. "to prevent the formation or progression ..." :Police Order 57, printed in newspapers, July 11 and 12, 1871.
4. Produce Exchange ...petition: *New York Tribune*, July 12, 1871.
5. Hoffman... counting Washington ... Congressmen S.S. Cox and Fernando Wood : See, for instance, letter from Cox to Hoffman, May 14, 1870. Hoffman papers, NYHS. Tammany had begun lining up Southern delegates for Hoffman's nomination as early, as seen in an interview with Jimmy O'Brien from January 1871: "The South is poor, and the delegations from the Southern States will go solid for Hoffman if Tammany wills it.... (this was said with a peculiar smile suggesting that Tammany was buying all the southern votes they'd need, and the south was happily taking the money)." *New York Herald*, January 8, 1871.

6. "the [Tammany] 'Ring' … will be …": *Cincinnati Commercial*, November 28, 1870, in the *New-York Times*, November 30, 1870.
7. "[Hoffman's] subserviency …": *London Times*, in *New York Tribune*, June 1, 1871.
8. "Senator Tweed, I propose to be governor …": Hudson, p. 32.
9. "I hereby give notice …": Hoffman proclamation, July 11, 1871. Newspapers, July 12, 1871; Lynch, p. 367.
10. "I may … conform my action …": *New York World*, July 13, 1871, in *New York Tribune*, 1871.
11. "The sight which was disclosed…": Walling, p. 158.
12. fatalities at almost 130 …: The *Sunday Irish Democrat* claimed 142 civilians killed, including 75 Irishmen, in the *New York Sun*, July 17, 1871.
13. "Excelsior": *New York Herald*, July 13, 1871.
14. "They did not even fight …": *New York Sun*, July 14, 1871.
15. "criminal weakness and vacillation ": *New York Tribune*, in Bernstein, p.231.
16. "instead of reefing down close …": *New York Sun*, July 17, 1871.
17. "Murdered by the Criminal Management …": Bowen, p.95.
18. Hoffman … "by order of his physician": *New York Sun*, July 14, 1871.
19. "There were three regiments of soldiers …": *New York Herald*, July 14, 1871. See sympathetic letter from Editor W.H. Hulbert of the *New York World* to Marble, July 15, 1871. Marble papers. LC.: "I agreed with P.B.[Sweeny] and Hall as to the wisdom of suppressing the Orangemen . P.B.S. went to Long Branch, Hoffman to Albany… Let us do justice to Tammany—it kept faith with us & kept us informed of what was going on."
20. "wept bitter tears over the ingratitude …": *New York Sun*, July 14, 1871. "I still believe that the Orange procession…" : *New York World*, in *NY Tribune*, July 14, 1871.
21. "But your position is a great deal more comfortable …": Letter form Sweeny to Hoffman, July 21, 1871. See also, *New York Sun*, July 14, 1871 (which reported "an envenomed hostility against Gov. Hoffman among the Irish.") and *New York Herald*, July 12, 1871, in Iver Bernstein, p. 231 (stating that many Catholics had expected the city to stand aside: "the city government… will do as they did in 1863—sit at home and drink punches and smoke cigars comfortably after dinner"). Sweeny, in the wreckage, considered retiring from politics altogether. His letter to Hoffman continued: "Your position relieves me of a great task which I had set for myself [engineering Hoffman's election as president] and leaves my future comparatively free…. I have bought a handsome residence at Lake Mahopac and *entre nous*, there, I will retire with my wife and child and try to get a little comfort and enjoyment out of life."
22. It was an unfortunate business …": *New York Tribune*, July 14, 1871.
23. Seventh Regiment … Thomas Nast: Paine, p. 172; *New-York Times*, July 15, 1871. Nast had joined the reserve regiment in 1866. See Notice from Regimental Secretary to Nast, May 23, 1866, in Nast Scrapbooks, NYPL.
24. "A correspondent wishes to know …": *New-York Times*, July 15, 1871.
25. "I was arrested two or three times …": Morphet p. 112.]

26. "Hot night," Jimmy O'Brien said: This version of the incident is taken from Berger, p. 42; Lynch, p. 362, who, in turn, took it from the *London World*, 1887
27. Jennings told this story to the *London World* in 1887…: See Paine, p. 168; Wingate, p. II, 154; *Harper's Weekly*, February 22, 1890; *New York World*, August 16, 1871; and Bigelow (Tilden writings), p. 588.
28. *New York Sun* … Charles Dana … out of the building: See Wingate, II, p. 154.
29. "[Jones] couldn't believe the steals …": O'Brien interview. *New York World*, August 16, 1871.
30. "Something that Wouldn't Blow Over …": *Harper's Weekly*, July 29, 1871.
31. "The New Horse Plague": *Harper's Weekly*, July 29, 1871.
32. "The old Colonel [Morgan] was angry …": Daniels, p. 24.
33. "The shares in the *New-York Times* …": *New-York Times*, July 19, 1871, in F. Hudson, p. 643.
34. "Two Thieves." "We shall prove …": *New-York Times*, July 19, 1871.
35. "[T]hey charged the money …": *New-York Times*, July 20, 1871.
36. "Will It 'Blow Over?'": *New-York Times*, July 21, 1871.

11. Disclosure *(pages 167–173)*

1. "THE SECRET ACCOUNTS": *New-York Times*, July 22, 1871.
2. "We have seen what a good thing …": *New-York Times*, July 26, 1871.
3. "314,145 chairs, and if placed …": *New-York Times*, July 26, 1871.
4. "Is not this Miller ….": *New-York Times*, July 23, 1871.
5. "would go nearly from New-York to New Haven …": *New-York Times*, July 26, 1871.
6. "Who is A.G. Miller?": *New-York Times*, July 24 and 29, 1871.
7. the "Company" in Ingersoll and Company: See Ingersoll testimony, Aldermen, p. 566-70.
8. "I don't want to see this man …": *Harper's Weekly*, February 22, 1890; Wingate, II, p. 152, See also Paine p. 170 and Davis, p. 103.
9. "at any valuation…" "This offer was made…": *Harper's Weekly*, February 22, 1890.
10. "For God's sake! Let me say…": Wingate, II, p. 152; *Harper's Weekly*, February 22, 1890.
11. "I have been over the hills with Greeley …": *Harper's Weekly*, February 22, 1890.
12. "[t]he public run instinctively …": Cortissoz, p. 151.
13. "We have scrupulously refrained …": Bowen, p. 106.
14. "We do not indorse …": *New York Tribune*, July 22, 1871.
15. "The bladder with beans …": *The Nation*, July 27, 1871.

12. Panic *(pages 174–190)*

1. "buncombe" … "Curses and indecent language…": Accounts of the Citizen Association meeting are from the *New York Tribune* and *New-York Times*, August 8, 1871.

2. "[A]ccusations are not proof": *New York Herald*, August 5, 1871.
3. "a reckless attempt to shake..": *New York World*, July 28, 1871, in Lynch, p. 366.
4. "the most brilliant dashing foray…": Conkling to Jones, July 28, 1871. Jones papers. NYPL.
5. city had bonds … debt had exploded … to over $97 million : See "Statement of the Dept of the City and County of New York," Hall papers, NYMA; for city financial structure, see *New-York Times*, July 20, 1871.
6. $40,000 in bonds … failed to receive a single bid : Strong, July 27 and 29, 1871, p. 376-377.
7. *Commercial and Financial Chronicle* warned… Berlin Stock Exchange banned …bonds from its official trading list.: Mandelbaum, p. 80.
8. "They distrust our securities ..": *New York Tribune*, July 29, 1871.
9. "[I]f our local government cannot …": Clews interview, *New York Herald*, September 19, 1871.
10. "insurrection of the capitalists"… lawsuit to block the Broadway widening job: See *New York Tribune* and other newspapers, August 1, 1871.
11. "[W]e want to know …": *New York Tribune*, July 29, 1871.
12. calls went out for city leaders to convene … on September 4 : See *New York Tribune*, August 4, 1871; Diary of George Templeton Strong, August 19, 1871, p. 379.
13. "Shocking levity": Bowen, p. 67, 97.
14. "indicate where the fraud …": *New York Tribune*, July 29, 1871.
15. "Is there any danger…" "Who is going to do it?" Garvey testimony, Hall trial, in *New-York Times*, October 26, 1872.
    This remark from Hall…: see Bigelow (Tilden writings), p. 590.]
16. "Look at that wall, gentlemen …": *New York Herald*, September 19, 1871.
17. "[H]e [the mayor] had been a twenty-year friend…": *Leader*, July 22, 1871, in the *New York Sun*, July 22, 1871.
18. "During the summer of 1870 …": *Leader*, July 22, 1871, in the *New York Sun*, July 22, 1871.
19. "I know that none of my friends …": Letter from Hall "To the Public," in *New York Sun*, July 24, 1871.
20. mayor's total assets as barely $70,000: Brown testimony, Hall Grand Jury, p. 51.
21. "ministerial" acts… "the malice of Mr. Jones" : Letter form Hall "To the Public," in *New York Sun*, July 24, 1871.
22. "*Are the figures …*": *New-York Times*, July 23, 1871.
23. "The defense set up by the mayor …": *New York Tribune*, July 29, 1871.
24. "I shall remain at my post…": *New-York Times*, July 30, 1871.
25. "My dear Sir … you may rest assured…": *New-York Times*, July 30, 1871.
26. "Being interviewed, [Hall] took the line…": *The Nation*, August 3, 1871. Another version was: "It will all blow over. These gusts of reform are wind and clatter. Next year we shall all be in Washington." Bowen, p. 110. And yet another: "The people's indignation will all blow over," says Boss Tweed; and his companions echo his words. *Syracuse Journal*, August 22, 1871, in *New-York*

Times, August 24, 1871. Another Hall-ism from this period: "We are likely to have what befell Adam—an early Fall." *New-York Times*, August 29, 1871, in Flick, p. 213.

27. "The most cordially hated man ...": *Harper's Weekly*, August 26, 1871.
28. Police Captain Ira Garland ... city officials removed: Paine, p. 179.
29. "Every stroke of his pencil ...": *Harper's Weekly*, August 26, 1871.
30. "Three Blind Mice": *Harper's Weekly*, July 22, 1871.
31. "Not a Bailable Case": *Harper's Weekly*, August 12, 1871.
32. "Nast-y artist of Harper's Hell Weekly": Bowen, p. 82. Tweed, in Albany, had put language in a school tax levy bill that winter calling Nast's drawings "vulgar and blasphemous" and designed to arouse "prejudices of the community against a wrong which exists only in their imaginations." Bowen, p. 81
33. "I used to walk down to the office ...": Harper, p. 294.
34. *"I hear you have been made an offer ...*: The story comes from Paine, p. 181-2, a biography written with Nast's active collaboration.
35. FN: "A million? Nast could have been bought...": Hershkowitz, p. 175.
36. "as individuals [are] corrupt ...": Letter to the editor from Nooney *New-York Times*, September 25, 1871.
37. "astounding insolence" ... "only by the permission ...": *Harper's Weekly*, in *New-York Times*, July 6, 1871.
38. "The American River Ganges": *Harper's Weekly*, September 30, 1871.
39. "doesn't care a straw for what is written ...": *Harper's Weekly*, August 26, 1871.
40. "if the people got used to seeing ...": Werner, p. 211.
41. guilt "*pro confesso*": Strong, July 26, 1871, p. 375.
42. FN: "Let's stop them d__d pictures... ": Payne, p. 179.
    "But they have eyes ...": Flick, p. 213
43. "This is not a question...": *Missouri Republican*, in *New-York Times*, August 24, 1871, in Callow, 268.
44. Tweed ... $118,000 ...into the club: See checks in Tweed confession, *New York Herald*, October 10, 1877; bills from Ingersolll, Watson & Company (furniture), June 1, 1871, and C. Boller (cabinets), August 16, 1871, in Tweed papers, NYHS.
45. Lower California Company: *New York Herald*, August 8, 1871.
46. Metropolitan Hotel... $450,000 on renovating: Tweed testimony, Aldermen, p. 310 and 371.
47. mayor appealed ..."large and influential committee...": Letter from Hall and Connolly to Dodge, in *New York Herald*, August 5, 1871.
48. Wall Street abruptly slapped him down: See letter from Opdyle to Hall and Connolly, in *New York Herald*, August 9, 1871. With Dodge away, the letter was signed by the Chamber's First Vice President: George Opdyke, New York's former mayor during the 1863 draft riots..
49. Hall and Connolly... Again ... asked business leaders to join him: Letter from Hall to Common Council, August 16, 1871, transmitted August 23, 1871, in *New York Sun* and other papers, August 24, 1871. The citizen chose as their

members on the committee bank presidents Lennox Kennedy (Bank of Commerce), Thomas Jeremiah (Bowery Savings Bank), and D. Bissenger (German Savings Bank), James Brown (Brown Brothers), chamber of commerce president William E. Dodge, and sugar merchant William A. Booth.

50. "The gross attacks of a partisan journal …": Letter from Hall to committee of aldermen, August 1871. NYMA.
51. "I am satisfied that if done at all …": Letter from Vanderbilt to Jones, undated. Jones papers, NYPL.
52. "The litigation promises …": *Sunday Mercury*, August 27, 1871, in the *New York Herald*, August 28, 1871.
53. "Property owners may well be alarmed ...": *New-York Times*, August 28, 1871. Jennings also used the Tweed sons' gala opening of the Metropolitan Hotel to attack. In "The Great Carpet Trick," he pointed to $386,821 worth of alleged city-paid overcharges for carpets: "What became of the carpets…? We cannot answer this. But Boss Tweed's son has just opened the Metropolitan Hotel." Jennings presented no other evidence to support this suggested Tweed family swindle. *New-York Times*, August 30, 1871
54. "It is no secret that the most influential …": *Evening Post*, in *New York Tribune*, August 21, 1871.
55. "Two Great Questions," … "Twas him." : *Harper's Weekly*, August 19, 1871.
56. "You have never done anything …": Harper, p. 292.
57. Tweed … transferring … real estate to his son Richard … Connolly's wife, transferred ownership of … United States treasury bonds: Tweed testimony, Alderman, p. 320,335,348,349,350,351, and 352; *New-York Times*, October 27 and 29, 1871; and, regarding Connolly, *New York Tribune*, September 12, 1871.
58. German Democratic Union … anti-Tweed resolutions : German immigrants had long felt much less enchanted with Tammany than the Irish. Many Germans had fled war, civil unrest, and anti-Catholic oppression in Europe and distrusted paternalistic government. See Bernstein, p. 222-223.
59. Council of Political Reform : See Hershkowitz, p. 183 and newspapers.
60. "They are since July public enemies…" "The *World* blundered terribly…": Letters from Croly ["DSC"] to Marble, August 13 and September 6, 1871. Marble papers. LC.

13. Tilden *(pages 191–212)*

1. "*Sam Tilden wants …*": T.P. Cook, p. 95.
2. "moral conviction of gross frauds": Bigelow (Tilden writings), p. 587.
3. "I think you had better note…": Letter from Tilden to Cassidy, August, 1871. Bigelow, (Tilden letters), p. 272-3.
4. "Where are the Honest Democrats?": *New-York Times*, August 8, 1871.
5. "Is it not a good time …": Letter from Church to Tilden, August 1, 1871. Bigelow (Tilden letters), p. 274.
6. "I told him I should appear …": Quote and Tilden movements from Bigelow (Tilden writings), p. 587-588; O'Brien interview, *New York World*, August 16, 1891.

7. "We have to face the question ...": Letter from Tilden (in NYC) to Purcell, August 12, 1871, in Bigelow (Tilden letters), p. 275.
8. Tilden buttonholed ... David Croly: McJimsey, p. 149.
9. "When the public mind ...": Letter from Seymour to Tilden, August 12, 1871, Bigelow (Tilden letters), p. 274.
10. Tilden ... had caught the fatal weakness : See Bigelow, (Tilden writings), p. 587.
11. "I propose now, gentlemen, ...": "An Appreciation" by James C. Carter, in Bigelow (Tilden Letters), p. xvi-xvii.
12. "If, by a violent blow ...": Flick, 97-98.
13. "Tilden is very positive in his views ...": *New York Tribune*, September 9, 1871.
14. "The *Times* rolls itself up ...": *New York Tribune*, August 21, 1871.
15. "political guerilla"... "English cockney proclivities": *New York Herald*, September 8, 1871.
16. *Times* circulation had jumped by 40 percent: Morphet, p. 140.
17. "A deadly disease is consuming ...": Accounts of the Cooper Union speeches are from the *New-York Times*, September 5, 1871.
18. "the ignorant Irish voting element": *The Nation*, August 24, 1871.
19. "the Anglo-Saxon race has never ...": *The Nation*, September 7, 1871.
20. "in our opinion, Hall, Connolly ...": *The Nation*, September 2, 1871, in Lynch, p. 371-372.
21. Played for suckers...: "The revulsion of feeling was all the more powerful because of the implicit character of the misplaced confidence which had preceded it," wrote *New-York Times* reporter John Foord. Foord, p. 93.
22. "Saints Lashing Sinners": *New York Sun*, September 5, 1871.
23. "followed the example of Mr. Tilden": *New York World*, September 5, 1871.
24. "I saw, as the roll proceeded, ...": Tweed interview, *New York Herald*, October 26, 1877. See also *New-York Times*, October 17, 1857 and September 21, 1860.]
25. "I was the best friend he ever had": Tweed testimony, Aldermen, p. 146.
26. "[Y]ou had to waste much time ...": Tweed testimony, Aldermen, p. 147.
27. "from 1868, and including the granting ...": Barnard testimony, Barnard Impeachment, p. 1638.
28. "I never called at her house ...": Barnard testimony, Barnard Impeachment, p. 1664.
29. "Why, I presume I got it out of my safe ...": Barnard testimony, Barnard Impeachment, p. 1667.
30. "Do you think Judge Barnard ...": *New York Tribune*, September 7, 1871.
31. "suffering from the convenient ...": *New York Tribune*, September 7, 1871.
32. "What of it; do you think that I can tell ...": Specifications, Barnard Impeachment, p.58. Another time, referring to a lawyer recently assaulted on the street, Barnard said from the bench: "My enemies are very unfortunate; one of them went home from his woman and fell down dead in his house; another tried to make a little capital by getting himself knocked in the head; but he got knocked too hard."

33. "[I]f the court should grant your injunction …": Barnard proceedings in *New York Herald*, September 8, 1871.
34. "Knowing Barnard as we do …": Lynch, p. 375. Another theory had it that Sweeny conceived the injunction and signaled Barnard to approve it to put pressure on Connolly and Tweed. See Wingate, III, p. 374.
35. "We owe to Barnard …": Tweed interview, *New York Herald*, October 26, 1877.
36. Tweed … "fatigued and worn": *New York Sun*, September 9, 1871.
37. Tweed had pulled his circle together several times: Records showed nomeetings of the Board of Apportionment in July or August 1871, but starting up again regularly on September 5, the day after the Cooper Union meeting. See affidavit of Richard Storrs, September 11, 1871. Boss Tweed in Court, Reel 1. "[W]e were in the habit of meeting daily, or at least three times a week—sometimes daily—at my private office," Tweed recalled. Aldermen, p. 141-2.
38. "That fellow was seized with the idea …": Tweed interview, *New York Herald*, October 26, 1877.
39. Connolly … "fatigued and careworn" … "I have no opinion to give,": *New York Sun*, September 9, 1871.
40. Tweed and Connolly both had hired lawyers: Tweed chose Willard O. Barrett, Connolly picked William A. Beach, and Mayor Hall relied on corporation counsel Richard O'Gorman.
41. "When the damaging evidences….": New York Tribune, September 9, 1871.
42. "Gentlemen, to resign would be to confess …": *New York Sun*, September 18, 1871.
43. "Mr. Sweeny was not greedy …": *New York Tribune*, September 9, 1871.
44. "If William M. Tweed and Richard B. Connolly have made…": *New York Herald*, September 8, 1871.
45. "the man who is his own lawyer ..": *New-York Times*, September 10, 1871.
46. "Yes you can": *New-York Times*, September 10, 1871.
47. "sink or swim with his colleagues,…": *New York Sun*, September 13, 1871.
48. "Well, what do you think of the matter ...": *New York Sun*, September 9, 1871. Reprinted in the *New-York Times* and other papers, September 10, 1871.
49. "typographic display": *New York Tribune*, September 13, 1871.
50. "Nothing to be ashamed of": *New York Tribune*, September 13, 1871.
51. "If I go to murder …": *New York Sun*, September 19, 1871.
52. breaking under strain: Said the normally-sympathetic *New York Sun*: "He shakes his fist, and stamps his foot, and threatens, and whines, and plays sick, and reveals the wounds which his public castigations have inflicted." *New York Sun*, September 11, 1871.
53. Lynes remembered: See Lynes testimony, in *New-York Times*, September 22, 1871.
54. "singularly unfortunate to himself": *New York Sun*, September 12, 1871.
55. Erie Railway and the Hannibal and St. Joseph ... tumbled in value … as did city bonds … Connolly might … dump bonds : *New York Tribune*, September 12, 1871.
56. "Too thin": *New York Tribune*, September 12, 1871.

57. "I have just been informed ...": Hall to Connolly, in *New York Sun* and other newspapers, September 12, 1871.
58. "Hall, don't send me that letter": *New York Sun*, September 18, 1871.
59. "You may mail it ...": *New York Sun*, September 18, 1871.
60. : "I am prepared to resign at once ...": *New York Tribune*, September 13, 1871.
61. "If Hall ever asks Tweed to resign ...": *New York Sun*, September 13, 1871.
62. "This is the flag ..." "with the air of a grand seigneur...": *New York Sun*, September 13, 1871.
63. "I am so overwhelmed with business ...": *New York Tribune*, September 13, 1871.

14. Coup d'Etat *(pages 213–219)*

1. *"Oh, yes, I am always cheerful ...":* *New-York Times*, September 20, 1871.
2. "Comptroller Connolly, one of the old school ...": Clipping from *The Star*, Hall scrapbooks, NYPL.
3. Connolly found himself threatened: Connolly had spent the weekend with lawyers hammering out an affidavit flatly denying all charges that his lawyers presented in Judge Barnard's courtroom that Monday. Affidavit of Controller Connolly, *New York Tribune* and other papers, September 12, 1871.
4. "headstrong woman, with a fair share of ability": *New York Tribune*, September 13, 1871. See also *New York Sun*, September 9, 1871.
5. Tuesday ... daily Board of Apportionment meeting : See accounts in *New York Tribune*, September 14, 1871.
6. refused to quit until "fully vindicated": *New-York Times*, September 13, 1871.
7. "I beg leave to differ from your Honor ...": Letter from Connolly to Hall, in *New-York Times*, September 13, 1871.
8. "Give us our money"... "If we don't get ...": *New York Tribune*, September 14, 1871.
9. Connolly ... warrant providing money for the mens' salaries, ...Broadway Bank: Incident is from the *New York Sun*, September 18, 1871.
10. "One evening Connolly came to see me ...": Havemeyer interview, *New York World*, September 20, 1871.
11. "They got together and talked ...": *New York World*, September 20, 1871.
12. "When rogues fall out ...": *New-York Times*, September 13, 1871.
13. "Wherever the gangrene of corruption ...": Tilden circular, September 11, 1871. Bigelow (Tilden letters), p. 276-278.
14. "I know nothing about it ...": *New-York Times*, September 15, 1871.
15. "I could not be his counsel...": Bigelow (Tilden writings), p. 591.
16. "[He] said it was crucifying him," ... "I put a little more backbone ...": *New York World*, September 20, 1871.
17. "if he threw himself upon the mercy ...": Bigelow (Tilden writings), p. 592.
18. three letters... Havemeyer to Connolly... Havemeyer to Andrew Green ... Connolly to Green: All three are in Bigelow (Tilden letters), p. 278-281, and newspapers, September 18, 1871.
19. "Of course, Mr. Havemeyer is not ...": *New York World*, September 18, 1871.

15. Numbers *(pages 220–241)*

1. "*Those were great days …*": Hudson, p. 37-38.
2. "*The excitement in political circles …*": Letter from Reid to Greeley, September 18, 1871, in Cortissoz, p. 154.
3. "The Municipal Muddle": *New York Herald*, September 17, 1871; see also *New York Sun*, September 18,1871, mentioning that it was the *Herald* that Hall read.
4. "This movement was about the last thing…": *New-York Times*, September 18, 1871.
5. "whitewashing parties …": Letter from Aspinwall to McClellan, September 18, 1871, in Sears, p. 393. See also W. Hunt to McClellan, September 18, 1871 and similar letters in McClellan papers. LC.
6. "I am advised that your action …": Letter from Hall to Connolly, September 18, 1871, in *New York Sun* and other newspapers, September 18, 1871.
7. "I therefore tender you …": Letter from Hall to McClellan, September 16, 1871, in *New York Sun* and other papers, September 18, 1871.
8. "I am directed by the Mayor t…": Letter from Joline to City Department Heads, September 18, 1871, in *New York Sun* and other newspapers, September 19, 1871.
9. "There is not a word of truth …": *New-York Times*, September 19, 1871.
10. "it would take too much time …": *New York Sun*, April 13, 1871.
11. New-York Times, September 19, 1871.
12. "Gentlemen, some of you yesterday …": Werner, p. 228; Wingate, III, p. 379.
13. "Hall is as crazy …": *New York World*, September 20, 1871.
14. "McClellan will have to walk …": *New York Sun*, September 19, 1871.
15. Tilden, Green … sought out during August : See letter from D.S.C. to Marble, August 13, 1871, Marble papers. LC.
16. Green had been visiting Tilden : *New York Sun*, September 18, 1871; Wingate, III, p. 378.
17. Mobs of hundreds gathered daily: See, for instance, *New-York Times*, October 13, 1871 describing the five hundred street diggers who marched from Central Park down Broadway behind fife and drum.
18. "inciting the laborers…" "[The workers] were instructed…": Unpublished manuscript, Green papers. NYHS. He described the scene in dramatic terms: "Let the reader picture to himself the spectacle of an army of ten to fifteen thousand laboring men turned adrift from their works at parks, streets, and boulevards, conscious only that somebody had cheated them out of their hard-earned money, and that there was money enough in the city to pay them could it only be got at."
19. Green …orders … forbid political monkey business on city payrolls: See Circular from Green to heads of Bureau, Department of Finance, from Green, October 10, 1871, in *New-York Times*, October 13, 1871.
20. "His hair was redolent …": *New York Sun*, September 19, 1871.
21. "They would not be mad enough …": *New York Sun*, September 19, 1871.
22. "I have not either in fact …": Letter from Connolly to Hall, September 18,

1871, 11:30 am, in *New York Sun* and other newspapers, September 19, 1871. Samuel Tilden, concerned with the festering legal uncertainly, sent word to Charles O'Conor, the 67-year-old dean of the New York Bar, asking him to issue a formal opinion confirming Green's right to the office. O'Conor's response, printed in the newspapers, would end any serious doubt on the issue. See Opinion of Charles O'Conor, in the *New York Sun* and other newspapers, September 19, 1871.

23. New charges … Connolly's own son J. Townsend had stolen … county vouchers : For charges and response, see *New York World* and *Sun*, September 21, 1871.
24. "I shall not part with your resignation …": Unpublished manuscript, Green papers. NYHS.
25. lip service … "He has documents …": *New York Sun*, September 19, 1871. Typical of the lip-service was E.L. Godkin in *The Nation*, November 2, 1871 ("Connolly is the only man of the [Tweed] party who has established the smallest title to any sympathy which a Christian can really give—that is, sympathy with a man who has done wrong, and is sorry for it, and shows that he is sorry by seeking to make amends") and Hevemeyer in the *New York World*, September 20, 1871 ("Why, Connolly is way ahead of all of them now … He has got the whip hand over the whole lot.").
26. Affidavit of Many Conway, September 20, 1871, in *New-York Times*, September 22, 1871. See generally coverage and court proceedings in the New-York Times and other papers, September 22 and 23, 1871.
27. Haggerty and Balch both would fight the charges: See Hershkowitz, p. 211-213, and Tweed confession, Supplementary Statement, in *New York Herald*, October 10, 1877.
28. "I have nothing to say …": *New-York Times*, September 13, 1871.
29. 1862 …Tweed … feuding with a rival Wigwam faction … Connolly switch sides: See Mushkat (Tammany, Evolution of a Political Machine), p. 342-346.
30. "untrue": Tweed affidavit, in *New York Tribune* and other papers, September 14, 1871.
31. "I don't intend at my time of life …": *New York Herald*, September 19, 1871; Hershkowitz, p. 186.
32. "As to the cry about thieving …": *New York World*, September 21, 1871.
33. "All my professional and personal ability …": Letter from Spencer to Tweed, October 27, 1871, in Hirsch, p. 277.
34. "a few political soreheads …": *New-York Times*, September 13, 1871.
35. new Central Tweed Organization : *New York World*, September 20, 1871.
36. Mr. Tweed is the most honorable man …": *New York Sun*, September 13, 1871.
37. twenty thousand people : Crowd estimate from *the New York Herald*, September 23, 1871;

    "Why, who is Roosevelt? ":*New York World*, September 21, 1871.
38. "a human sea, surging …": *New York World*, September 23, 1871. Crowd estimate from Lynch, p. 377.
39. "like a statue, while the storm …": *New York Sun*, September 23, 1871.

40. "At home again, among the friends …": For Tweed's speech, see *New York World* and *Sun*, September 23, 1871, Lynch, 377-378, and Hershkowitz, p. 160. Note slight wording variations in each source.
41. "Last year my majority …": *New York World* and *Sun*, September 23, 1871.
42. "hard-fisted bruisers ..": *The Nation*, November 9, 1871.
43. "offices, sinecures, contracts …": *The Nation*, October 12, 1871.
44. "Go ahead and kick us out …": Hershkowitz, p. 199. See also, *New-York Times*, October 4, 1871.
45. Tweed … counted only forty ... firmly hostile: Alexander, p. 269.
46. Dewitt … petition signed by all sixteen Tammany delegates… "no delegation be deemed …": Letter from Tammany delegates and proceedings in the *New-York Times* and *New York Tribune*, October 5, 1871.
47. "The man from Kings…": *New York Tribune*, October 5, 1871.
48. "This is the perfection of discipline …": *The Nation*, October 12, 1871.
49. Seymour … left the hall in disgust, : Seymour was also prompted by hostile treatment of his ally Francis Kernan.
50. "cursing in [Tilden's] face …": Letter from Marble to Tilden, October 11, 1871, never sent. Marble papers. LC.
51. "I am free to avow …": Flick, p. 219-220, *New York Tribune* and *New York World*, October 6, 1871.
52. "The excitement threatened…": Alexander, p. 273, and generally p. 269-273.
53. "troublesome old fools." …: "I should like some …": *New York Tribune*, October 6, 1871.
54. "A number of active leading men ...": Telegram from Richmond to Tilden, September 29, 1871. Tilden papers. NYPL. See also letter from Marble to Tilden, never sent. October 11, 1871. Marble papers. LC. ("[Y]our presence or your absence, your action or your inaction, your leadership of all the anti-corruption forces will make the difference of success or failure in an effort for good government & a Dem. Triumph."]
55. "I beg to send you herewith my check …": Letter from Belmont to Tilden, November 1, 1871. Tilden papers. NYPL.
56. "*You* must not be allowed to spend…": Letter from Royal Phelps to Tilden, November 4, 1871. Bigelow (Tilden letters), p. 287.
57. "The only way is for you …": Roosevelt to Tilden, September 26, 1871. Tilden papers, NYPL.
58. "Action and not words …": Telegram Tilden to Kernan, September 30, 1871. Bigelow (Tilden letters) p. 282.
59. "The anti-Tammany men …": Letter from Seymour to Tilden, October 8, 1871. Tilden letters, p. 284.
60. Tilden … state assemblyman: Tilden decided to seek the seat from the 18th district around 22nd Street, the same neighborhood as Jimmy O'Brien's state senate district, rather than Gramercy Park. To quality, he listed O'Brien's house as his residence and, according to O'Brien, two jointly funded their campaign largely by redirecting Tammany bribes paid to local hacks to *oppose* the reformers. "You'll be astonished to know that the money by which we carried

that election was supplied by the Tweed ring itself," O'Brien later claimed. Tilden, he said, knew nothing about it. : O'Brien interview, *New York World*, August 16, 1891.

61. "Are you going to send selfish ...": *New-York Times*, October 29, 1871.
62. "These men had pretended to be your friend ...": *New-York Times*, October 11, 1871.
63. "They betrayed the Democratic Party....": *New-York Times*, October 17, 1871.
64. Tilden ... $10,000 for expenses " Alexander, p.267.
65. Tilden ... Broadway Bank records: Background on this process is from Tilden affidavit, October 24, 1871 and worksheets in Tilden papers, boxes 22, 23, and 24. NYPL. These original worksheets are, incidentally, are a fascinating read for anyone with a background in accounting or finance
66. Smith, ... Parkhurst ... confirmed : See statements of Smith and Parkhurst, in the *New-York Times* and other newspapers, October 28, 1871.
67. "Mr. Tilden is busily engaged ...": *New York Herald*, October 22, 1871.
68. "Indeed, we will be successful ...": *New-York Times*, October 13, 1871; see also October 12, 1871.
69. "Identification of the parties..."... New-York Printing Company: These tables were published in newspapers (see e..g. *New York Times*, October 26, 1871), and, in original and printed forms, are in box 23, Tilden papers, NYPL, and Bigelow (Tilden writings), ""Figures That Could Not Lie," p. 505.
70. "They will act with promptness...": Tilden interview in *New-York Times*, October 20, 1871.

16. Personal Knowledge *(pages 242–246)*

1. "I have nothing to say except ...": *New-York Times*, October 4, 1871.
2. "I am here, Sir, to disappoint ...": *New-York Times*, October 5, 1871. The Committee of Seventy, had originally asked that Hall be arrested, but the judge had refused: See proceedings in the New-York Times, October 3, 1871.
3. "There is a new Grand Jury ...": *New-York Times*, October 5, 1871.
4. *Times* ... charged Judge Barnard ...selecting ... General William Hall, ...": See *New-York Times*, October 5, 1871.
5. Each would ... deny ... "personal" evidence : See, for instance, testimony of Committee of Seventy Chairman Henry Stebbins ["I have no facts of my own knowledge."] and Samuel Tilden ["only the opinion founded on documentary evidence." Some insisted that Hall's signatures approving exorbitant payouts made a solid enough case. See testimony of James O'Brien testimony ("A man of Mr. Hall's position would not [sign such warrants] without he would be patted on the back, that he would be made Governor, or that he would have some emoluments") and William Copeland ("I do not think that Mr. Hall, nor Mr. Connolly, or anybody else would sign away one hundred thousand dollars in warrants, without looking to see what it was about.") Hall Grand Jury, p. 19, 32, 38,44.
6. "Jennings was paid $50,000 for his work ...": Quote from the *Star* is from *The New-York Times Jubilee Supplemen, 1851-1901*, p. 15. Samuel Tilden claims that, in mid-September, he met Jones and editor Louis Jennings privately in

Andrew Green's office and Jennings had commiserated that "the contest was too exhausting to be continued very long." The *Times* later denied the story. Bigelow (Tilden writings), p. 589; *New-York Times*, February 4, 1873.

7. "Mr. Jones, what is your business …": Jones testimony, Hall Grand Jury, p. 45, et seq.
8. "it is known to the whole of this public …": Jones testimony, Hall Grand Jury, p. 47 and 48.
9. "A. Oakey Hall has been careless …": Hall Grand July, p. 62.
10. "Whitewashing Hall": *Tribune*, November 18, and *New-York Times*, November 19, 1871.
11. "destitute of any moral purpose…" "They should have subpoenaed …": *Tribune*, November 20, 1871. Other writers had similarly have criticized Jones' performance before the Grand Jury. S Bowen, 126-129; Hershkowitz, p. 195-6.
12. Nast… Greeley applying pails of "whitewash" : *Harper's Weekly*, December 16, 1871.

17. Marked Man *(pages 247–257)*

1. "*The best philosopher…*" :*New-York Times*, November 26, 1868.
2. Judge Learned … bail … one million dollars : Order of Judge W.J. Learned, October 25, 1871, in New-York Times, October 28, 1871. The fact that they'd used a judge in far-off Albany caused some to joke that they should have gone further and used a judge from Buffalo "nearer to the Great Fall" (Niagara Falls). *New York Herald*, October 27, 1871.
3. "white-coated roughs…" "What, arrest our Boss?" : *New-York Times*, October 27, 1871.
4. "Tweed! Why he is the incarnation …": New-York Times, October 27, 1871.
5. 1,500 … rally at Centre and Pearl Streets: *New York Herald*, October 20, 1871.
6. Tweed Club on East Broadway … "men above suspicion" : *New York Herald*, October 24, 1871.
7. Green and the mayor locked horns… claims to six charities : *New York Herald*, October 21, 1871.
8. Tweed… blackmail threat from Jimmy O'Brien … $350,000 claim : Tweed testimony, aldermen, p. 52-59.
9. "The Tammany 'braves' looked …": *New-York Times*, October 13, 1871.
10. Tweed … lost $4 million … Western railroad stock : *New-York Times*, October 13, 1871.
11. Tweed … urgent notes to friends … bail: See letters from Tweed to J. McB. Davidson and Hugh Hastings, October 27, 1871, Tweed papers, Historical Society of Pennsylvania.
12. Tweed… transfer …seven most valuable real estate holdings : *New-York Times*, October 27, 1871; Tweed testimony, aldermen, p. 320, 335, 348, 349, 350, 351, 352.
13. Tweed… $22,359 … salaries for Public Works …employees : *New-York Times* and *Herald*, October 27, 1871.

14. Tweed ... burning his personal records: Tweed testimony, aldermen, p. 151,281, 291; Ingersoll statement, *New-York Times*, June 3, 1875.
15. "Yes, the exhibit [Tilden's table] does look bad ...": *New-York Times*, October 27, 1871.
16. "Although 'interviewed' and badgered...": Strong, October 28, 1871, p. 395.
17. "Good by, my son ...": *New-York Times*, October 29, 1871. The reporter's name is unknown.
18. "You have never misrepresented me ...": *New-York Times*, October 31, 1871.
19. "Well, they've been talking about this...": *New York Tribune*, October 27, 1871.
20. "Good morning, Mr. Tweed": Accounts of the arrest are from the *New-York Times* and *Tribune*, October 28, 1871.
21. "You're my man"... "a deliciously cool joke": *New York Tribune*, October 28, 1871.
22. "What for, I would like to know...": *New York Herald*, October 31, 1871.
23. "Japanese Custom in New York": *Leslie's Illustrated*, October 7, 1871.
24. "The Only Thing That They Respect or Fear": *Harper's Week*, October 21, 1871.
25. "City Treasury"... "Empty" ... "Full" : Paine, p. 189.
26. the *New-York Times* ...charging fraud: New-York Times, November 9, 1871.
27. "He will be back here." ..."Ingersoll will be back" : *New-York Times*, October 29, 1871.
28. Ingersoll ...sold four of his lots ...$45,000: Clipping from *Real Estate Record* of October 21, 1871, in Tilden papers, box 23, NYPL.
29. Hilton resigned... Parks Department: Letter from Henry Hilton to Hall, November 10, 1871, in Hall papers. NYMA.
30. Sweeny ... resigned as Parks Commissioner: Letter from Peter B. Sweeny to Hall, in Hall papers. November 1, 1871, NYMA. Sweeny had been complaining for weeks about pressure being put on his to step aside. See Letter from Sweeny to Marble, September 27, 1871.. Marble papers. LC. ("A Gentleman called on me this evening and stated that the Report is in circulation, that I am negotiating with—Tilden, Havemeyer & yourself fort a general resignation in consideration of general confirmation of past offenses.... Is that fair on the part of Tilden & Co.?")
31. Hall ...appointed Andrew H. Green ...comptroller: Order of November 18, 1871, Hall papers. NYMA.
32. Connolly had resigned: Letter from Connolly to Hall, October 31, 1871, Hall papers. NYMA.
33. "Mr. Connolly, I've got an unpleasant duty to perform": This account is from the *New York Tribune*, June 9, 1880.
34. "I must pay $1,500,000 or go to jail," "Richard, go to jail!": See *New York Tribune*, June 15, 1877 and June 9, 1880, and *New-York Times*, November 26 and 27, 1871.
35. "Dick cut and ran": Letter from Greeley to Whitelaw Reid, in Cortissoz, p. 152.
36. Tweed ... resigned ... Commissioner of Public Works: Letter from Tweed to

Hall, December 28, 1871. Hall papers. NYMA; *New-York Times*, December 30, 1871.

37. Tweed ... transferred.... fifteen ... holdings ...Richard: Tweed testimony, aldermen, p. 306, 307, 321,324, 328, 329, 330, 331,332, 336, 342, 345, 346, 347, 353, 354, 355.
38. "Must I go to prison tonight?" Hershkowitz, p. 202.
39. Judge George Barnard ... *habeas corpus* ... $5,000: *New-York Times* and other newspapers, December 17, 1871.
40. Tammany Sachems ... Grand Sachem ... Tammany's General Committee: *New York Herald*, January 1, 1871, and *New-York Times*, December 30 and 31, 1871.
41. "What the divil's the use ...": *New-York Times*, December 31, 1871.

18. Law *(pages 261–279)*

1. "*It is a great, a splendid ...*": *New-York Times*, November 8, 1871.
2. "*I have got twenty more years ...*": *New York Herald*, February 1, 1873.
3. "Gentlemen, have you agreed...": Court proceedings from *New York Herald*, February 1, 1873.
4. "More counts than in a German principality": Breen, p. 422.
5. "We are not here to try any petty question...": Peckham statement in *New York Herald*, January 14, 1873. Peckham and prosecutors apparently had rejected an all-money deal brokered by Tweed's lawyers in early 1872 under which Tweed, Sweeny, and Connolly, would settle their cases by paying $4.5 million total to restitution. *New-York Times*, February 7, 1872.
6. Davis ... legislation ...naturalize new citizens: See *New-York Times*, April 19, 1870.
7. Committee of Seventy ..."reform": See *New-York Times*, October 27 and 30, 1872; Breen, p. 423.
8. Tweed's ... fortune at $20 to $25 million : *New York Tribune*, October 19, 1871.
9. "We haven't sympathized very much" : Hershkowirtz, p. 243.
10. "His language was blasphemous": Lynch, p. 393. Garvey had been indicted on forgery charges for accepting payments for Phillip Donnarumma, T.C. Cashman, and R.J. Hennessay, falsely signing their names.
11. "Oh, I feel all right, ...": *New York Herald*, January 16, 1873.
12. "I expected an acquittal" ... "I only know what they tell me"... "It was only a political trial": : Tweed interview, *New York Herald*, February 1, 1873.
13. "I myself was almost exhausted": Tweed interview, *New York Herald*, October 26, 1877.
14. "When you were a boy ...": *New York Sun*, January 8, 1872; Swanberg, p. 274.
15. "Tammany don't amount...": *New York Herald*, October 10, 1872.
16. "I am not now in politics": *New York Herald*, September 4, 1872.
17. Tweed kept ...land ...Queens and Putnam counties: Tweed testimony, Aldermen, p. 306.
18. Gould ... withdrawn ... Erie Railway: *New York Tribune*, November 17, 1871. Tweed replaced him with lawyer Jacob Vanderpeol, registrar Charles Cornell, and contractor Charles Devlin.

19. "The Finger of Scorn:" *Harper's Weekly*, January 4, 1873; in Bowen, p. 186. On handing over his desk to new mayor William Havemeyer, Hall said: "Mr. Mayor, I desire to restore you to that vacant chair and to give you the keys of your private office and wish you a very Happy New Year." Bowen, p. 185.
20. "I am inundated with ball tickets …": Bowen, p. 189.
21. George Barnard… Albert Cardozo: Barnard Impeachment: Cardfozo Impeachment The charges against Cardozo principally involved his role in the Gould-Fisk 1869 attempted gold market corner, but also included that, during 1868 through 1871, Cardozo (a) appointed 511 referees in real estate disputes, including 33 to Tweed's son William Jr.,(b) discharged 134 convicted prisoners serving terms of Blackwell's Island allegedly in exchange for payoffs.
22. "I had a very pleasant chat …": Paine, 222-223.
23. "[Tilden] denounced …" "Just at present "Mr. Tilden was throughout…" : *New-York Times* editorials, December 24, 26, and 29, 1872.
24. "*The New York City 'Ring:'* See Bigelow (Tilden writings), p. 552 et seq.
25. "The Tobacco Manufacturers Association": *New-York Times*, June 19, 1872.
26. "The Cat's Paw" "Save me from my tobacco Partner": *Harper's Weekly*, August 10 and November 2, 1872.
27. "I have been so bitterly…": Letter from Greeley to Tappan, November 8, 1872. Greeley papers, LC,
28. "the biggest club in New York …": *New-York Times*, October 19, 1872.
29. State's $6.3 million civil suit … tying it up in appeals: Tweed's lawyers argued that the state had no standing in the case since the alleged victim had been New York county, not the state, and the county was not a party. Ultimately, New York's court of appeals agreed. See e.g. Townsend. 108.
30. Tweed … travel … Boston… Chicago … California … Canada: See *New-York Times*, April 12, April 14, April 24, 1873, Lynch, 394, Hershkowitz, p. 248.
31. "[B]read and butter is one …": *New-York Times*, November 13, 1873.
32. Peckham …complained … jury … "corrupt.": See *New York World*, November 20, 1873.
33. Davis … "unqualified and decided opinion…": Statement of Tweed's lawyers in the *New-York Times* and other newspapers, November 30, 1873.
34. "to vindicate the dignity of the court…": Proceedings from *New-York Times*, November 6, 1873.
35. "The trial must proceed" … "I will give no time…": Proceedings in *New York World*, November 6, 1873.
36. Pinkerton detectives … lawyers to investigate each … juror : Hershkowirtz, p. 251-252.
37. Davis …dropped Lubry from the panel: Proceedings in *New-York Times*, November 13, 1873; Lynch, p. 394.
38. "Some of them…" "on account of his moral character": Proceedings in *New-York Times*, November 14, 1873.
39. FN: Garvey … "The job has been put up…": Werner, p. 233; Wingate, III, p. 383; *New York Herald*, November 18, 1873.

40. "Gentlemen of the Jury": Proceedings in *New York World*, November 20, 1873.
41. "I hope you will bear up ...": Lynch, p. 395.
42. "Physical and mental prostration …": *New York World*, November 23, 1873.
43. "Your motion is perfectly starting …": Proceedings in *New York Sun*, November 24, 1871.
44. "Your Honor, we are taught …": Proceedings in newspapers; Lynch, p. 396.
45. "could have no legitimate effect ..": Proceedings in *New-York Times*, November 23, 1873; Hershkowitz, p. 259-260.
46. "he grew red and excited ..." *New York Sun*, November 24, 1873.
47. "Few honest men could have looked …": *New York World*, November 23, 1873.
48. "It is the duty of this court …": Proceedings in *New-York Times*, November 23, 1873.
49. Davis … charge them with contempt … fine three … $250 apiece: *New-York Times*, November 25 and 30, 1873.
50. "utterly broken": *New-York Times*, November 23, 1873.
51. Tweed hid his face in his hands: Breen, p. 467.
52. "Dick is living in clover …": *New York Sun*, November 24, 1873; Hershkowitz, p. 260.
53. "I can't help my looks…" "He had no business…": *New York Sun*, November 24, 1873.
54. "John, how are you?" …"Yes, Mr. Tweed…": *New York Sun*, November 24, 1873.

19. Prison *(pages 280–293)*

1. "*The reporters did this*": *New York Sun*, November 25, 1873.
2. "as well as I can be …": *New York Sun*, November 25, 1873.
3. "The sight or thought of William M. Tweed …": *New York World*, November 20, 1873.
4. Barlow sent Brennan a blistering … "that William M. Tweed be at once removed…": Letters between Barlow and Brennan, November 28, 1873, in the *New-York Times*, November 29, 1873.
5. "Perhaps I ought to be grateful …": *New-York Times*, November 30, 1873.
6. Blackwell's Island: See Jackson, p.1020-1021, and *New-York Times*, November 27, 1873.
7. "You have brought me here …": Report of Commissioner Stern, from *New York Sun*, April 10, 1871.
8. "Tweed would have been killed …": *New York Sun*, April 6, 1874.
9. "A woman comes [to Tweed's room] …": *New York Sun*, April 18, 1874.
10. "The sentence which consigned Tweed …": Report of Commissioner Stern, in *New York Sun*, April 10, 1871.
11. "William M. Tweed might, in the eyes…": *New-York Times*, April 10, 1874. See also *New-York Times*, April 5,6,10,17, and December 11, 15, 31, 1874.
12. inmates … faked … cases of smallpox: *New-York Times*, April 17, 1874.
13. "There he goes." "There's the old man": Description of Tweed from *New York Sun*, June 20, 1874.

14. Tweed … letter to his sister-in-law Margaret: Letter to Margaret Tweed, March 21, 1874, in Hershkowitz, p. 266.
15. Tweed's … testimony: Proceedings from the *New York Herald*, June 20, 1874. Asked if officials from the Tweed Association had asked him to contribute money to the club, Tweed said: "I should think they did… they called so often, I got tired of them and would not see them." Asked if he'd refused the request, he said: "I did, because I hadn't it. I was in trouble about the negotiation of property." The trial would end on a jury deadlock.
16. "expression of almost tearful pleasure …": *New York Herald*, June 20, 1874.
17. "enforced regularity of the life …": *New York Herald*, December 18, 1874.
18. "We have got it!" ... "Well, I expected it …": *New-York Times*, June 16, 1875.
18. "grim satisfaction [of a] public humiliation …": Letter from O'Conor to Noah Davis, June 30, 1875, in *New-York Times*, July 16, 1875. See also Townsend, p. 110.
20. "He was the best…" "He stood his imprisonment…": *New-York Times*, June 16, 1875.
21. "You are my prisoner…" "Oh, I know that…": *New York Sun*, June 23, 1875.
22. "His hair has become white": *New-York Times*, June 23, 1875.
23. "walked briskly and with an upright bearing…": *New York Sun*, June 23, 1875.
24. "We do not now believe—…": *New-York Times*, November 26, 1875; Bowen, p. 201.
25. "because he is the only leading member …": *New-York Times*, June 16, 1875.
26. The warden had allowed Tweed this privilege: Warden Dunham acknowledged four occasions; interviews by *New York Times* reporters confirmed seven sightings including Thanksgiving Day. *New-York Times*, December 6, 1875.
27. Joseph Johnson … "merely nominal": *New-York Times*, December 6, 1875. On "Mrs. MacMacMullin, see letter from Carolyn O'Brien Bryant to Charles Fairchild, in *New-York Times*, July 19, 1877.

20. Escape *(pages 294–314)*

1. *"Now, is it likely …"*: *New-York Times*, December 30, 1871.
2. *"I shall follow him wherever …"*: *New York Sun*, December 5, 1875.
3. Tweed had kept his plan utterly secret: There is no definitive account of Tweed's escape and flight, through Tweed, speaking through lawyer John Townsend, described as "perfectly correct" the narrative that appeared in *Harper's Weekly*, April 14, 1877. (Tweed testimony, Aldermen, p. 373-375.) See also *New York Herald*, September 13, 1876, and sources cited below. For a different slant, see the tale told by Captain James Bryan of the schooner *Joe Kelly*, who spoke to a reporter twelve years after the fact and claimed to have personally carried Tweed from Coney Island to Cuba, in *New York Tribune*, April 1, 1888.
4. "GONE AT LAST": *New York Herald*, December 5, 1875.
5. Tweed … in Canada, Long Island, Savannah, Cuba, Texas: See *New-York Times*, December 16, 23, 25, and 29, 1875. Even now, some New Yorkers sympathized with him. James Gordon Bennett Jr.'s *New York Herald* argued that

Tweed had acted only to strengthen his hand in negotiating with prosecutors or to get vengeance on former allies "who have of late, to use the vernacular, 'gone back on him.'" *New York Herald*, December, 14, 1875.

6. "What could I do with myself?": *Harper's Weekly*, April 14, 1877.
7. "I am ruined" … "like an insane man": Keeper Hagen's statement, in *New York Herald*, December, 5, 1875.
8. "Flight is always interpreted…" "a great mistake": Hershkowitz, p. 285 and 286.
9. "letting all the alleged wrongdoers go free…": Proceedings in *The Daily Register*, March 4, 1876.
10. Theories … Hunt's actual identity: See, for instance, letter from Adee to Fish, September 7 and 11, 1877. NARA; Lynch, p. 300; Transcript of Young's interview with Hamilton Fish, November 29, 1877. Fish papers. LC.
11. Spain … no extradition treaty: At the time, the United States had extradition treaties with fifteen governments: eight European (Great Britain, France, Germany, Austria, Italy, Norway and Sweden, the Swiss confederation, and Belgium), two West Indian, and one each in Central and South America and South Africa, plus similar arrangements with Mexico and the Sandwich Islands.
12. "I should have lived in Spain…": Tweed interview, *New York Herald*, October 26, 1877.
13. "terribly sunburnt, his face being as brown…": *New York Herald*, September 13, 1876.
14. "As soon as I got free …": Tweed interview, *New York Herald*, October 26, 1877.
15. "I felt indisposed to talk …": Tweed interview, *New York Herald*, October 26, 1877.
16. "Sir!" he'd screamed, "a man who is not …": Flick, p. 274.
17. the "Era of Good Stealings": See generally Summers.
18. FN: "When Dr. Johnson defined patriotism…": *New-York Times*, September 27, 1877.
19. "You and Tweed went to Philadelphia …": *The Daily Register*, February 29 and March 1, 1876.
20. "The sheriff alone …": *New York Herald*, December 87, 1875.
21. "Tweed-le-dee and Tilden-Dum": *Harper's Weekly*, July 1, 1876; Paine, p. 336.
22. "Jon Brown, New Court House…": Hershkowitz, p. 287.
23. New York sheriff's wanted poster: Wanted Poster, December 6, 1875. Tweed collection, NYPL. It described Tweed as "very portly, ruddy complexion, has rather large, coarse, prominent features and large prominent nose; rather small blue or grey eyes, grey hair, from originally auburn color; head nearly bald on top from forehead back to crown, and bare part of ruddy color; head projecting toward the crown."
24. "Vessel Arrived Safely": Hall to Fish, July 28, 1876, NARA, in Hershkowitz, p. 287-288.
25. "If Secor is Tweed…": Fish to Hall, July 11, 1876, in Hershkowitz, p. 288.

26. "No sooner had I got to Havana …": *New York Tribune*, November 16, 1876.
27. "[H]is wife had great influence …": Memo on Fish-Young interview, November 29, 1877. Fish papers, LC.
28. "had rec'd orders to let Secor …": Transcript of Fish-Young interview, November 29, 1877. Fish papers. LC.
29. "I thought Tweed was a persecuted …": Transcript of Fish-Young interview, November 29, 1877. Fish papers. LC. See also Hall to Cadwalader, September 21, 1876, and memos, November 29, 1876, State Department Archives. NARA.
30. "I am at this moment in receipt …": Fish to DA Phelps, July 28, 1876. Tweed papers, NYHS.
31. "I try to eat what is provided …": Tweed journal, in *Harper's Weekly*, April 14, 1877.
32. "the old fellow [Tweed] had no coat …": *New York Tribune*, November 16, 1876; Lynch, p. 400.
33. "Mr. Tweed, put on your coat ..": *New York Tribune*, November 16, 1876.
34. "I think it will be advisable …": Grant to Fish, September 13, 1876. Fish papers. LC.
35. "Ascertain secretly and cautiously …": Fish to Cushing, August 2, 1876. State Department archives. NARA.
36. Hunter to Adee, September 9, 1876. State Department archives. NARA.
37. Adee… asked … Don Benigno S. Suarez… *Harper's Weekly* : Letter from Adee to Nast, January 28, 1892, in Paine, p. 336;
38. "The generous conduct of the Spanish ..": Adee to Fish September 27, 1876. NARA.
39. "I hope you will find …": Adee to Franklin, September 22, 1876. NARA
40. "Tweed, traveling as Secor, …": Adee to Fish, September 7, 1876. NARA.
41. "Luggage should be guarded …": Fish to Adee telegrams, September 17 and 18, 1876. NARA.
42. *New York Herald* … denied … access: See Adee to Fish, September 12 and 26, 1877. NARA.
43. "Say also [to the Spanish] … Hunt: Fish to Adee telegram, September 17, 1876. NARA.
44. "Hunt" … question forever unanswered: See Hershkowitz, p. 298-299; and *Harper's Weekly*, April 14, 1877 claiming Hunt first learned at Vigo of Tweed actual identity and became indignant, fearing jail as an accessory.
45. "Twid"… a kidnapper or child abuser: Adee to Fish, September 11, 1876, NARA..
46. Tilden-Hayes campaign: See Roy Morris, Jr.; Boller, ch. 23.
47. "The word 'reform' is not popular ..": Letter from Seymour to Tilden, October 25, 1876. Bigelow (Tilden letters), p. 470; Flick, p. 307.
48. "Turn the rascals out ": Flick, p. 308.
49. "Tilden and Tweed; The Twin Leaders …": *New-York Times*, July 7, 1876.
50. "Samuel J. Tilden was personally …": *New-York Times*, July 11, 1876.

51. "The capture of Tweed is no accident …": *New York Sun*, September 17, 1876.
52. "a Naval vessel should be …": Grant to Fish, September 7, 1876. Fish papers, LC.
53. "The [New York] Herald is very anxious …": Grant to Fish, September 13, 1876. Fish papers. LC.
54. "These details, from a stranger …": Adee to Fish, September 18, 1876. NARA.
55. "His behavior was that of a perfect gentleman ..": Lynch, p. 401.
56. "He evidently regards himself …": *New York Tribune*, November 16, 1876.
57. Suicide … "wicked": Lynch, p. 401.
58. "hurricane": See *New York Sun*, November 24, 1876.
59. "very amusing remarks signifying…": *New York Tribune*, November 24, 1876.
60. "It's the old man. I found him …": *New York Tribune*, November 24, 1876.
61. "[w]alking slowly… stooping …": *New York Sun*, November 24, 1876.
62. Is Reilly elected Sheriff? …" "I see they've got the wires…" "careworn ….": *New York Sun*, November 24, 1876.
63. "Hooray for the 'ould Boss'" *New York Sun*, November 24, 1876.
64. "Yes, gentlemen; Tweed is locked up …": *New York Tribune*, November 24, 1876.
65. "Well, I thought I'd come back …": *New York Sun*, November 24, 1876.
66. "He is crushed and broken...": *New York Sun*, November 24, 1876.
67. "His curious, ill-conceived escape …": Hershkowitz, p. 295.
68. "I did not escape from the jail": For quote and $60,000 cost, Tweed testimony, Aldermen, p. 373-4.
69. "No, sir…. Tweed shall not escape …": *New York Sun*, November 25, 1876.

21. Lawyers *(pages 315–332)*

1. "*For Tweed there was some sympathy* …": *New York Tribune*, June 8, 1877.
2. "*The abuse you get only shows* …": Barlow to Fairchild, June 25, 1877; Fairchild papers, NYHS.
3. "*These men are dead socially* …": *New York Tribune*, June 8, 1877.
4. "If Mr. Tweed had known …": *New York Herald*, October 26, 1877.
5. "lost their brightness," … "remarkable possession…": *New York Sun*, November 28, 1876.
6. "I can't get the motion …": *New York Sun*, November 25, 1876.
7. "try to cheer him up": *New York Tribune*, November 27, 1876. Weeds claims that he also visited Tweed three times during his imprisonment on Blackwell's Island and suggested shortly after Tweed's escape from Ludlow Street that Tweed only wanted "to make a clean breast of it… provided he can secure freedom from himself and for some of his particular friends." See Weed interview in *New York Herald*, December, 14, 1875.
8. FN: Release… under … "60-Days Act": See *New York Tribune*, July 30, 1877; New-York Times, February 21, 1878.
9. "I have recklessly parted …": Tweed testimony, Aldermen, p. 307 and 310.
10. "Sir; Physically and financially …": Tweed to Ingersoll, January 10, 1877. Tweed papers, NYHS.

11. "the name of T—d rendered it difficult:" Letter from Margaret Tweed to Tweed, in Hershkowitz, p. 308.
12. "Personally, Tweed was the pluckiest man ...": *New York Tribune*, April 13, 1878.
13. "At first it was not an easy matter ...": Townsend, p. 118.
14. "The drunken Democrat [from] the Galena gutter": Letter from O'Conor to Samuel Reid, November 24, 1876, in *New-York Times*, December 6, 1876.
15. no effort ... extradite Sweeny or Connolly: Tilden tried to cool this issue by asking Hamilton Fish in September to hand over "this great criminal" Tweed to local authorities immediately upon his return to the country.
16. "[T]he spectacle of Tweed upon his knees ...": Townsend, p. 118-119.
17. "I take the liberty of addressing you...": Letter from Tweed to O'Conor, December 5, 1876, in Townsend, p. 119, *Harper's Weekly*, April 14, 1877, and newspapers.
18. "I've got secrets enough of his...": *New York Tribune*, November 16, 1878. See also *New-York Times*, December 15, 1875: ("If Governor Tilden knew that a full and true story of the Tammany Ring, by Tweed, was to appear in The Times next Saturday, we do not believe he would get much sleep on Friday night.")
19. "about nine out of ten men ...": Flick, p. 260.
20. "I... caution the public against a pretended confession ...": Letter from Hewitt in *New-York Times* and other newspapers, November 5, 1876.
21. Sweeny full immunity ... "unmolested": The document, signed by Fairchild, DA Benjamin Phelps, William Whitney, and Peckham, is in the Fairchild papers, NYHS.
22. Critics sneered at the ... deal: See, for instance, *New-York Times*, December 29, 1876: ("As the election is now over and there is no longer the necessity for a pretense of a Democratic 'war on the thieves,' Gov. Tilden has interposed no obstacle.")
23. O'Conor ... letter resigning from the Tweed prosecution: On the O'Conor-Tilden meeting, see *New York Tribune*, July 2, 1877; Lynch, 405; and Townsend, 121.
24. "He attracts few people": Flick, p. 362.
25. Townsend ... fee ... ten promissory notes: Townsend insisted on collateral for the fee, which Tweed's friend Benjamin Fairchild provided in the form of a deed on land near Jamaica, Long Island. See *New-York Times*, November 13, 1878 and January 9, 1879.
26. Field asked Tweed ... $1,000 ... Tweed refused: Letters between Field and Tweed, February 1877, reprinted in Townsend, p. 124 through 126.
27. "Of course Tweed was aware ...": Townsend, p. 121.
28. "I... talked with him awhile": Fairchild testimony to state assembly, in *New-York Times*, May 2, 1877.
29. notes from the meeting: Document dated February 21, 1877, in Fairchild papers, NYHS.
30. Bryant ... article on his jailbreak: *Harper's Weekly*, April 14, 1877.
31. "[H]e refused to lead...": *New York Star*, August 4, 1886, in Flick, p. 401.

32. "Unwilling to bargain ...": Morris Jr., p. 252.
33. "Physically he was an old ...": Flick, p. 417.
34. "[Fairchild] accepted Tilden's invitation ...": Bryant to Townsend, March 15, 1877, in Townsend, p. 130.
35. "The understanding is absolute ...": Bryant to Townsend, March 22, 1877, in Townsend, p. 131.
36. "The talk of a compromise ...": Letter from Whitney to Fairchild, March 31, 1877, Fairchild papers, NYHS.
37. "I saw [Tweed] again at the jail ...": Fairchild testimony to state assembly, in *New-York Times*, May 2, 1877.
38. "Mr. Fairchild did not fix any date ...": Townsend, p. 132.
39. "*Buckingham* ...": G. Union [Bryant] to Luke Grant [Tweed], April 5, 1877, in Townsend, p. 132.
40. "confession": For full text, see *New York Herald*, October 10, 1877.
41. "He says he has no doubt ...": Letter from Townsend to Tweed, April 15, 1877, in Townsend, p. 133.
42. "in Tilden's hands": Lettter from Townsend to Tweed, April 15, 1877, in Townsend, p. 133.
43. "Since his troubles ...": *New York World*, April 17, 1877.
44. FN: "I notice that the 'World' has several columns...": Letter from Townsend to Fairchild, April 17, 1877, Fairchild papers, NYHS.
45. "It is pretty well understood ...": *New-York Times*, April 20, 1877.
46. Dirt... against ... Woodin ...Weed ... New York Central Railroad: Letter from Townsend to Fairchild, June 20, 1877, in *New-York Times* and other papers, June 21, 1877.
47. "My mind is not easy ...": Letter from Tweed to Townsend, May 4, 1877, in Townsend, p. 133.
48. "He is suffering intensely from diabetes...": Letter from Schirmer to Townsend, May 10, 1877, in Townsend, p. 136, and Lynch, p. 408.
49. "If possible, have the Counsel ...": Letter from Tweed to Townsend, May 4, 1877, in Townsend, p. 133.
50. "Tweed's testimony will so key up...: Letter from Whitney to Fairchild, May 25, 1877, Fairchild papers, NYHS.
51. "Pursuant to your suggestion ...": Letter from Peckham to Fairchild, May 3, 1877. Fairchild papers, NYHS.
52. "Whitney & I saw [Tweed] ...": Peckham to Fairchild, May 18, 1877. Fairchild papers, NYHS.
53. "I consulted with several people ...": Fairchild testimony to state assembly, in *New-York Times*, May 2, 1877.
54. Peckham ...meeting secretly with Sweeny's agents: Peckham testimony, Aldermen, p. 870-872.
55. Peckham ... gloomy picture of the evidence: Fairchild Report in *New York Tribune*, November 30, 1877.
    Peckham had bank records: See financial spreadsheets in box 23, Tilden papers, NYPL.

56. "In my view the trial ...": Letter from Peckham to Fairchild, May 25, 1877. Fairchild papers, NYPL.
57. Sweeny ... "laughing and talking": *New York Tribune*, June 7, 1877.
58. "It may be proper for me to say ...": *New York Tribune*, June 7, 1877.
59. "[A]ny settlement [was on] condition ...": *New York Tribune*, June 7, 1877
60. "I was no party... to any agreement ...": *New York Tribune*, June 8, 1877.
61. Pechkam ... hadn't objected: Judge Westbrook himself went further and said that Sweeny's lawyers had requested the language in a private meeting with Peckham present and "Mr. Peckham, I think, said nothing about it." *New York Tribune*, June 14, 1877.
62. Smith Ely, Jr.,... Sweeny ... offered ... $600,000 : *New York Tribune*, June 9, 1877.
63. Kelly accused prosecutors ...Sweeny ... l back channel: *New York Tribune*, June 7, 1877.
64. "I am just informed ...": Letter from Townsend to Fairchild, June 6, 1877. Fairchiild papers, NYHS.
65. "After careful examination...": Letter from Fairchild to Townsend, June 12, 1877, Fairchild papers, NYHS.
66. Fairchild ... leaked ... at the Manhattan Club: Letter from Townsend to Fairchild, June 20, 1877, in *New-York Times* and other papers, June 21, 1877.
67. FN: "If it be shown that through incompetence...": Townsend to Fairchild, June 20, 1877, in *New-York Times* and other papers, June 21, 1877. Peckham, in turn, would callTownsend's attack "[U]ngentlemanly." Peckham to Fairchild, June 21, 1877; Fairchild papers, NYHS.

FN: "The copy submitted to Mr. Fairchild...": *New York Tribune*, June 14, 1877.

68. FN: Fairchild ... published a report: Fairchild Report in *New York Tribune*, November 30, 1877.
69. FN: Carolyn O'Brien Bryant ...scathing ... letters: See *New-York Times*, July 18, 19 and 20, 1877; *New York Tribune*, July 18, 1877.
70. "You have refused to let Tweed...": Letter from Whitney to Fairchild, July 20, 1877, Fairchild papers, NYHS.
71. "That Fairchild attempted ...": Hirsch (Whitney), p. 125.
72. "The worst feature of [the Tweed ring crimes] ...": *New York Tribune* and other papers, December 5, 1877; Townsend, p. 145.

22. Clean Breast *(pages 333–344)*

1. "*I can't; I am in the same condition* ...": Tweed testimony, Aldermen, p. 148.
2. "*Nathaniel Sands was taken care of* ...": Tweed testimony, Aldermen, p. 223.
3. "My defenses ... have been disclosed ...": Letter from Tweed to Townsend, June 13, 1877, in *New York Tribune*, June 14, 1877. On subsequent judgments, see *New-York Times*, February 14, 1878.
4. FN: Honest John" ... accused by Mayor William Havemeyer ... "Fraud permeates every part ...": See Werner, p. 278-279; *New-York Times* and other newspapers, December 1 and 2, 1874.
5. "I never dictate ...": Kelly interview, *New York World*, October 18, 1875.

6. "John Kelly is a man ...": *New-York Times*, October 27, 1875.
7. Lewis ... star witness ... the former Boss himself: Lewis obtained a judicial summons to compel Tweed to testify, though Tweed had not asked for it. In his application, Lewis felt obliged to say it was "in good faith, and without any fraud or connivance between the said committee ... and the said William M. Tweed."
8. "He stoops more than usual ...": *New York Herald*, September 4, 1877.
9. I believe you are a native..."“I am, sir.": Tweed testimony, aldermen, p. 12
10. "Mr. Tweed manifested no nervousness ...": *New York Sun*, September 13, 1877.
11. "the most timid never dreaded...": *New York Tribune*, September 17, 1877.
12. "There is not a word of truth in it": *New York Sun*, September 8, 1877.
13. "There is no truth ...": *New York Sun*, September 13, 1877.
14. Tweed ... producing ... sales document... "That settles ...": The document, an assignment of the claim to Tweed's secretary Foster Dewey, is in Tweed testimony, Aldermen, p.59; the quote is from *New York Sun*, September 16, 1877.
15. "it is simply and wholly false...": Argus, in *New York Sun*, September 30, 1877.
16. "Men whom I have benefited in every way ...": Tweed testimony, Aldermen, p.234 and 239.
17. Several hundred persons..." "Every seat ...": *New York Sun* and *New York Herald*, September 22, 1877.
18. "He seemed bursting ...": *New York Tribune*, September 13, 1877.
19. "jaunty air" "the promptness with which his answers...": *New-York Times*, September 16, 1877.
20. "Well, you must recollect that if I don't answer ...": Tweed testimony, Aldermen, p. 108.
21. "men who could inform me ...": Tweed testimony, Aldermen, p. 211.
22. : "Must I sit here and be abused ...": Tweed testimony, Aldermen, p. 123.
23. "I have read it [the list] ...": Tweed testimony, Aldermen, p. 273, 261.
24. "What I swore then was false; ...": *New-York Times*, September 22, 1877. Tweed testimony, Alderman, p. 167.
25. "I cannot say anything against ...": Tweed testimony, Aldermen, p. 290.
26. "on the contrary, he was always quarreling ...": Tweed testimony, Aldermen, p. 119-120.
27. "How much was true? ...": Hershkowitz, p. 335.
28. Sweeny ... hiding behind ... immunity: The committee issued a subpoena demanding he appear, but Sweeny sent a lawyer to protest saying Sweeny had come to American under protection of prosecutors. "Mr. Sweeny ... has had no notification from any source that the immunity thus assured would at any time expire, according to its provisions," the lawyer argued, and it would be "oppressive" to make him speak. Aldermen, p. 767-775.
29. Taintor ...had examined ... $30 million is city payments: Taintor testimony, p. 403-404.
   $200 million ... Matthew O'Rourke: See New York Herald, January 13, 1901; Callow, p. 164; Lynch, p. 16.

30. "At present all the thieves ...": Aldermen report, p. 26-27.
31. "incomprehensible"..."to save some shred ...": Aldermen report, p. 29.
32. "almost a nonentity" ... "a poor stick" ... "I was pretty well acquainted ..." "I was a Douglas democrat..." "I have gained...": Tweed interview, *New York Herald*, October 26, 1877.
33. "I think, [he] has been crazy..." "a hard, overbearing..." "I was always ambitious ..." "Nothing. My vanity sees nothing...": Tweed interview, *New York Herald*, October 26, 1877.
34. I should go to New Orleans..." "My son-in-law is in business...": *New York Herald*, October 26, 1877.
35. "I never bother my head ...": Tweed testimony, Aldermen, p. 116.
36. aldermen ... voted 13 to 6 ... to free Tweed: See Aldermen proceedings, *New-York Times*, January 5, 1878.
37. "[Schoonmaker] will, it is believed ...": *New-York Times*, November 11, 1877.
38. "Tweed's case must stand ...": *New-York Times*, February 9, 1878.
39. "I feel it to be my duty both ...": Letter from Kelly to Schoonmaker, March 21, 1878, in Townsend, p. 149, *New York World*, March 27, 1878..
40. Schoonmaker ... understanding with Kelly and Townsend: See letter from Townsend to Schoomnmaker, in the *New York Herald*, April 14, 1878.
41. "It is doubtless true that Mr. Kelly promised...": *Utica Observer*, in *New-York Times*, April 5, 1878.
42. "That gentleman [Schoonmaker] gave assurance ...": Townsend, p. 151.
43. "Of what use to the Attorney General ...": Letter from Fairchild to Schoonmaker, April 1, 1878. Fairchild papers, NYHS, and newspapers. See, for instance, *New York World*, April 2, 1878..
44. "I saw at once that ...": *New York Herald*, April 13, 1878.
45. "as many as five hundred times ...": Werner, p. 257.
46. Dewey ... Tweed ...out names of people ...one out of every four : *New York Sun*, April 13, 1878.
47. "I felt I could be to him of no further use...": *New York Tribune*, April 13, 1878.

23. Legacy *(pages 345–362)*

1. "*The politicians who make a lastin'* ...": Plunkett, p. 35 and 83.
2. "*Tammany Hall, for years, has unfairly* ...": *New-York Times*, February 13, 1961.
3. "*There is no boss over me*": *New-York Times*, January 14, 1960.
4. "*[I]f Tammany could lay its hands*...": *New-York Times*, October 22, 1954.
5. "[H]is life, as a whole ...": *New York Tribune*, April 13, 1878.
6. "The bulk of the poorer voters...": *The Nation*, April 18, 1878.
7. "It was broadly stated...": *New York Herald*, April 13, 1878.
8. "Schoonmaker had been just as bad as Fairchild...": *Brooklyn Eagle*, April 14, 1876.
9. "Undoubtedly [Tweed] was not a malignant scoundrel": *Harper's Weekly*, May 4, 1878.
10. "To prove that this life...": *New York World*, April 15, 1878.

11. "It is a mercy to him…": *New York World*, April 15, 1878.
12. "almost exclusively of the poorer classes": *New-York Times*, April 18, 1878.
13. "the only mourners at Tweed's funeral…": *New York Sun*, April 18, 1878.
14. "If he had died in 1870…": *New York Sun*, April 18, 1878.
15. Greenwood Cemetery … "any person … " no "striking monument": *New York World*, April 15, 1878.
16. Greenwich estate … to … Joseph Millbank for … $75,000: *New-York Times*, March 4, 1879
17. Knickerbocker Life Insurance Company … decided to cancel payment:: On the insurance dispute, see *New-York Times*, March 13 and May 14, 1878 and June 14, 1879.
18. "[Y]ou were the only officer…": "Letter from Edelstein to Kelly, May 7, 1878.
19. "A. Oakey Hall was a great jurist …": Goldman, p. 11-12.
20. Hall sued … British writer … James Bryce: Bowen, p. 250-263.
21. "Mr. Hall was innocent of the charge …": *New-York Times*, October 8, 1898; Bowen, p. 278..
22. Hall … scrapbooks of newspaper clippings: The Hall scrapbooks are in the rare books collection of the NYPL.
23. "solidly built, [his] head liberally covered...": *New York World*, October 14, 1889.
24. "after seven years …": *New York World*, October 14, 1889. See also Sweeny to Hoffman, January 1, 1881. Hoffman papers, NYPL. ("You once asked me if I did not feel a better man for all my trials. Surely—much better than if all had gone well with me.")
25. "There is nothing against Mr. Sweeny….": Sweeny letter to the *New York World*, August 15, 1891.
26. "One of the 'Big Four'": Sweeny obituary, *New-York Times*, September 1, 1911.
27. "shunned by everybody …": Wingate, III, p. 416; Werner, p. 269.
28. "He was a very old man …": *New York Tribune*, December 5, 1877. On Connolly's later years generally, see *New-York Times*, June 1, 1880
29. Andrew H. Green: See generally Foord and *Gotham Gazette*, November 11, 2003 ("Honor Andrew Haskell Green")
30. "cipher" telegrams sent by Tilden's agents: See Kluger, p. 136-138; Flick, 429-436.
31. "I am going there to find out …": Paine, p. 559.
32. "Tweed Ring" … plunder … $200 million … the legend: See New York Herald, January 13, 1901; Callow, p. 164; Lynch, p. 16.
33. "A Worse Fraud…": See, for instance, *New-York Times*, July 24, 1879, or *New York Sun*, November 24, 1876.
34. "A villain of more brains…": *The Nation*, April 18, 1878.
35. "The politician who steals …": Plunkett, p. 32.
36. Tweed … easy to envision … walking away : As late as September 27, two months after the *New-York Times* disclosures, three weeks the reformers'

Cooper Union meeting, and two weeks after the voucher robberies, parties leaders were still working behind the scenes to arrange a way to settle the scandal. See letter from August Belmont to Manton Marble, September 27, 1871. Marble papers. LC. ("If Hall will throw himself in the arms of Tilden, O'Conor, Havemeyer & Sweeny and Tweed resign was can probably save the State.")

37. value of real estate …tripled … to over $80 million … value of property …rose 82.5 percent: Message from Governor John Hoffman, December 28, 1871; Public Papers of John T. Hoffman, p. 318, 321. Hoffman papers, NYSL.
38. "Mr. Tweed has frequently told me…": Garvey testimony, Aldermen, p. 564.
39. "large and centralized schemes ,,,": Kessner, p. 153.
40. "ruling vast bodies of human beings …": Wingate, p. 419.
41. "Tweed was a bold, bad, able man…": *The Nation*, July 29, 1875.
42. "Why, bless you, I've seen him wade…": *Brooklyn Eagle*, April 14, 1876.
43. "If I could have bought newspapermen …": Hudson, p. 25.
44. "Tweed's testimony, his confession …": Hershkowitz, p. 336.
45. "Honest John" Kelly … restore discipline: See Werner, p. 276: "He found it a horde. He left it a political army."
46. De Sapio … cover of *Time Magazine* : *Time Magazine*, August 22, 1955. He once told reporters he preferred his job running Tammany over even a possible cabinet seat should Harriman be elected president. *New-York Times*, June 18, 1956.
47. Courthouse … budgeted … at $250,000, costs … topped $4 million …$12 million or more: The low-end number is from Hershkowitz, p. 113; the end end from the New-York Times, August 2, 1871.

ACKNOWLEDGEMENTS

Delving into the complexities of Boss Tweed and following his winding trail of legend and scandal was an enormous undertaking that I could not have faced or accomplished alone without the many people who helped me along the way. To all of you, a heartfelt *thank you*.

As a writer, I benefited from the talents of many who read my manuscript and gave me their feedback from a variety of viewpoints. As experienced hands in the writers' craft, Sky Beaven, Lawrence Ellsworth, Cynthia Gayton, Clyde Linsley, George Manno, Ilya Verbitsky, and Michael Williams of the Washington Independent Writers History Small Group reviewed my chapters as they came off the printer. So too did historians Jamie Morris, David Bridges, and Jim Percoco and the editor Ellen E.M. Roberts of "Where Books Begin." My colleagues David Durkin and Robert Hahn at Olsson, Frank, and Weeda, P.C., gave me their sharp eyes as lawyers and readers in reviewing large portions of the early draft of the book. Once the manuscript was complete, three accomplished academics gave me the honor of sharing with me their special insights. Roy Morris Jr. gave me his perspectives on the role of Samuel Tilden, and Tyler Anbinder commented on the portrayal of nineteenth-century New York City. Leo Hershkowitz, in addition to his notes on the manuscript, shared with me his well-researched thoughts on the Boss himself, and his doubts as to whether Tweed actually committed the famous crimes attributed to him and the campaign waged against him by enemies and prosecutors whose abuses often seemed to overshadow the original charges. I thank all of you for your time and help; the final book is a far better product because of your input.

Research on Boss Tweed must begin and end in New York City, where Tweed's footprints remain vivid and ubiquitous. I enjoyed having the opportunity to explore New York's great research institutions and benefited from guides who went far out of their way to help me navigate their extensive resources: David Smith of the New York Public Library, Jan Hilley of the New-York Historical Society, Lora Korbut of the *New York Times* archives, Alden James of the National Arts Club (formerly Samuel Tilden's home on Gramercy Park), and Cindy Lyon of the New York State Library in Albany. In Washington, D.C., the staffs of the Library Congress manuscript, newspaper, microform, and print rooms once again handled my barrages of requests with skill and good nature, as they have done for me on many projects in the past, and the research assistants at the National Archives and Records Administration guided me through the complex web of federal records from the 1860s and 1870s.

The team at Carroll & Graf Publishers once again did a solid job transforming my work into a high quality, polished final book and giving it visibility across the country. I particularly thank my editor Philip Turner, who supported and encouraged me in this project from the beginning, the associate editor Keith Wallman who made sure all the details got attended, the publicist Wendie Carr who gave the book its place in the public eye, and the copy editor Phil Gaskill. They all took this project under their wing and made it fly. Jeff Gerecke, my literary agent, did his usual excellent job of arranging the business end of the publication; his friendship and guidance over the years have been invaluable.

Finally, for this new Viral History Press edition, I thank Catherine Zaccarine of Zaccarine Design, Inc., a very talented designer who took my old titles and tranformed them into these fine new editions.

I thank my colleagues at my law firm, Olsson, Frank, and Weeda, P.C., in Washington, D.C. who have consistently given me the warmest support as I have pursued my writing ambitions. And, finally, to my wife, Karen, thanks again for being a good sport and understanding my quest with grace and humor.

To all of you and to many more, thank you.

ILLUSTRATION CREDITS

p. frontpiece, 6, 15, 33, 34, 38, 50, 72, 113, 137, 139, 180, 184, 189, 211, 253, 254, 259, 308, 356: Library of Congress.

p. 59, 89, 121, 151, 164, 171, 182, 268: General Research Division, The New York Public Library, Astor, Lenox, and Tilden Foundations.

p. 62, 68, 264 (Peckham): Breen, 1899.

p. 95, 224, 257, 264 (Davis): Print Collection, Miriam and Ira D. Wallach Division of Arts, Prints and Photographs, the New York Public Library, Astor, Lenox and Tilden Foundations.

p.143: Courtesy of Leo Hershkowitz.

p. 168, 241: Supplied by Project Information and Learning.

p. 300: Rare books Division, The New York Public Library, Astor, Lenox, and Tilden Foundations.

INDEX

M

N

O

P

R

S

T

U

V

W

Y

CPSIA information can be obtained at www.ICGtesting.com
Printed in the USA
LVOW07s1817130114

369230LV00006B/1439/P